Instructional Textbooks

Comics and Sequential Art
Graphic Storytelling and Visual Narrative
Expressive Anatomy for Comics and Narrative

Other Books by Will Eisner

Fagin the Jew
Last Day in Vietnam
Eisner/Miller
The Spirit Archives
Will Eisner Sketchbook
Will Eisner's Shop Talk
Hawks of the Seas
The Princess and the Frog
The Last Knight
Moby Dick
Sundiata

to The HEART of the STORM

Will Eisner

W. W. NORTON & COMPANY
New York • London

First published as a Norton paperback 2008

Printed in the United States of America

For information about permission to reproduce selections from this book,
write to Permissions, W. W. Norton & Company, Inc.,
500 Fifth Avenue, New York, NY 10110

For information about special discounts for bulk purchases, please contact
W. W. Norton Special Sales at specialsales@wwnorton.com or 800-233-4830

Manufacturing by RR Donnelley, Willard
Production manager: Devon Zahn

Library of Congress Cataloging-in-Publication Data

Eisner, Will.
To the heart of the storm / Will Eisner.
p. cm.
Originally published: Princeton, Wis. : Kitchen Sink Press, 1991.
ISBN 978-0-393-32810-3 (pbk.)
1. Graphic novels. I. Title.
PN6727.E4T6 2008
741.5'973—dc22

2008029327

W. W. Norton & Company, Inc.
500 Fifth Avenue, New York, N.Y. 10110
www.wwnorton.com

W. W. Norton & Company Ltd.
Castle House, 75/76 Wells Street, London W1T 3QT

1 2 3 4 5 6 7 8 9 0

DEDICATION

This book is dedicated to Ann, my wife and loving companion.
Her caring, wisdom, perspective and unflagging support during
our years of journey together carried me through the many
creative storms along the way.

Acknowledgments

My gratitude to Dave Schreiner, who edited this book and persevered with me through the painful revisions. His judgment is unfailingly dependable.

My thanks also to Cat Yronwode, who once again provided me with priceless editorial advice as generously as she had in many of my former works.

Introduction

I grew up in the safety of America during the brewing of the storm that culminated in World War II. It was a voyage through a time of social awakenings and pervading concern with economic survival. At the same time, one could hear the rumblings and feel the shock waves from the distant Holocaust.

When I began work on this book, I intended to deliver a narrowly focused fictional experience of that climate, but in the end, it metamorphosed into a thinly disguised autobiography. In such a work, fact and fiction became blended with selective recall and result in a special reality. I came to rely on the truthfulness of visceral memory.

Perhaps the most indelible of my memories of those years was the insidious prejudice that permeated my world. Revisiting it brought me to the realization that primal prejudice has different meanings. To other than whites, it is racism; to the ethnically different, it is nationalism; to Jews, it is anti-Semitism.

This book, completed in the 90th year of the Twentieth Century, documents my coming of age into the dawn of what is generally regarded as a new era. From its beginnings, America managed to sustain and advance the dream of cultural and racial integration. America likes to see itself now as the world's champion of human rights. In these times, more African Americans unapologetically describe themselves by the color of their skin; Hispanics proudly display their culture and language, and young Jews boldly appear in the streets wearing a badge of their faith, the yarmulke. There are acknowledged civil rights, anti-discrimination laws, interfaith forums, intermarriage and a vigilant free press that quickly publicizes racial incidents.

Whether all this is proof of a new prejudice-free world, or simply evidence that the same old hatreds are still within us, is arguable. I cling to the hope that kids growing up today can no longer easily assume a social superiority with its license to discriminate.

But, just in case this view is not too sanguine, I share with you my journey To the Heart of the Storm.

Will Eisner

Florida, 1990

To the Heart of the Storm

IT WAS A TIME OF THUNDER AND LIGHTNING. THE WAR THAT HAD RAVAGED EUROPE SINCE 1939 NOW ENGULFED AMERICA. THERE WORLD WAR II SET IN MOTION THE DRAFTING OF ITS CITIZENS FOR MILITARY SERVICE. YOUNG MEN REGISTERED WITH THEIR LOCAL DRAFT BOARDS.

THERE THEY WERE CLASSIFIED FOR SERVICE. THOSE SELECTED WERE TOLD TO REPORT TO RECRUITING POINTS WHERE THEY WERE EXAMINED, INDUCTED AND ASSIGNED TO BRANCHES. THEY WERE THEN UNIFORMED, GROUPED, AND HERDED ONTO TROOP TRAINS COMMANDEERED FOR SHIPPING SOLDIERS TO UNANNOUNCED DESTINATIONS.

FOR THESE YOUNG PEOPLE IT WAS AN UNFORGETTABLE JOURNEY TO A NEW LIFE. BEHIND THEM WERE THE YEARS OF THEIR YOUTH AND THE

TIME OF GROWING UP. ABOARD THE TRAINS THAT SNAKED ALONG THE RIVERBEDS, SOMBER RECRUITS STARED OUT OF THE GRIMY WINDOWS. IT WAS A TIME TO REFLECT, TO TAKE INVENTORY, NOT AS DYING MEN—FOR THEY HAD STILL TO FACE THAT—BUT RATHER TO SHORE UP THEIR STRENGTH AGAINST WHAT LAY AHEAD. THEY KNEW INSTINCTIVELY THAT THEIR VALUES AND PREJUDICES WOULD SOON BE TESTED AND THAT PERHAPS NOT AGAIN IN THE RUSH OF LIVING WOULD THERE BE SUCH A MOMENT AS THIS.

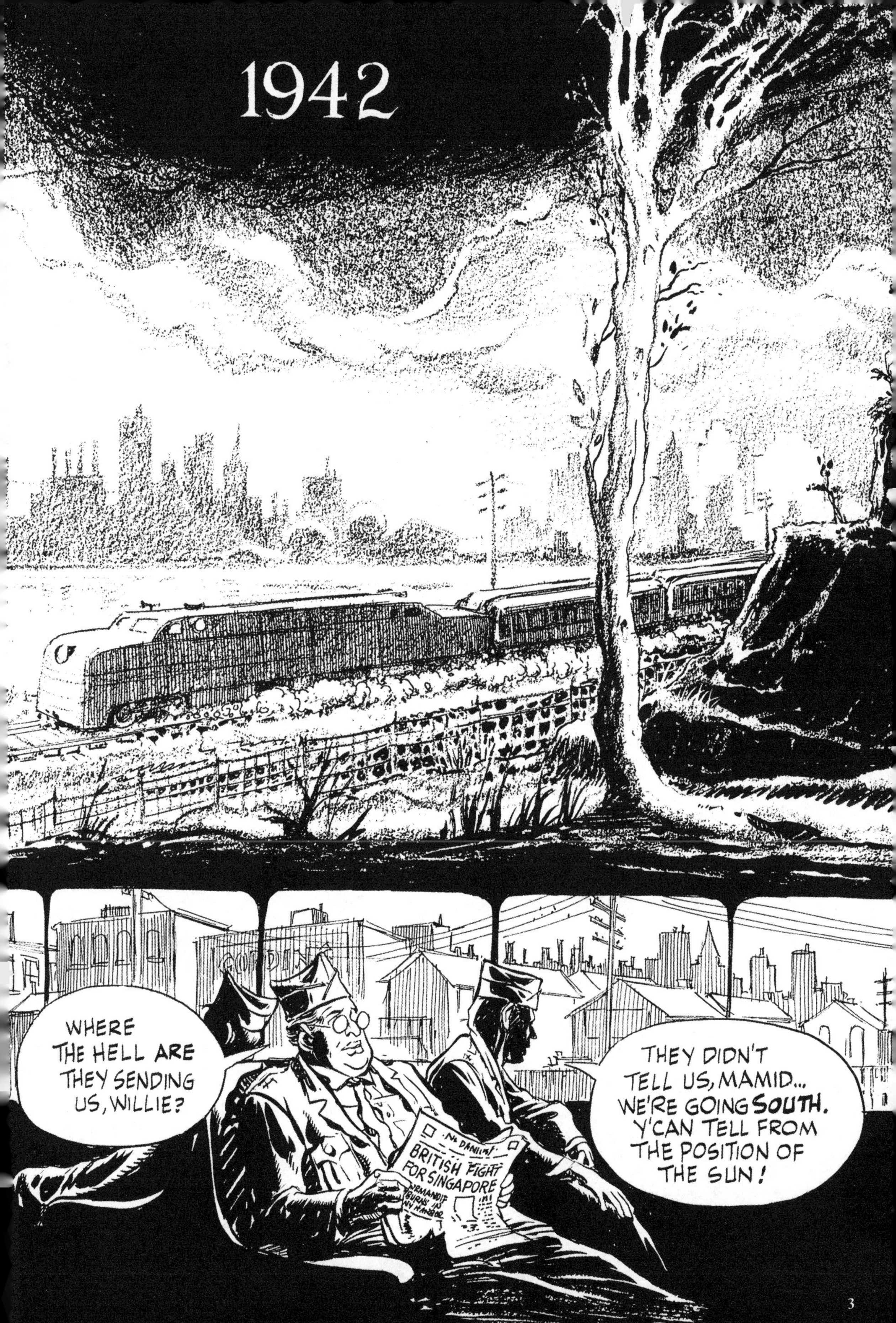
1942
WHERE THE HELL ARE THEY SENDING US, WILLIE?
BRITISH FIGHT FOR SINGAPORE
THEY DIDN'T TELL US, MAMID... WE'RE GOING SOUTH. Y'CAN TELL FROM THE POSITION OF THE SUN!

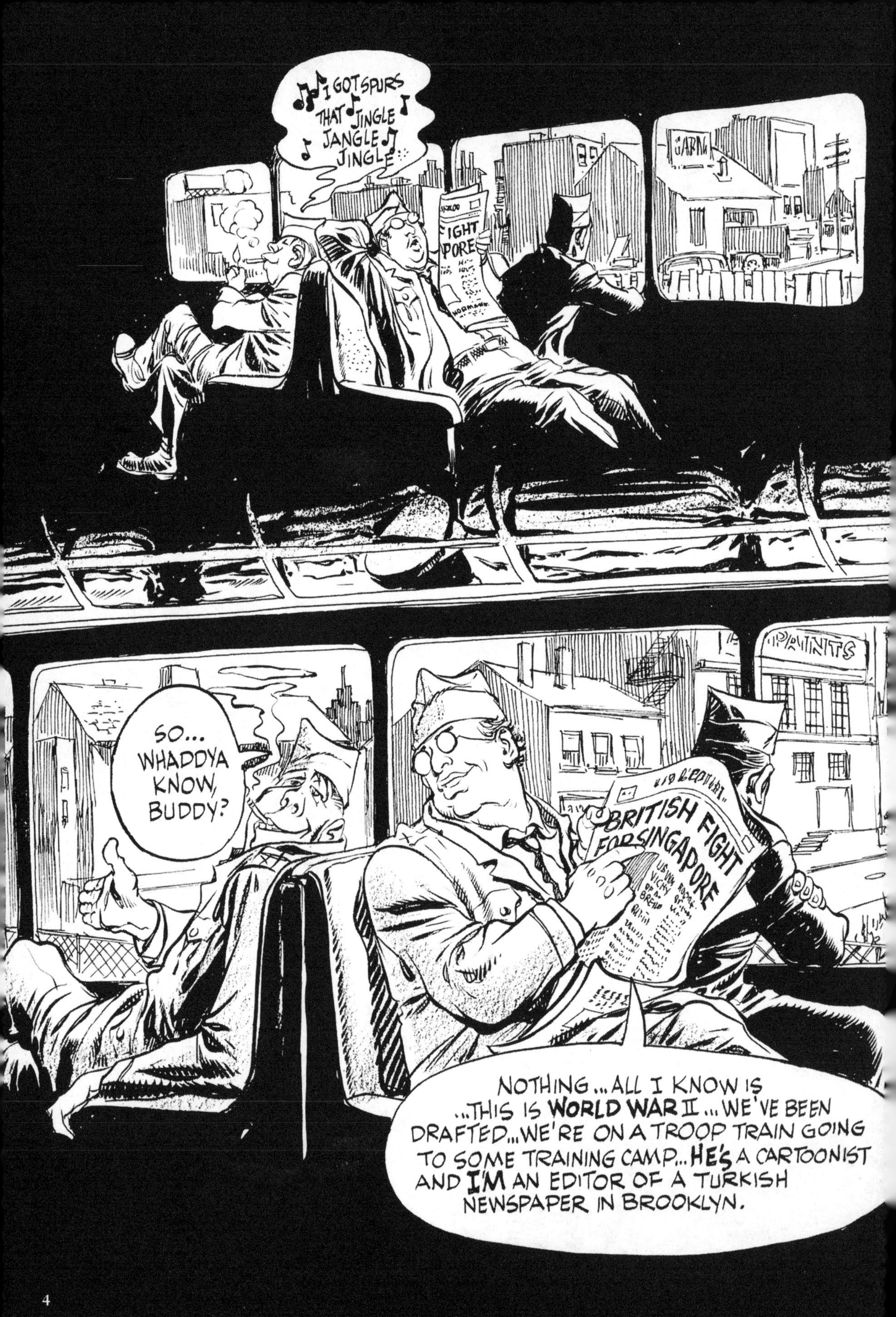
I GOT SPURS THAT JINGLE JANGLE JINGLE
FIGHT
PORE
PAINTS
SO... WHADDYA KNOW, BUDDY?
BRITISH FIGHT FOR SINGAPORE
NOTHING... ALL I KNOW IS ..THIS IS **WORLD WAR II** ... WE'VE BEEN DRAFTED... WE'RE ON A TROOP TRAIN GOING TO SOME TRAINING CAMP... **HE'S** A CARTOONIST AND **I'M** AN EDITOR OF A TURKISH NEWSPAPER IN BROOKLYN.

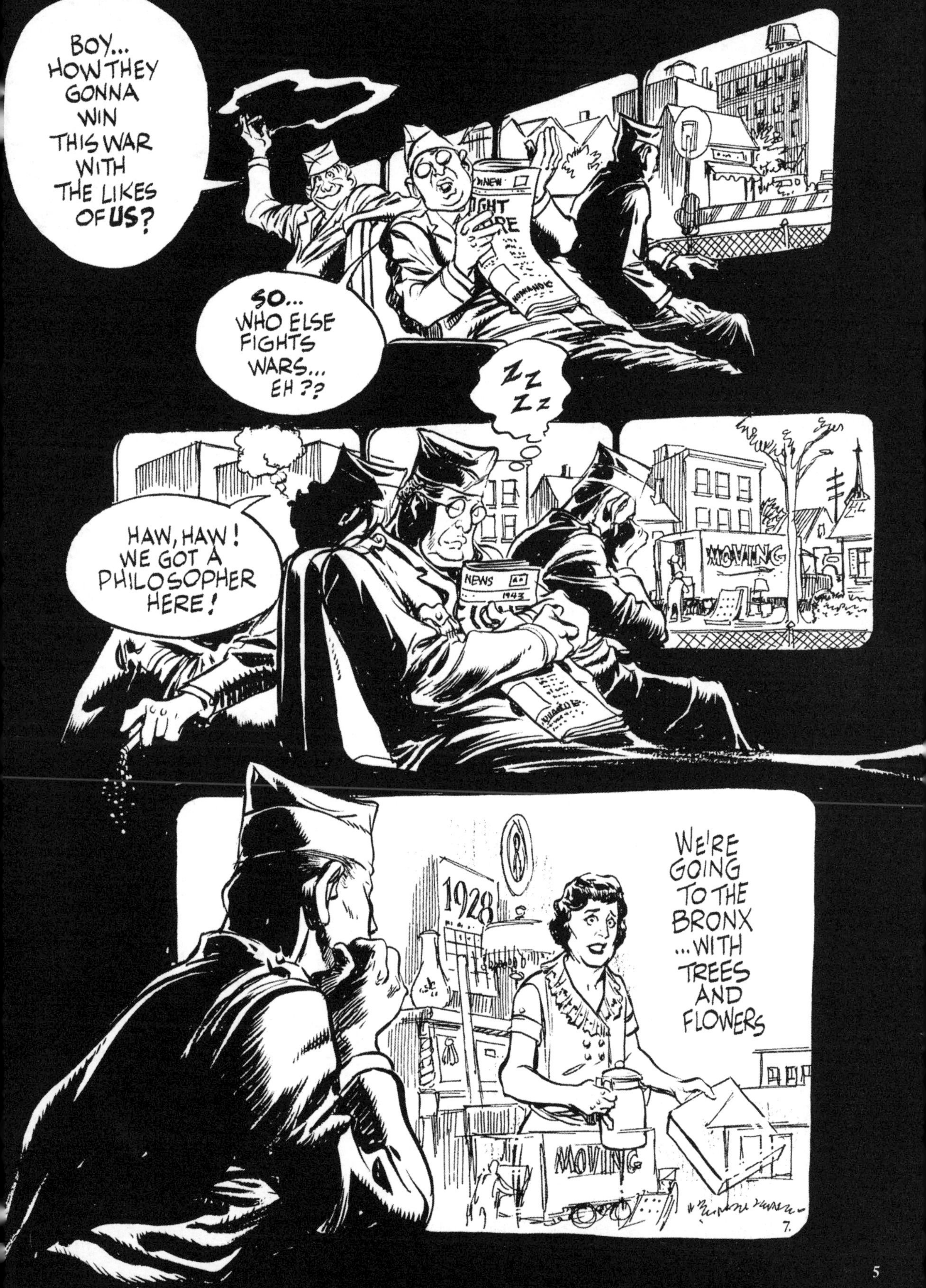
BOY... HOW THEY GONNA WIN THIS WAR WITH THE LIKES OF US?
SO... WHO ELSE FIGHTS WARS... EH ??
Z Z Z Z
HAW, HAW! WE GOT A PHILOSOPHER HERE!
NEWS
1943
MOVING
1928
WE'RE GOING TO THE BRONX ...WITH TREES AND FLOWERS
MOVING
7.

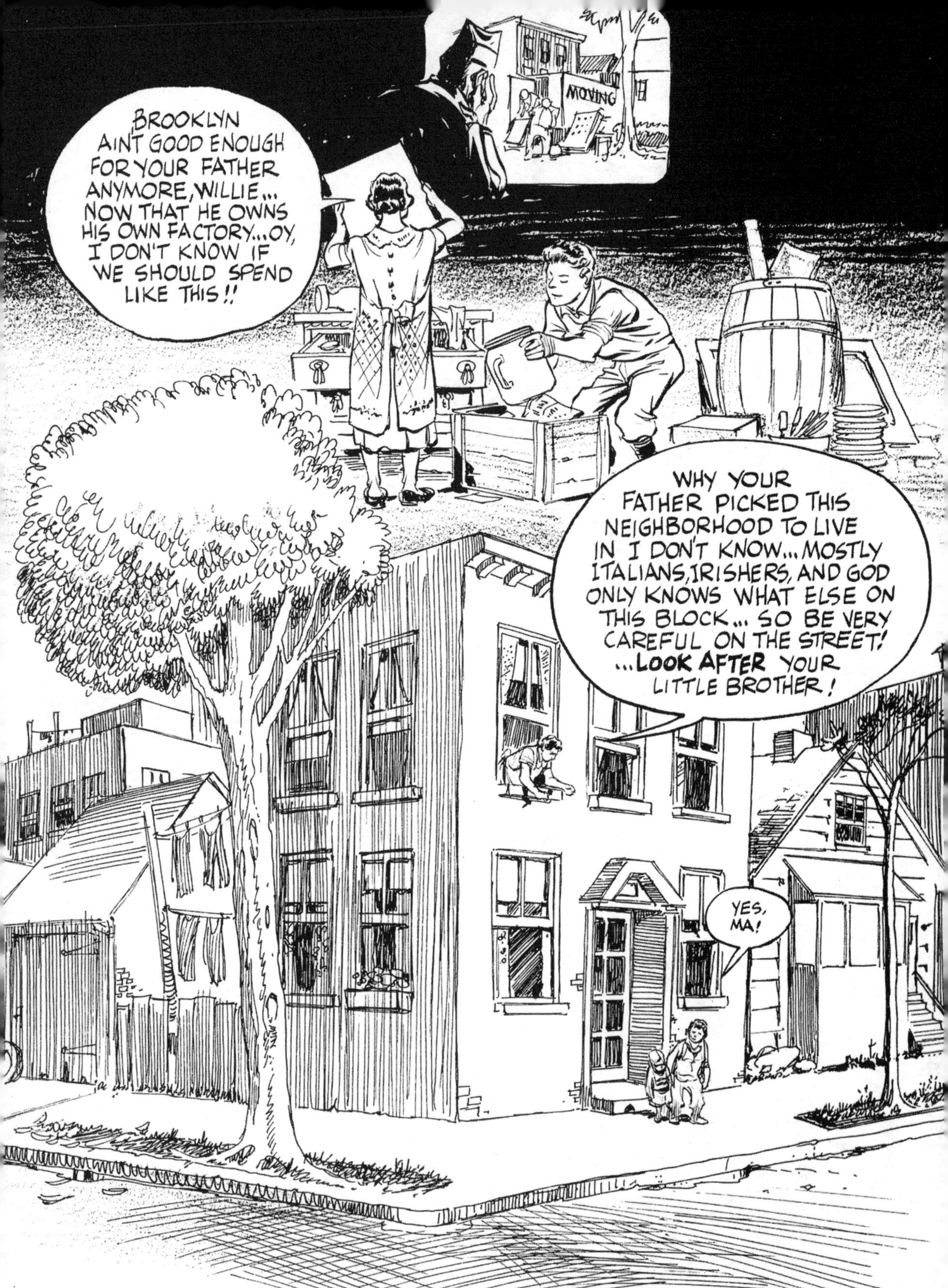
MOVING
BROOKLYN AIN'T GOOD ENOUGH FOR YOUR FATHER ANYMORE, WILLIE... NOW THAT HE OWNS HIS OWN FACTORY...OY, I DON'T KNOW IF WE SHOULD SPEND LIKE THIS!!
WHY YOUR FATHER PICKED THIS NEIGHBORHOOD TO LIVE IN I DON'T KNOW... MOSTLY ITALIANS, IRISHERS, AND GOD ONLY KNOWS WHAT ELSE ON THIS BLOCK... SO BE VERY CAREFUL ON THE STREET! ...**LOOK AFTER** YOUR LITTLE BROTHER!
YES, MA!

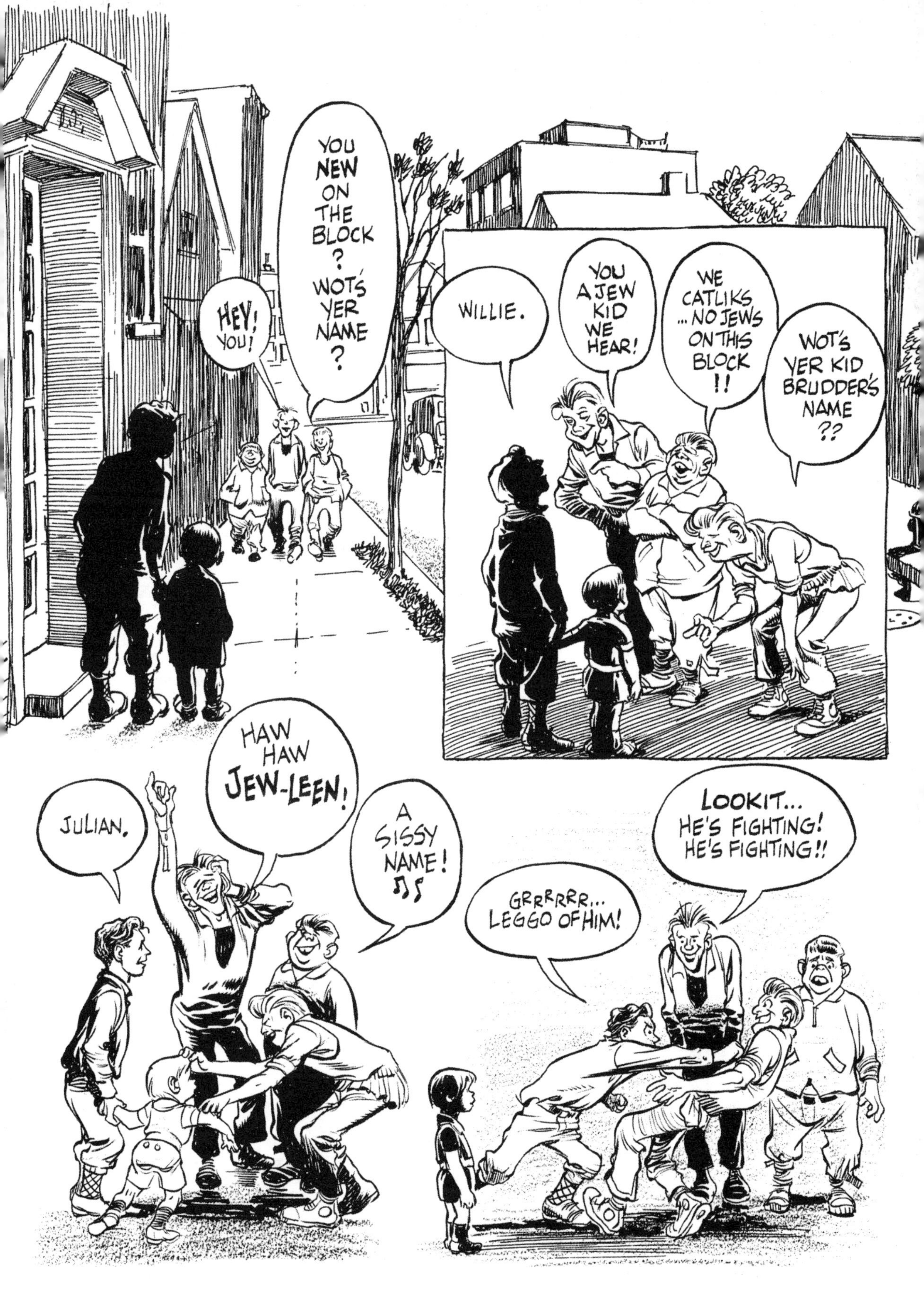
HEY! YOU!
YOU NEW ON THE BLOCK? WOT'S YER NAME?
WILLIE.
YOU A JEW KID WE HEAR!
WE CATLIKS ...NO JEWS ON THIS BLOCK!!
WOT'S YER KID BRUDDER'S NAME??
JULIAN.
HAW HAW JEW-LEEN!
A SISSY NAME!
GRRRRRR... LEGGO OF HIM!
LOOKIT... HE'S FIGHTING! HE'S FIGHTING!!

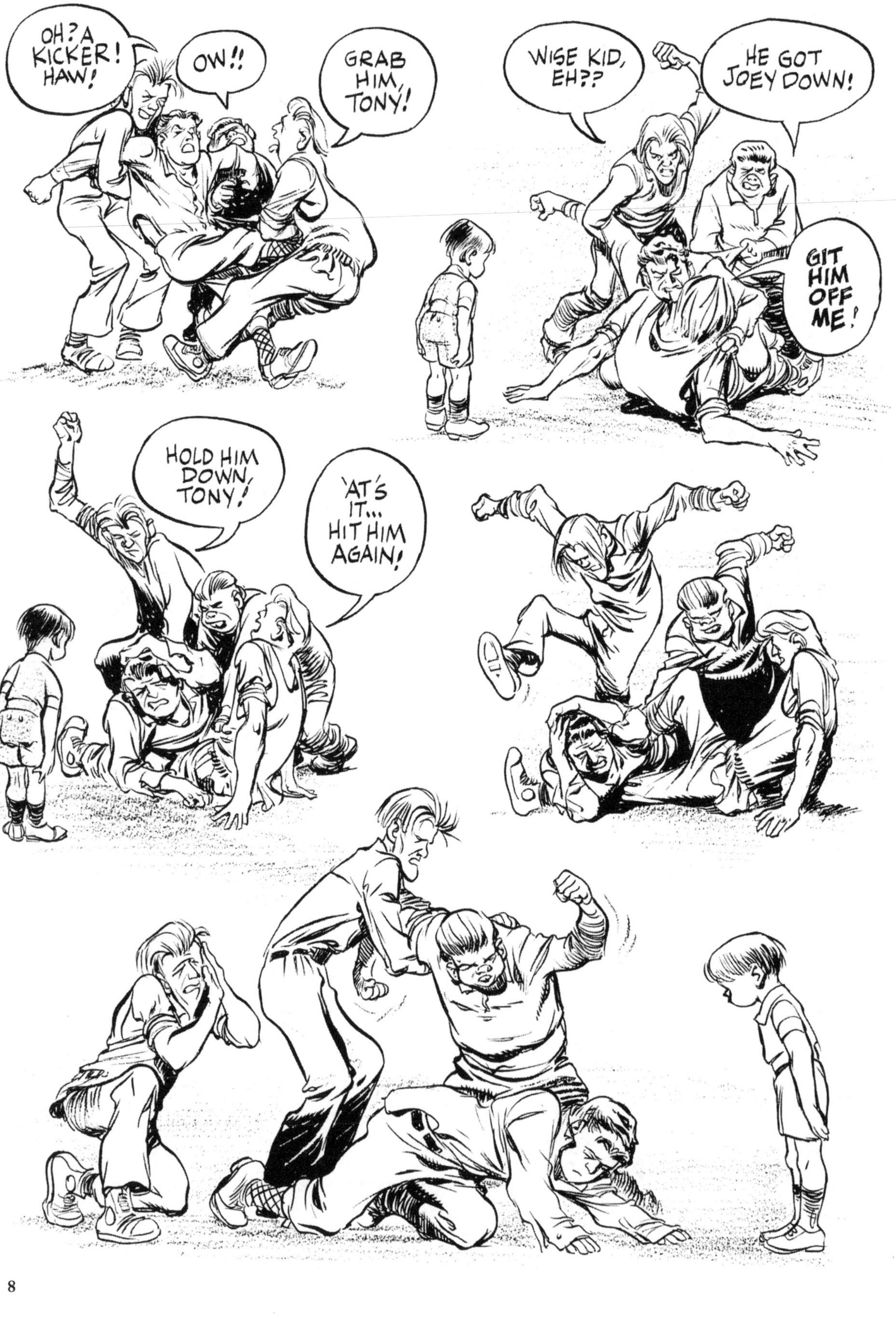
OH? A KICKER! HAW!
OW!!
GRAB HIM, TONY!
WISE KID, EH??
HE GOT JOEY DOWN!
GIT HIM OFF ME!
HOLD HIM DOWN, TONY!
'AT'S IT... HIT HIM AGAIN!

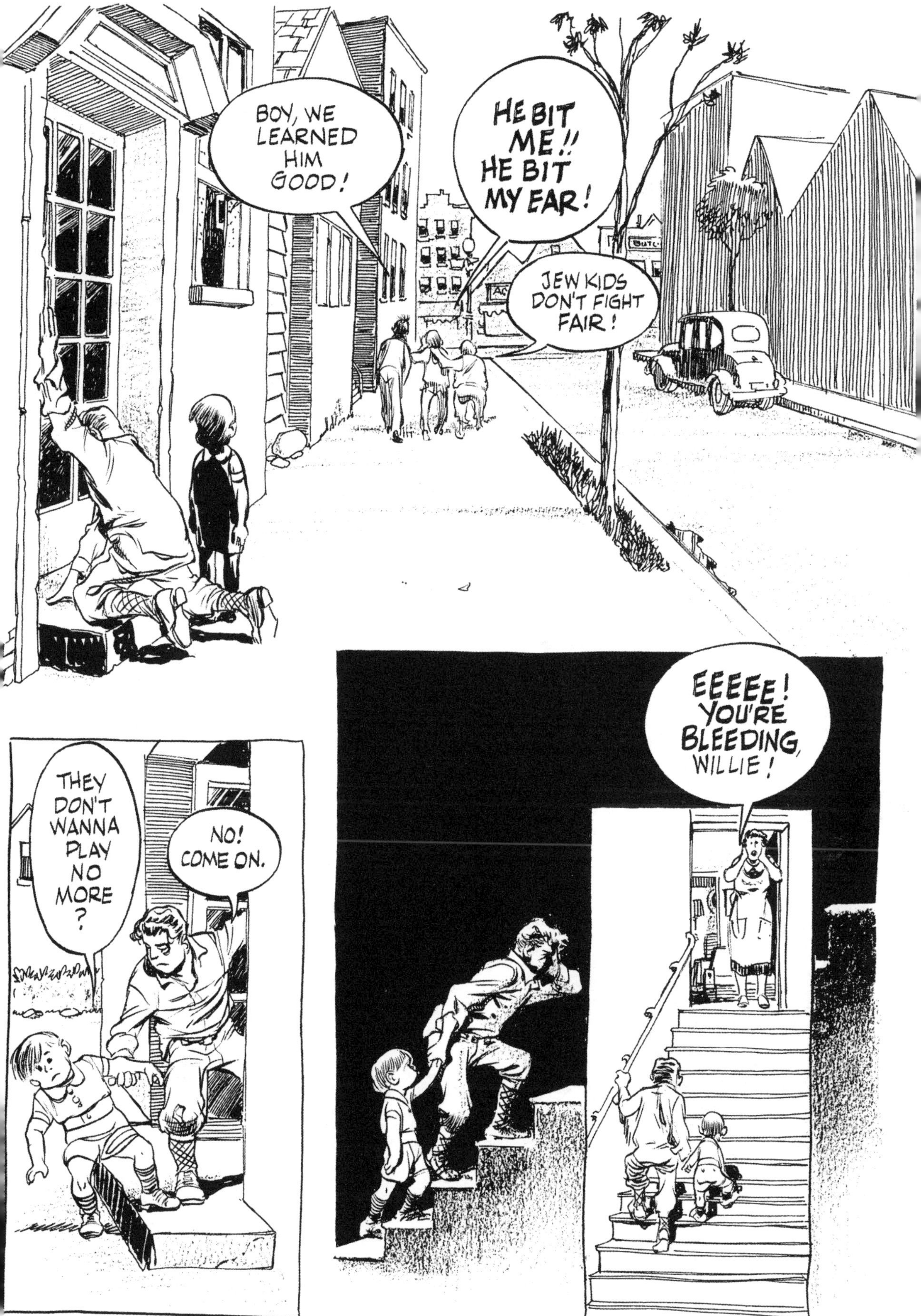
BOY, WE LEARNED HIM GOOD!
HE BIT ME!! HE BIT MY EAR!
JEW KIDS DON'T FIGHT FAIR!
THEY DON'T WANNA PLAY NO MORE?
NO! COME ON.
EEEEE! YOU'RE BLEEDING, WILLIE!

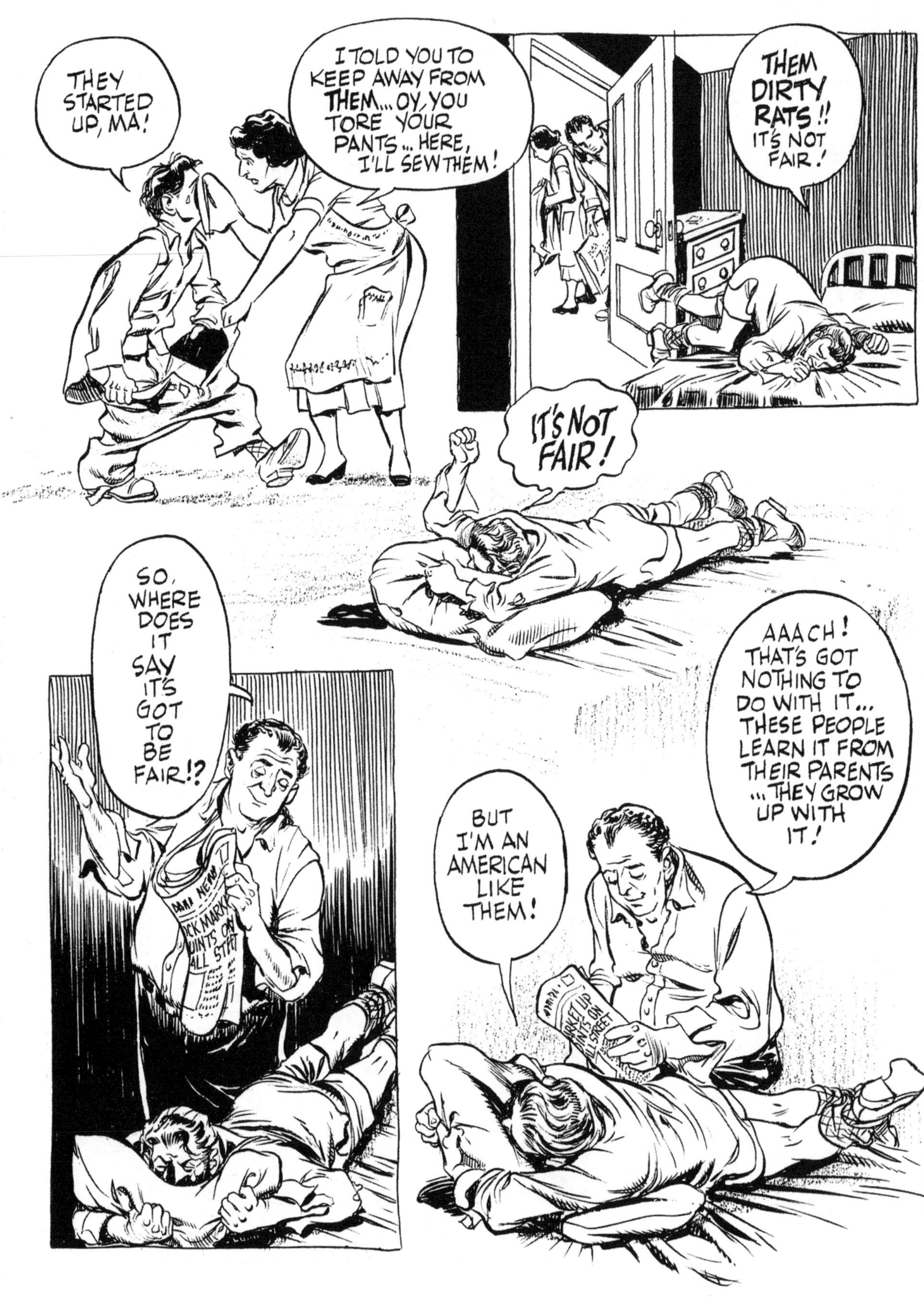
THEY STARTED UP, MA!
I TOLD YOU TO KEEP AWAY FROM THEM... OY, YOU TORE YOUR PANTS... HERE, I'LL SEW THEM!
THEM DIRTY RATS!! IT'S NOT FAIR!
IT'S NOT FAIR!
SO, WHERE DOES IT SAY IT'S GOT TO BE FAIR!?
AAACH! THAT'S GOT NOTHING TO DO WITH IT... THESE PEOPLE LEARN IT FROM THEIR PARENTS ...THEY GROW UP WITH IT!
BUT I'M AN AMERICAN LIKE THEM!

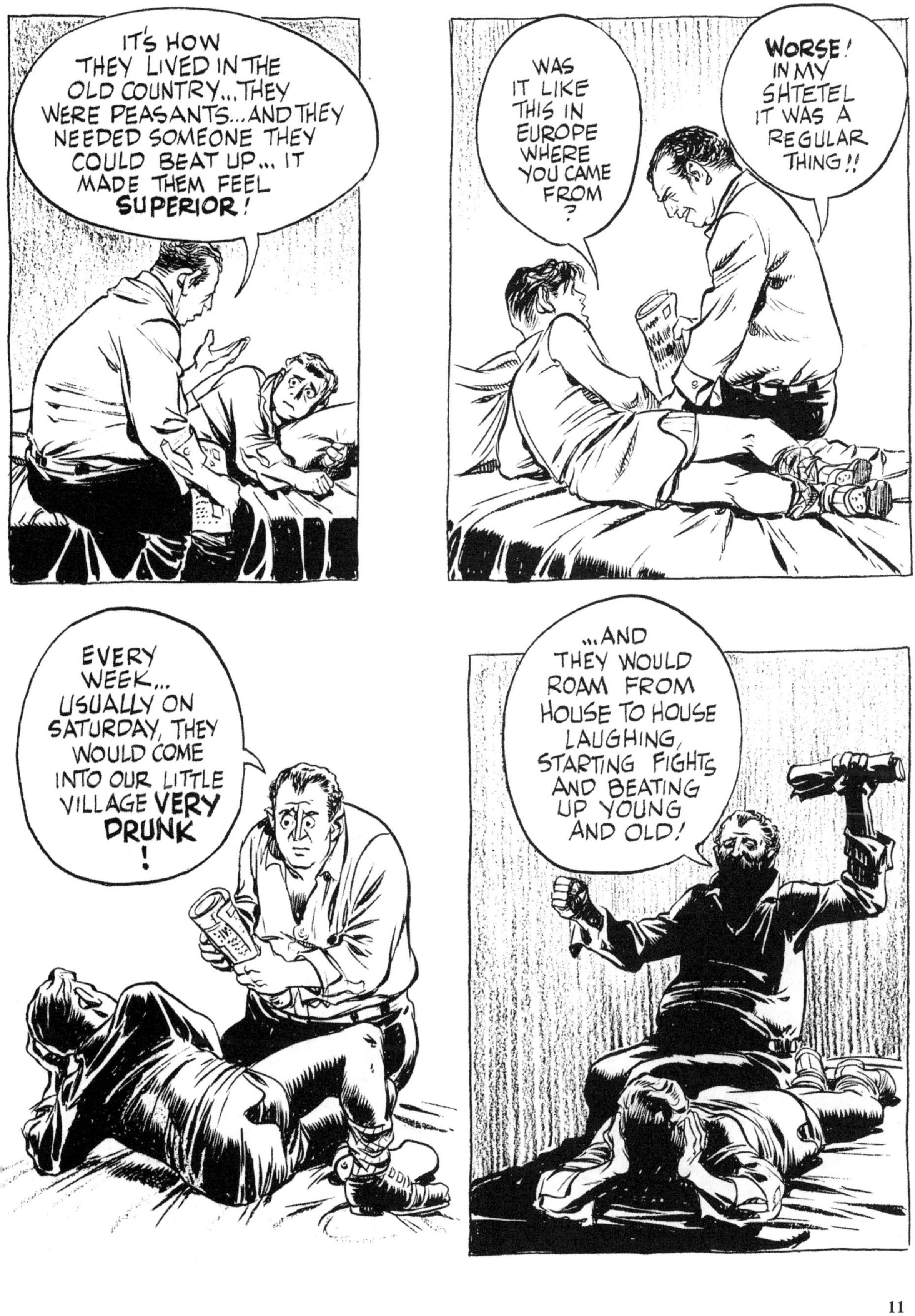
IT'S HOW THEY LIVED IN THE OLD COUNTRY...THEY WERE PEASANTS...AND THEY NEEDED SOMEONE THEY COULD BEAT UP... IT MADE THEM FEEL SUPERIOR!
WAS IT LIKE THIS IN EUROPE WHERE YOU CAME FROM?
WORSE! IN MY SHTETEL IT WAS A REGULAR THING!!
EVERY WEEK... USUALLY ON SATURDAY, THEY WOULD COME INTO OUR LITTLE VILLAGE VERY DRUNK!
...AND THEY WOULD ROAM FROM HOUSE TO HOUSE LAUGHING, STARTING FIGHTS AND BEATING UP YOUNG AND OLD!

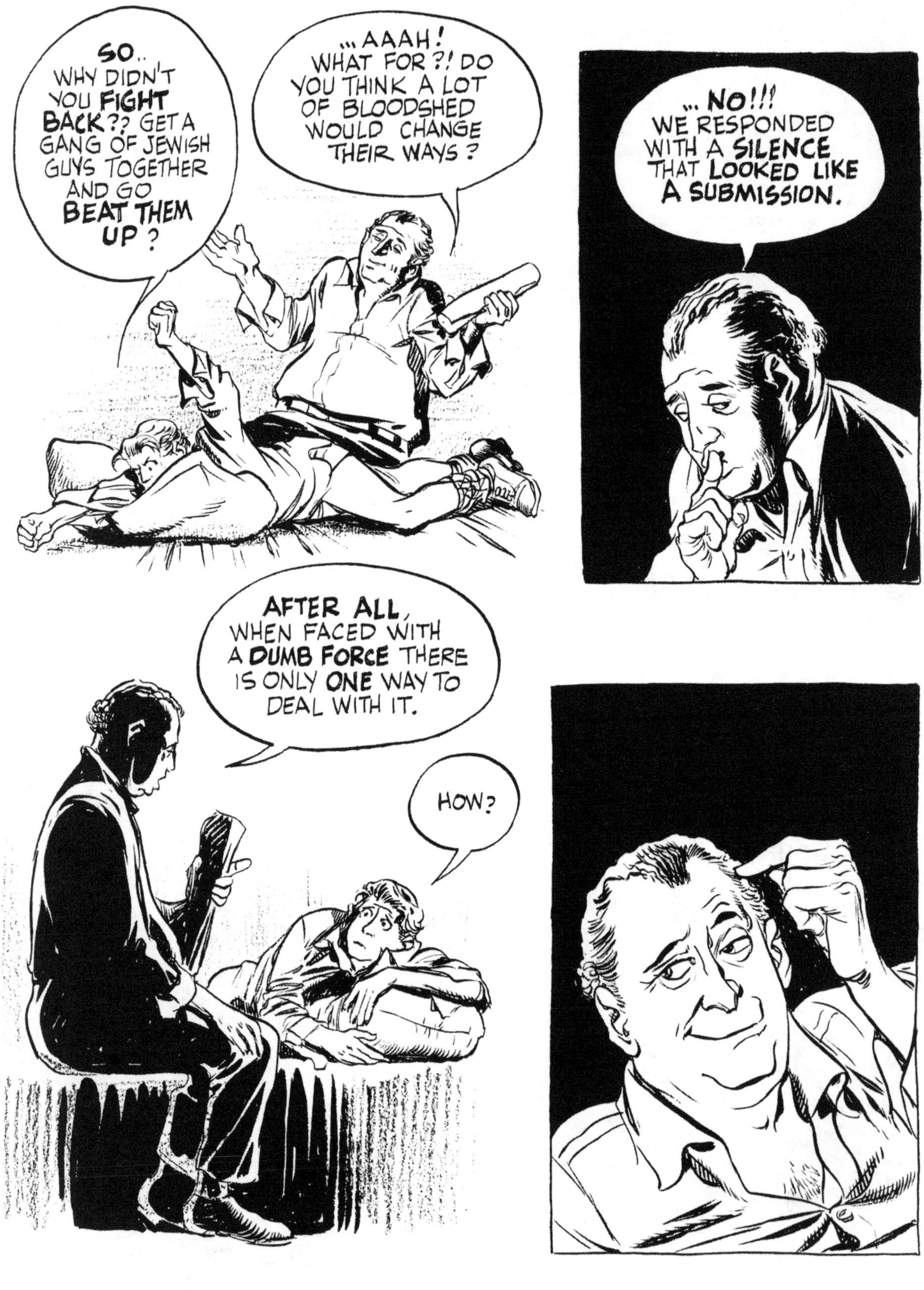
SO.. WHY DIDN'T YOU FIGHT BACK?? GET A GANG OF JEWISH GUYS TOGETHER AND GO BEAT THEM UP?
... AAAH! WHAT FOR?! DO YOU THINK A LOT OF BLOODSHED WOULD CHANGE THEIR WAYS?
... NO!!! WE RESPONDED WITH A SILENCE THAT LOOKED LIKE A SUBMISSION.
AFTER ALL, WHEN FACED WITH A DUMB FORCE THERE IS ONLY ONE WAY TO DEAL WITH IT.
HOW?

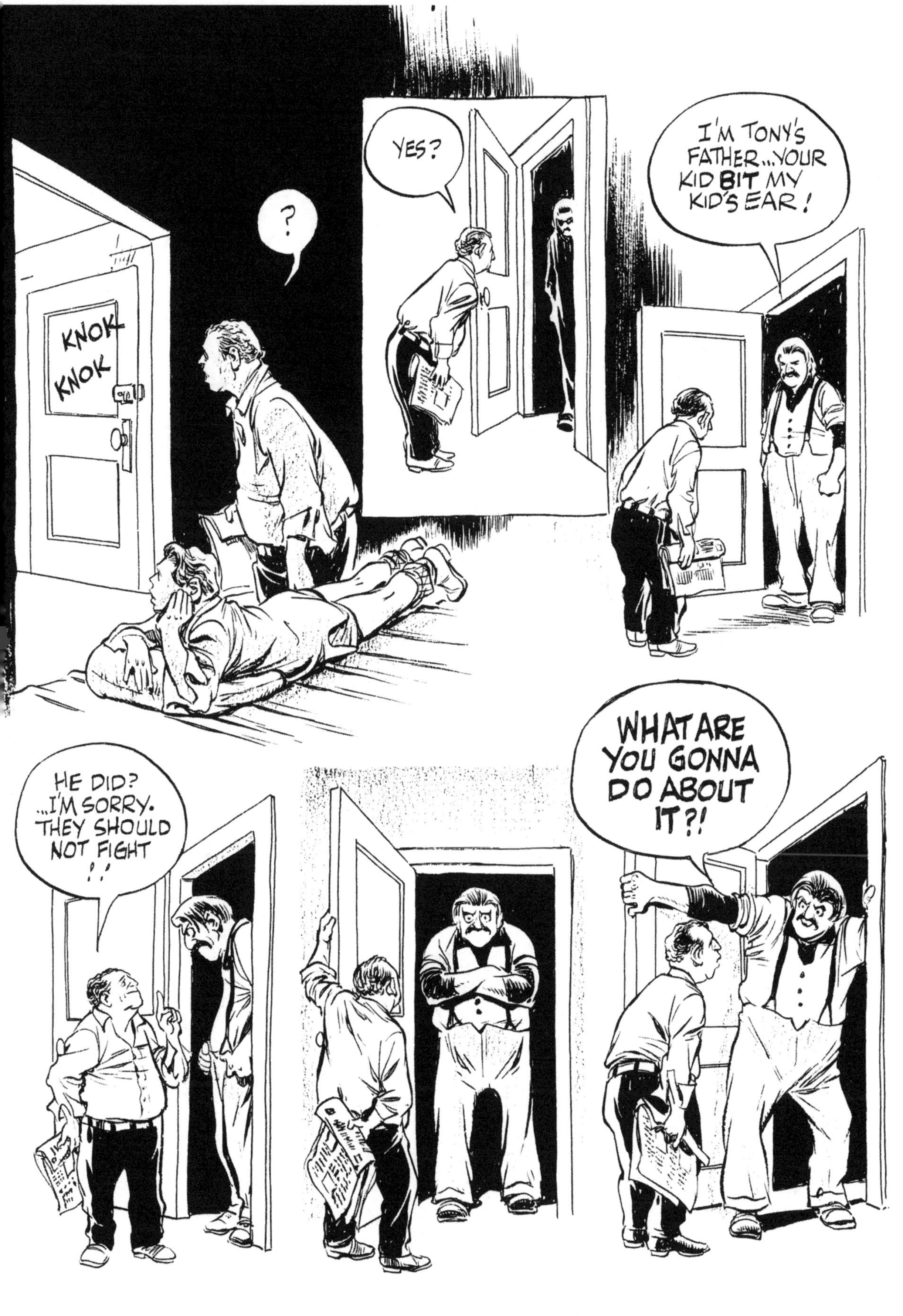
KNOK
KNOK
?
YES?
I'M TONY'S FATHER...YOUR KID BIT MY KID'S EAR!
HE DID? ...I'M SORRY. THEY SHOULD NOT FIGHT !!
WHAT ARE YOU GONNA DO ABOUT IT?!

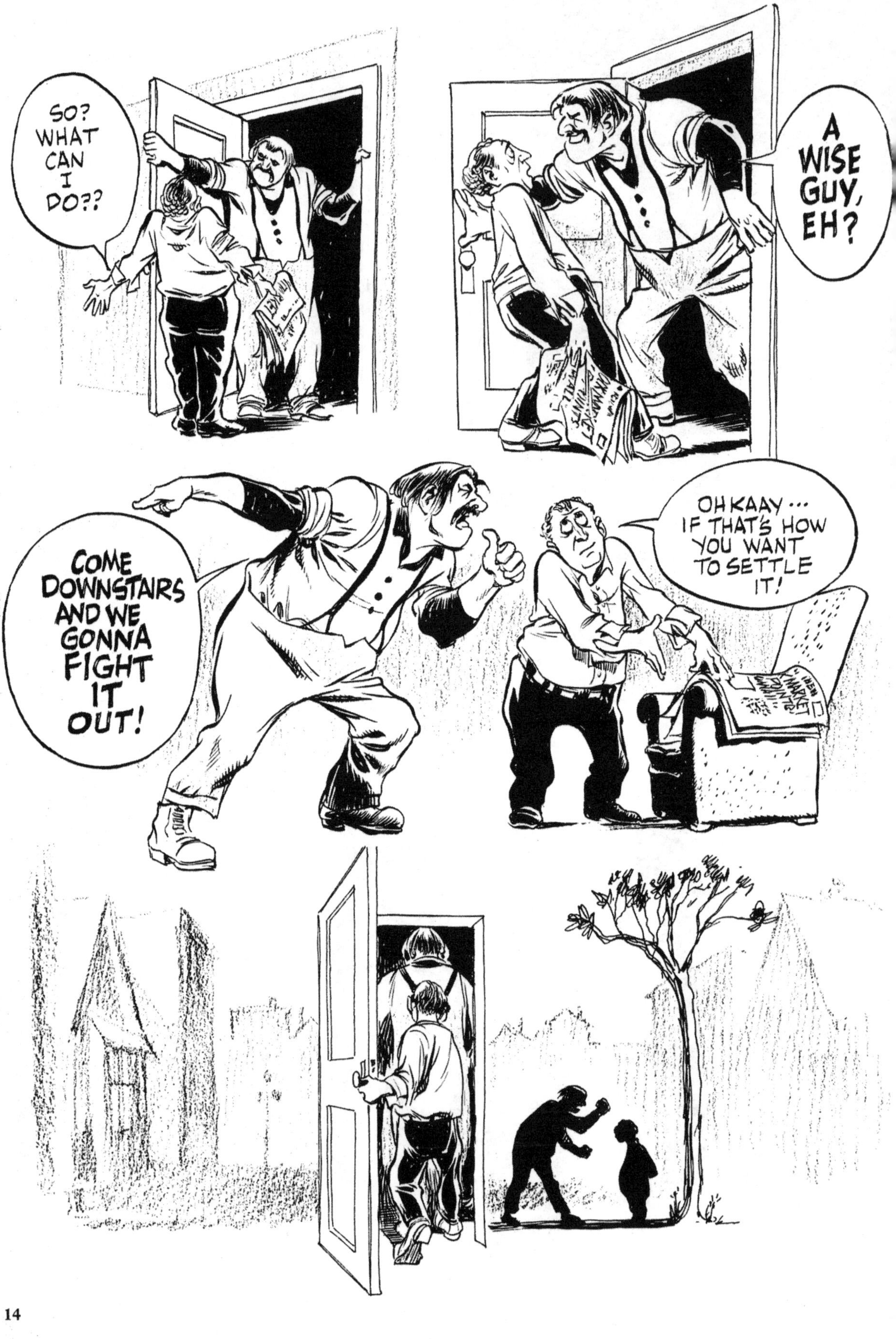
SO? WHAT CAN I DO??
A WISE GUY, EH?
COME DOWNSTAIRS AND WE GONNA FIGHT IT OUT!
OH KAAY... IF THAT'S HOW YOU WANT TO SETTLE IT!

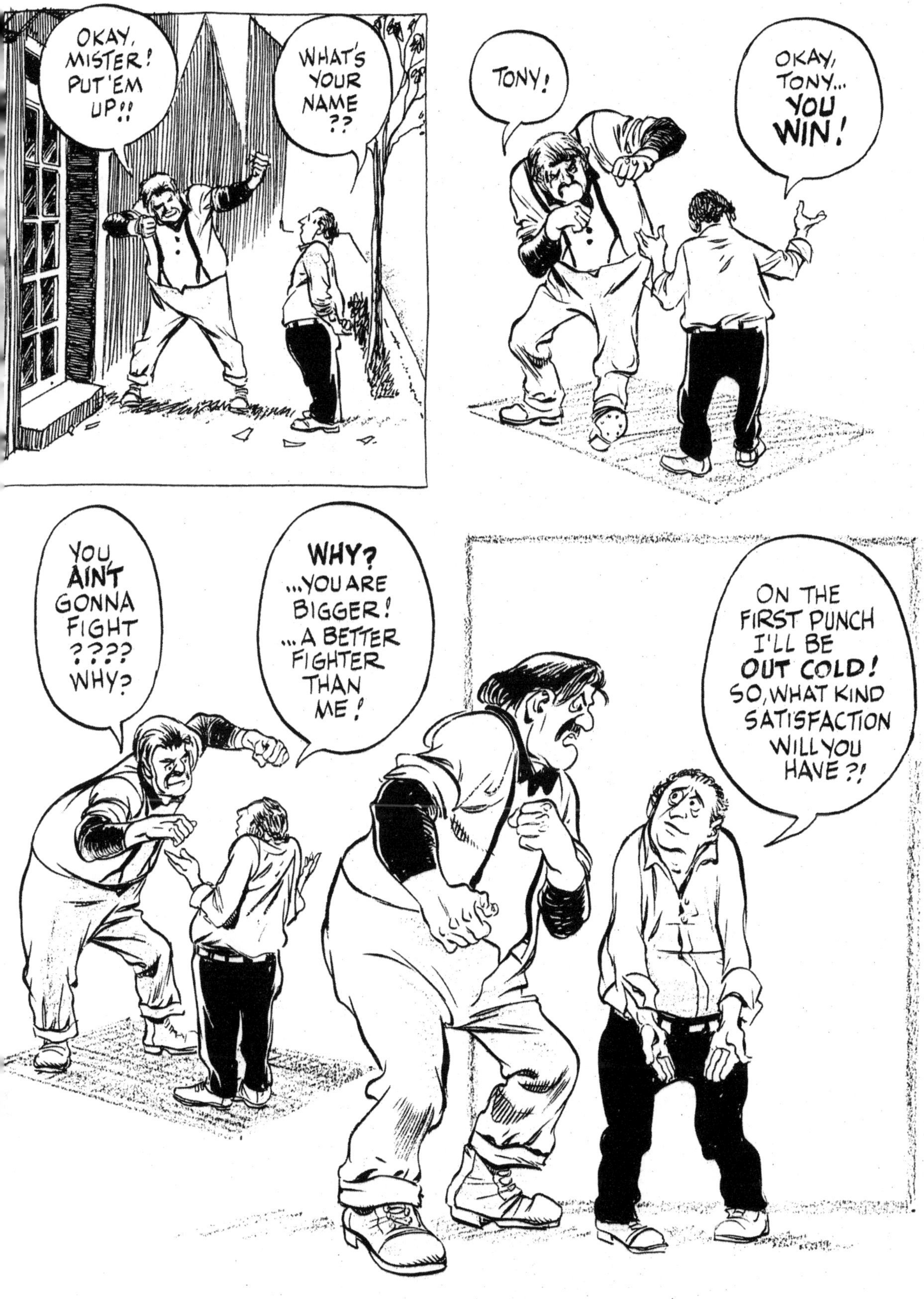

OKAY, MISTER! PUT 'EM UP!!
WHAT'S YOUR NAME ??
TONY!
OKAY, TONY... YOU WIN!
YOU AIN'T GONNA FIGHT ???? WHY?
WHY? ...YOU ARE BIGGER! ...A BETTER FIGHTER THAN ME!
ON THE FIRST PUNCH I'LL BE OUT COLD! SO, WHAT KIND SATISFACTION WILL YOU HAVE?!

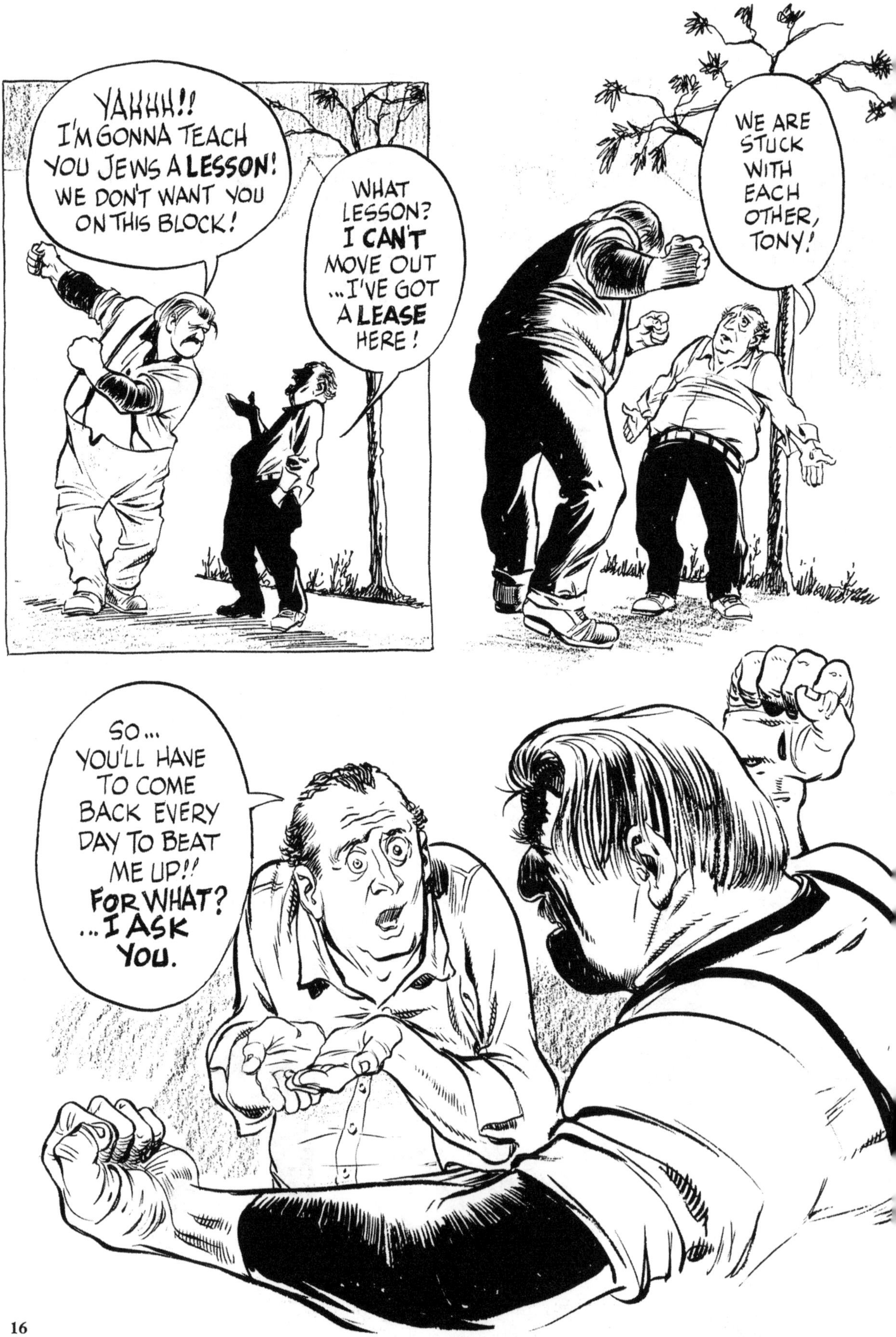
YAHHH!! I'M GONNA TEACH YOU JEWS A **LESSON**! WE DON'T WANT YOU ON THIS BLOCK!
WHAT LESSON? **I CAN'T** MOVE OUT ...I'VE GOT A **LEASE** HERE!
WE ARE STUCK WITH EACH OTHER, TONY!
SO... YOU'LL HAVE TO COME BACK EVERY DAY TO BEAT ME UP!! **FOR WHAT?** ...**I ASK YOU**.

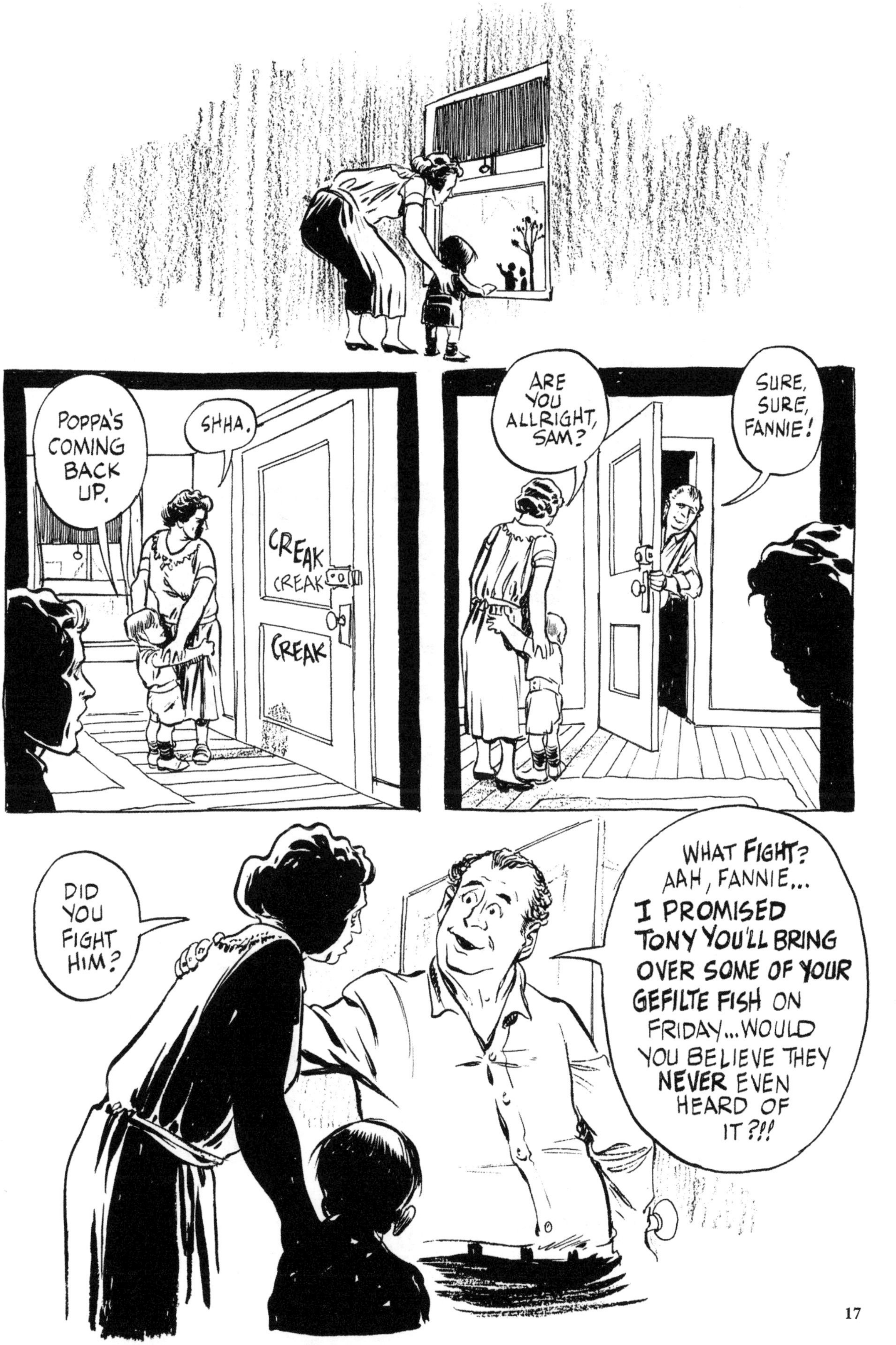
POPPA'S COMING BACK UP.
SHHA.
CREAK
CREAK
CREAK
ARE YOU ALLRIGHT, SAM?
SURE, SURE, FANNIE!
DID YOU FIGHT HIM?
WHAT FIGHT? AAH, FANNIE... I PROMISED TONY YOU'LL BRING OVER SOME OF YOUR GEFILTE FISH ON FRIDAY... WOULD YOU BELIEVE THEY NEVER EVEN HEARD OF IT?!!

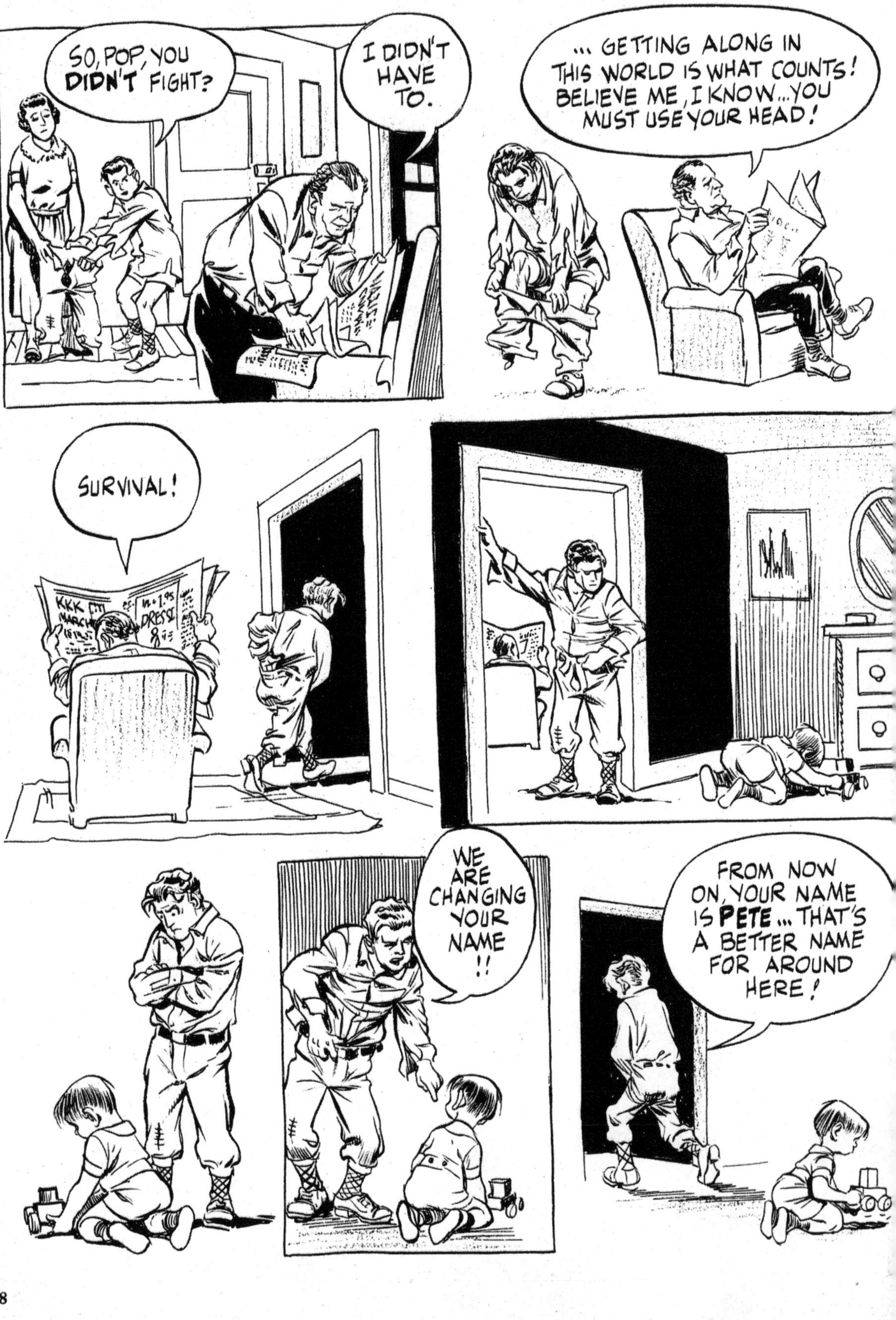
SO, POP, YOU DIDN'T FIGHT?
I DIDN'T HAVE TO.
... GETTING ALONG IN THIS WORLD IS WHAT COUNTS! BELIEVE ME, I KNOW... YOU MUST USE YOUR HEAD!
SURVIVAL!
WE ARE CHANGING YOUR NAME !!
FROM NOW ON, YOUR NAME IS PETE ... THAT'S A BETTER NAME FOR AROUND HERE!

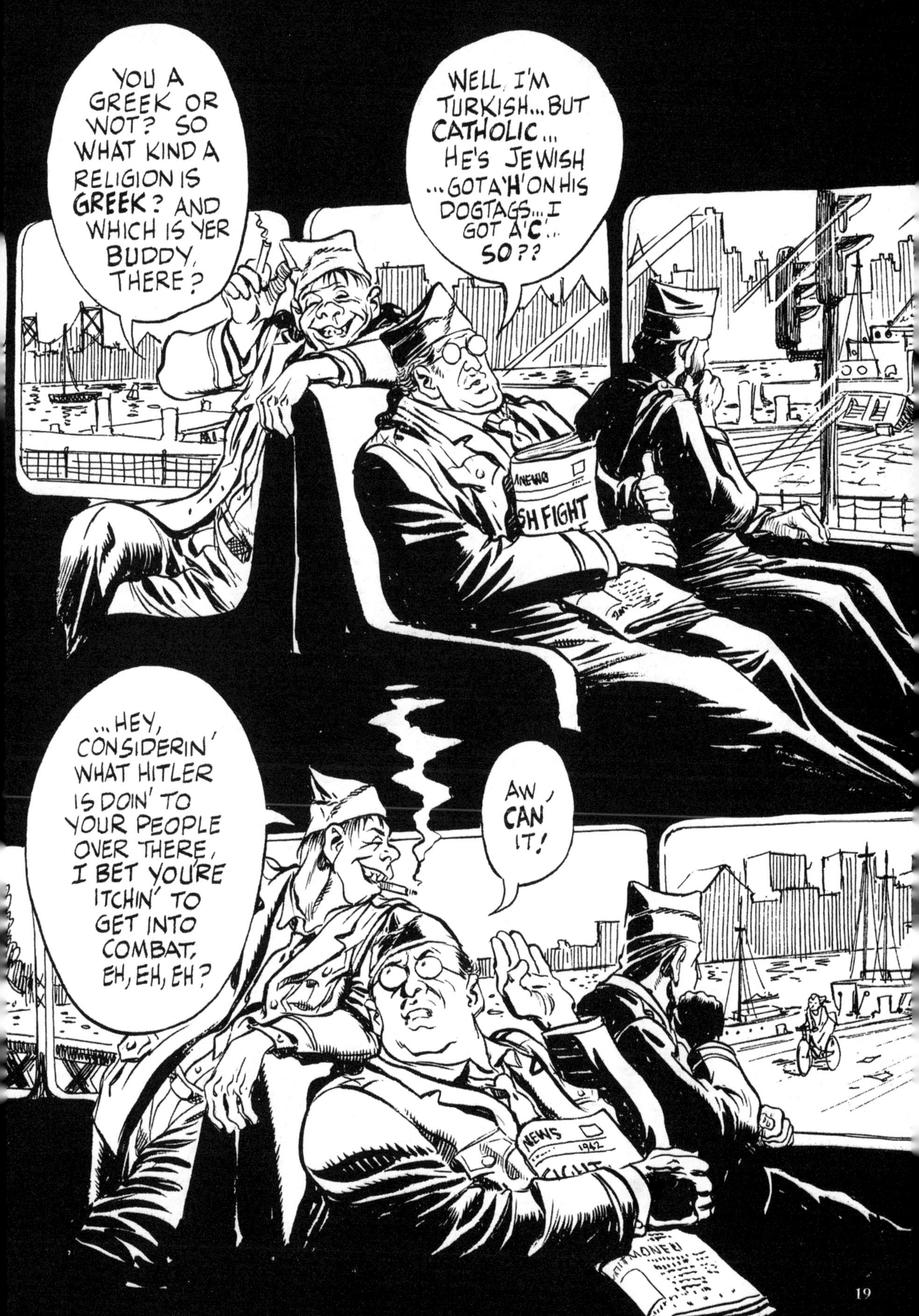
YOU A GREEK OR WOT? SO WHAT KIND A RELIGION IS GREEK? AND WHICH IS YER BUDDY, THERE?
WELL, I'M TURKISH... BUT CATHOLIC... HE'S JEWISH ...GOT A 'H' ON HIS DOGTAGS... I GOT A 'C'... SO??
NEWS
SH FIGHT
...HEY, CONSIDERIN' WHAT HITLER IS DOIN' TO YOUR PEOPLE OVER THERE, I BET YOU'RE ITCHIN' TO GET INTO COMBAT, EH, EH, EH?
AW, CAN IT!
NEWS
1942

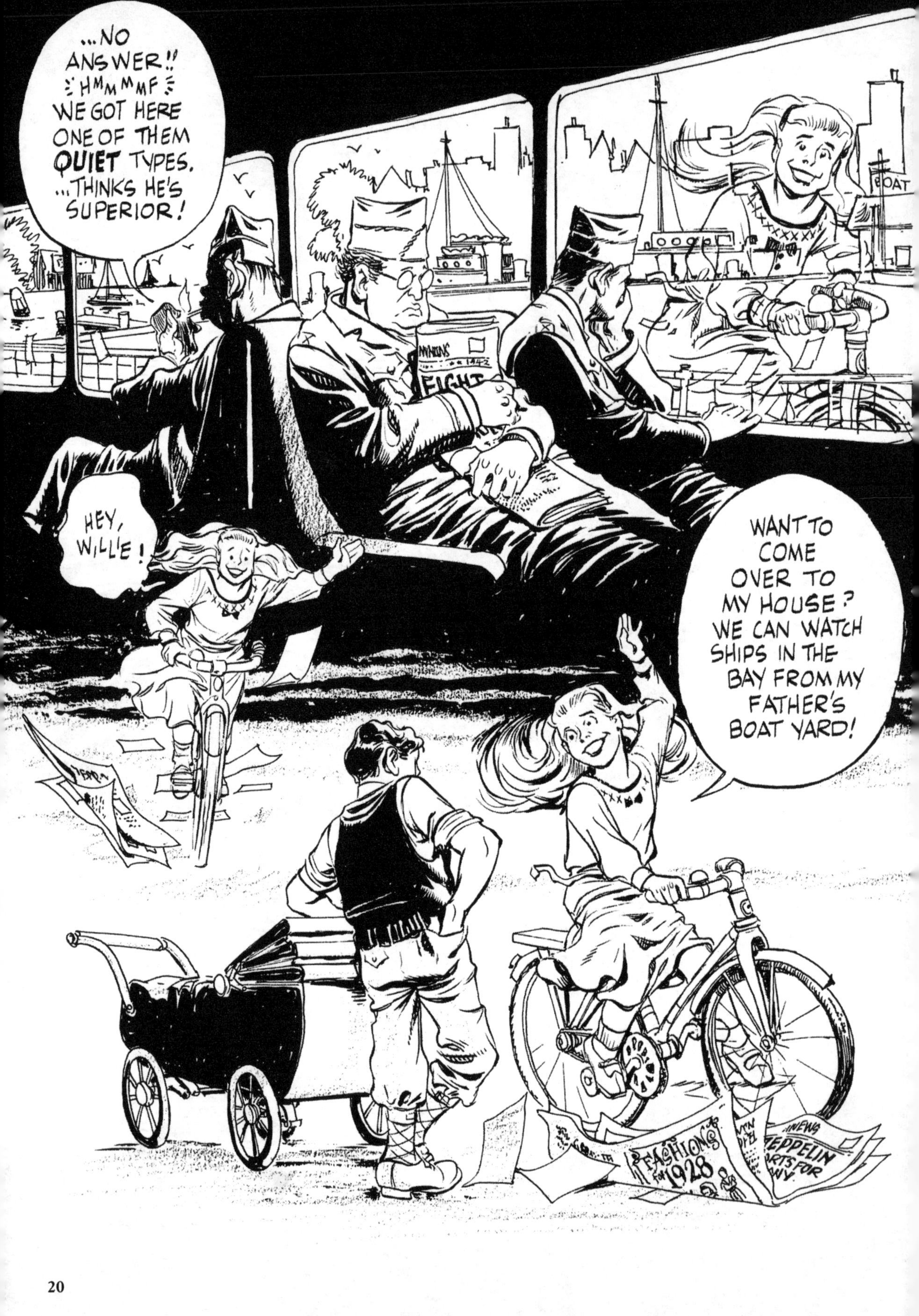
...NO ANSWER!! HMMMMF WE GOT HERE ONE OF THEM **QUIET** TYPES. ...THINKS HE'S SUPERIOR!
BOAT
1942
FIGHT
HEY, WILLIE!
WANT TO COME OVER TO MY HOUSE? WE CAN WATCH SHIPS IN THE BAY FROM MY FATHER'S BOAT YARD!
FASHIONS for 1928
NEWS
ZEPPELIN

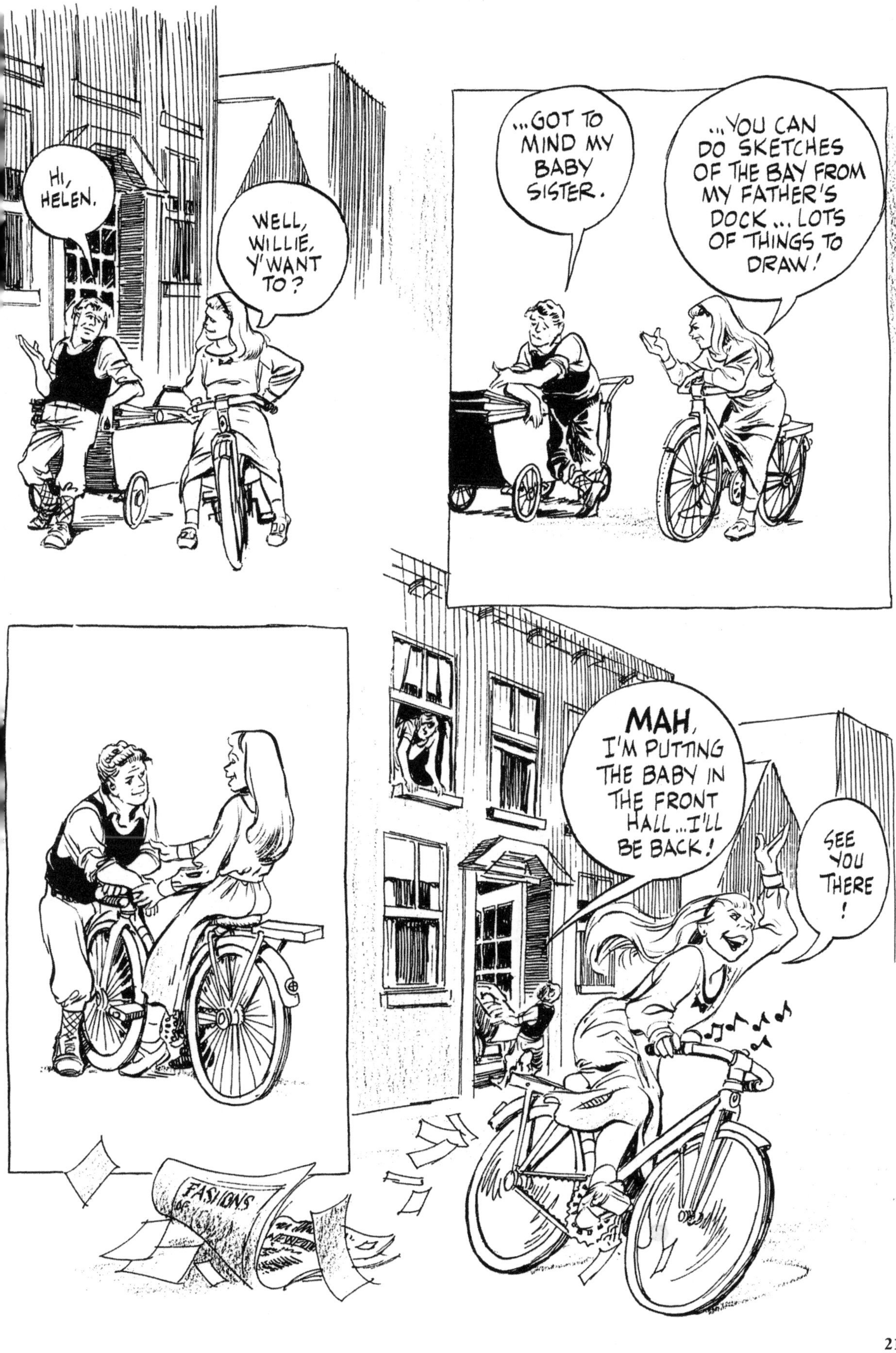
HI, HELEN.
WELL, WILLIE, Y'WANT TO?
...GOT TO MIND MY BABY SISTER.
...YOU CAN DO SKETCHES OF THE BAY FROM MY FATHER'S DOCK... LOTS OF THINGS TO DRAW!
MAH, I'M PUTTING THE BABY IN THE FRONT HALL...I'LL BE BACK!
SEE YOU THERE!
FASHIONS

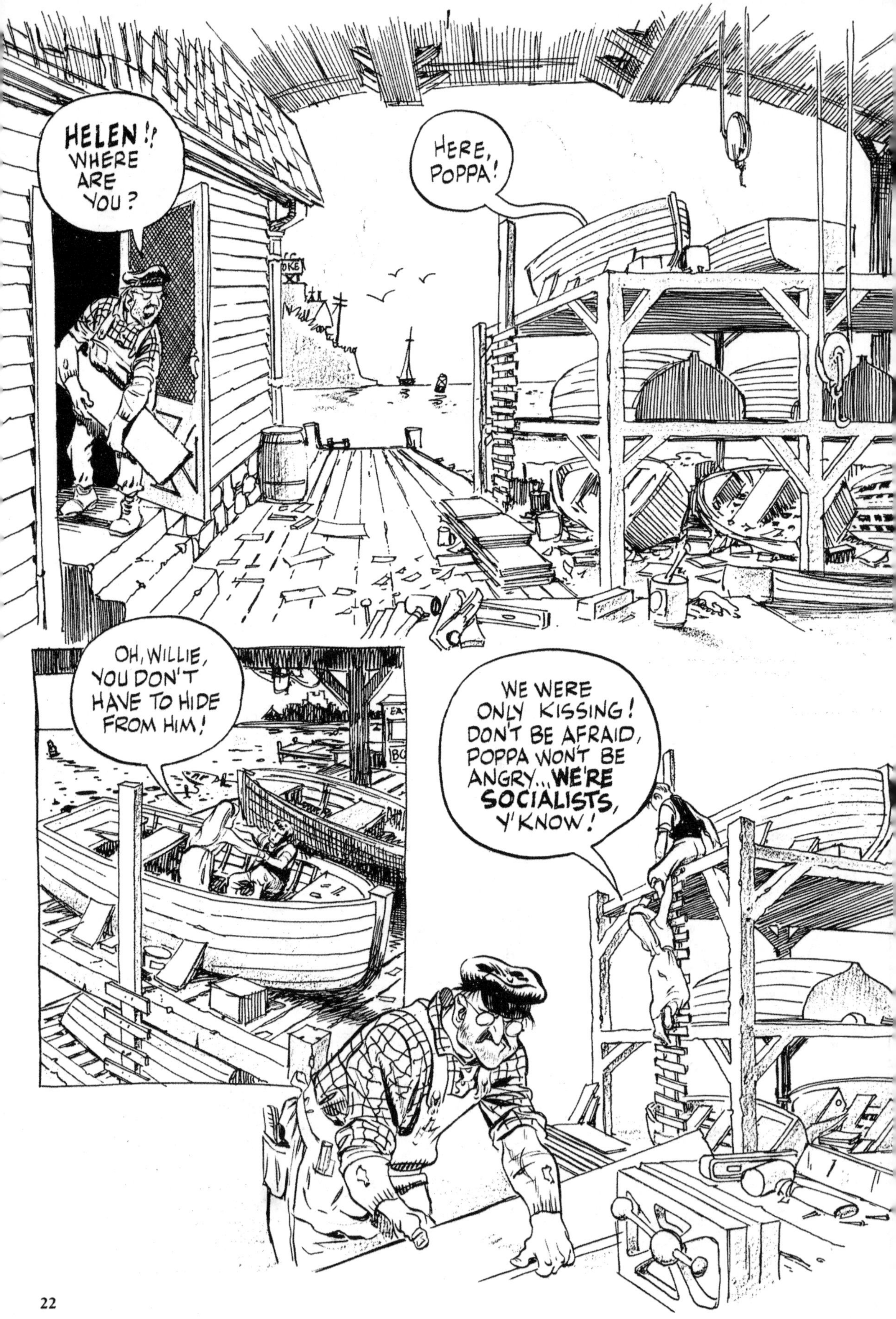
HELEN!! WHERE ARE YOU?
HERE, POPPA!
OH, WILLIE, YOU DON'T HAVE TO HIDE FROM HIM!
WE WERE ONLY KISSING! DON'T BE AFRAID, POPPA WON'T BE ANGRY... **WE'RE SOCIALISTS**, Y'KNOW!

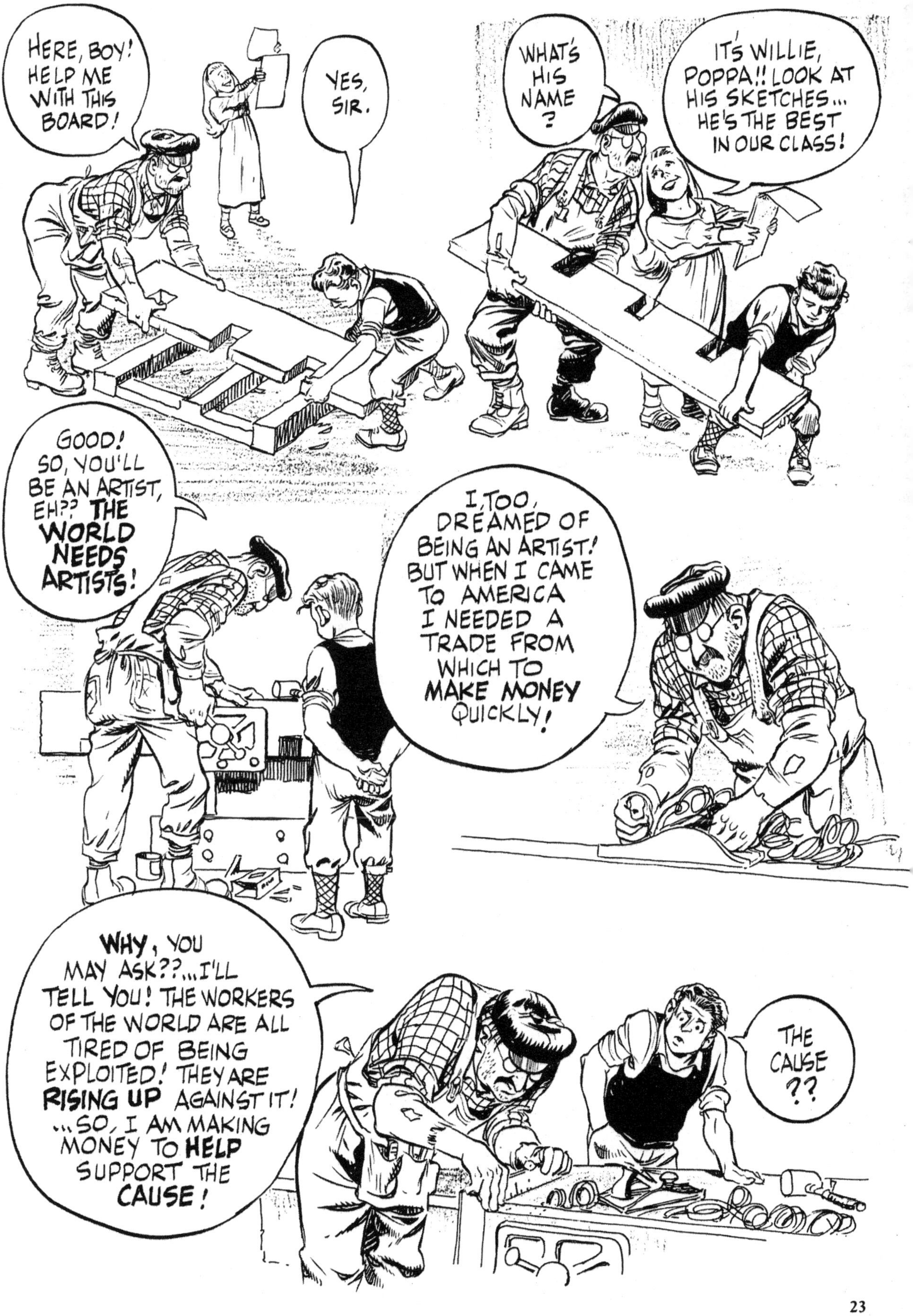
HERE, BOY! HELP ME WITH THIS BOARD!
YES, SIR.
WHAT'S HIS NAME ?
IT'S WILLIE, POPPA!! LOOK AT HIS SKETCHES... HE'S THE BEST IN OUR CLASS!
GOOD! SO, YOU'LL BE AN ARTIST, EH?? THE WORLD NEEDS ARTISTS!
I, TOO, DREAMED OF BEING AN ARTIST! BUT WHEN I CAME TO AMERICA I NEEDED A TRADE FROM WHICH TO MAKE MONEY QUICKLY!
WHY, YOU MAY ASK??...I'LL TELL YOU! THE WORKERS OF THE WORLD ARE ALL TIRED OF BEING EXPLOITED! THEY ARE RISING UP AGAINST IT! ...SO, I AM MAKING MONEY TO HELP SUPPORT THE CAUSE!
THE CAUSE ??

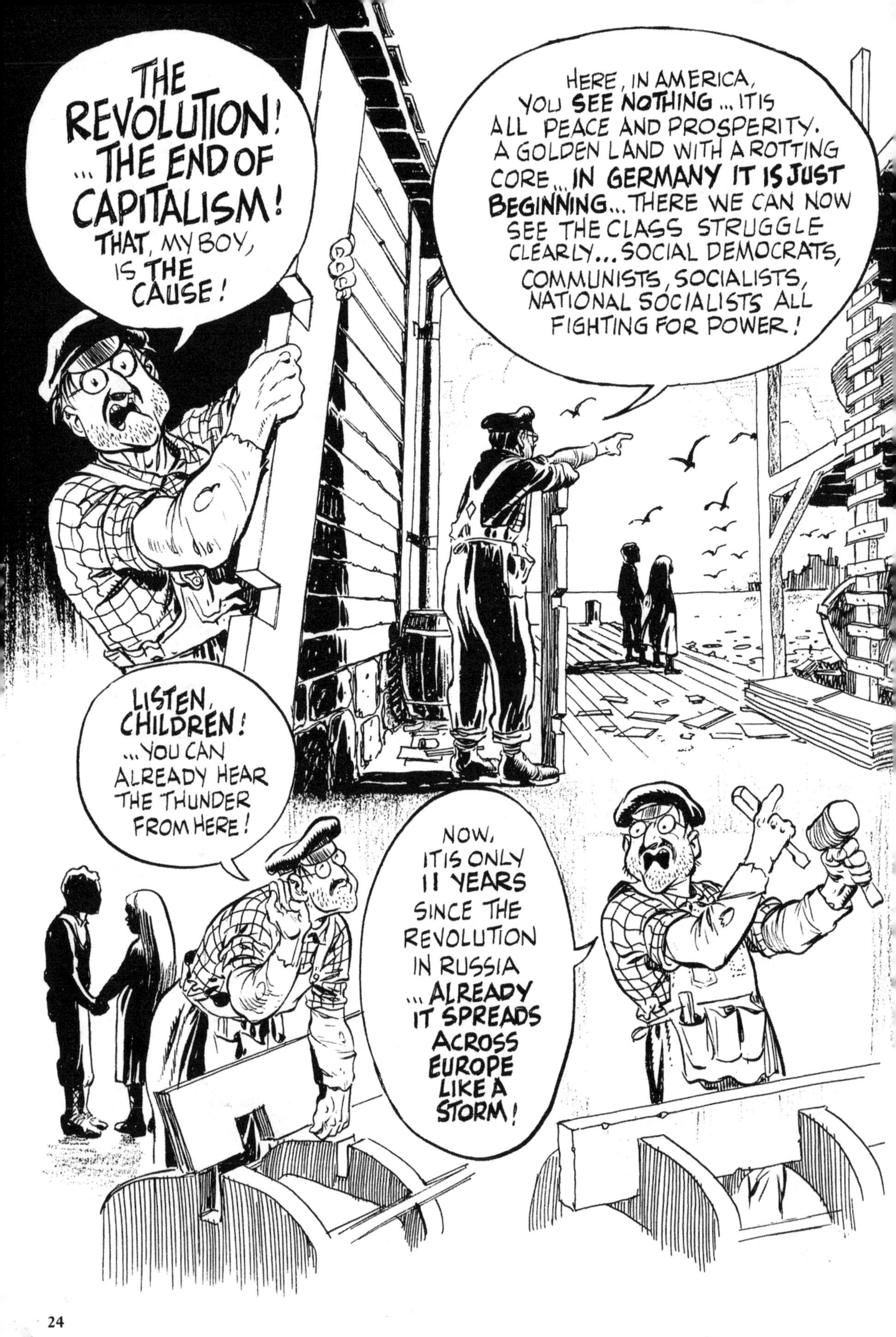
THE REVOLUTION! ... THE END OF CAPITALISM! THAT, MY BOY, IS THE CAUSE!
HERE, IN AMERICA, YOU SEE NOTHING ... IT IS ALL PEACE AND PROSPERITY. A GOLDEN LAND WITH A ROTTING CORE ... IN GERMANY IT IS JUST BEGINNING ... THERE WE CAN NOW SEE THE CLASS STRUGGLE CLEARLY ... SOCIAL DEMOCRATS, COMMUNISTS, SOCIALISTS, NATIONAL SOCIALISTS ALL FIGHTING FOR POWER!
LISTEN, CHILDREN! ... YOU CAN ALREADY HEAR THE THUNDER FROM HERE!
NOW, IT IS ONLY 11 YEARS SINCE THE REVOLUTION IN RUSSIA ... ALREADY IT SPREADS ACROSS EUROPE LIKE A STORM!

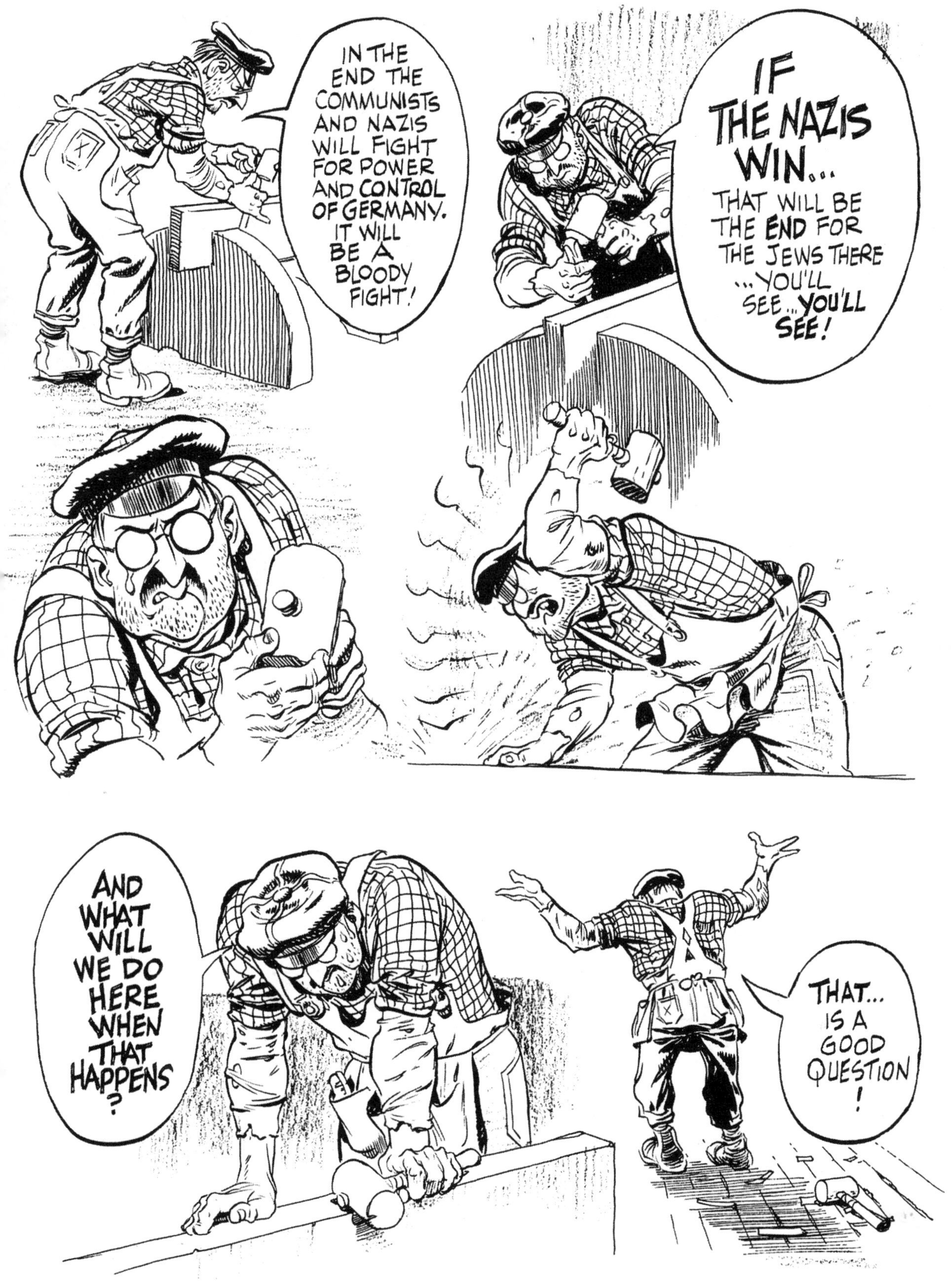
IN THE END THE COMMUNISTS AND NAZIS WILL FIGHT FOR POWER AND CONTROL OF GERMANY. IT WILL BE A BLOODY FIGHT!
IF THE NAZIS WIN... THAT WILL BE THE END FOR THE JEWS THERE ...YOU'LL SEE...YOU'LL SEE!
AND WHAT WILL WE DO HERE WHEN THAT HAPPENS?
THAT... IS A GOOD QUESTION!

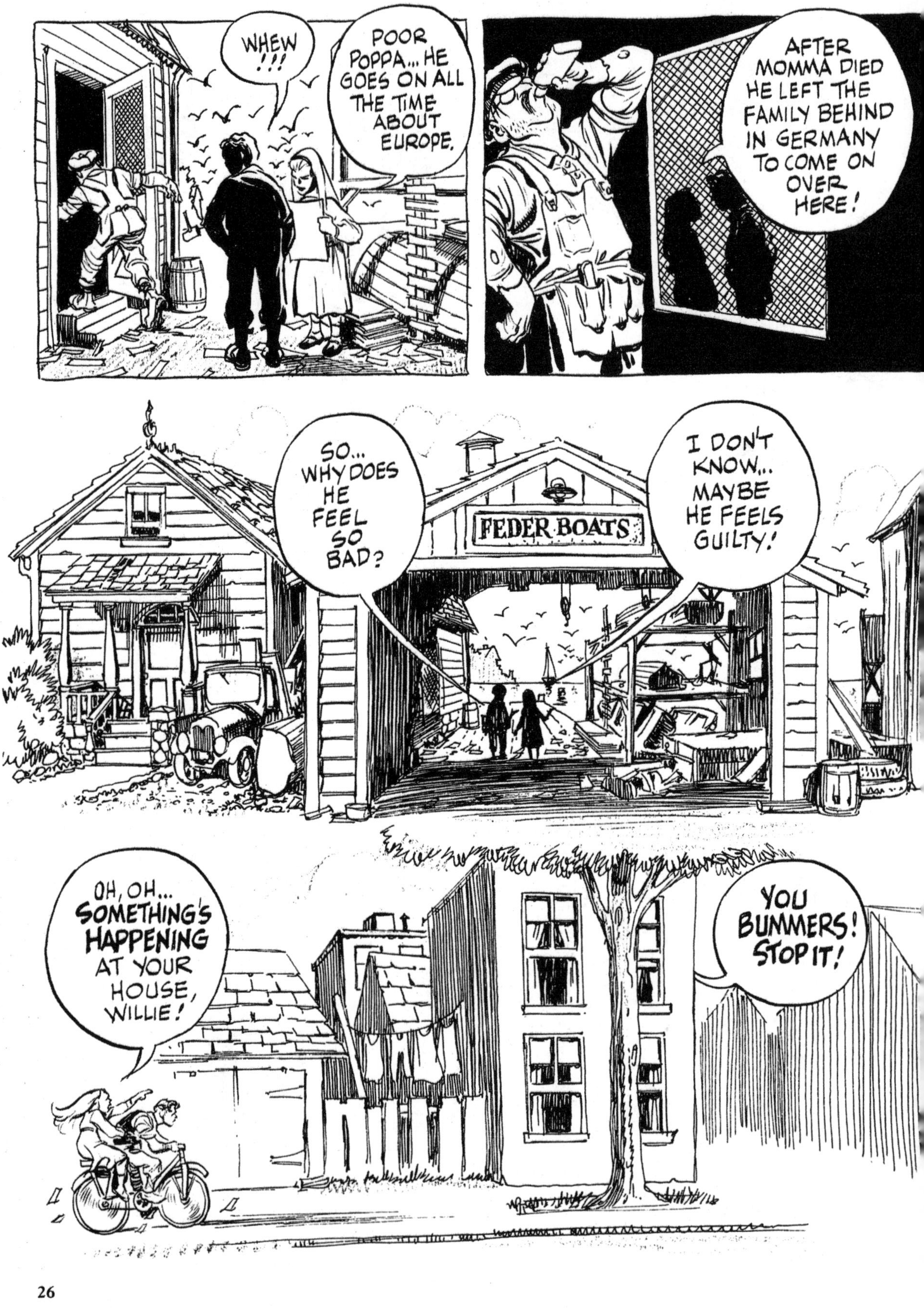
WHEW !!!
POOR POPPA... HE GOES ON ALL THE TIME ABOUT EUROPE.
AFTER MOMMA DIED HE LEFT THE FAMILY BEHIND IN GERMANY TO COME ON OVER HERE!
SO... WHY DOES HE FEEL SO BAD?
FEDER BOATS
I DON'T KNOW... MAYBE HE FEELS GUILTY!
OH, OH... SOMETHING'S HAPPENING AT YOUR HOUSE, WILLIE!
YOU BUMMERS! STOP IT!

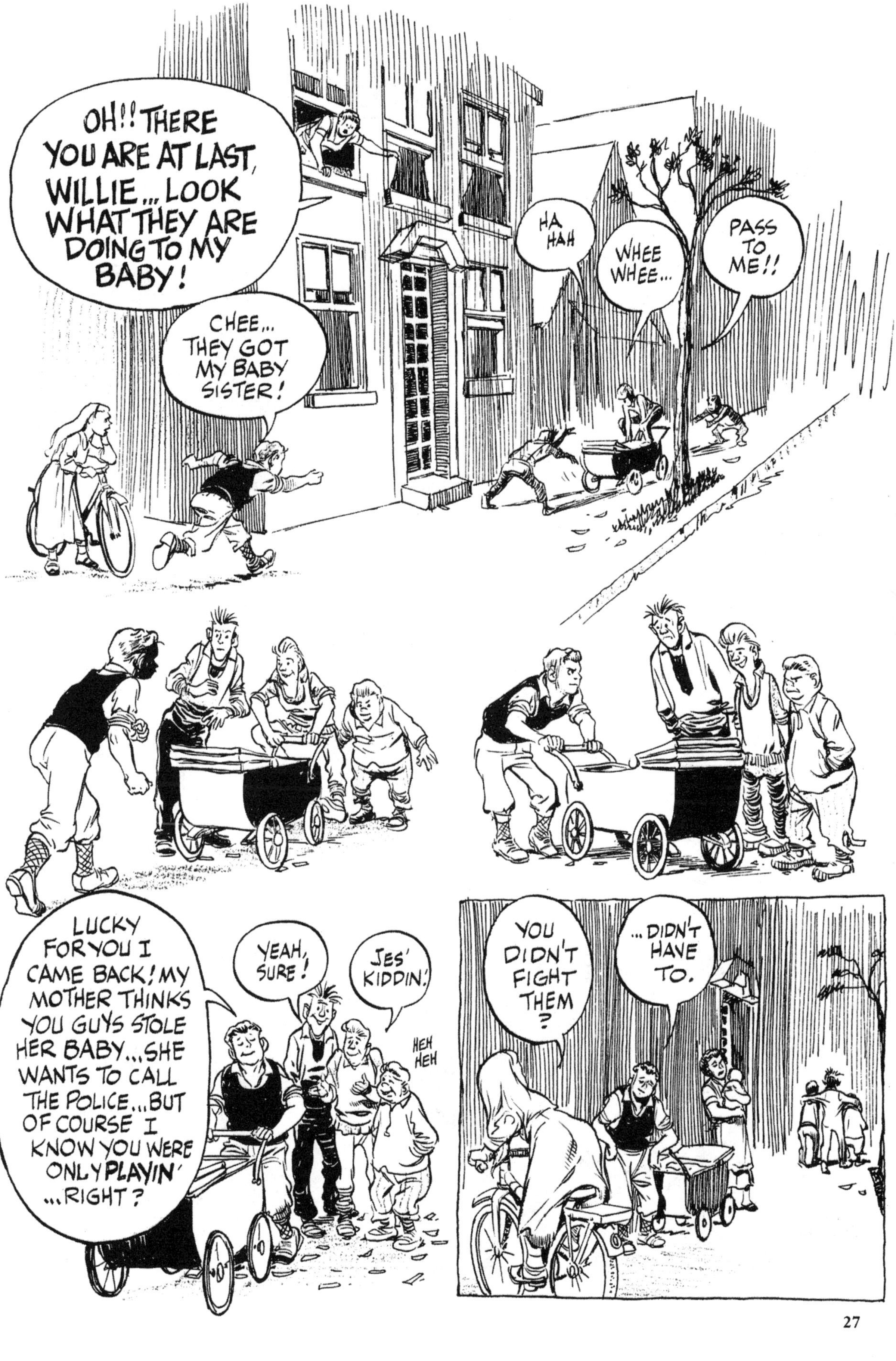
OH!! THERE YOU ARE AT LAST, WILLIE... LOOK WHAT THEY ARE DOING TO MY BABY!
CHEE... THEY GOT MY BABY SISTER!
HA HAH
WHEE WHEE...
PASS TO ME!!
LUCKY FOR YOU I CAME BACK! MY MOTHER THINKS YOU GUYS STOLE HER BABY... SHE WANTS TO CALL THE POLICE... BUT OF COURSE I KNOW YOU WERE ONLY **PLAYIN'** ...RIGHT?
YEAH, SURE!
JES' KIDDIN'!
HEH HEH
YOU DIDN'T FIGHT THEM?
...DIDN'T HAVE TO.

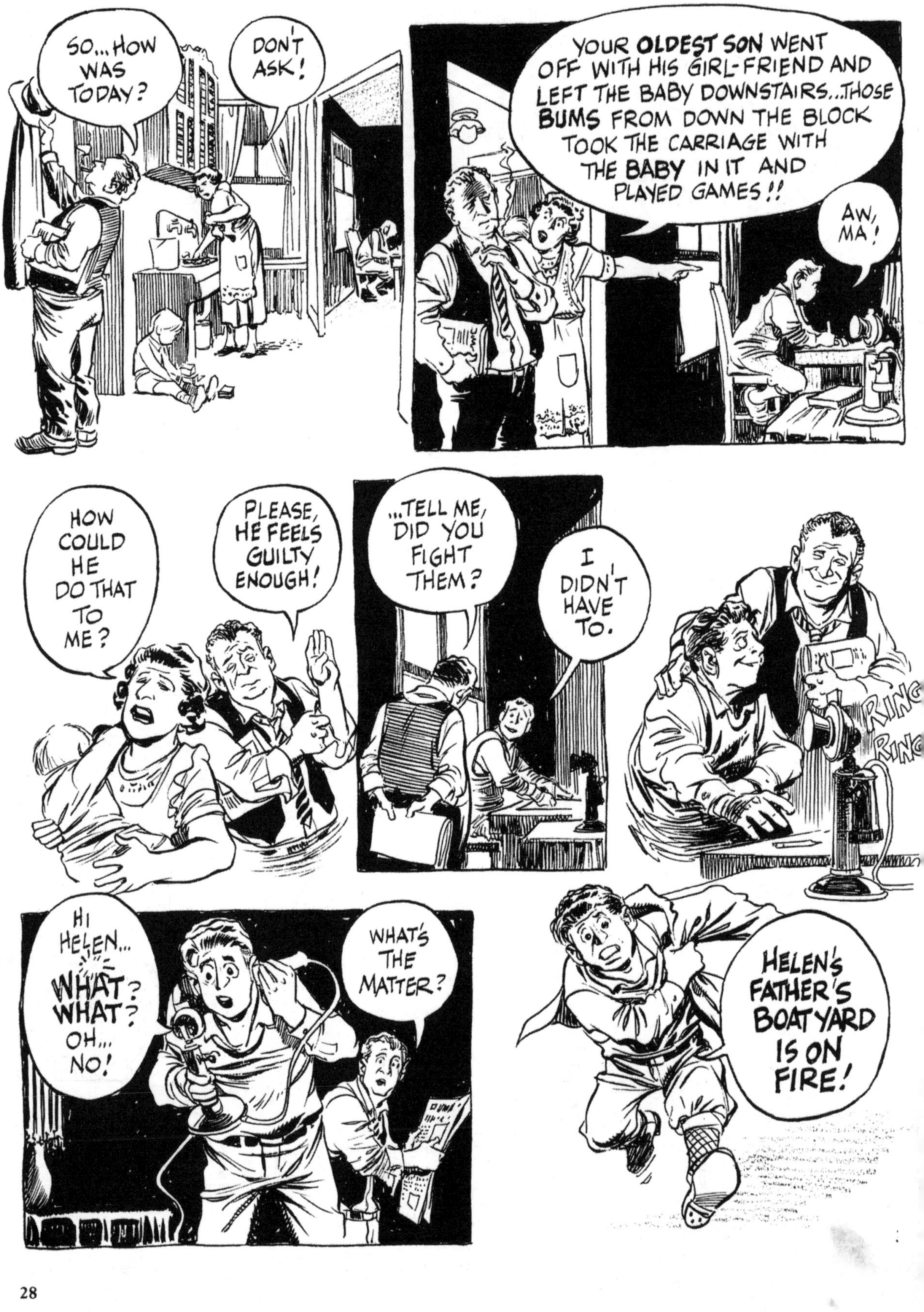
SO... HOW WAS TODAY?
DON'T ASK!
YOUR OLDEST SON WENT OFF WITH HIS GIRL-FRIEND AND LEFT THE BABY DOWNSTAIRS... THOSE BUMS FROM DOWN THE BLOCK TOOK THE CARRIAGE WITH THE BABY IN IT AND PLAYED GAMES!!
AW, MA!
HOW COULD HE DO THAT TO ME?
PLEASE, HE FEELS GUILTY ENOUGH!
...TELL ME, DID YOU FIGHT THEM?
I DIDN'T HAVE TO.
RING
RING
HI HELEN... WHAT? WHAT? OH... NO!
WHAT'S THE MATTER?
HELEN'S FATHER'S BOATYARD IS ON FIRE!

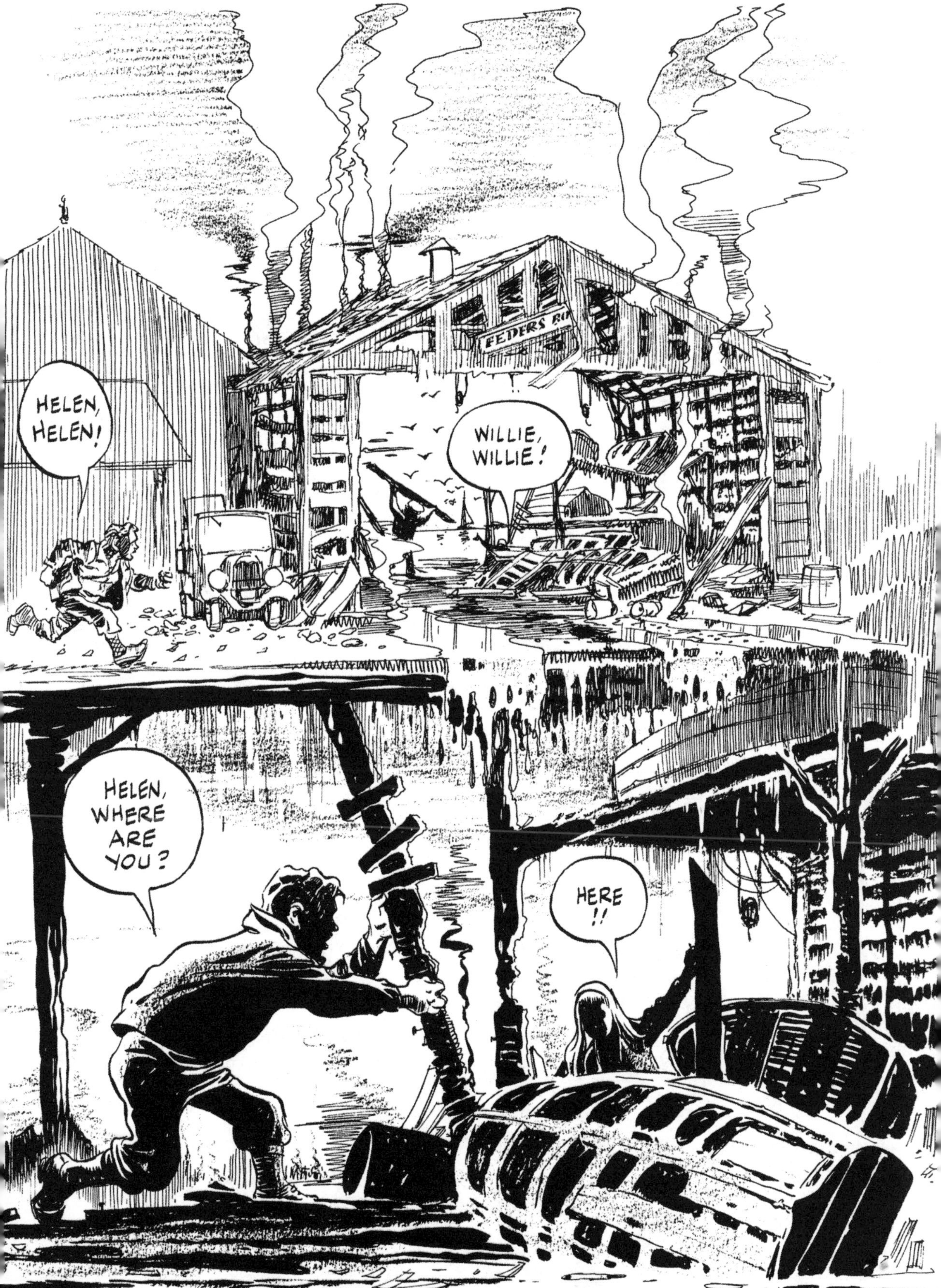
HELEN, HELEN!
WILLIE, WILLIE!
HELEN, WHERE ARE YOU?
HERE !!

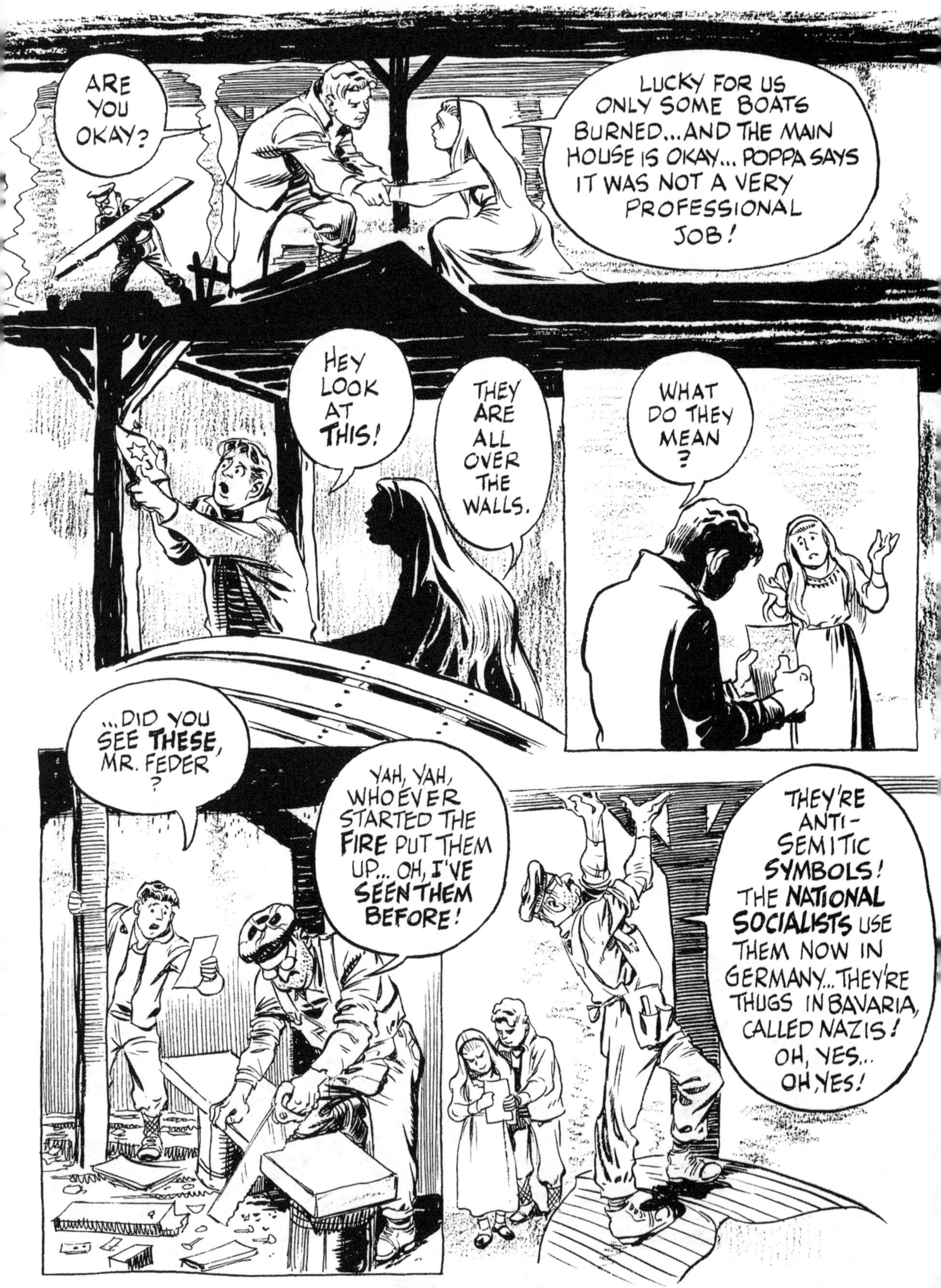

ARE YOU OKAY?
LUCKY FOR US ONLY SOME BOATS BURNED... AND THE MAIN HOUSE IS OKAY... POPPA SAYS IT WAS NOT A VERY PROFESSIONAL JOB!
HEY LOOK AT THIS!
THEY ARE ALL OVER THE WALLS.
WHAT DO THEY MEAN ?
...DID YOU SEE THESE, MR. FEDER ?
YAH, YAH, WHOEVER STARTED THE FIRE PUT THEM UP... OH, I'VE SEEN THEM BEFORE!
THEY'RE ANTI-SEMITIC SYMBOLS! THE NATIONAL SOCIALISTS USE THEM NOW IN GERMANY... THEY'RE THUGS IN BAVARIA, CALLED NAZIS! OH, YES... OH, YES!

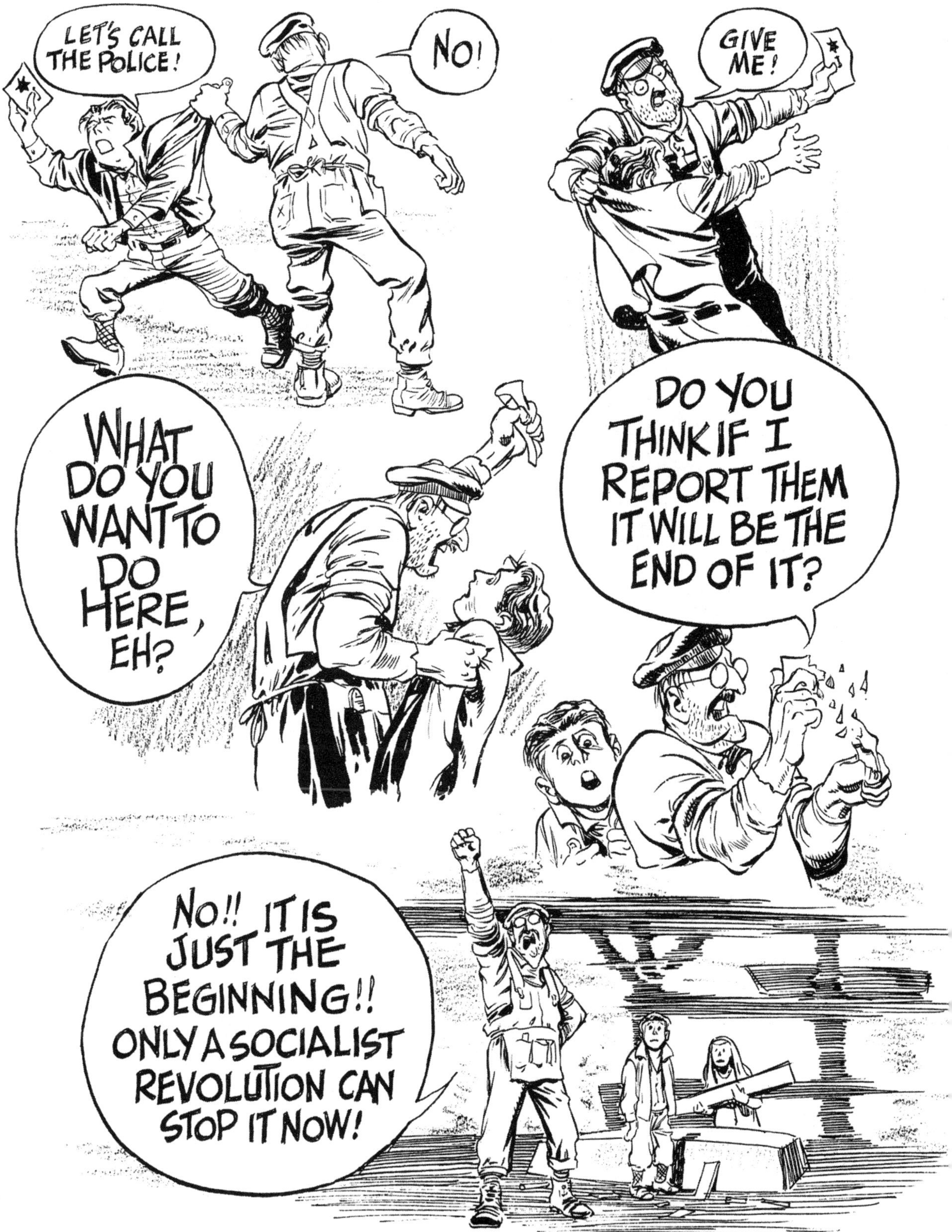
LET'S CALL THE POLICE!
NO!
GIVE ME!
WHAT DO YOU WANT TO DO HERE, EH?
DO YOU THINK IF I REPORT THEM IT WILL BE THE END OF IT?
NO!! IT IS JUST THE BEGINNING!! ONLY A SOCIALIST REVOLUTION CAN STOP IT NOW!

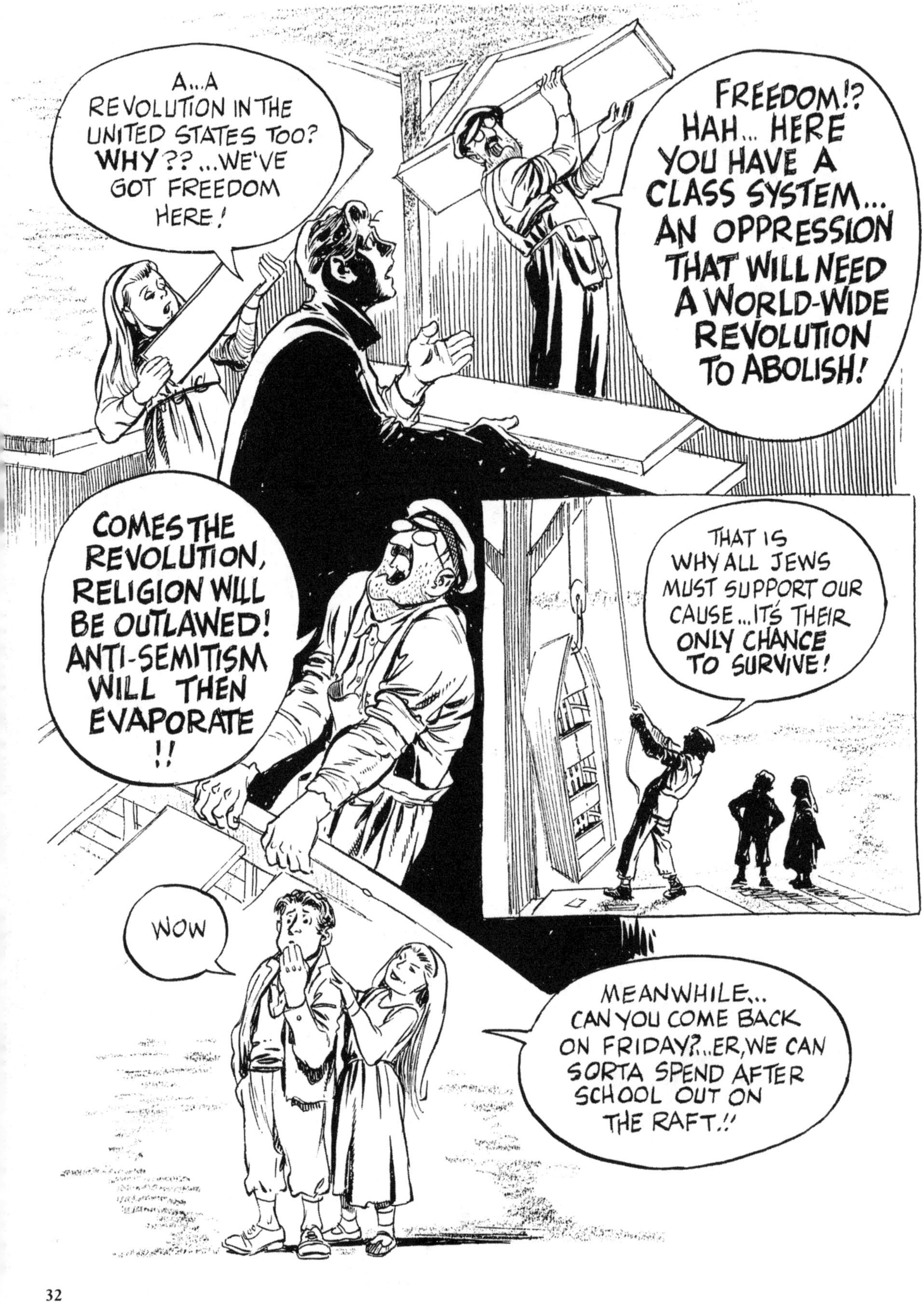
A...A REVOLUTION IN THE UNITED STATES TOO? WHY?? ...WE'VE GOT FREEDOM HERE!
FREEDOM!? HAH... HERE YOU HAVE A CLASS SYSTEM... AN OPPRESSION THAT WILL NEED A WORLD-WIDE REVOLUTION TO ABOLISH!
COMES THE REVOLUTION, RELIGION WILL BE OUTLAWED! ANTI-SEMITISM WILL THEN EVAPORATE !!
THAT IS WHY ALL JEWS MUST SUPPORT OUR CAUSE...IT'S THEIR ONLY CHANCE TO SURVIVE!
WOW
MEANWHILE... CAN YOU COME BACK ON FRIDAY?...ER, WE CAN SORTA SPEND AFTER SCHOOL OUT ON THE RAFT!!

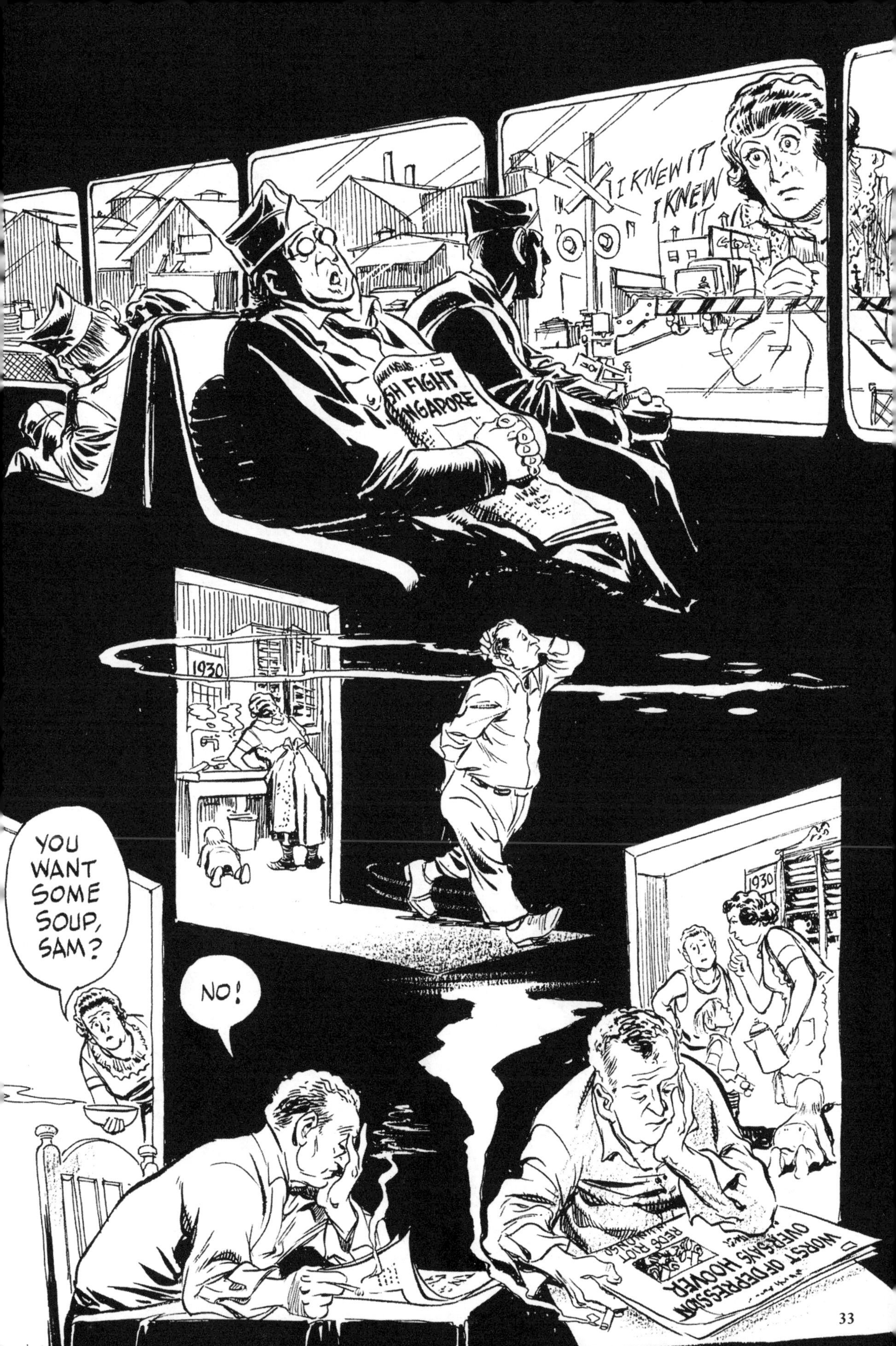
I KNEW IT
I KNEW IT
SH FIGHT
NGAPORE
1930
YOU WANT SOME SOUP, SAM?
NO!
1930
WORST OF DEPRESSION OVER SAYS HOOVER
REDS RIOT

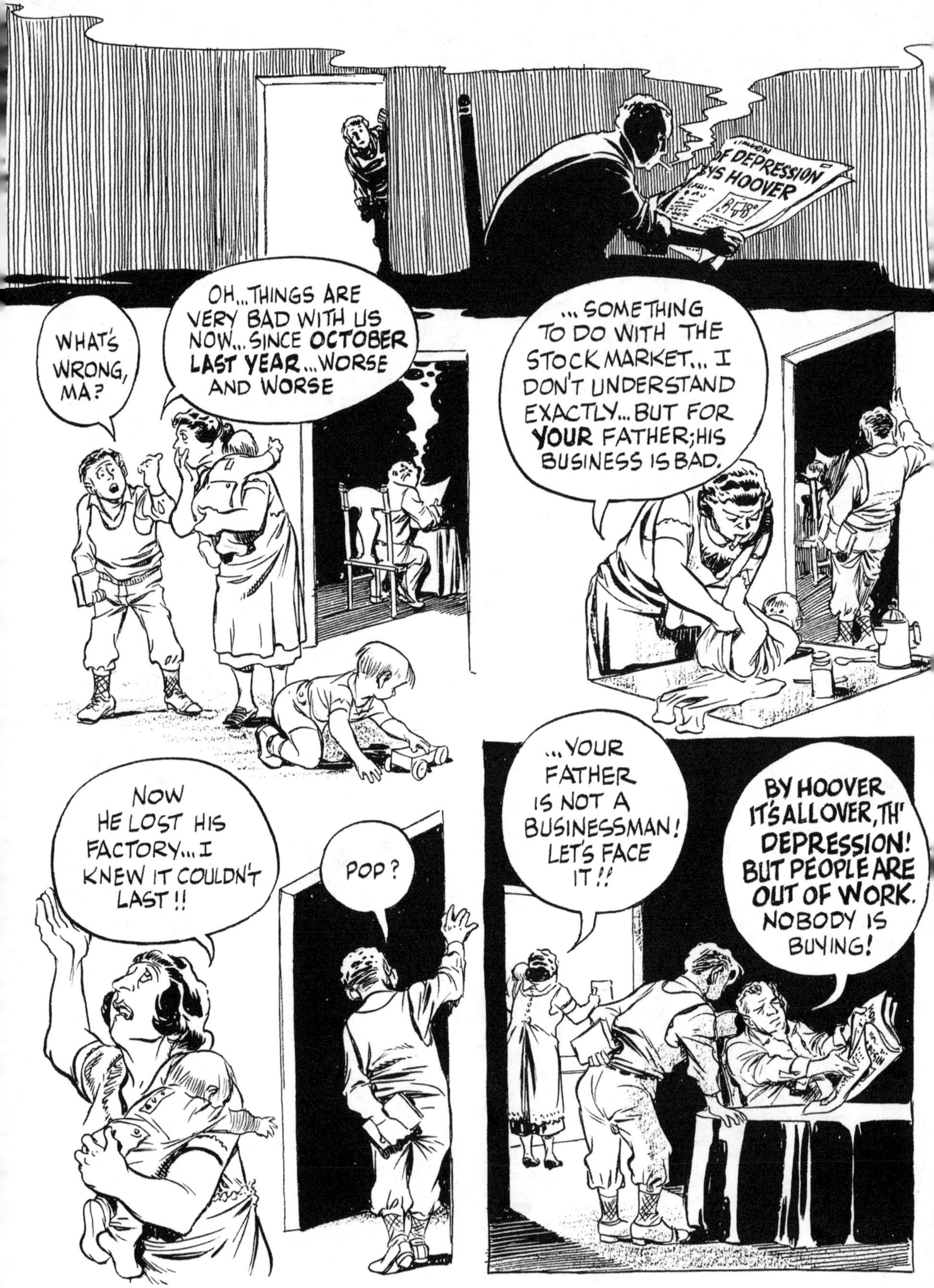
OF DEPRESSION
SAYS HOOVER
WHAT'S WRONG, MA?
OH...THINGS ARE VERY BAD WITH US NOW...SINCE OCTOBER LAST YEAR...WORSE AND WORSE
...SOMETHING TO DO WITH THE STOCK MARKET... I DON'T UNDERSTAND EXACTLY...BUT FOR YOUR FATHER; HIS BUSINESS IS BAD.
NOW HE LOST HIS FACTORY...I KNEW IT COULDN'T LAST!!
POP?
...YOUR FATHER IS NOT A BUSINESSMAN! LET'S FACE IT!!
BY HOOVER IT'S ALL OVER, TH' DEPRESSION! BUT PEOPLE ARE OUT OF WORK. NOBODY IS BUYING!

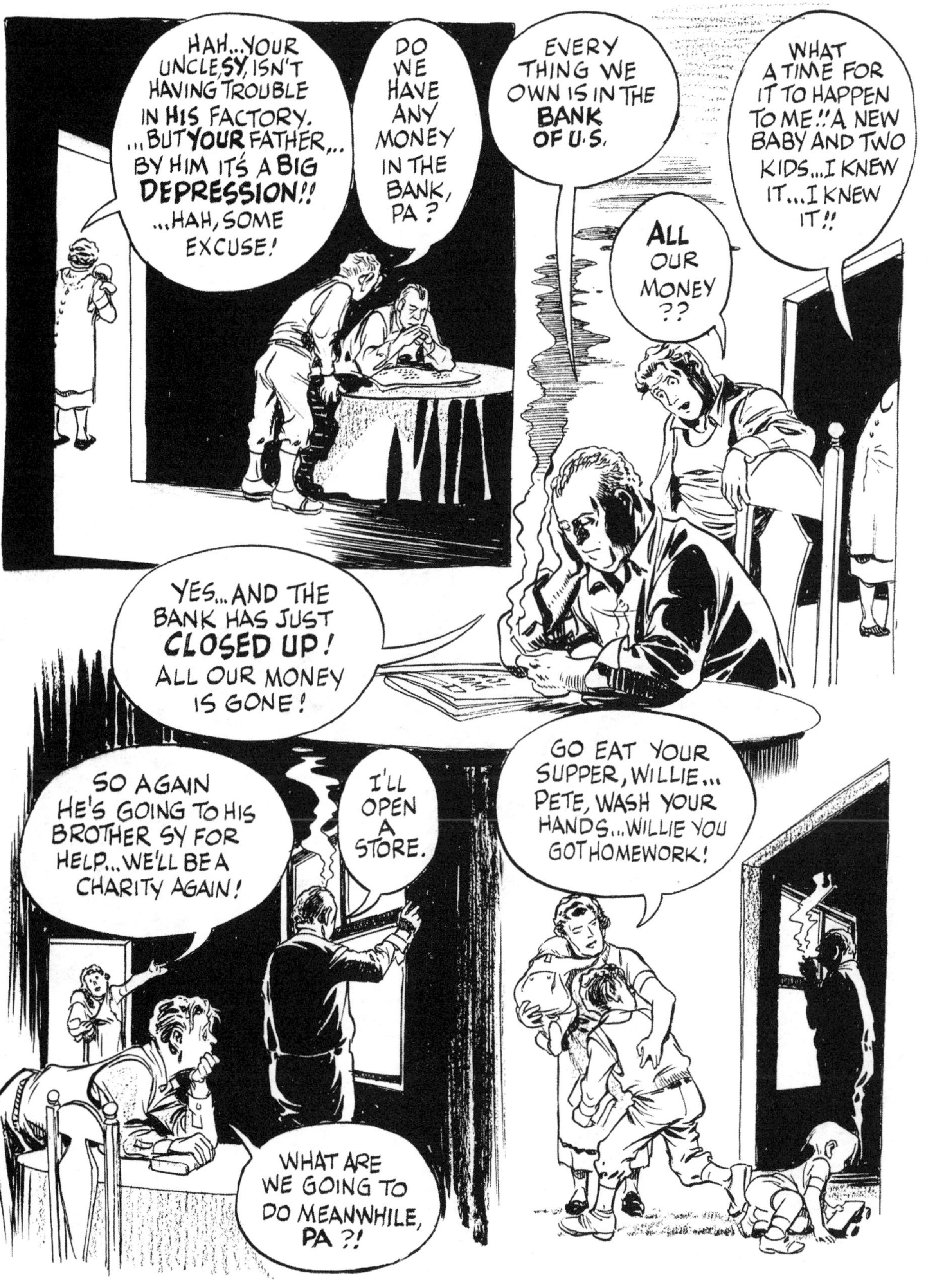
HAH...YOUR UNCLE,SY, ISN'T HAVING TROUBLE IN HIS FACTORY. ...BUT YOUR FATHER,... BY HIM IT'S A BIG DEPRESSION!! ...HAH, SOME EXCUSE!
DO WE HAVE ANY MONEY IN THE BANK, PA ?
EVERY THING WE OWN IS IN THE BANK OF U.S.
WHAT A TIME FOR IT TO HAPPEN TO ME!! A NEW BABY AND TWO KIDS...I KNEW IT...I KNEW IT!!
ALL OUR MONEY ??
YES...AND THE BANK HAS JUST CLOSED UP! ALL OUR MONEY IS GONE!
SO AGAIN HE'S GOING TO HIS BROTHER SY FOR HELP...WE'LL BE A CHARITY AGAIN!
I'LL OPEN A STORE.
WHAT ARE WE GOING TO DO MEANWHILE, PA ?!
GO EAT YOUR SUPPER, WILLIE... PETE, WASH YOUR HANDS...WILLIE YOU GOT HOMEWORK!

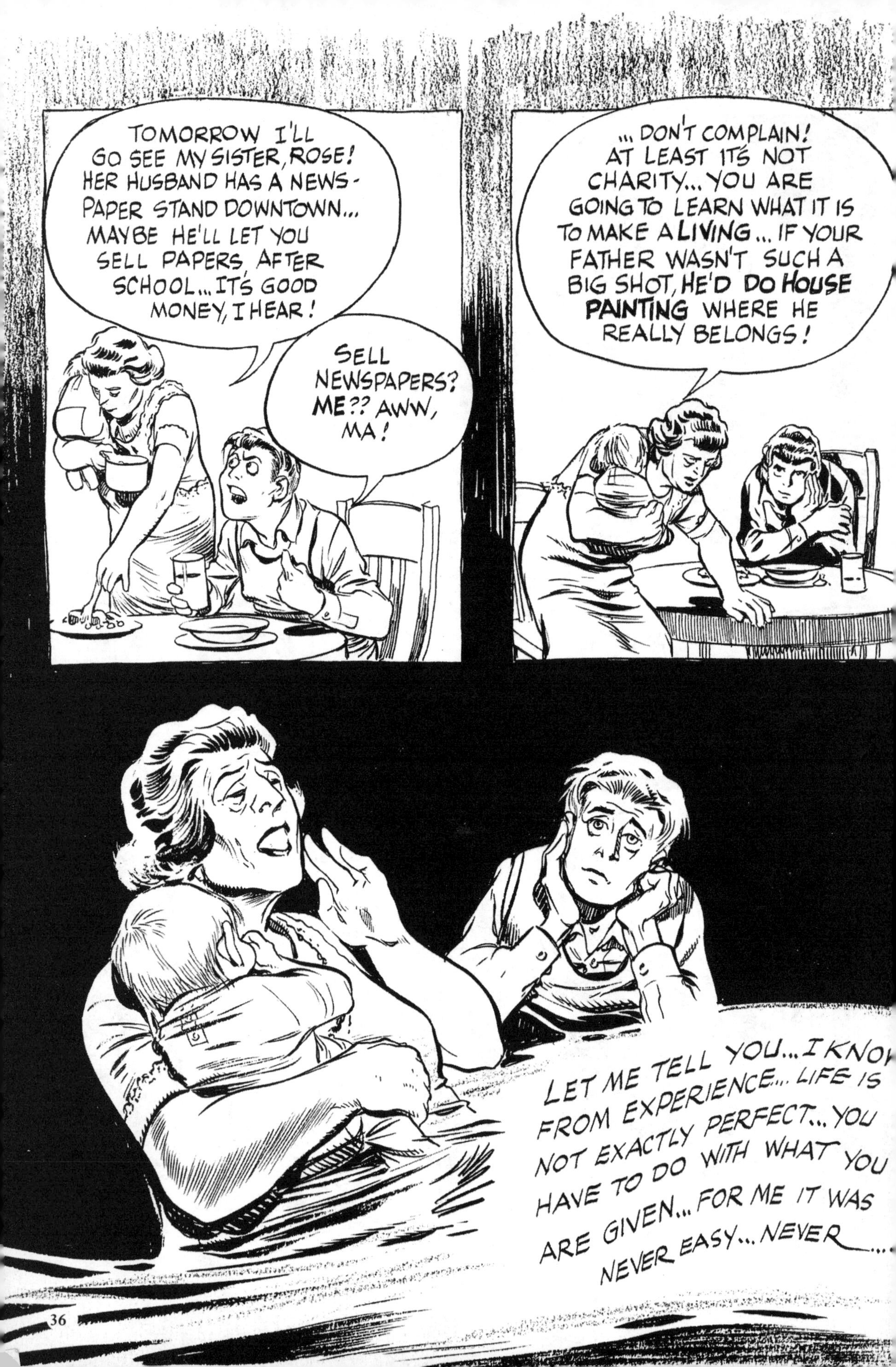
TOMORROW I'LL GO SEE MY SISTER, ROSE! HER HUSBAND HAS A NEWS-PAPER STAND DOWNTOWN... MAYBE HE'LL LET YOU SELL PAPERS, AFTER SCHOOL... IT'S GOOD MONEY, I HEAR!
SELL NEWSPAPERS? **ME**?? AWW, MA!
... DON'T COMPLAIN! AT LEAST IT'S NOT CHARITY... YOU ARE GOING TO LEARN WHAT IT IS TO MAKE A **LIVING**... IF YOUR FATHER WASN'T SUCH A BIG SHOT, **HE'D DO HOUSE PAINTING** WHERE HE REALLY BELONGS!
LET ME TELL YOU... I KNO FROM EXPERIENCE... LIFE IS NOT EXACTLY PERFECT... YOU HAVE TO DO WITH WHAT YOU ARE GIVEN... FOR ME IT WAS NEVER EASY... NEVER....

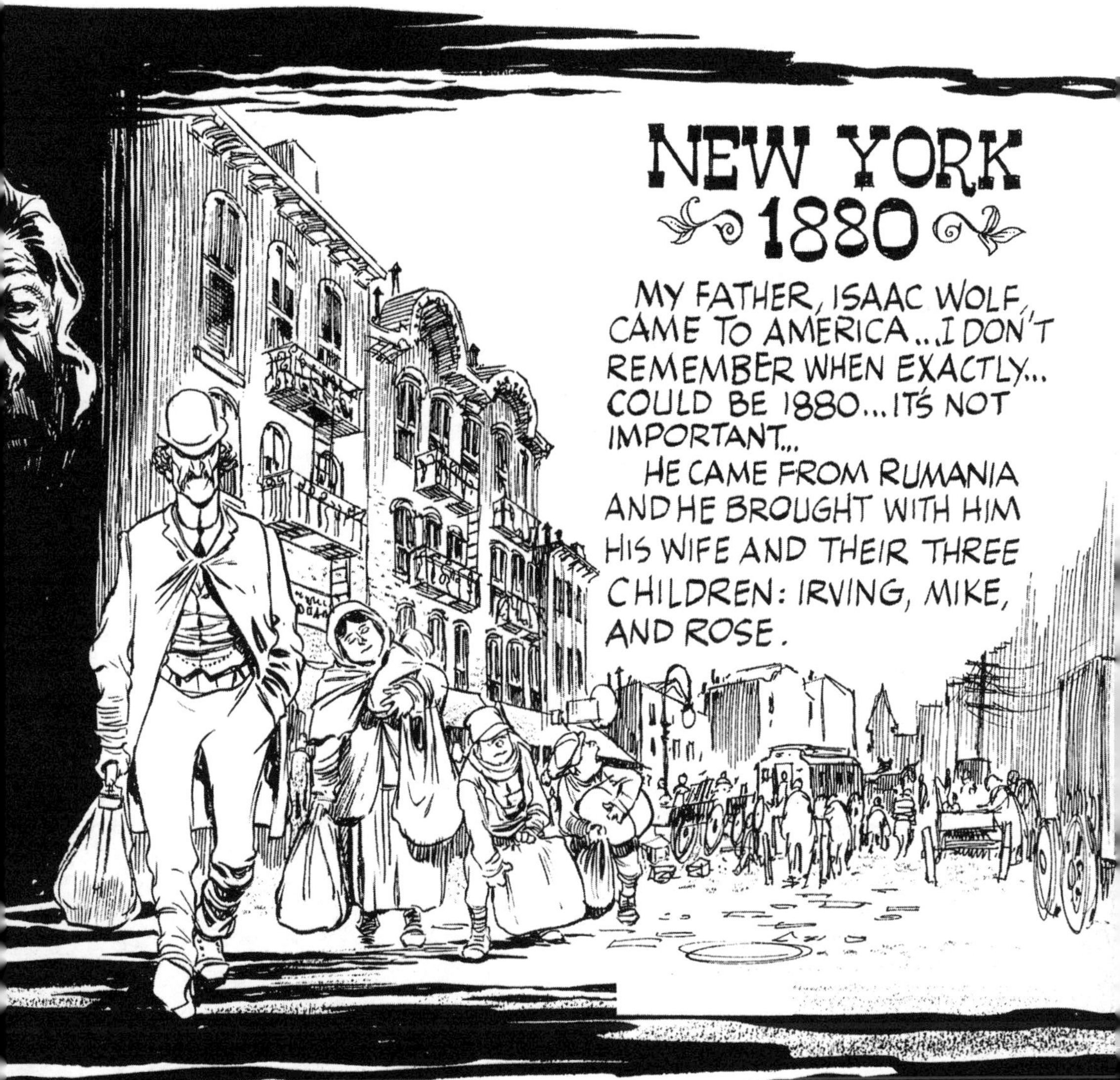
NEW YORK
1880
MY FATHER, ISAAC WOLF, CAME TO AMERICA...I DON'T REMEMBER WHEN EXACTLY... COULD BE 1880...IT'S NOT IMPORTANT...
HE CAME FROM RUMANIA AND HE BROUGHT WITH HIM HIS WIFE AND THEIR THREE CHILDREN: IRVING, MIKE, AND ROSE.

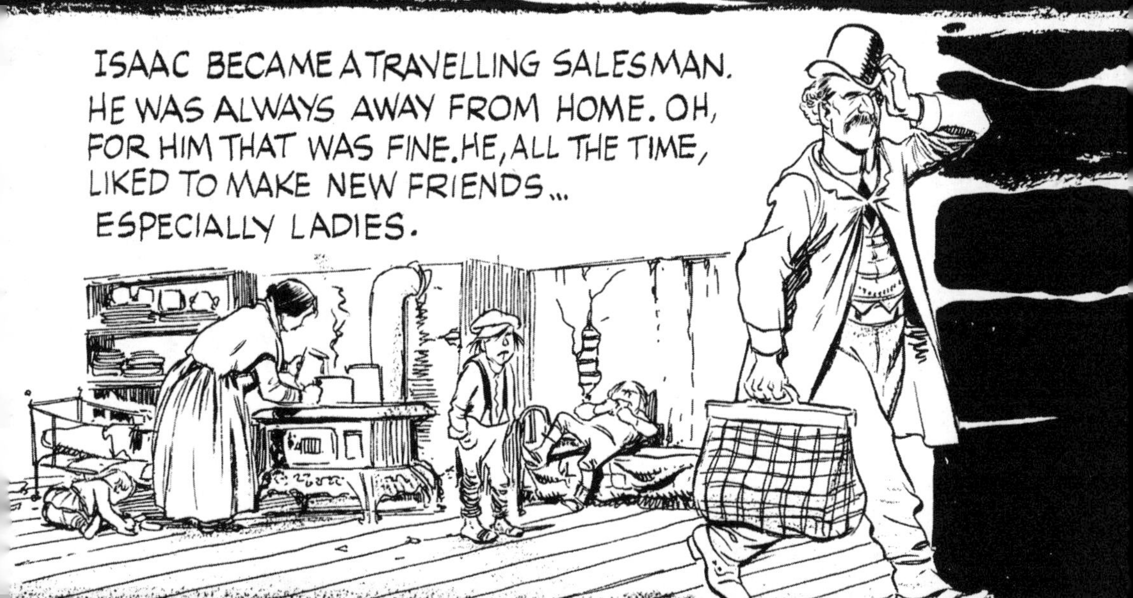
ISAAC BECAME A TRAVELLING SALESMAN. HE WAS ALWAYS AWAY FROM HOME. OH, FOR HIM THAT WAS FINE. HE, ALL THE TIME, LIKED TO MAKE NEW FRIENDS... ESPECIALLY LADIES.

BUT ISAAC'S WIFE DIED, OF THE FLU, I THINK ... WHICH IN THOSE DAYS WAS VERY COMMON!! BY THEN ISAAC WOLF WAS 70 YEARS OLD.

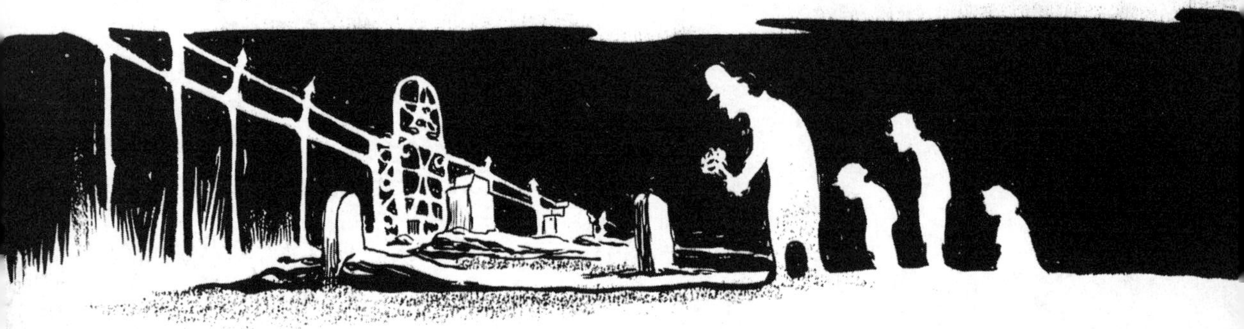

SO, RIGHT AWAY ISAAC WENT BACK TO RUMANIA TO MARRY HIS WIFE'S YOUNGER SISTER AND BROUGHT HER OVER. NOT ONLY WAS IT THE **RIGHT** THING TO DO - ACCORDING TO OUR CUSTOM - BUT HE NEEDED SOMEONE TO TAKE CARE OF HIS KIDS!

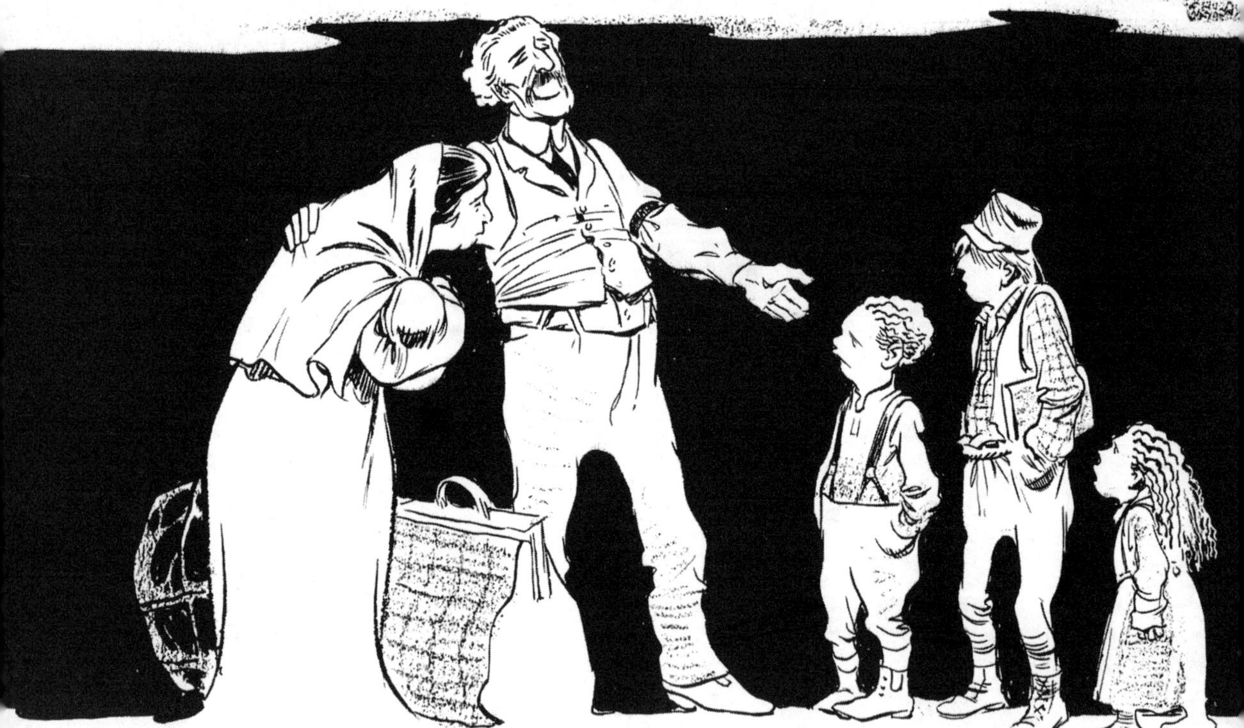

HOO-HAH!...FATHER WAS A VIGOROUS MAN FOR HIS AGE... SO ON THE BOAT COMING OVER WITH HIS NEW WIFE, I WAS BORN!

BY THE TIME ISAAC WOLF REACHED 80, MY MOTHER HAD TWO MORE CHILDREN BY HIM. WE DIDN'T SEE HIM MUCH. HE JUST CAME HOME TO MAKE BABIES – LITTLE ELSE. IT SEEMED TO ME HE DIDN'T GET OLDER LIKE OTHER MEN. SOON, THERE WERE SIX KIDS IN THE HOUSE... IRVING, MIKE, AND ROSE FROM HIS FIRST WIFE AND ME, GOLDIE, AND BOBBY FROM THE NEW ONE.

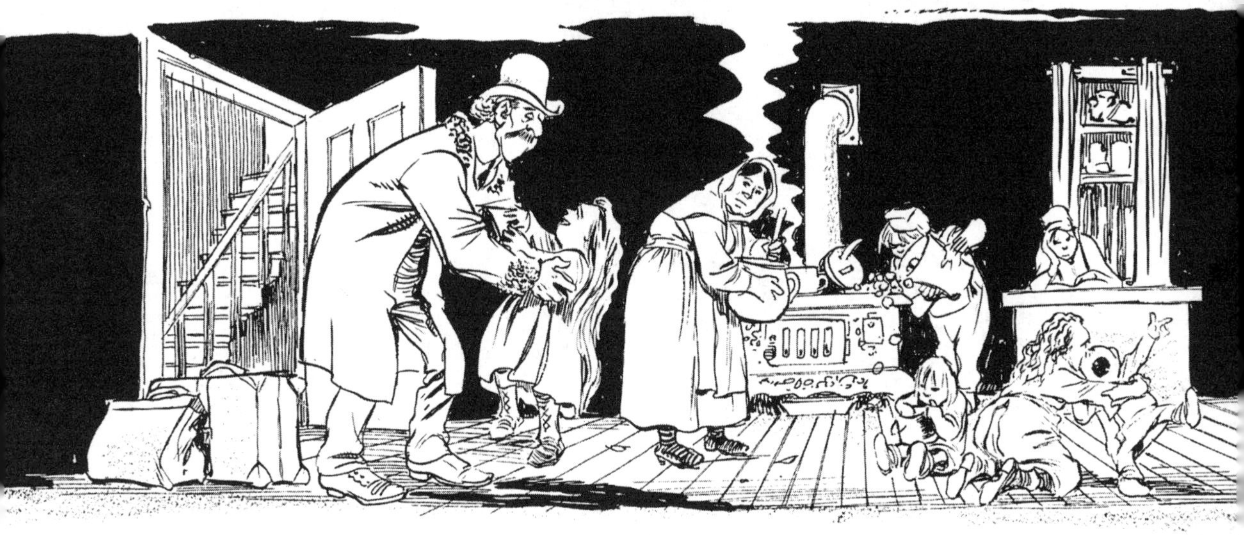

MOTHER WAS A SICKLY WOMAN AND TAKING CARE OF ALL THOSE KIDS WAS KILLING HER.

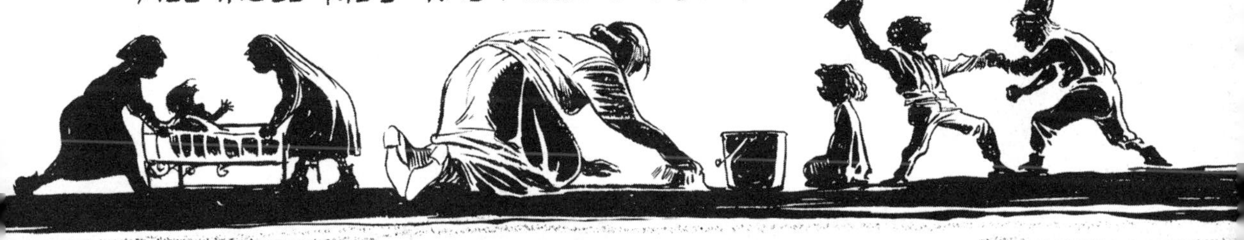

ON MY TENTH BIRTHDAY, MY MOTHER DIED.

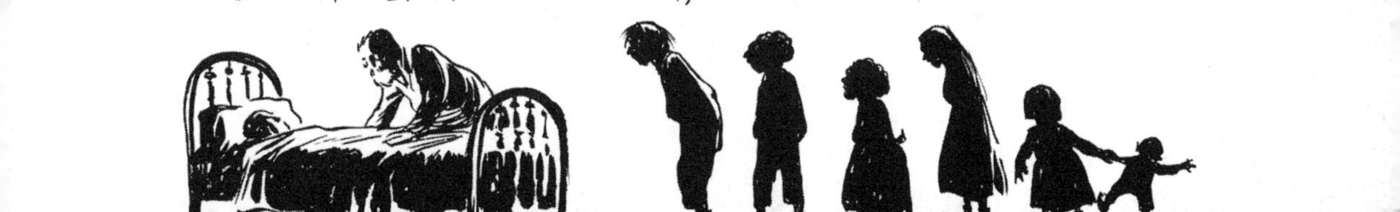

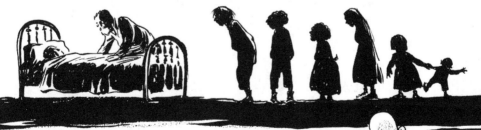

ALSO THAT YEAR ISAAC WOLF DIED SOMEWHERE ON THE ROAD.

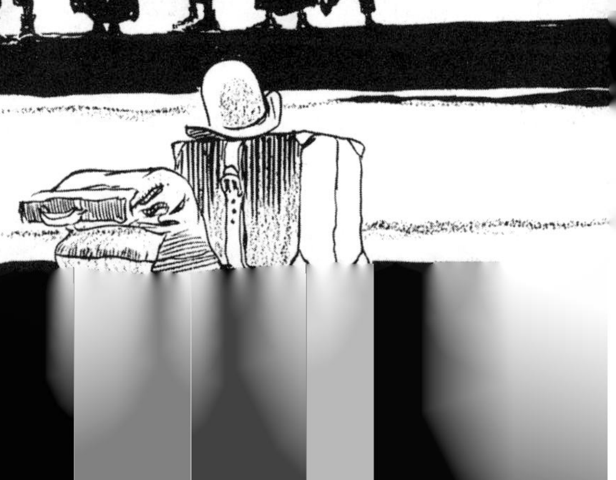

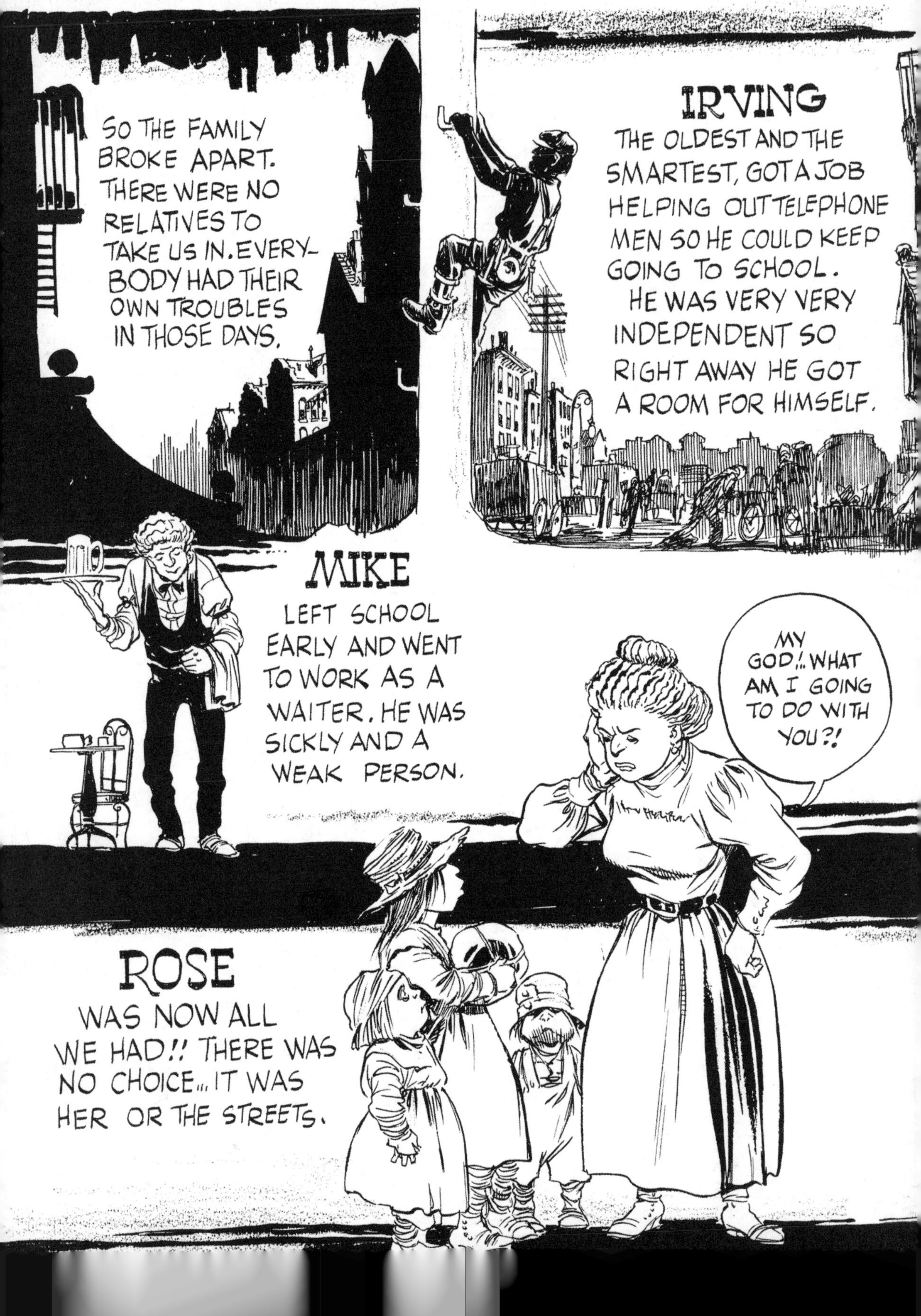
SO THE FAMILY BROKE APART. THERE WERE NO RELATIVES TO TAKE US IN. EVERY-BODY HAD THEIR OWN TROUBLES IN THOSE DAYS.
IRVING
THE OLDEST AND THE SMARTEST, GOT A JOB HELPING OUT TELEPHONE MEN SO HE COULD KEEP GOING TO SCHOOL. HE WAS VERY VERY INDEPENDENT SO RIGHT AWAY HE GOT A ROOM FOR HIMSELF.
MIKE
LEFT SCHOOL EARLY AND WENT TO WORK AS A WAITER. HE WAS SICKLY AND A WEAK PERSON.
MY GOD!.. WHAT AM I GOING TO DO WITH YOU?!
ROSE
WAS NOW ALL WE HAD!! THERE WAS NO CHOICE... IT WAS HER OR THE STREETS.

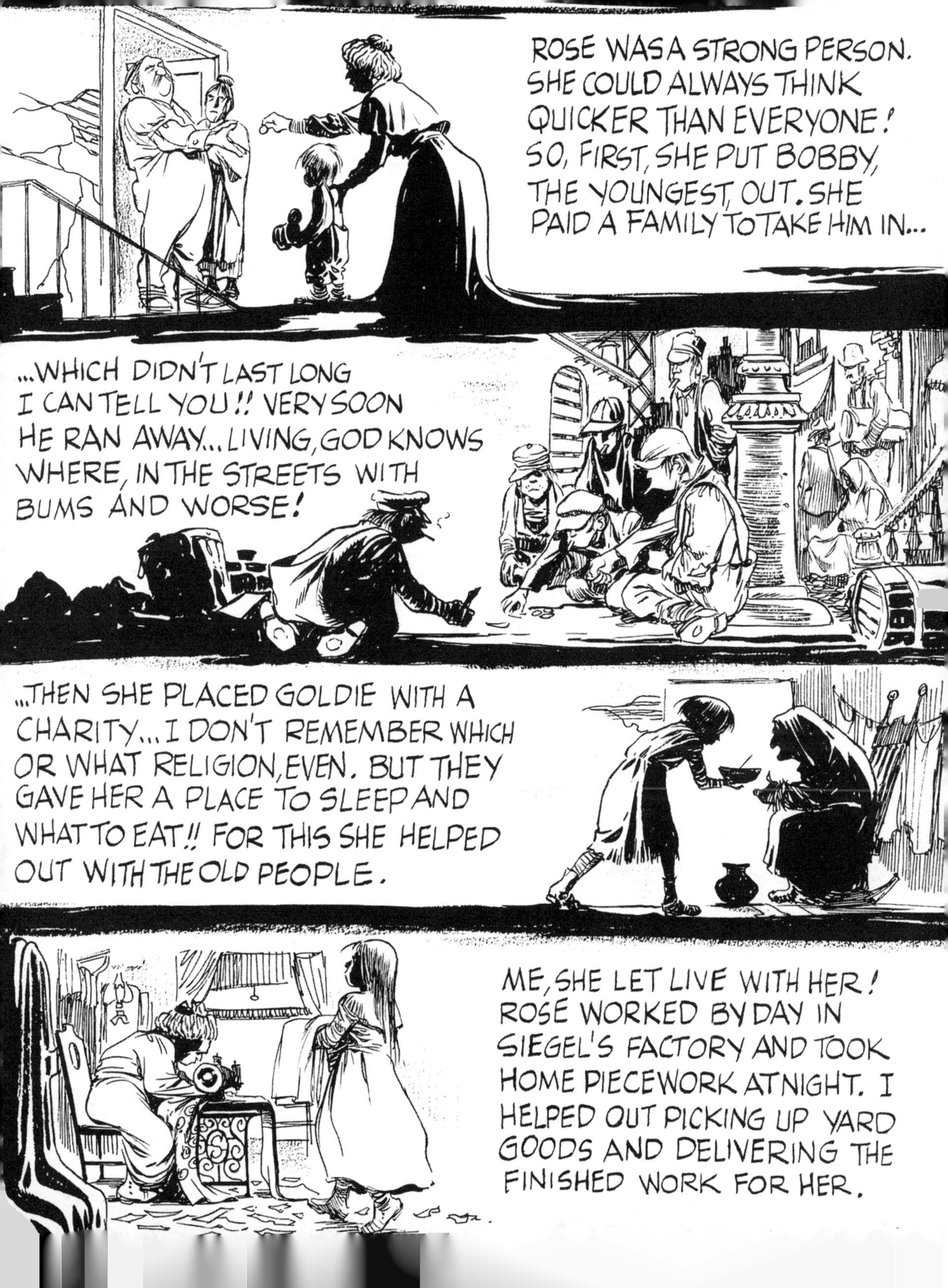
ROSE WAS A STRONG PERSON. SHE COULD ALWAYS THINK QUICKER THAN EVERYONE! SO, FIRST, SHE PUT BOBBY, THE YOUNGEST, OUT. SHE PAID A FAMILY TO TAKE HIM IN...
...WHICH DIDN'T LAST LONG I CAN TELL YOU!! VERY SOON HE RAN AWAY... LIVING, GOD KNOWS WHERE, IN THE STREETS WITH BUMS AND WORSE!
...THEN SHE PLACED GOLDIE WITH A CHARITY... I DON'T REMEMBER WHICH OR WHAT RELIGION, EVEN. BUT THEY GAVE HER A PLACE TO SLEEP AND WHAT TO EAT!! FOR THIS SHE HELPED OUT WITH THE OLD PEOPLE.
ME, SHE LET LIVE WITH HER! ROSE WORKED BY DAY IN SIEGEL'S FACTORY AND TOOK HOME PIECEWORK AT NIGHT. I HELPED OUT PICKING UP YARD GOODS AND DELIVERING THE FINISHED WORK FOR HER.

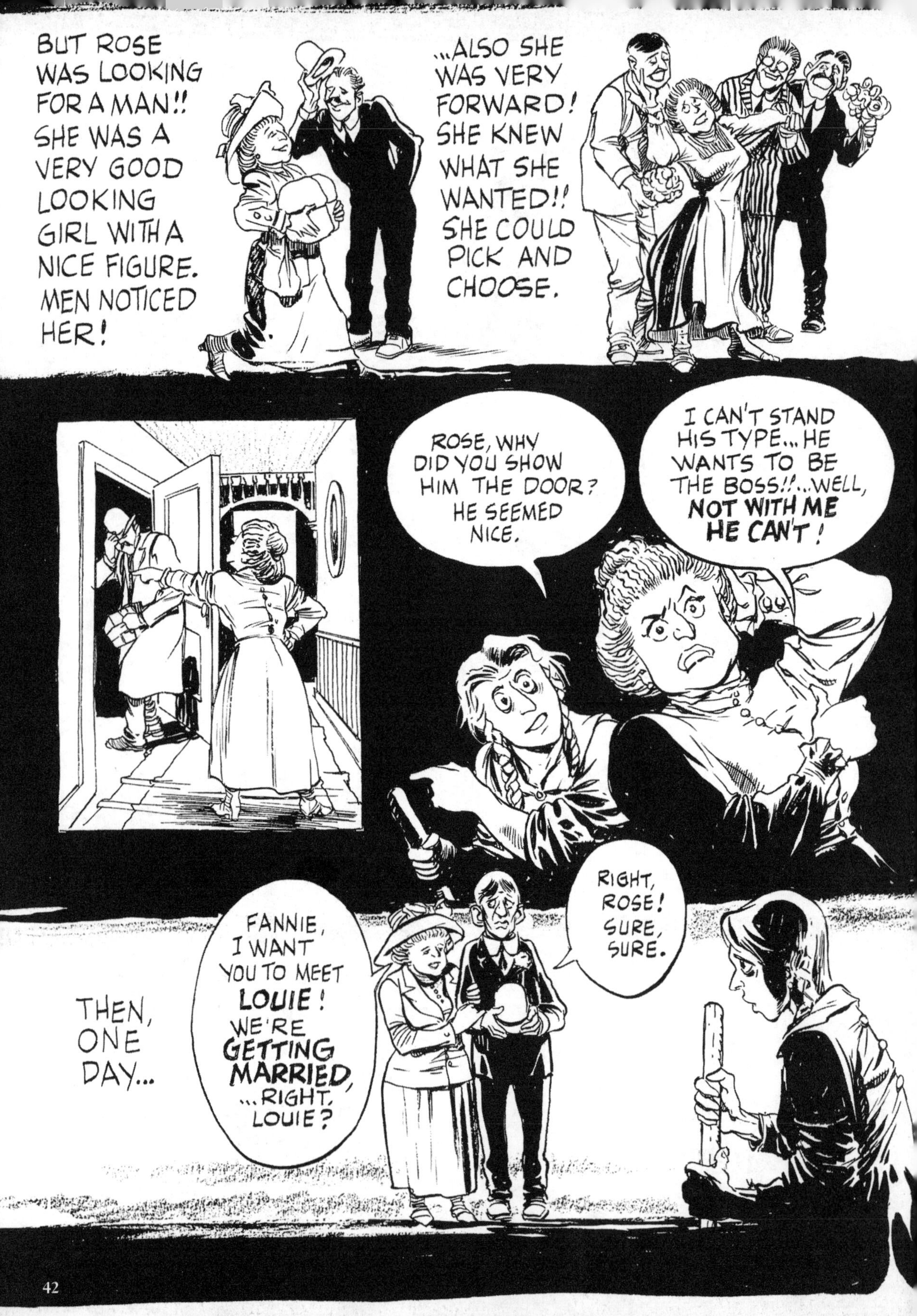
BUT ROSE WAS LOOKING FOR A MAN!! SHE WAS A VERY GOOD LOOKING GIRL WITH A NICE FIGURE. MEN NOTICED HER!
...ALSO SHE WAS VERY FORWARD! SHE KNEW WHAT SHE WANTED!! SHE COULD PICK AND CHOOSE.
ROSE, WHY DID YOU SHOW HIM THE DOOR? HE SEEMED NICE.
I CAN'T STAND HIS TYPE... HE WANTS TO BE THE BOSS!!...WELL, NOT WITH ME HE CAN'T!
THEN, ONE DAY...
FANNIE, I WANT YOU TO MEET LOUIE! WE'RE GETTING MARRIED, ...RIGHT, LOUIE?
RIGHT, ROSE! SURE, SURE.

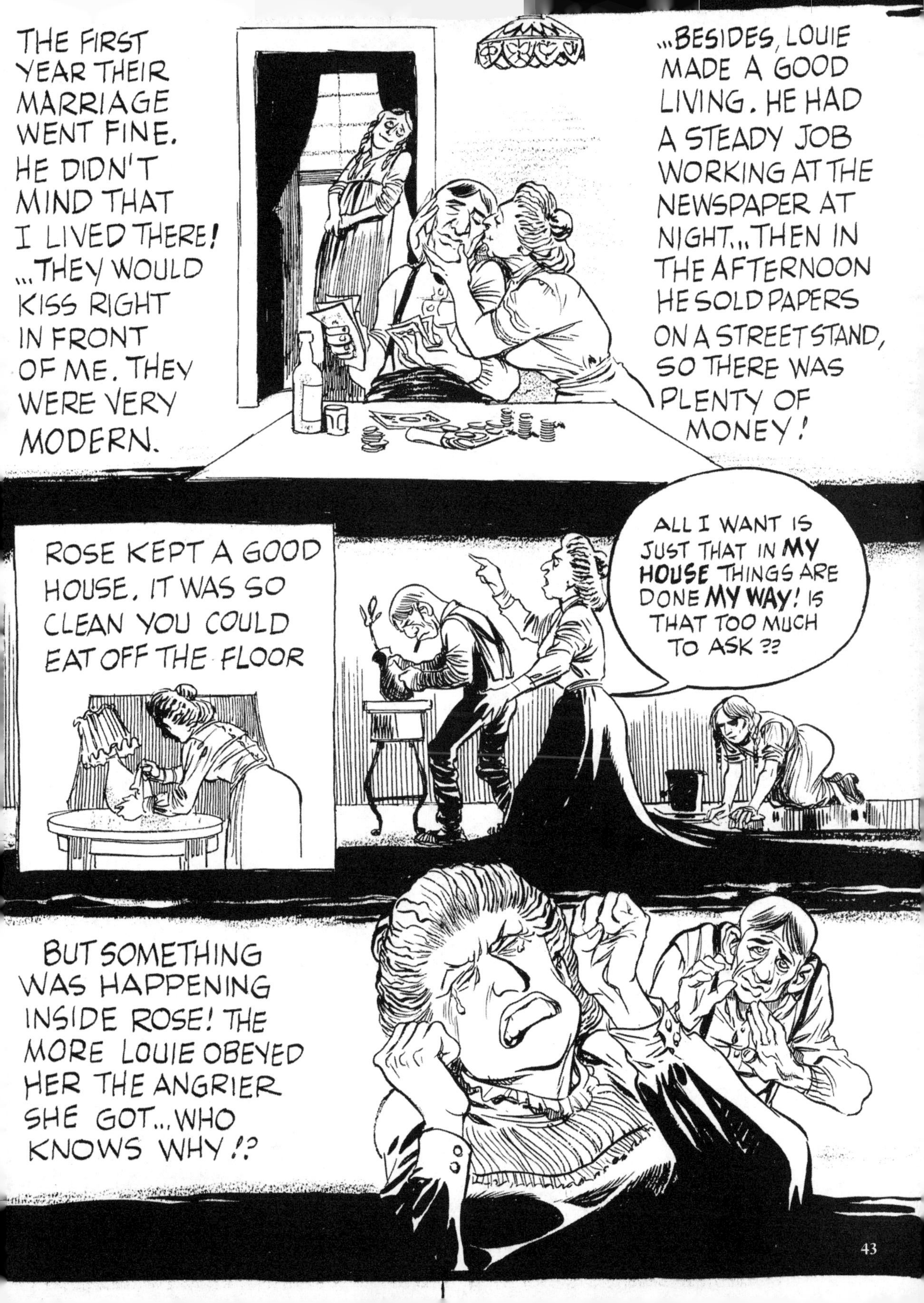
THE FIRST YEAR THEIR MARRIAGE WENT FINE. HE DIDN'T MIND THAT I LIVED THERE! ...THEY WOULD KISS RIGHT IN FRONT OF ME. THEY WERE VERY MODERN.
...BESIDES, LOUIE MADE A GOOD LIVING. HE HAD A STEADY JOB WORKING AT THE NEWSPAPER AT NIGHT... THEN IN THE AFTERNOON HE SOLD PAPERS ON A STREET STAND, SO THERE WAS PLENTY OF MONEY!
ROSE KEPT A GOOD HOUSE. IT WAS SO CLEAN YOU COULD EAT OFF THE FLOOR
ALL I WANT IS JUST THAT IN MY HOUSE THINGS ARE DONE MY WAY! IS THAT TOO MUCH TO ASK ??
BUT SOMETHING WAS HAPPENING INSIDE ROSE! THE MORE LOUIE OBEYED HER THE ANGRIER SHE GOT... WHO KNOWS WHY !?

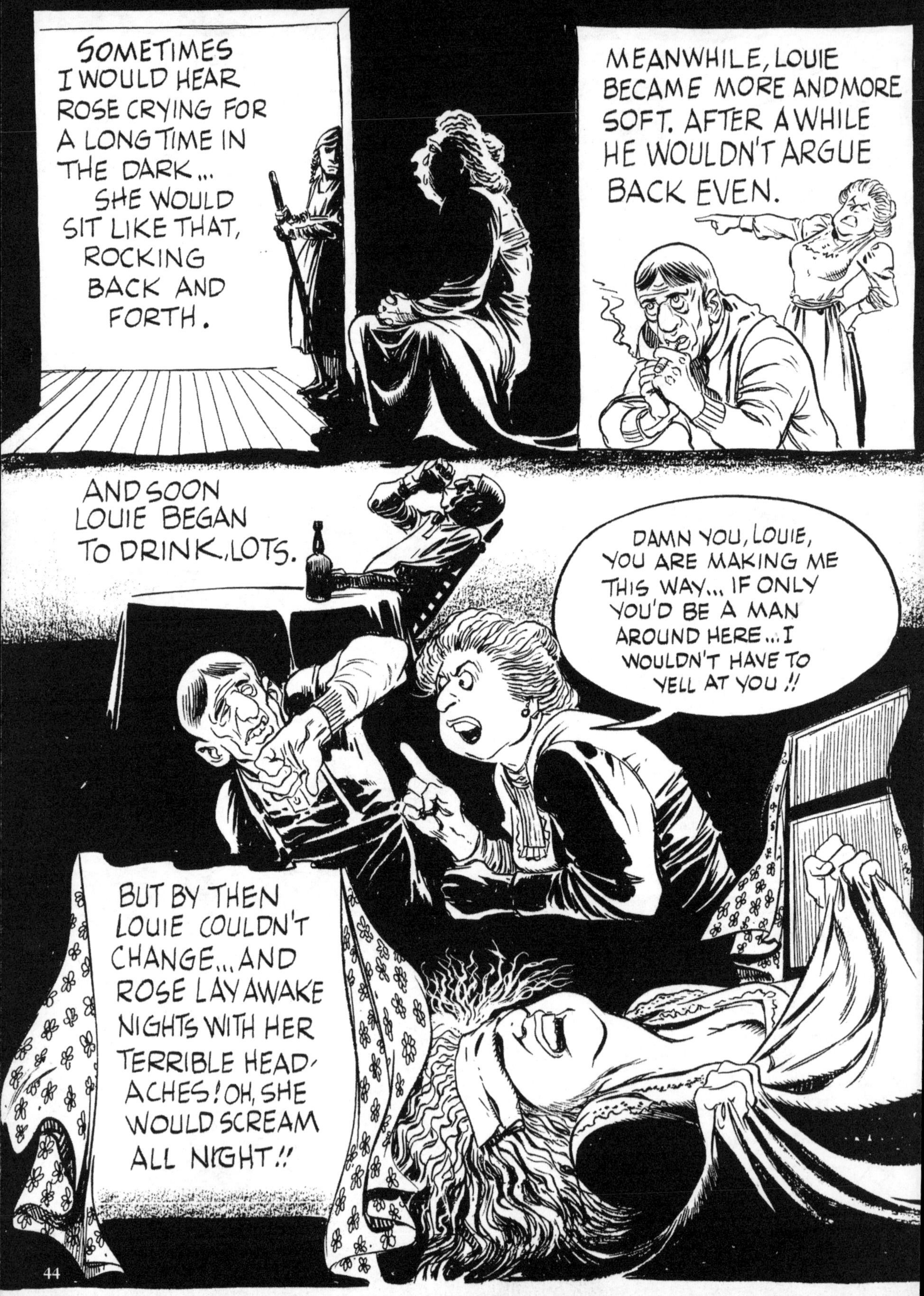
SOMETIMES I WOULD HEAR ROSE CRYING FOR A LONG TIME IN THE DARK... SHE WOULD SIT LIKE THAT, ROCKING BACK AND FORTH.
MEANWHILE, LOUIE BECAME MORE AND MORE SOFT. AFTER A WHILE HE WOULDN'T ARGUE BACK EVEN.
AND SOON LOUIE BEGAN TO DRINK, LOTS.
DAMN YOU, LOUIE, YOU ARE MAKING ME THIS WAY... IF ONLY YOU'D BE A MAN AROUND HERE... I WOULDN'T HAVE TO YELL AT YOU!!
BUT BY THEN LOUIE COULDN'T CHANGE... AND ROSE LAY AWAKE NIGHTS WITH HER TERRIBLE HEAD-ACHES! OH, SHE WOULD SCREAM ALL NIGHT!!

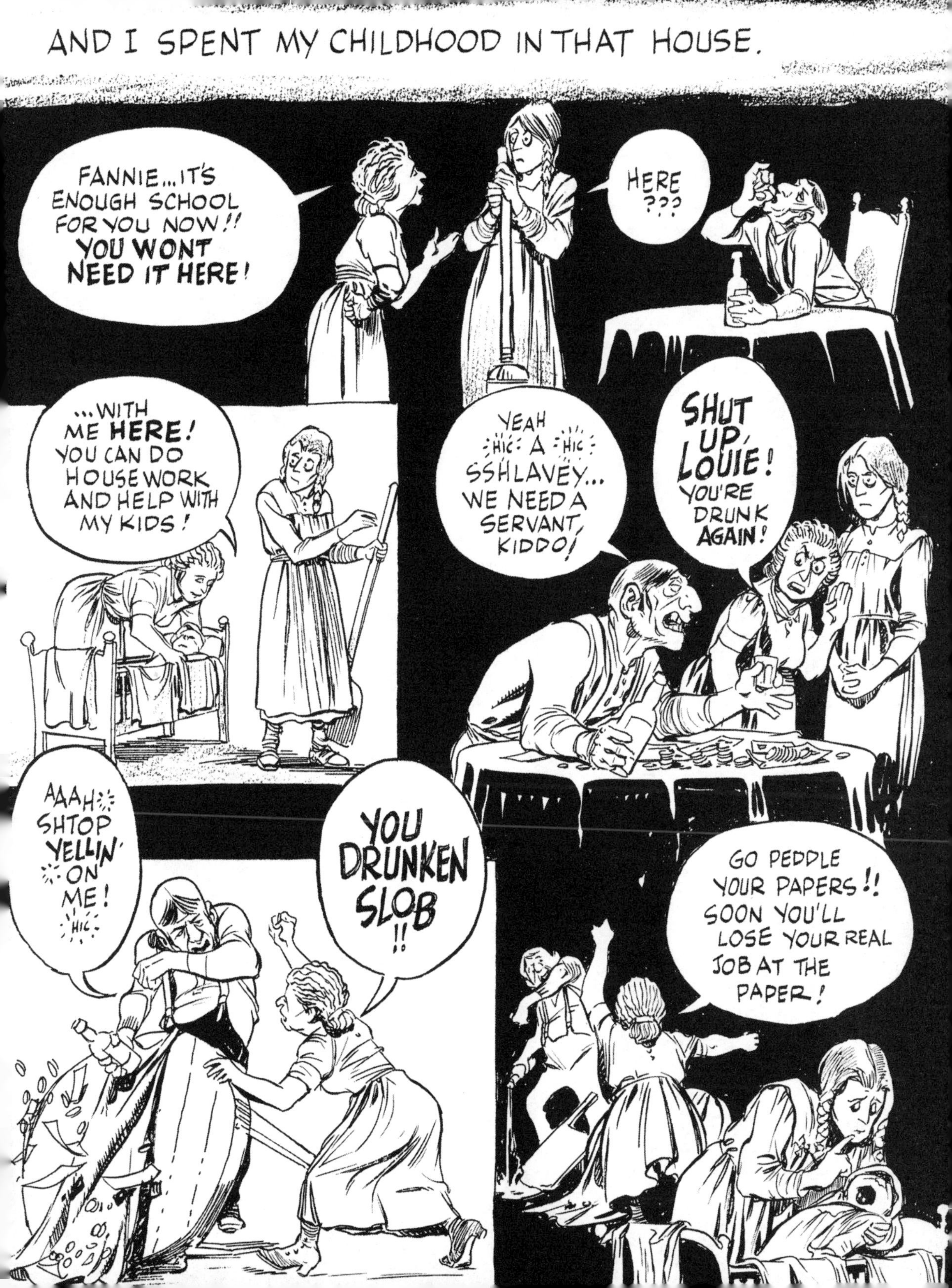
AND I SPENT MY CHILDHOOD IN THAT HOUSE.
FANNIE...IT'S ENOUGH SCHOOL FOR YOU NOW!! YOU WONT NEED IT HERE!
HERE ???
...WITH ME HERE! YOU CAN DO HOUSEWORK AND HELP WITH MY KIDS!
YEAH HIC A HIC SSHLAVEY... WE NEED A SERVANT, KIDDO!
SHUT UP, LOUIE! YOU'RE DRUNK AGAIN!
AAAH SHTOP YELLIN' ON ME! HIC
YOU DRUNKEN SLOB !!
GO PEDDLE YOUR PAPERS!! SOON YOU'LL LOSE YOUR REAL JOB AT THE PAPER!

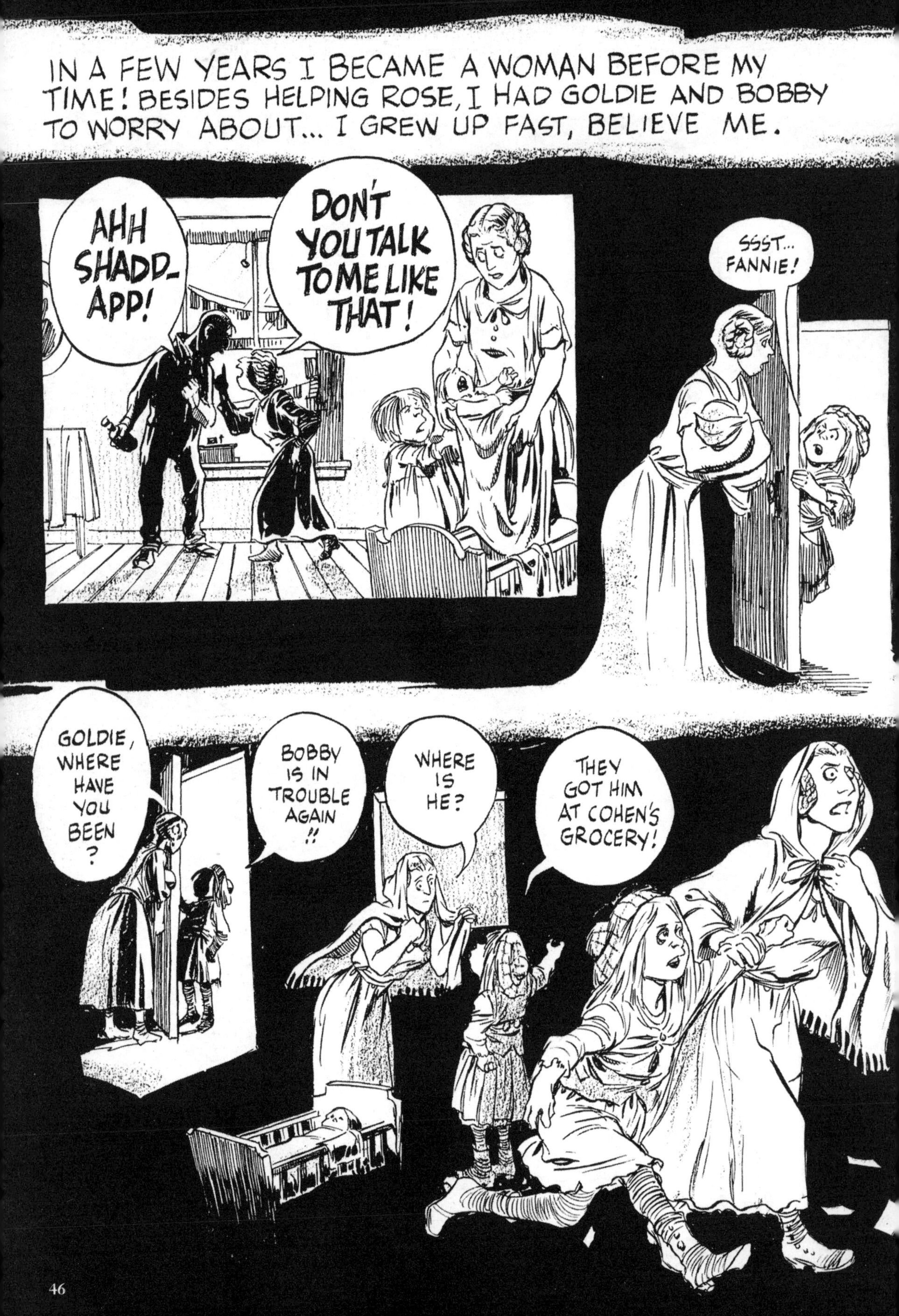
IN A FEW YEARS I BECAME A WOMAN BEFORE MY TIME! BESIDES HELPING ROSE, I HAD GOLDIE AND BOBBY TO WORRY ABOUT... I GREW UP FAST, BELIEVE ME.
AHH SHADD-APP!
DON'T YOU TALK TO ME LIKE THAT!
SSST... FANNIE!
GOLDIE, WHERE HAVE YOU BEEN ?
BOBBY IS IN TROUBLE AGAIN !!
WHERE IS HE?
THEY GOT HIM AT COHEN'S GROCERY!

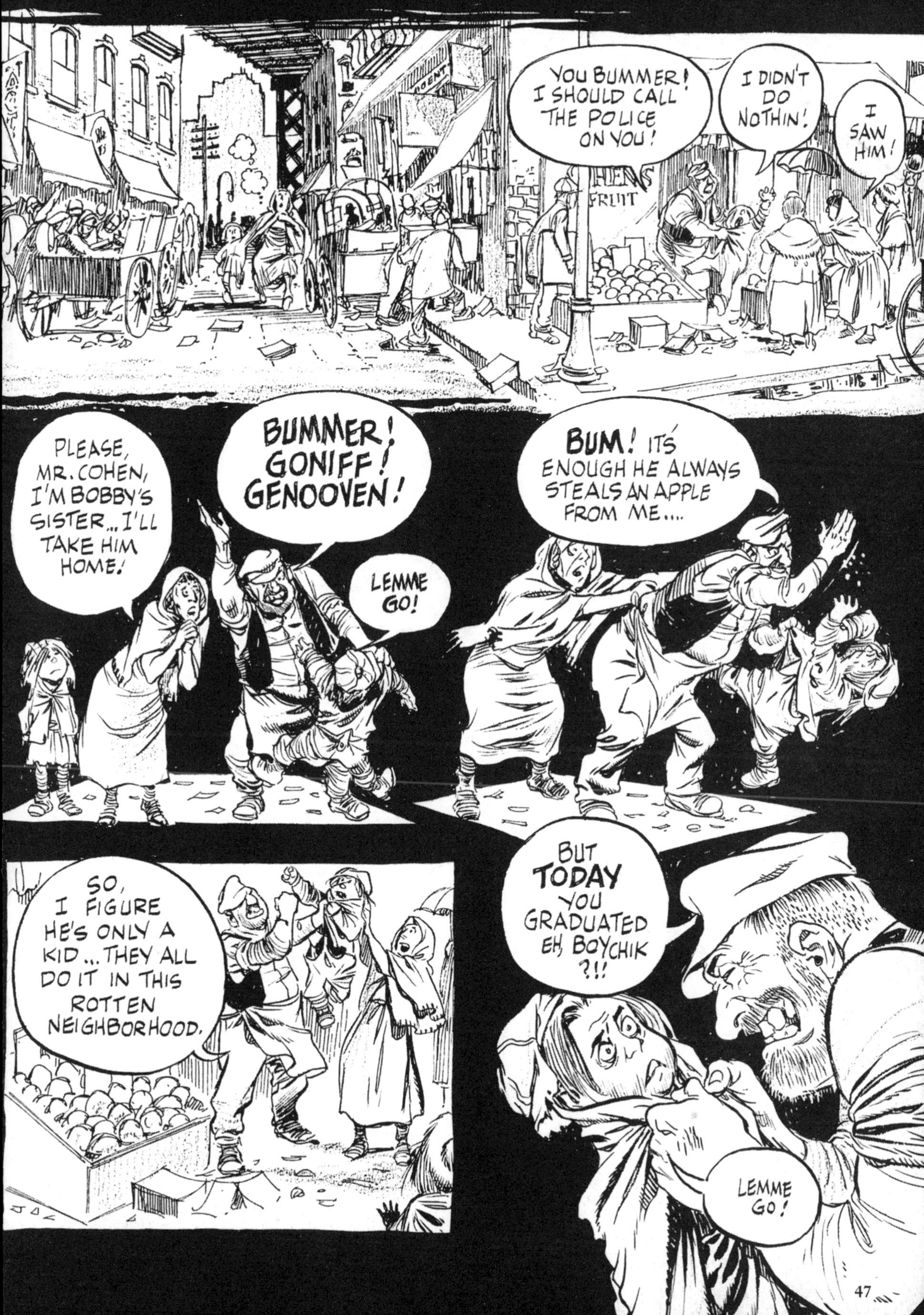
YOU BUMMER! I SHOULD CALL THE POLICE ON YOU!
I DIDN'T DO NOTHIN!
I SAW HIM!
PLEASE, MR. COHEN, I'M BOBBY'S SISTER... I'LL TAKE HIM HOME!
BUMMER! GONIFF! GENOOVEN!
LEMME GO!
BUM! IT'S ENOUGH HE ALWAYS STEALS AN APPLE FROM ME....
SO, I FIGURE HE'S ONLY A KID... THEY ALL DO IT IN THIS ROTTEN NEIGHBORHOOD.
BUT TODAY YOU GRADUATED EH, BOYCHIK ?!!
LEMME GO!

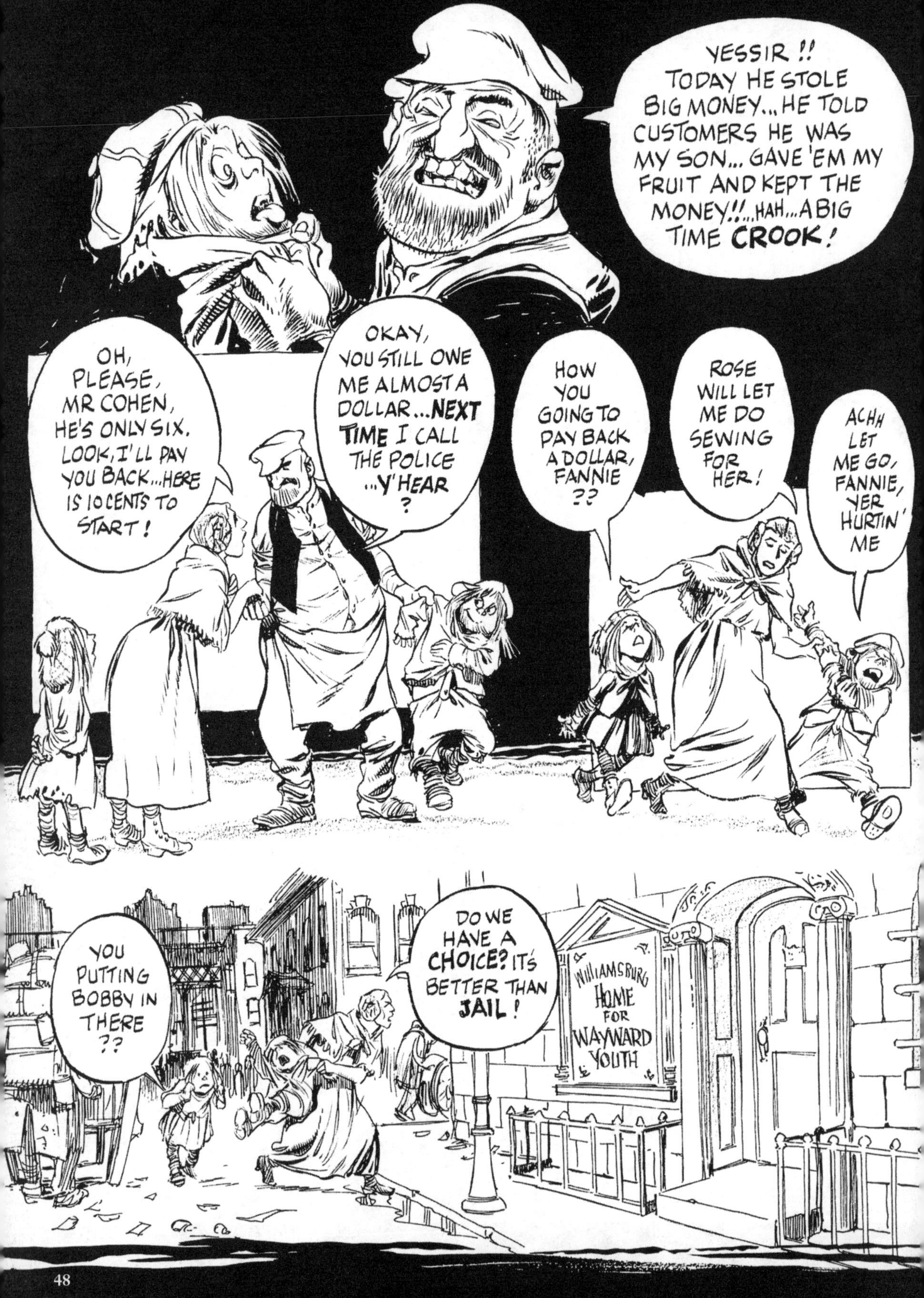
YESSIR !! TODAY HE STOLE BIG MONEY... HE TOLD CUSTOMERS HE WAS MY SON... GAVE 'EM MY FRUIT AND KEPT THE MONEY!!...HAH...A BIG TIME CROOK!
OH, PLEASE, MR COHEN, HE'S ONLY SIX. LOOK, I'LL PAY YOU BACK...HERE IS 10 CENTS TO START!
OKAY, YOU STILL OWE ME ALMOST A DOLLAR...NEXT TIME I CALL THE POLICE ...Y'HEAR ?
HOW YOU GOING TO PAY BACK A DOLLAR, FANNIE ??
ROSE WILL LET ME DO SEWING FOR HER!
ACHH LET ME GO, FANNIE, YER HURTIN' ME
YOU PUTTING BOBBY IN THERE ??
DO WE HAVE A CHOICE? IT'S BETTER THAN JAIL!
WILLIAMSBURG HOME FOR WAYWARD YOUTH

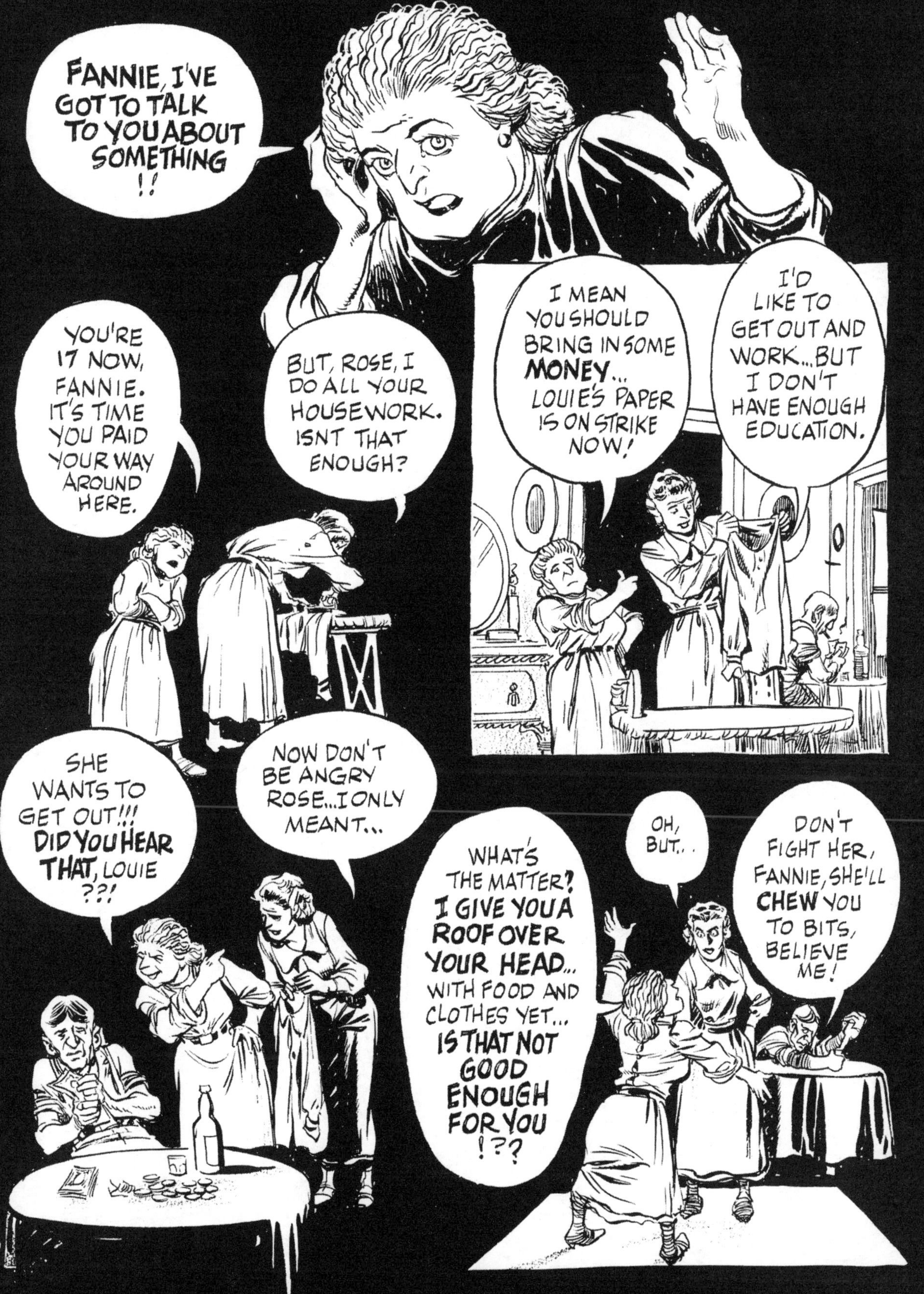
FANNIE, I'VE GOT TO TALK TO YOU ABOUT SOMETHING !!
YOU'RE 17 NOW, FANNIE. IT'S TIME YOU PAID YOUR WAY AROUND HERE.
BUT, ROSE, I DO ALL YOUR HOUSEWORK. ISNT THAT ENOUGH?
I MEAN YOU SHOULD BRING IN SOME **MONEY**... LOUIE'S PAPER IS ON STRIKE NOW!
I'D LIKE TO GET OUT AND WORK... BUT I DON'T HAVE ENOUGH EDUCATION.
SHE WANTS TO GET OUT!!! **DID YOU HEAR THAT**, LOUIE ??!
NOW DON'T BE ANGRY ROSE... I ONLY MEANT...
WHAT'S THE MATTER? **I GIVE YOU A ROOF OVER YOUR HEAD**... WITH FOOD AND CLOTHES YET... **IS THAT NOT GOOD ENOUGH FOR YOU** !??
OH, BUT...
DON'T FIGHT HER, FANNIE, SHE'LL **CHEW** YOU TO BITS, BELIEVE ME!

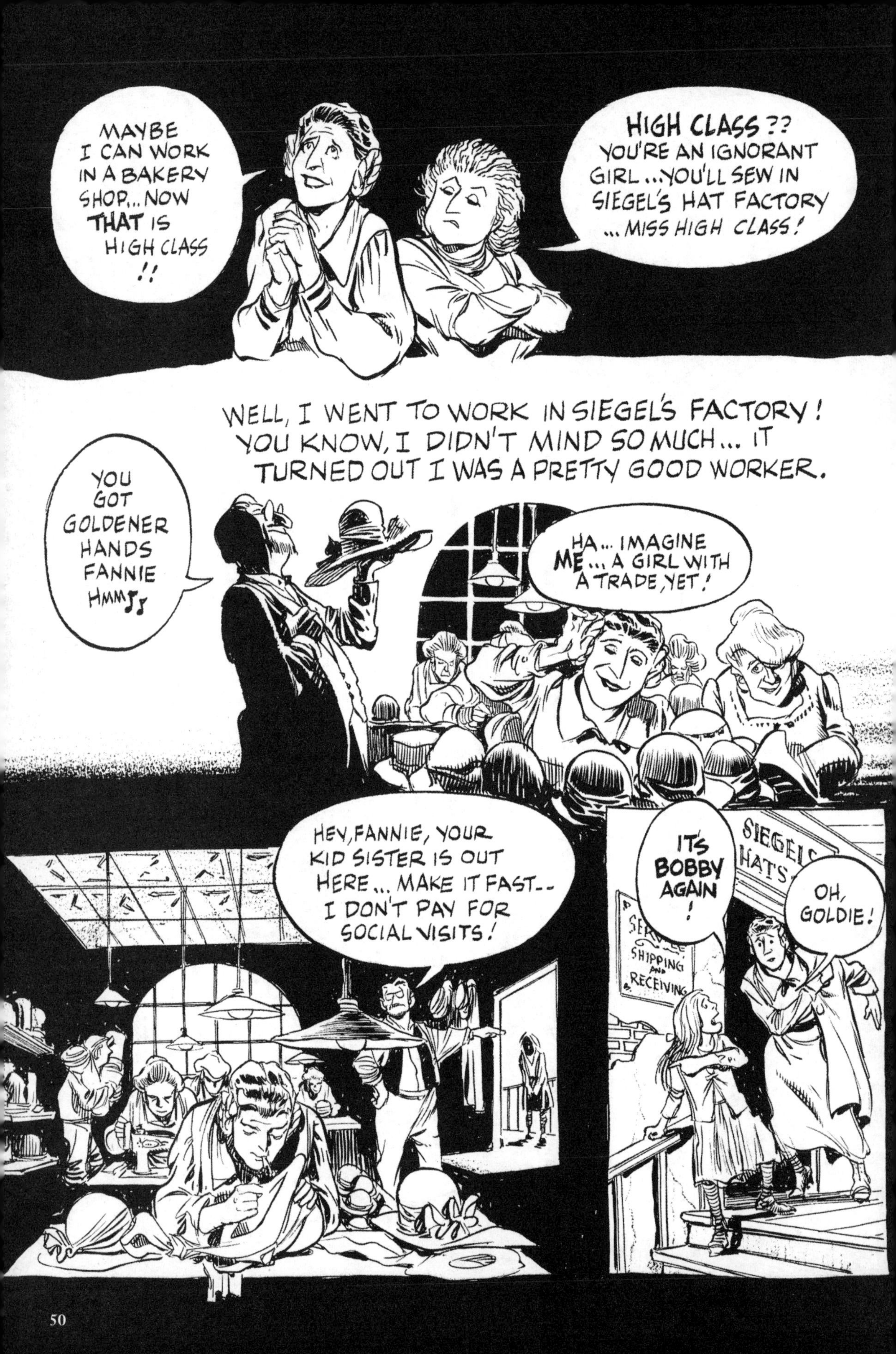
MAYBE I CAN WORK IN A BAKERY SHOP... NOW THAT IS HIGH CLASS !!
HIGH CLASS ?? YOU'RE AN IGNORANT GIRL ...YOU'LL SEW IN SIEGEL'S HAT FACTORY ...MISS HIGH CLASS!
WELL, I WENT TO WORK IN SIEGEL'S FACTORY! YOU KNOW, I DIDN'T MIND SO MUCH... IT TURNED OUT I WAS A PRETTY GOOD WORKER.
YOU GOT GOLDENER HANDS FANNIE HMM
HA... IMAGINE ME... A GIRL WITH A TRADE, YET!
HEY, FANNIE, YOUR KID SISTER IS OUT HERE... MAKE IT FAST-- I DON'T PAY FOR SOCIAL VISITS!
IT'S BOBBY AGAIN !
OH, GOLDIE!
SHIPPING AND RECEIVING

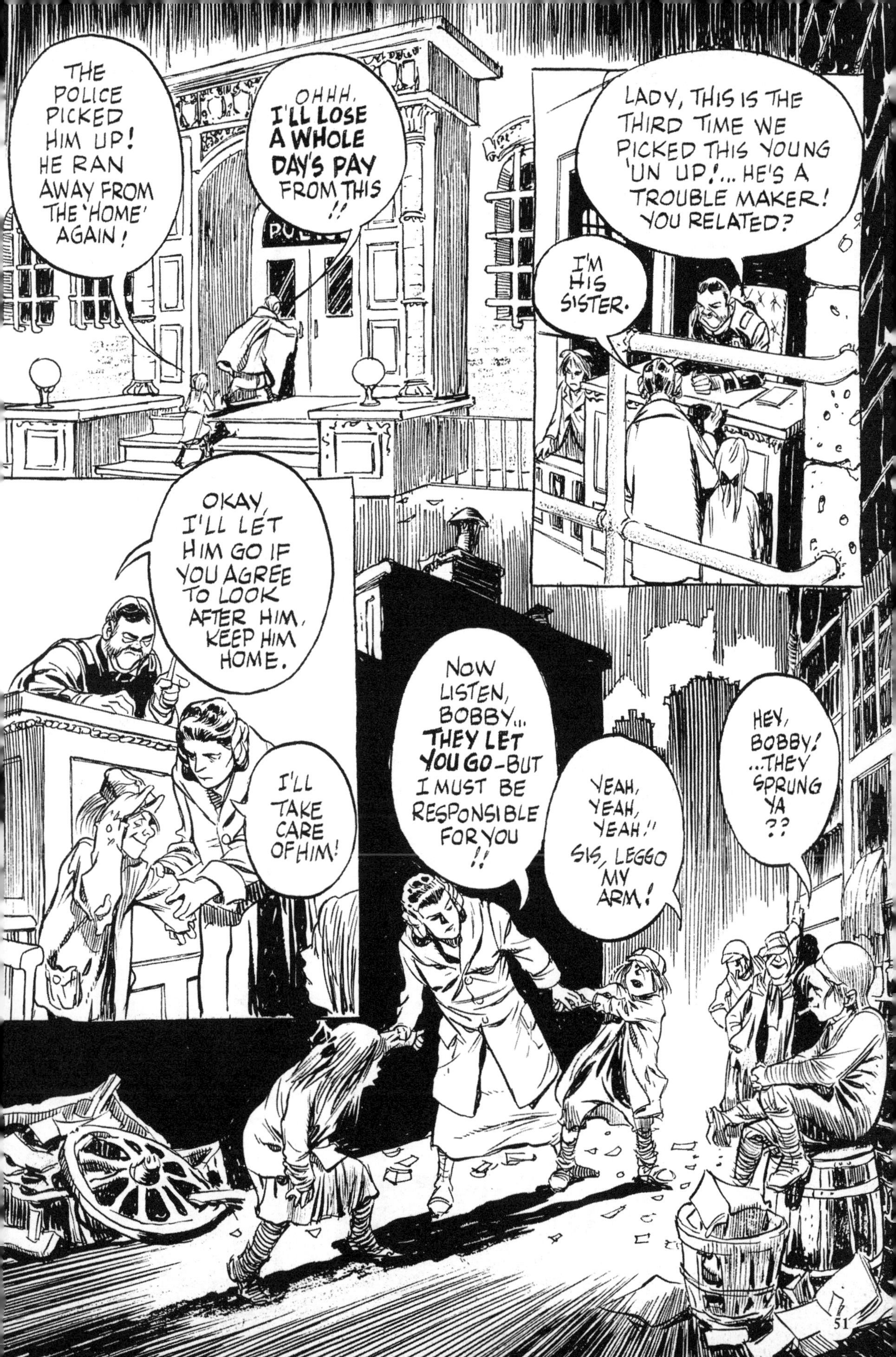
THE POLICE PICKED HIM UP! HE RAN AWAY FROM THE 'HOME' AGAIN!
OHHH. I'LL LOSE A WHOLE DAY'S PAY FROM THIS!!
LADY, THIS IS THE THIRD TIME WE PICKED THIS YOUNG 'UN UP!... HE'S A TROUBLE MAKER! YOU RELATED?
I'M HIS SISTER.
OKAY, I'LL LET HIM GO IF YOU AGREE TO LOOK AFTER HIM. KEEP HIM HOME.
I'LL TAKE CARE OF HIM!
NOW LISTEN, BOBBY... THEY LET YOU GO-BUT I MUST BE RESPONSIBLE FOR YOU!!
YEAH, YEAH, YEAH!! SIS, LEGGO MY ARM!
HEY, BOBBY! ...THEY SPRUNG YA??

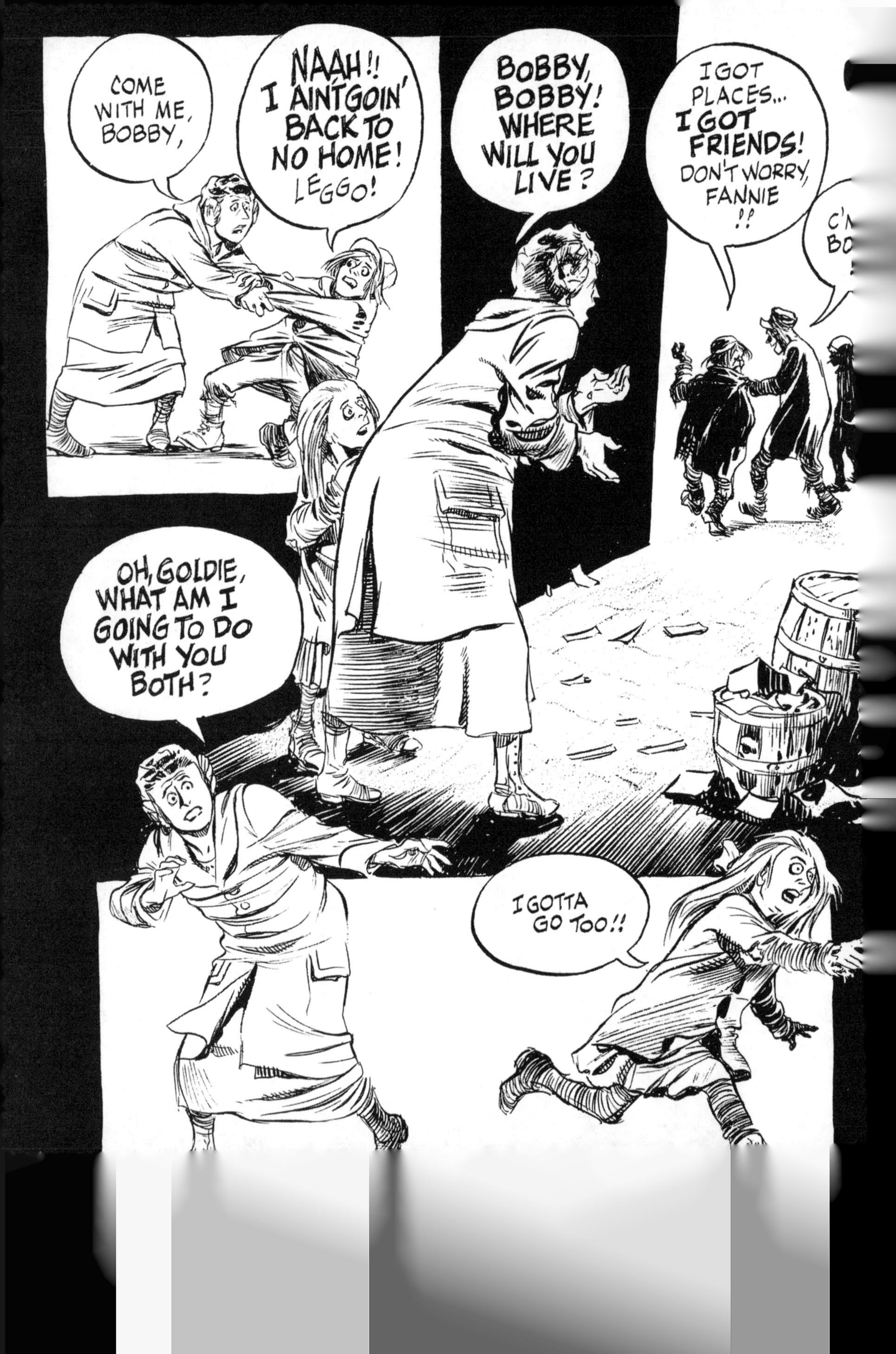
COME WITH ME, BOBBY,
NAAH!! I AIN'T GOIN' BACK TO NO HOME! LEGGO!
BOBBY, BOBBY! WHERE WILL YOU LIVE?
I GOT PLACES... I GOT FRIENDS! DON'T WORRY, FANNIE !!
OH, GOLDIE, WHAT AM I GOING TO DO WITH YOU BOTH?
I GOTTA GO TOO!!

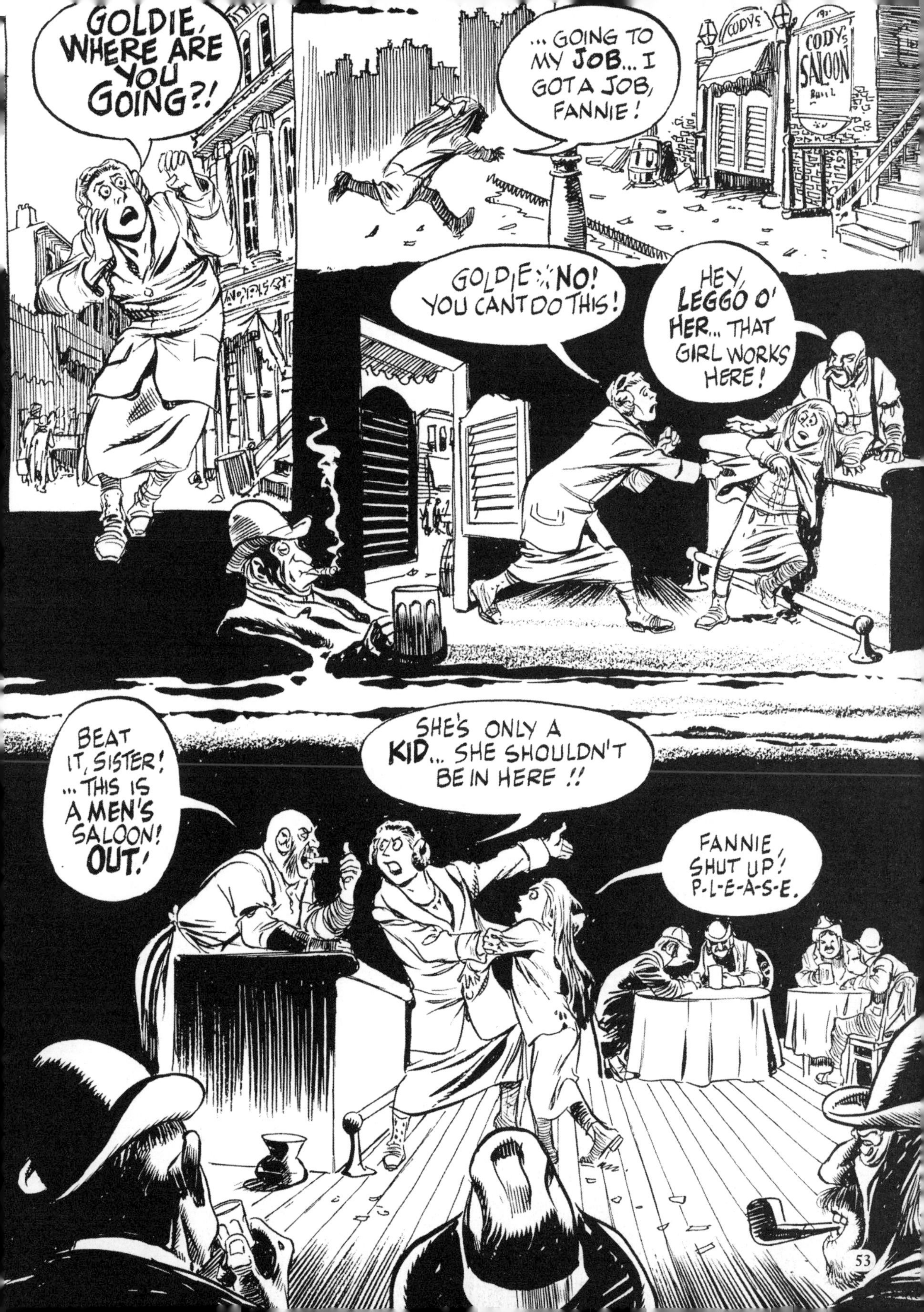
GOLDIE, WHERE ARE YOU GOING?!
... GOING TO MY JOB... I GOT A JOB, FANNIE!
CODY'S
CODY'S SALOON
GOLDIE NO! YOU CANT DO THIS!
HEY, LEGGO O' HER... THAT GIRL WORKS HERE!
BEAT IT, SISTER! ... THIS IS A MEN'S SALOON! OUT!
SHE'S ONLY A KID... SHE SHOULDN'T BE IN HERE !!
FANNIE SHUT UP! P-L-E-A-S-E.

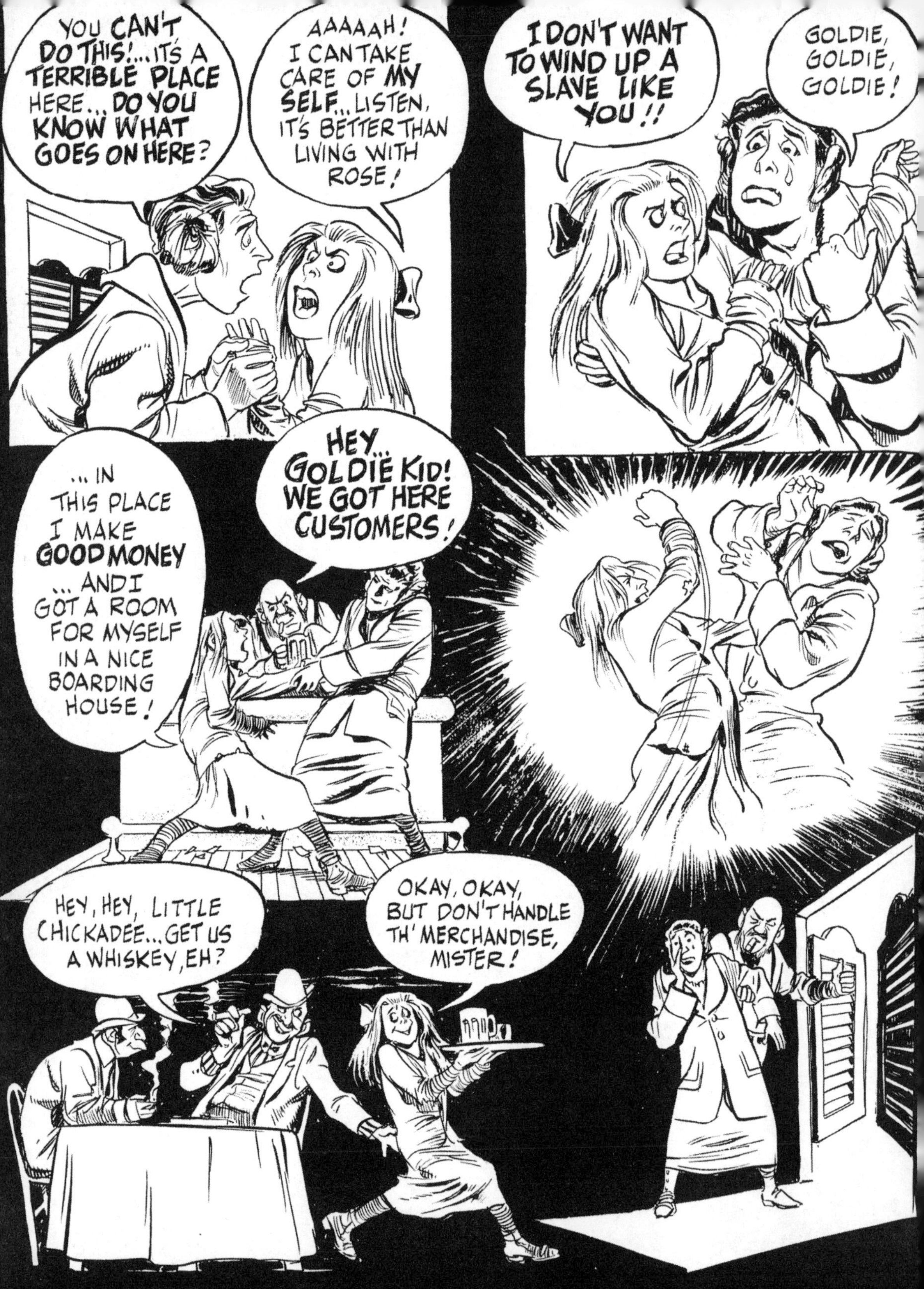
YOU CAN'T DO THIS!...IT'S A TERRIBLE PLACE HERE... DO YOU KNOW WHAT GOES ON HERE?
AAAAAH! I CAN TAKE CARE OF MY SELF...LISTEN, IT'S BETTER THAN LIVING WITH ROSE!
I DON'T WANT TO WIND UP A SLAVE LIKE YOU!!
GOLDIE, GOLDIE, GOLDIE!
...IN THIS PLACE I MAKE GOOD MONEY ...AND I GOT A ROOM FOR MYSELF IN A NICE BOARDING HOUSE!
HEY... GOLDIE KID! WE GOT HERE CUSTOMERS!
HEY, HEY, LITTLE CHICKADEE...GET US A WHISKEY, EH?
OKAY, OKAY, BUT DON'T HANDLE TH' MERCHANDISE, MISTER!

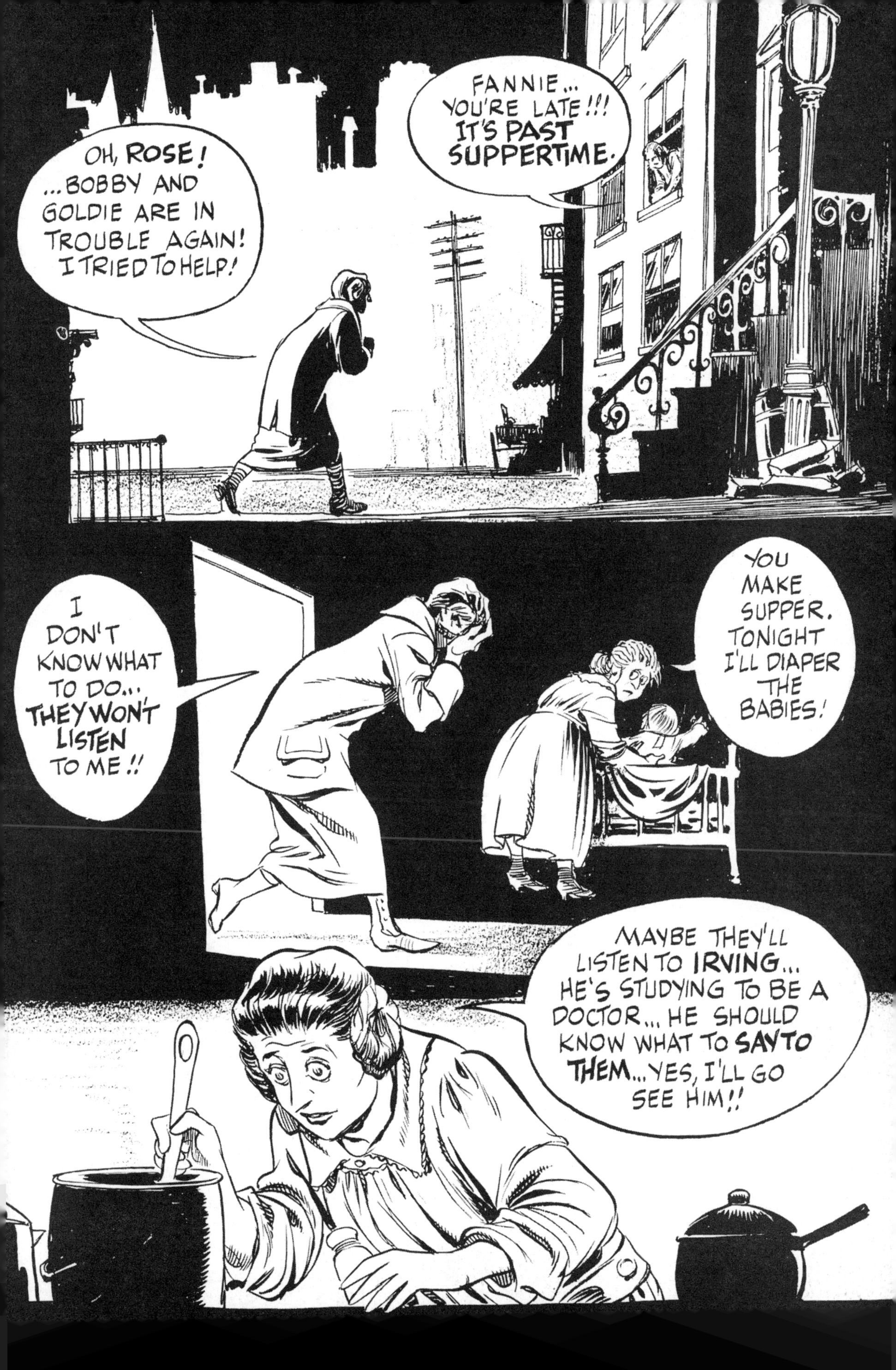
OH, ROSE! ...BOBBY AND GOLDIE ARE IN TROUBLE AGAIN! I TRIED TO HELP!
FANNIE... YOU'RE LATE!!! IT'S PAST SUPPERTIME.
I DON'T KNOW WHAT TO DO... THEY WON'T LISTEN TO ME!!
YOU MAKE SUPPER. TONIGHT I'LL DIAPER THE BABIES!
MAYBE THEY'LL LISTEN TO IRVING... HE'S STUDYING TO BE A DOCTOR... HE SHOULD KNOW WHAT TO SAY TO THEM... YES, I'LL GO SEE HIM!!

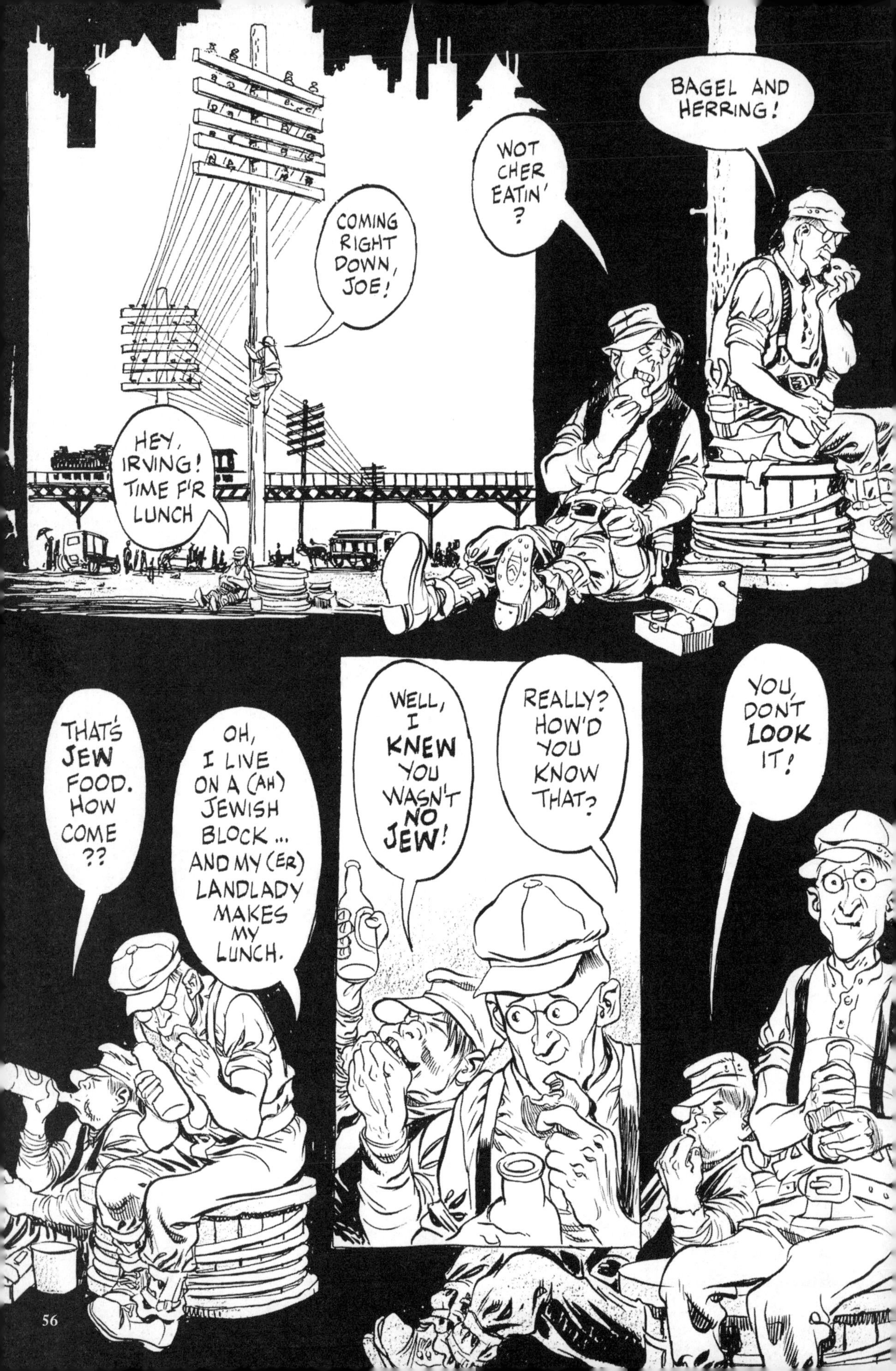
HEY, IRVING! TIME F'R LUNCH
COMING RIGHT DOWN, JOE!
WOT CHER EATIN' ?
BAGEL AND HERRING!
THAT'S JEW FOOD. HOW COME ??
OH, I LIVE ON A (AH) JEWISH BLOCK... AND MY (ER) LANDLADY MAKES MY LUNCH.
WELL, I KNEW YOU WASN'T NO JEW!
REALLY? HOW'D YOU KNOW THAT?
YOU, DON'T LOOK IT!

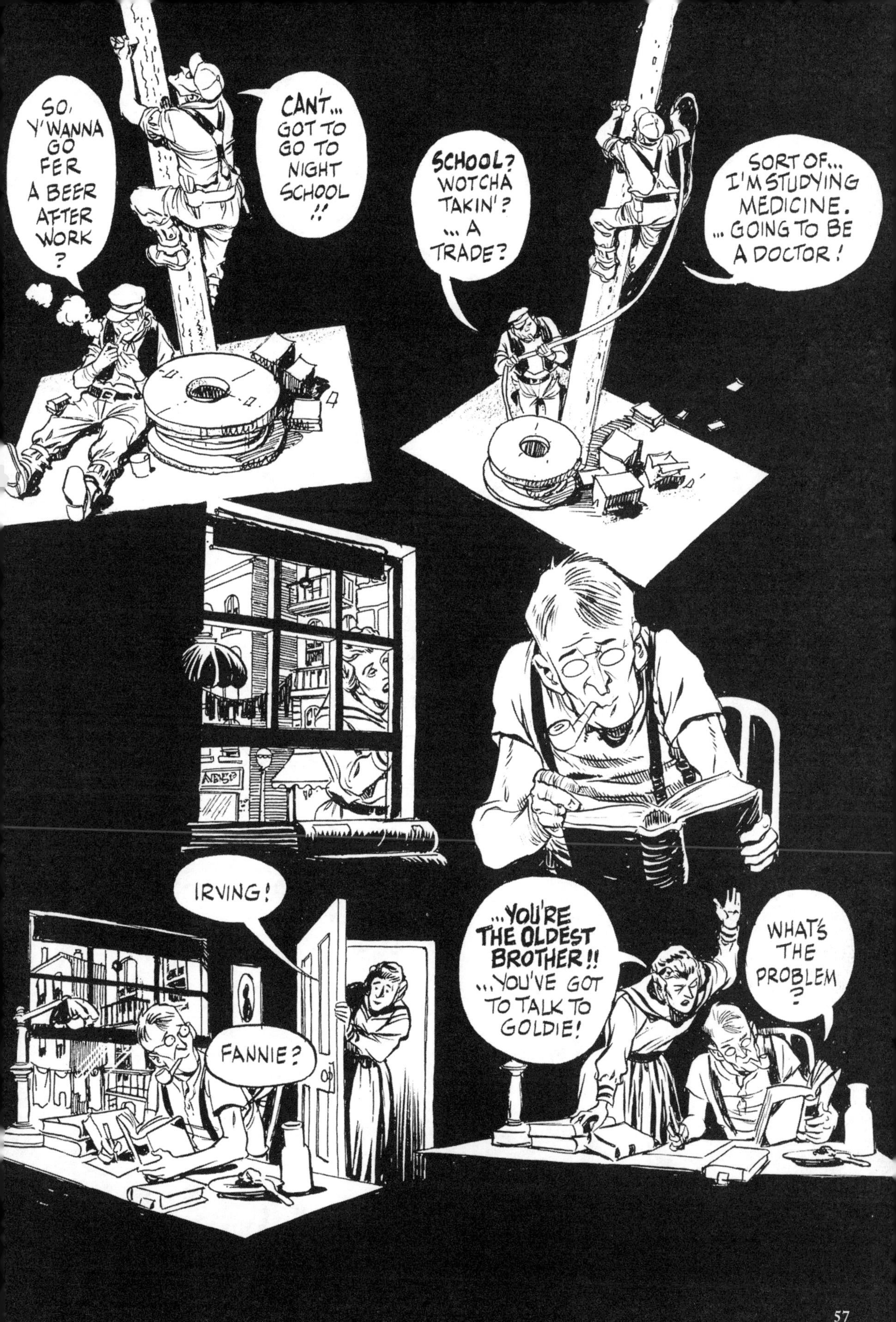
SO, Y'WANNA GO FER A BEER AFTER WORK ?
CAN'T... GOT TO GO TO NIGHT SCHOOL !!
SCHOOL? WOTCHA TAKIN'? ... A TRADE?
SORT OF... I'M STUDYING MEDICINE. ... GOING TO BE A DOCTOR!
IRVING!
FANNIE?
... YOU'RE THE OLDEST BROTHER!! ... YOU'VE GOT TO TALK TO GOLDIE!
WHAT'S THE PROBLEM ?

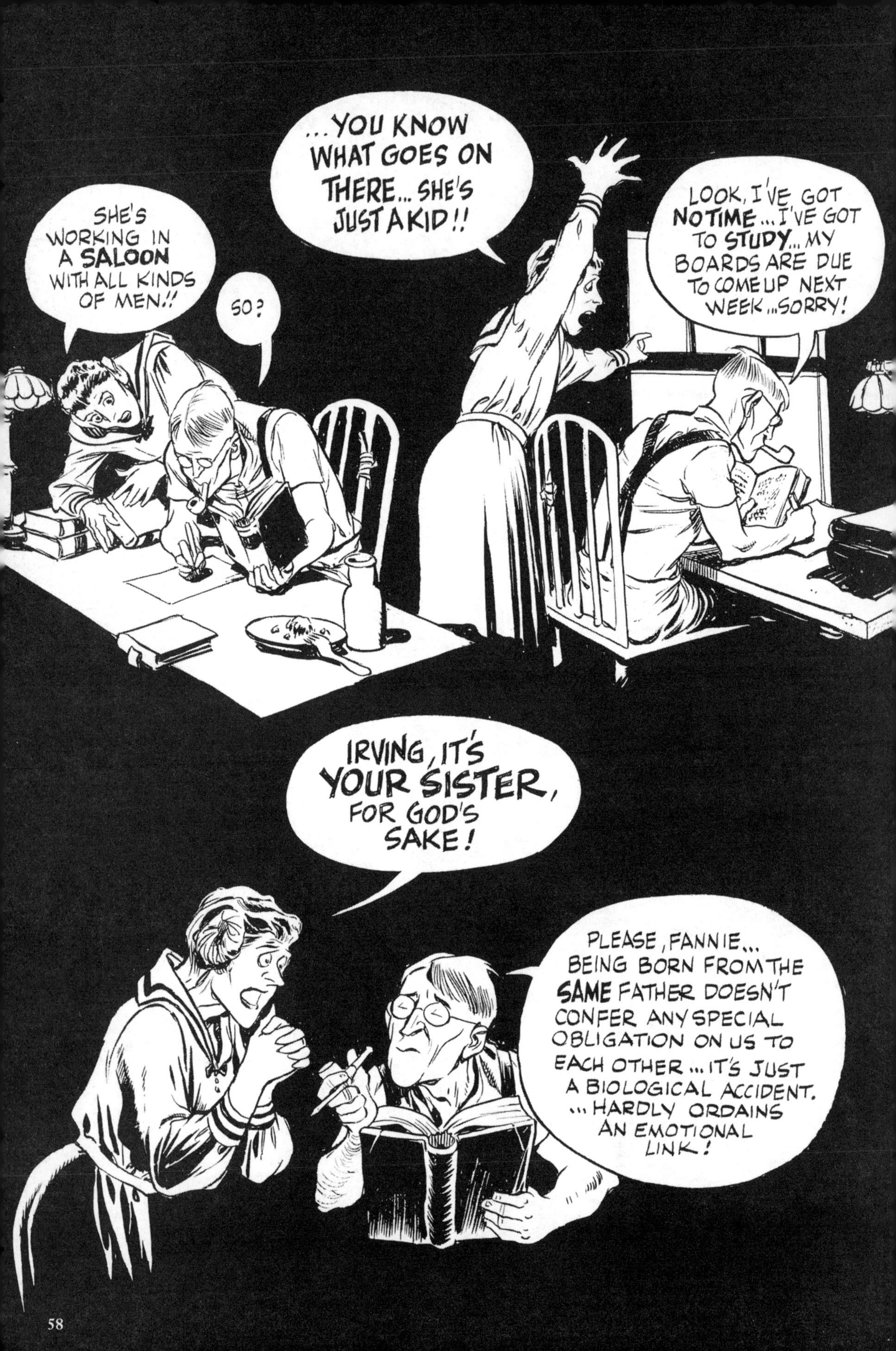
SHE'S WORKING IN A **SALOON** WITH ALL KINDS OF MEN!!
SO?
...YOU KNOW WHAT GOES ON THERE... SHE'S JUST A KID!!
LOOK, I'VE GOT **NO TIME**... I'VE GOT TO **STUDY**... MY BOARDS ARE DUE TO COME UP NEXT WEEK... SORRY!
IRVING, IT'S **YOUR SISTER**, FOR GOD'S SAKE!
PLEASE, FANNIE... BEING BORN FROM THE **SAME** FATHER DOESN'T CONFER ANY SPECIAL OBLIGATION ON US TO EACH OTHER... IT'S JUST A BIOLOGICAL ACCIDENT. ... HARDLY ORDAINS AN EMOTIONAL LINK!

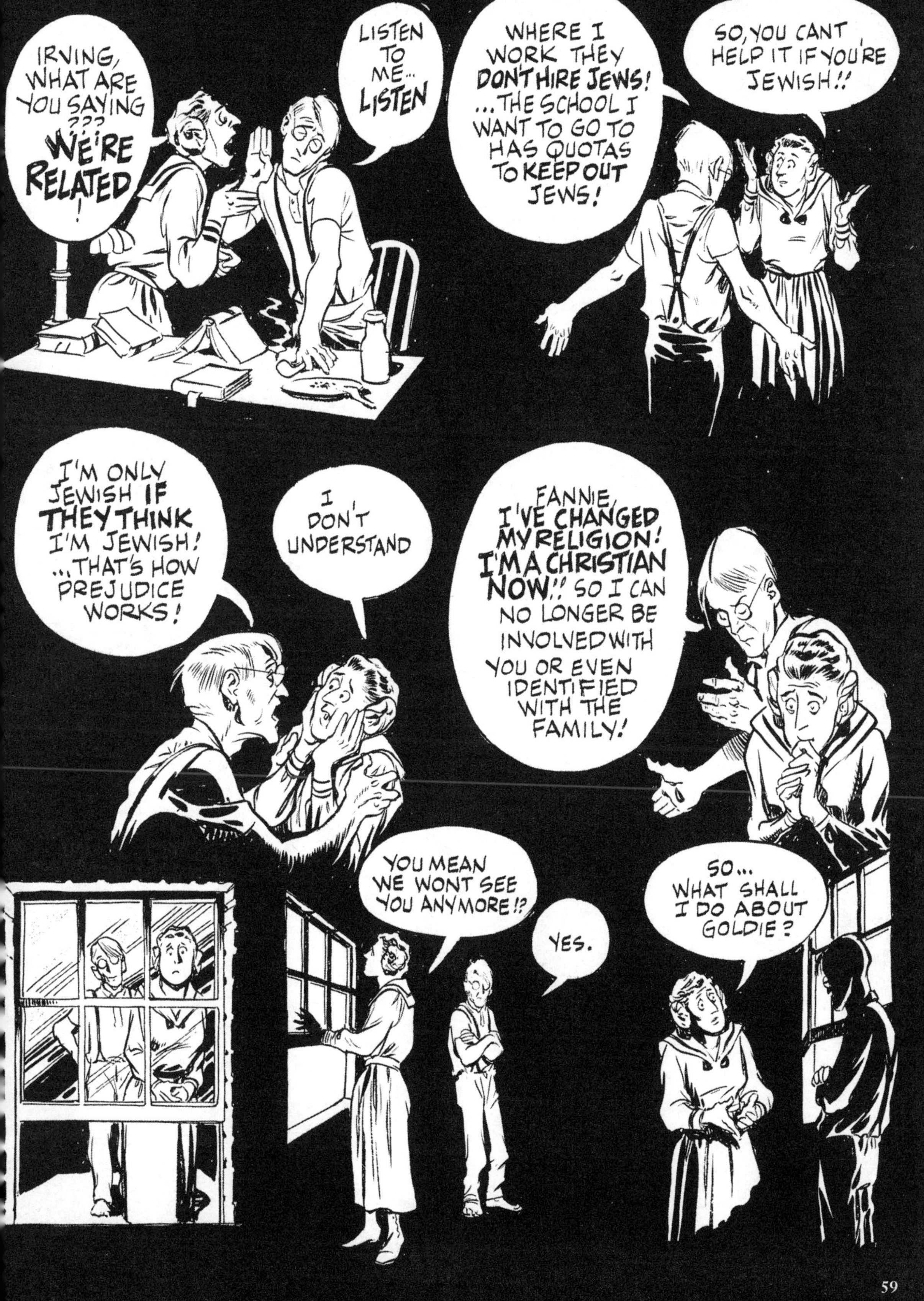
IRVING, WHAT ARE YOU SAYING ??? WE'RE RELATED!
LISTEN TO ME... LISTEN
WHERE I WORK THEY DON'T HIRE JEWS! ...THE SCHOOL I WANT TO GO TO HAS QUOTAS TO KEEP OUT JEWS!
SO, YOU CANT HELP IT IF YOU'RE JEWISH!!
I'M ONLY JEWISH IF THEY THINK I'M JEWISH! ...THAT'S HOW PREJUDICE WORKS!
I DON'T UNDERSTAND
FANNIE, I'VE CHANGED MY RELIGION! I'M A CHRISTIAN NOW!! SO I CAN NO LONGER BE INVOLVED WITH YOU OR EVEN IDENTIFIED WITH THE FAMILY!
YOU MEAN WE WONT SEE YOU ANYMORE!?
YES.
SO... WHAT SHALL I DO ABOUT GOLDIE?

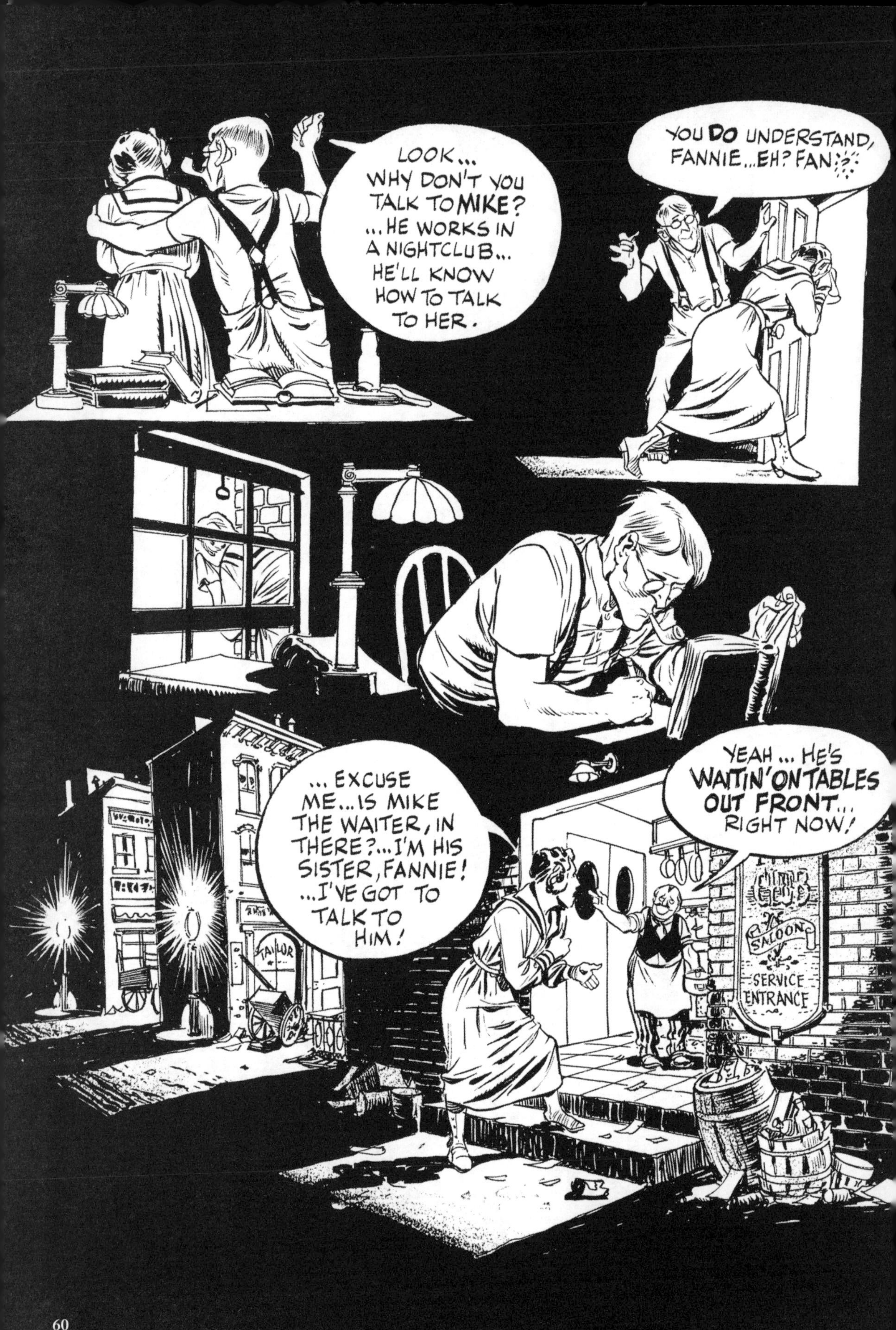
LOOK... WHY DON'T YOU TALK TO MIKE? ...HE WORKS IN A NIGHTCLUB... HE'LL KNOW HOW TO TALK TO HER.
YOU DO UNDERSTAND, FANNIE...EH? FAN...?
...EXCUSE ME...IS MIKE THE WAITER, IN THERE?...I'M HIS SISTER, FANNIE! ...I'VE GOT TO TALK TO HIM!
YEAH ... HE'S WAITIN' ON TABLES OUT FRONT... RIGHT NOW!
TAILOR
SALOON
SERVICE ENTRANCE

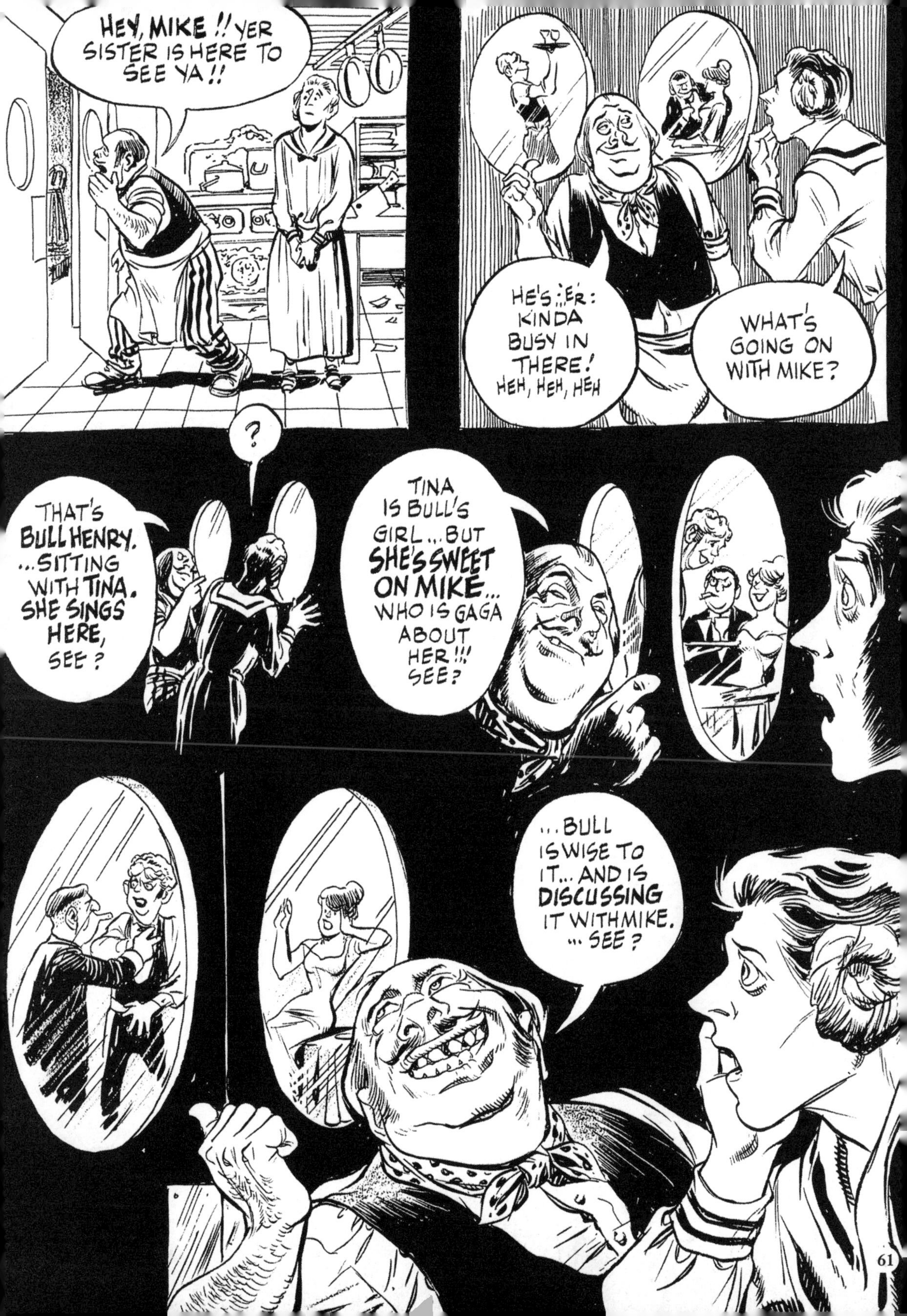
HEY, MIKE !! YER SISTER IS HERE TO SEE YA !!
HE'S ...ER... KINDA BUSY IN THERE! HEH, HEH, HEH
WHAT'S GOING ON WITH MIKE?
?
THAT'S BULL HENRY. ...SITTING WITH TINA. SHE SINGS HERE, SEE?
TINA IS BULL'S GIRL... BUT SHE'S SWEET ON MIKE... WHO IS GAGA ABOUT HER!!! SEE?
...BULL IS WISE TO IT... AND IS DISCUSSING IT WITH MIKE. ... SEE?

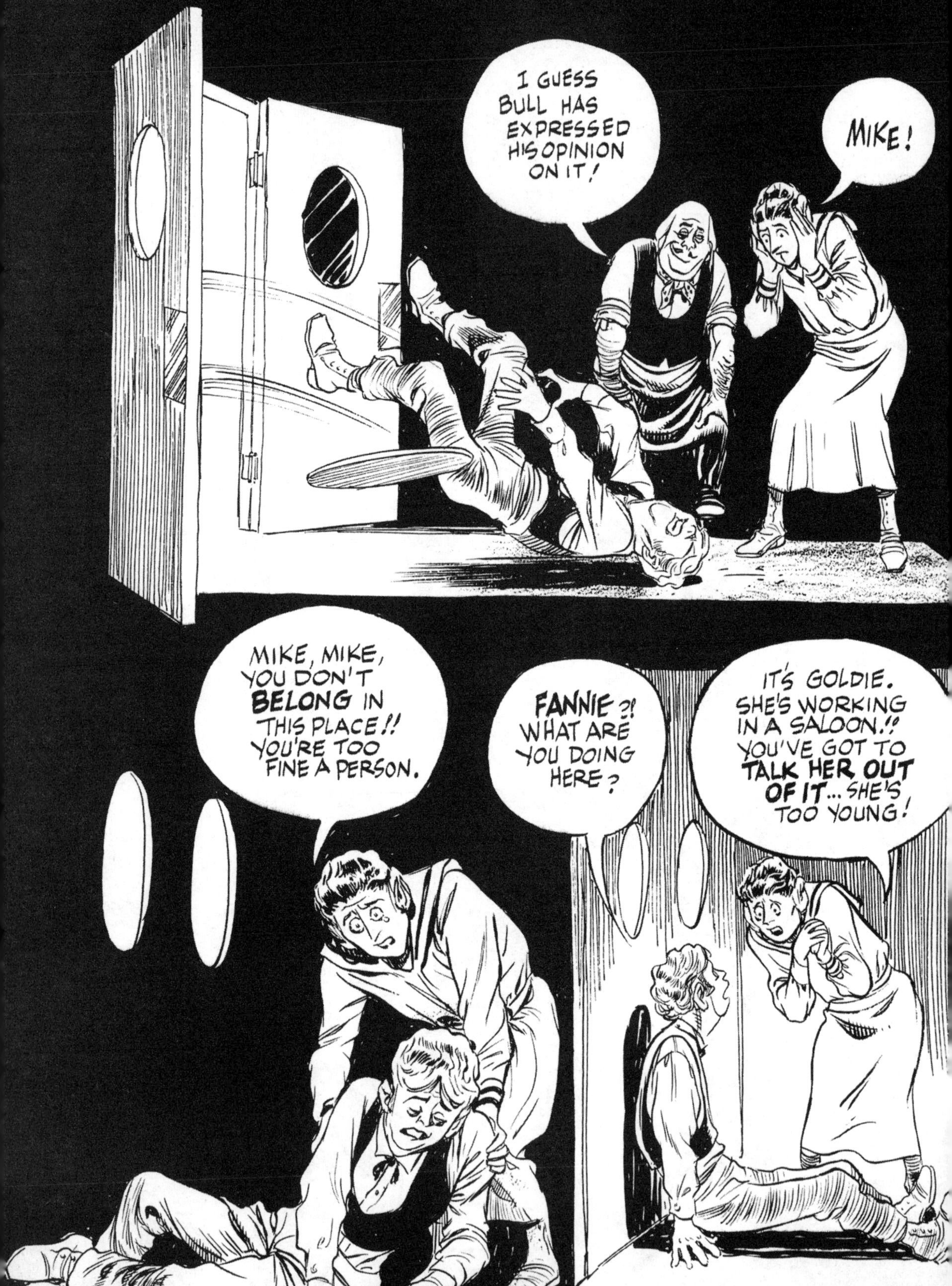
I GUESS BULL HAS EXPRESSED HIS OPINION ON IT!
MIKE!
MIKE, MIKE, YOU DON'T **BELONG** IN THIS PLACE!! YOU'RE TOO FINE A PERSON.
FANNIE?! WHAT ARE YOU DOING HERE?
IT'S GOLDIE. SHE'S WORKING IN A SALOON!? YOU'VE GOT TO **TALK HER OUT OF IT**... SHE'S TOO YOUNG!

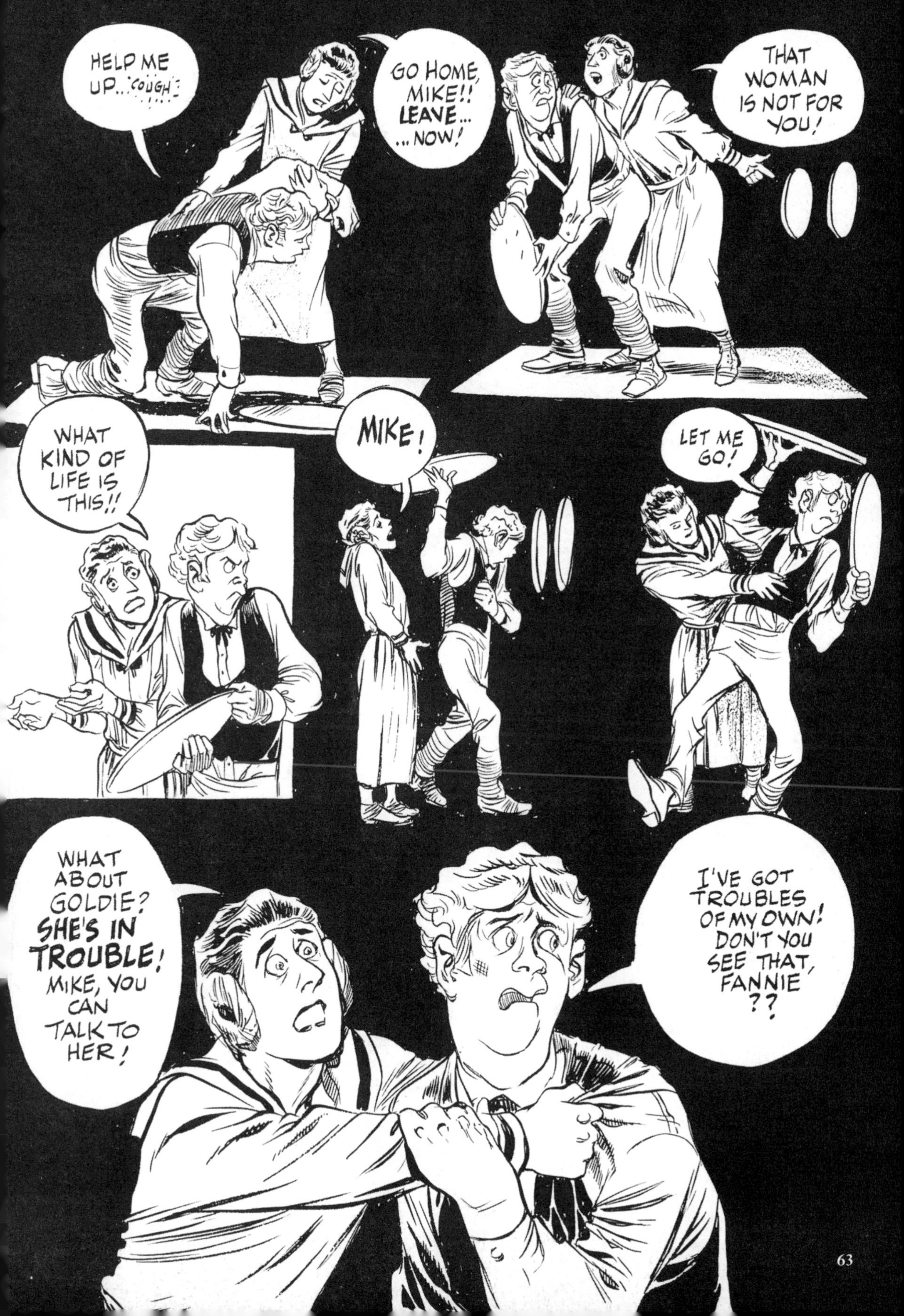
HELP ME UP... COUGH
GO HOME, MIKE!! LEAVE... ...NOW!
THAT WOMAN IS NOT FOR YOU!
WHAT KIND OF LIFE IS THIS!!
MIKE!
LET ME GO!
WHAT ABOUT GOLDIE? SHE'S IN TROUBLE! MIKE, YOU CAN TALK TO HER!
I'VE GOT TROUBLES OF MY OWN! DON'T YOU SEE THAT, FANNIE??

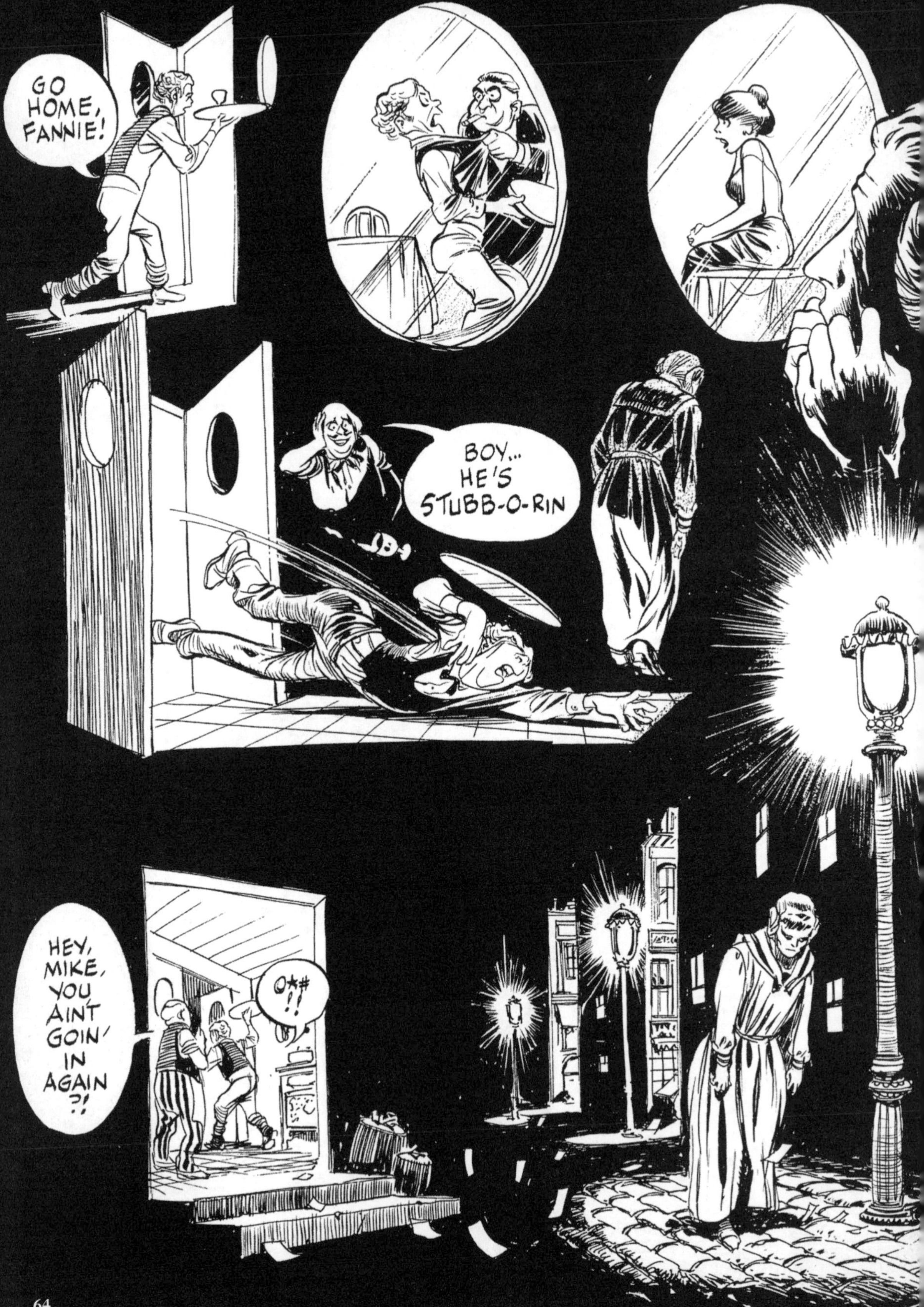
GO HOME, FANNIE!
BOY... HE'S STUBB-O-RIN
HEY, MIKE, YOU AIN'T GOIN' IN AGAIN ?!
@*# !!

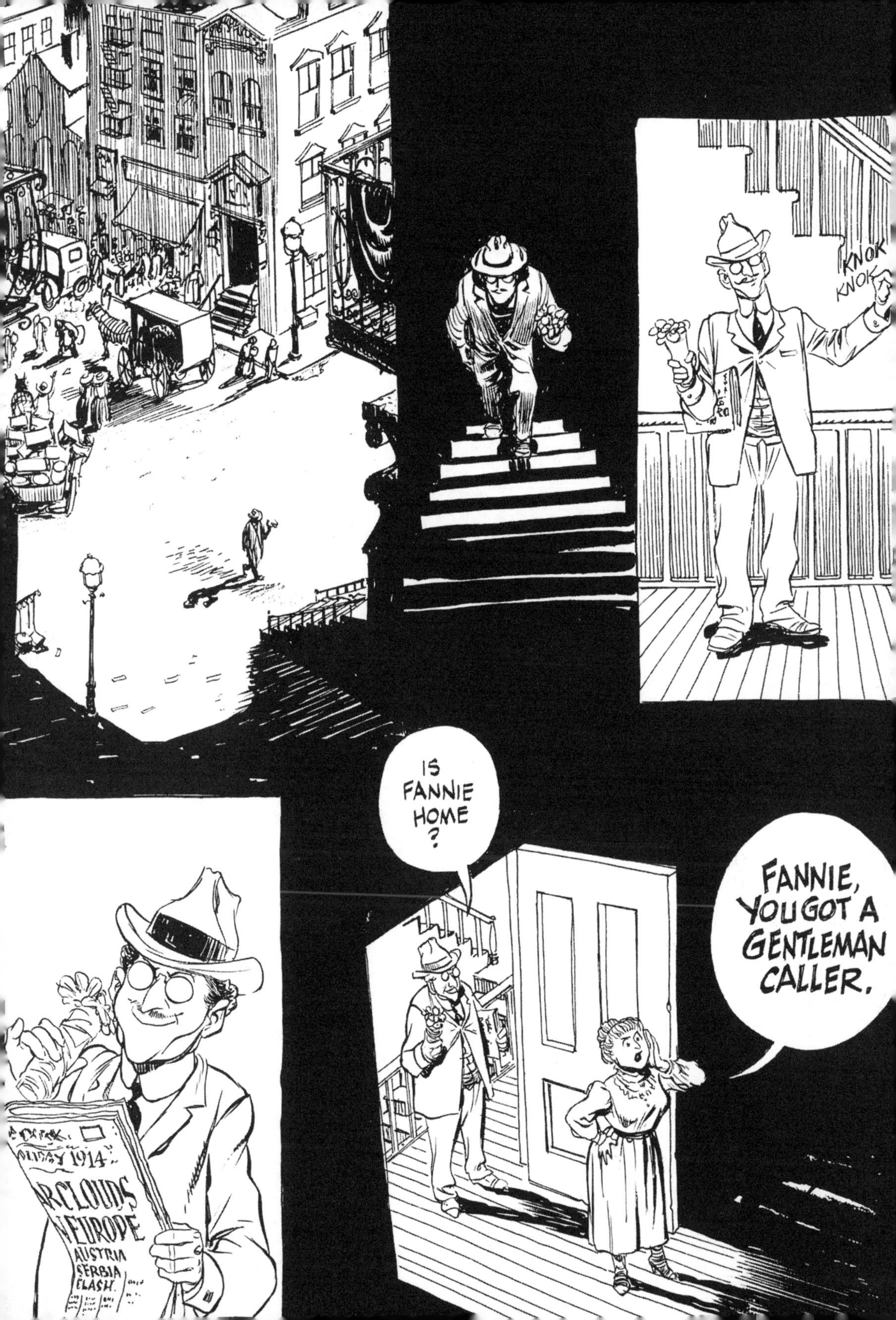
KNOK
KNOK
ONDAY 1914
ARCLOUDS
N EUROPE
AUSTRIA
SERBIA
FLASH.
IS FANNIE HOME?
FANNIE, YOU GOT A GENTLEMAN CALLER.

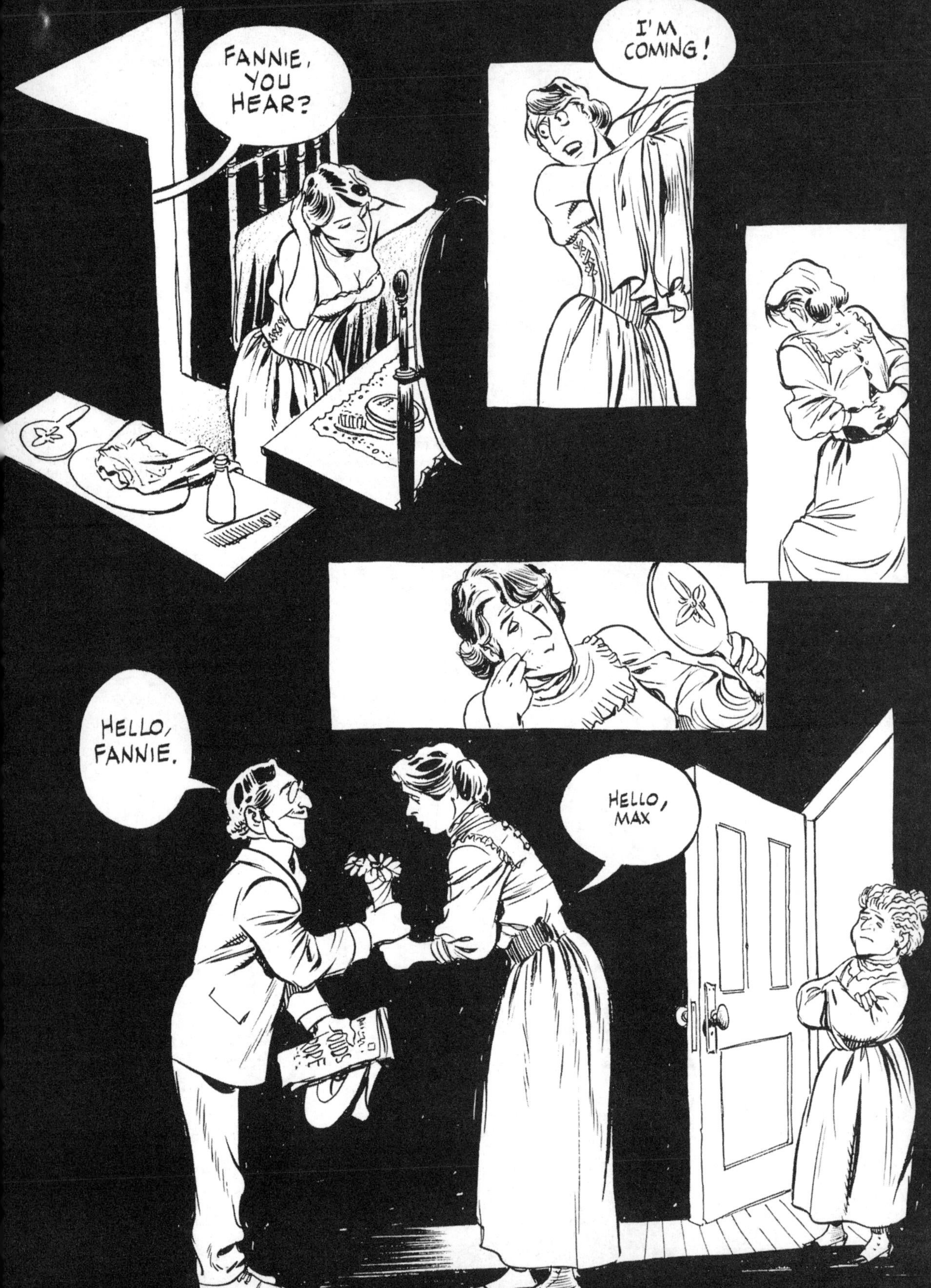
FANNIE, YOU HEAR?
I'M COMING!
HELLO, FANNIE.
HELLO, MAX

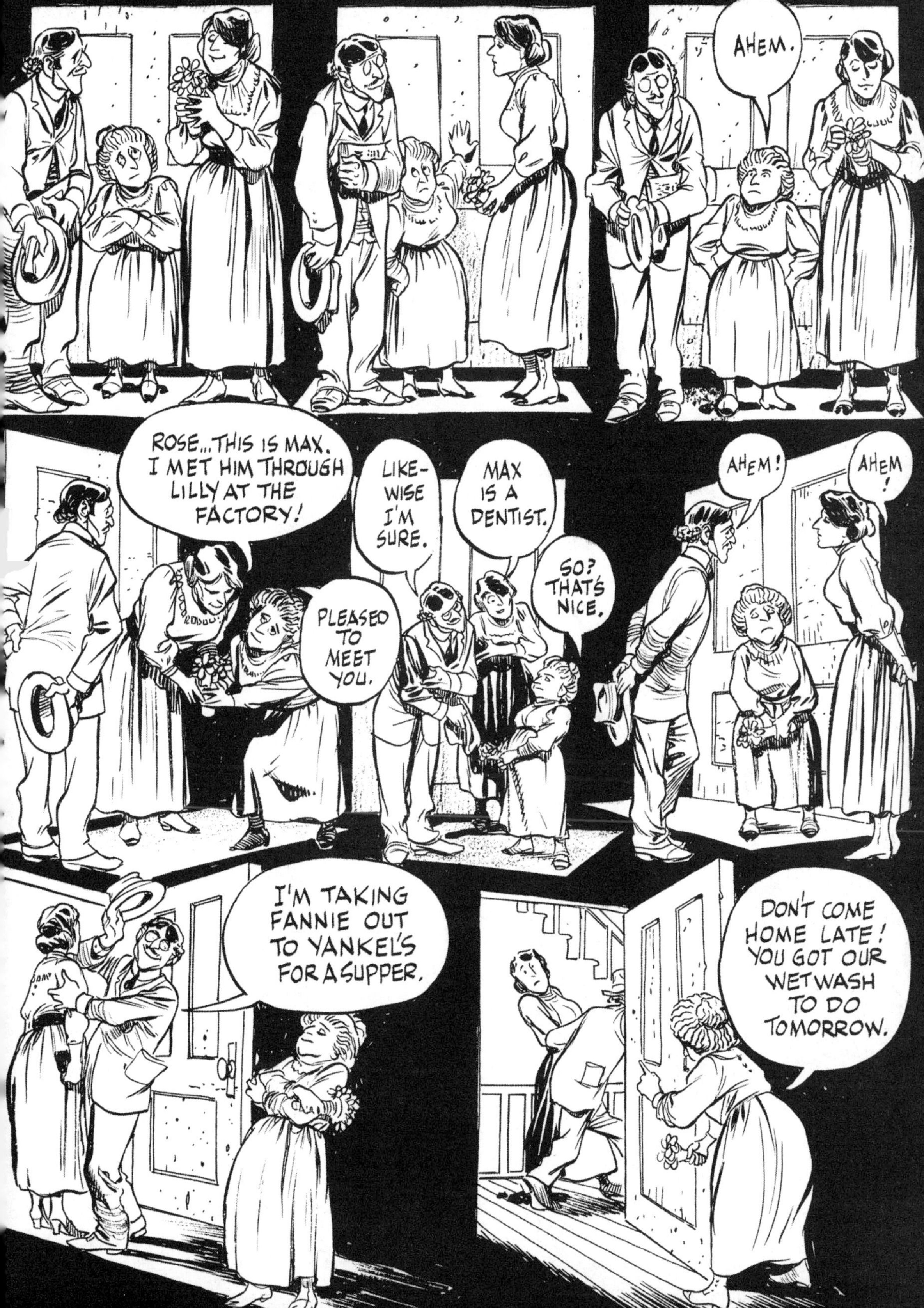
AHEM.
ROSE... THIS IS MAX. I MET HIM THROUGH LILLY AT THE FACTORY!
PLEASED TO MEET YOU.
LIKE-WISE I'M SURE.
MAX IS A DENTIST.
SO? THAT'S NICE.
AHEM!
AHEM!
I'M TAKING FANNIE OUT TO YANKEL'S FOR A SUPPER.
DON'T COME HOME LATE! YOU GOT OUR WETWASH TO DO TOMORROW.

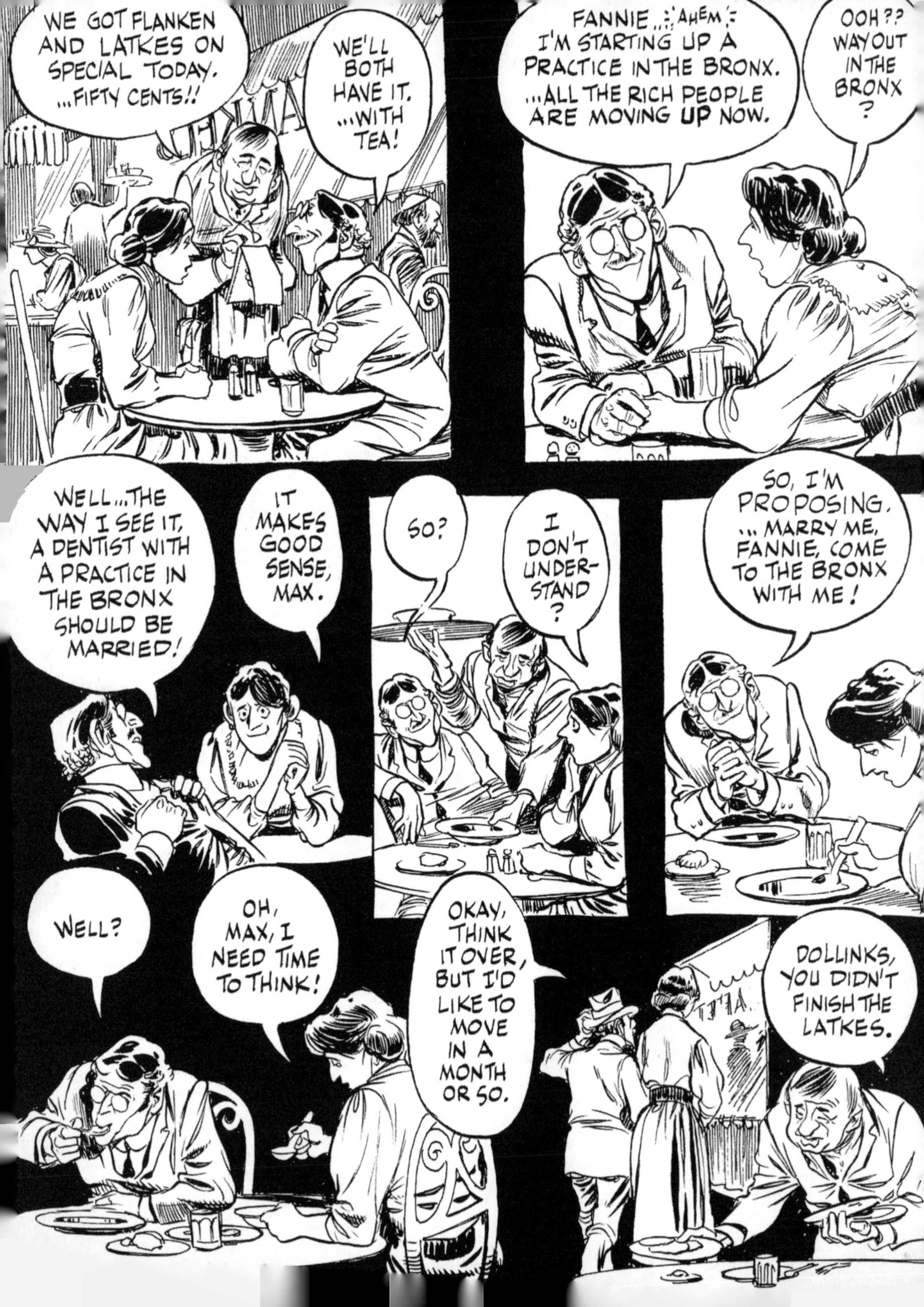
WE GOT FLANKEN AND LATKES ON SPECIAL TODAY. ...FIFTY CENTS!!
WE'LL BOTH HAVE IT. ...WITH TEA!
FANNIE... AHEM I'M STARTING UP A PRACTICE IN THE BRONX. ...ALL THE RICH PEOPLE ARE MOVING UP NOW.
OOH?? WAY OUT IN THE BRONX?
WELL...THE WAY I SEE IT, A DENTIST WITH A PRACTICE IN THE BRONX SHOULD BE MARRIED!
IT MAKES GOOD SENSE, MAX.
SO?
I DON'T UNDERSTAND?
SO, I'M PROPOSING. ... MARRY ME, FANNIE, COME TO THE BRONX WITH ME!
WELL?
OH, MAX, I NEED TIME TO THINK!
OKAY, THINK IT OVER, BUT I'D LIKE TO MOVE IN A MONTH OR SO.
DOLLINKS, YOU DIDN'T FINISH THE LATKES.

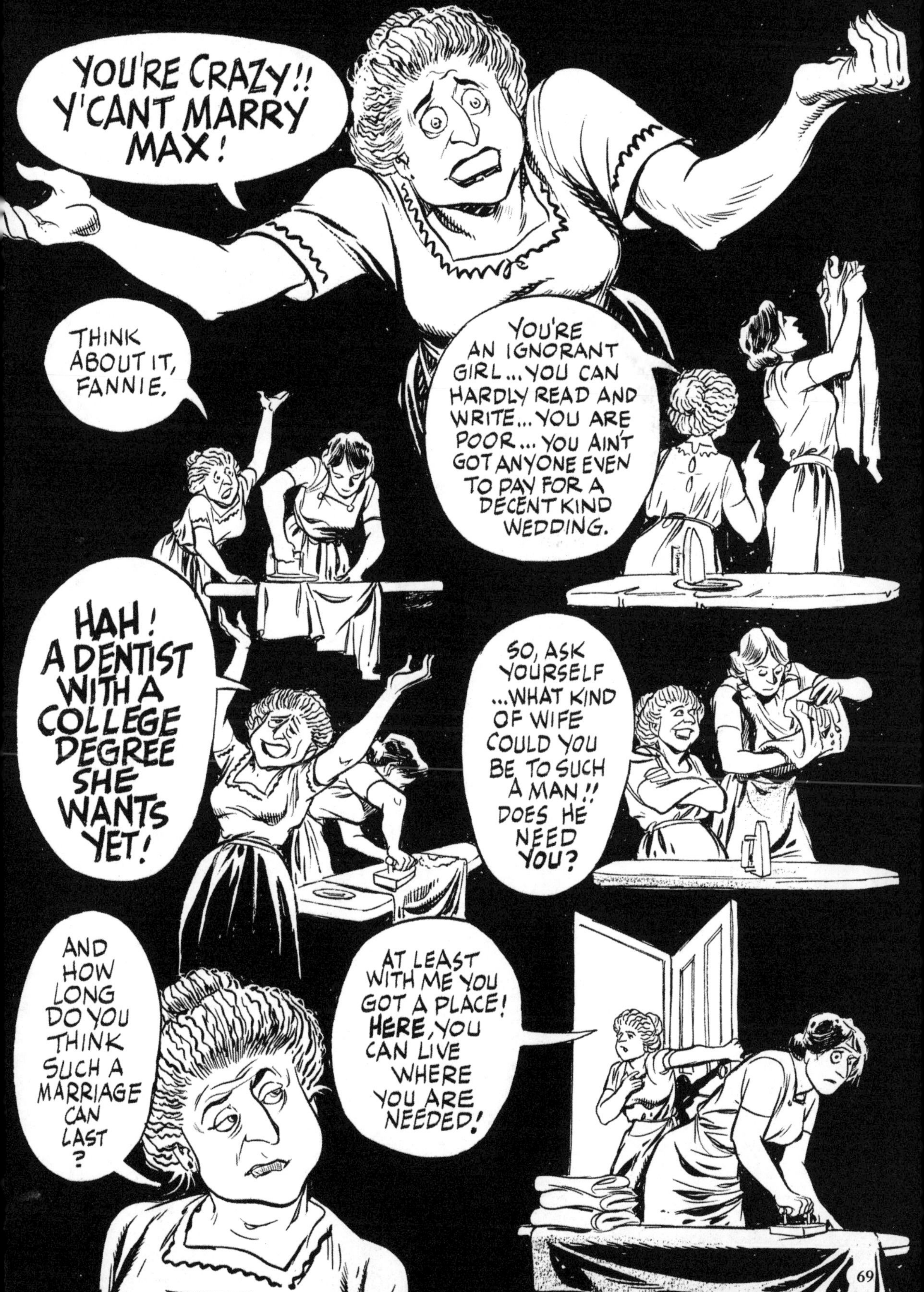
YOU'RE CRAZY!! Y'CAN'T MARRY MAX!
THINK ABOUT IT, FANNIE.
YOU'RE AN IGNORANT GIRL... YOU CAN HARDLY READ AND WRITE... YOU ARE POOR... YOU AIN'T GOT ANYONE EVEN TO PAY FOR A DECENT KIND WEDDING.
HAH! A DENTIST WITH A COLLEGE DEGREE SHE WANTS YET!
SO, ASK YOURSELF ...WHAT KIND OF WIFE COULD YOU BE TO SUCH A MAN!! DOES HE NEED YOU?
AND HOW LONG DO YOU THINK SUCH A MARRIAGE CAN LAST?
AT LEAST WITH ME YOU GOT A PLACE! HERE, YOU CAN LIVE WHERE YOU ARE NEEDED!

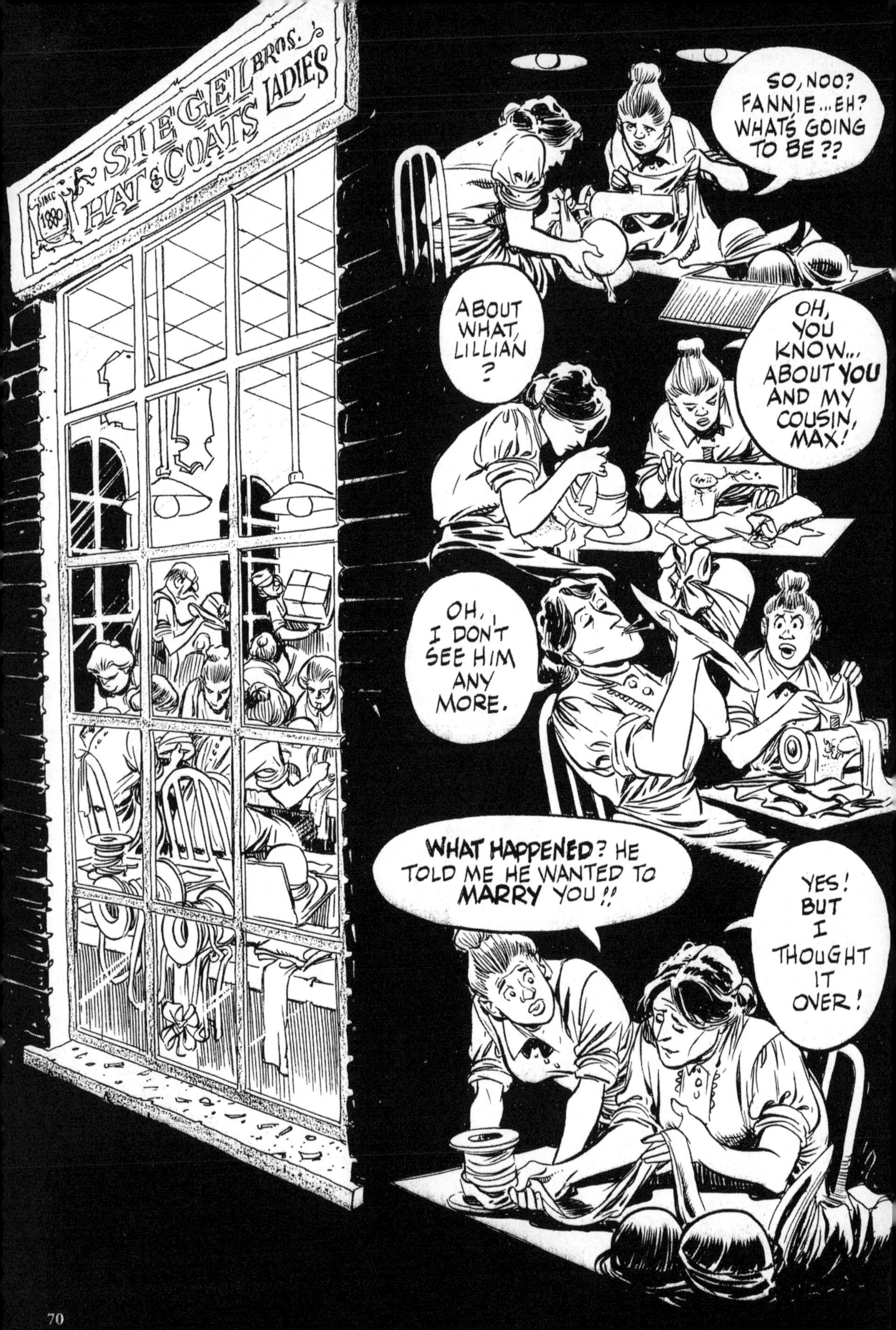
SINCE 1880
SIEGEL BROS. LADIES HAT & COATS
SO, NOO? FANNIE...EH? WHAT'S GOING TO BE ??
ABOUT WHAT, LILLIAN ?
OH, YOU KNOW... ABOUT YOU AND MY COUSIN, MAX!
OH, I DON'T SEE HIM ANY MORE.
WHAT HAPPENED? HE TOLD ME HE WANTED TO MARRY YOU !!
YES! BUT I THOUGHT IT OVER!

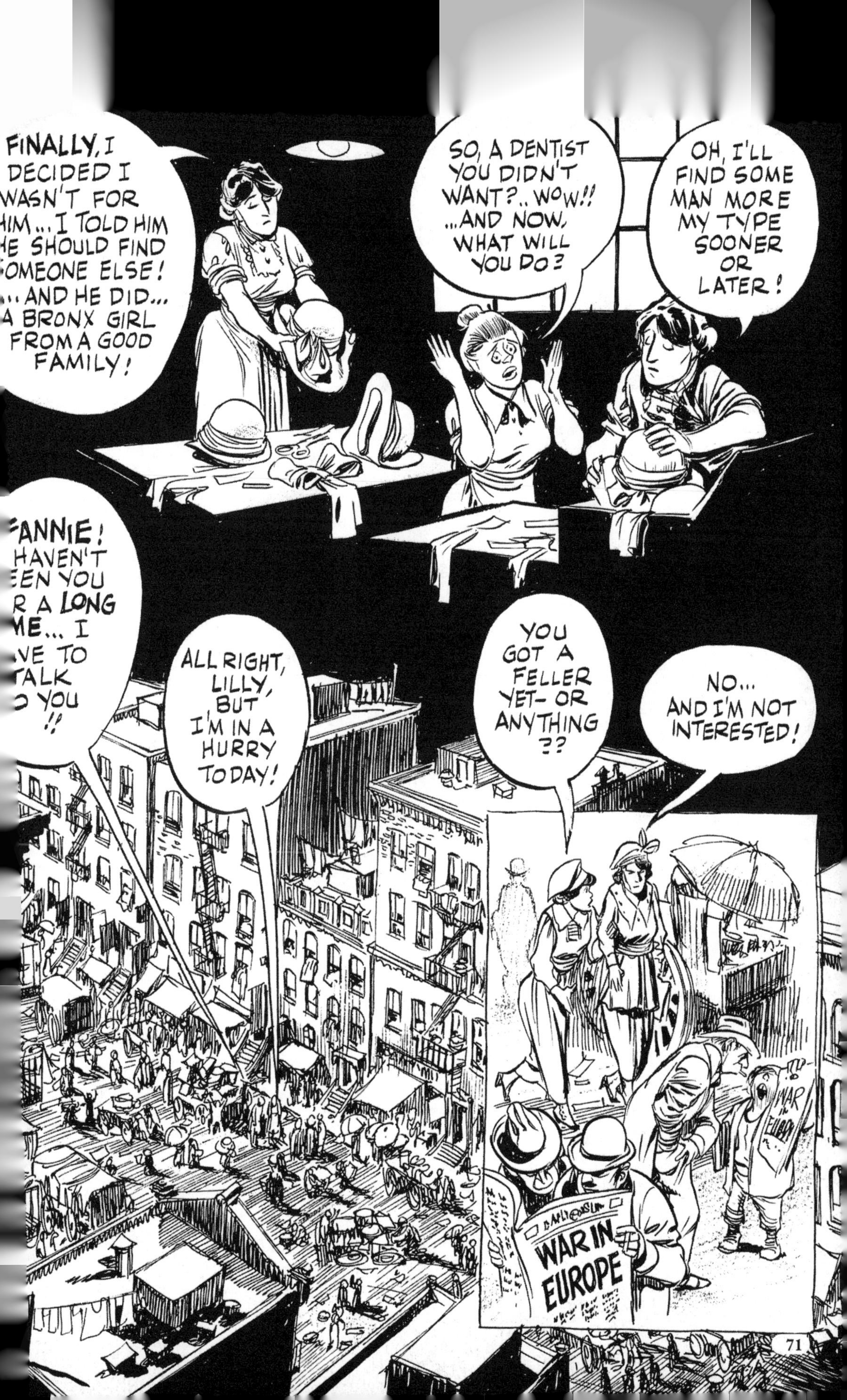
FINALLY, I DECIDED I WASN'T FOR HIM... I TOLD HIM HE SHOULD FIND SOMEONE ELSE! ...AND HE DID... A BRONX GIRL FROM A GOOD FAMILY!
SO, A DENTIST YOU DIDN'T WANT?.. WOW!! ...AND NOW, WHAT WILL YOU DO?
OH, I'LL FIND SOME MAN MORE MY TYPE SOONER OR LATER!
FANNIE! HAVEN'T EEN YOU R A LONG ME... I VE TO TALK O YOU !!
ALL RIGHT, LILLY, BUT I'M IN A HURRY TODAY!
YOU GOT A FELLER YET- OR ANYTHING ??
NO... AND I'M NOT INTERESTED!
WAR IN EUROPE

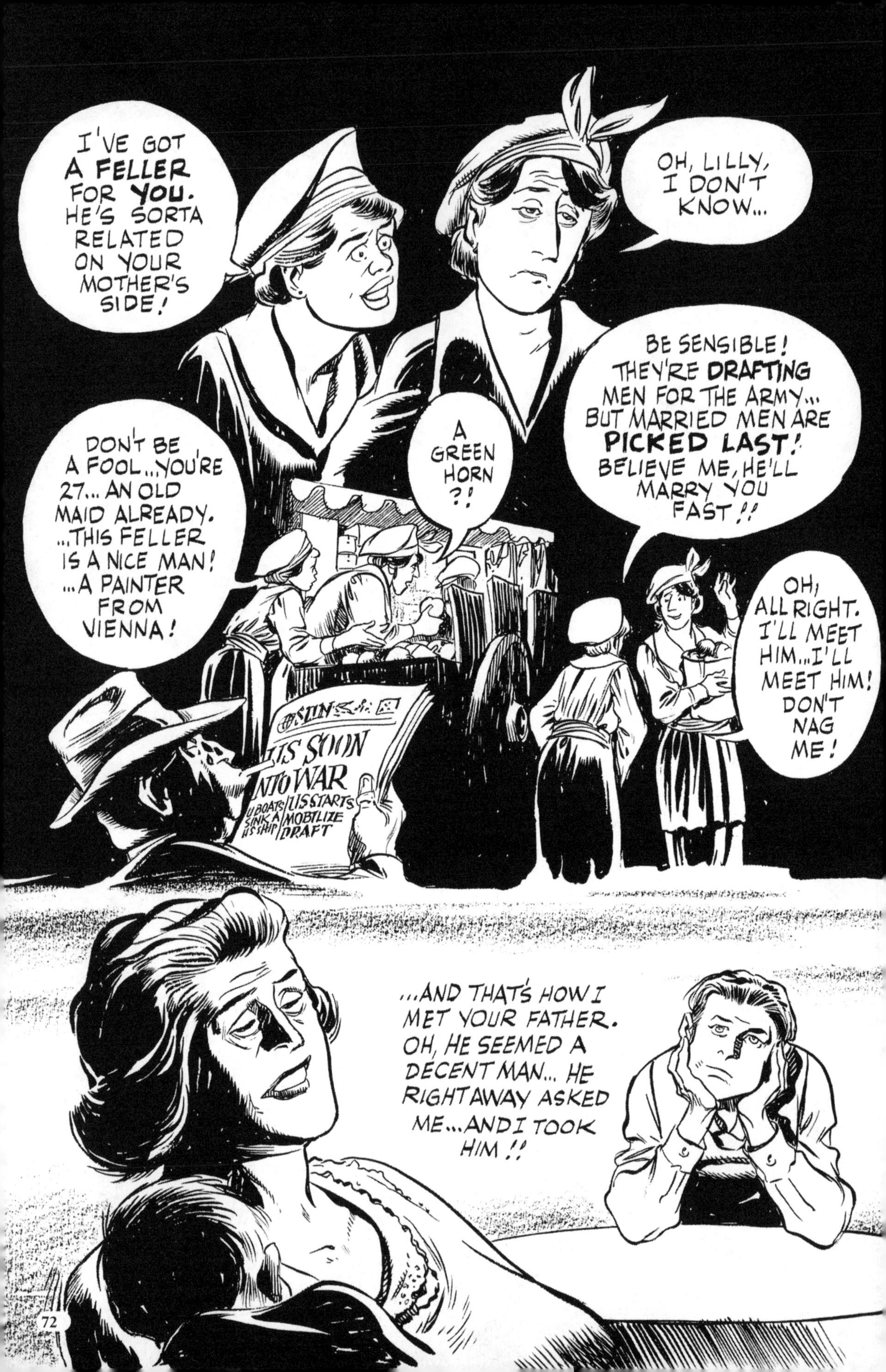
I'VE GOT A FELLER FOR YOU. HE'S SORTA RELATED ON YOUR MOTHER'S SIDE!
OH, LILLY, I DON'T KNOW...
BE SENSIBLE! THEY'RE DRAFTING MEN FOR THE ARMY... BUT MARRIED MEN ARE PICKED LAST! BELIEVE ME, HE'LL MARRY YOU FAST!!
A GREEN HORN ?!
DON'T BE A FOOL... YOU'RE 27... AN OLD MAID ALREADY. ...THIS FELLER IS A NICE MAN! ...A PAINTER FROM VIENNA!
OH, ALL RIGHT. I'LL MEET HIM... I'LL MEET HIM! DON'T NAG ME!
SUN
U.S. SOON INTO WAR
U BOATS SINK A US SHIP
US STARTS MOBILIZE DRAFT
...AND THAT'S HOW I MET YOUR FATHER. OH, HE SEEMED A DECENT MAN... HE RIGHTAWAY ASKED ME... AND I TOOK HIM!!

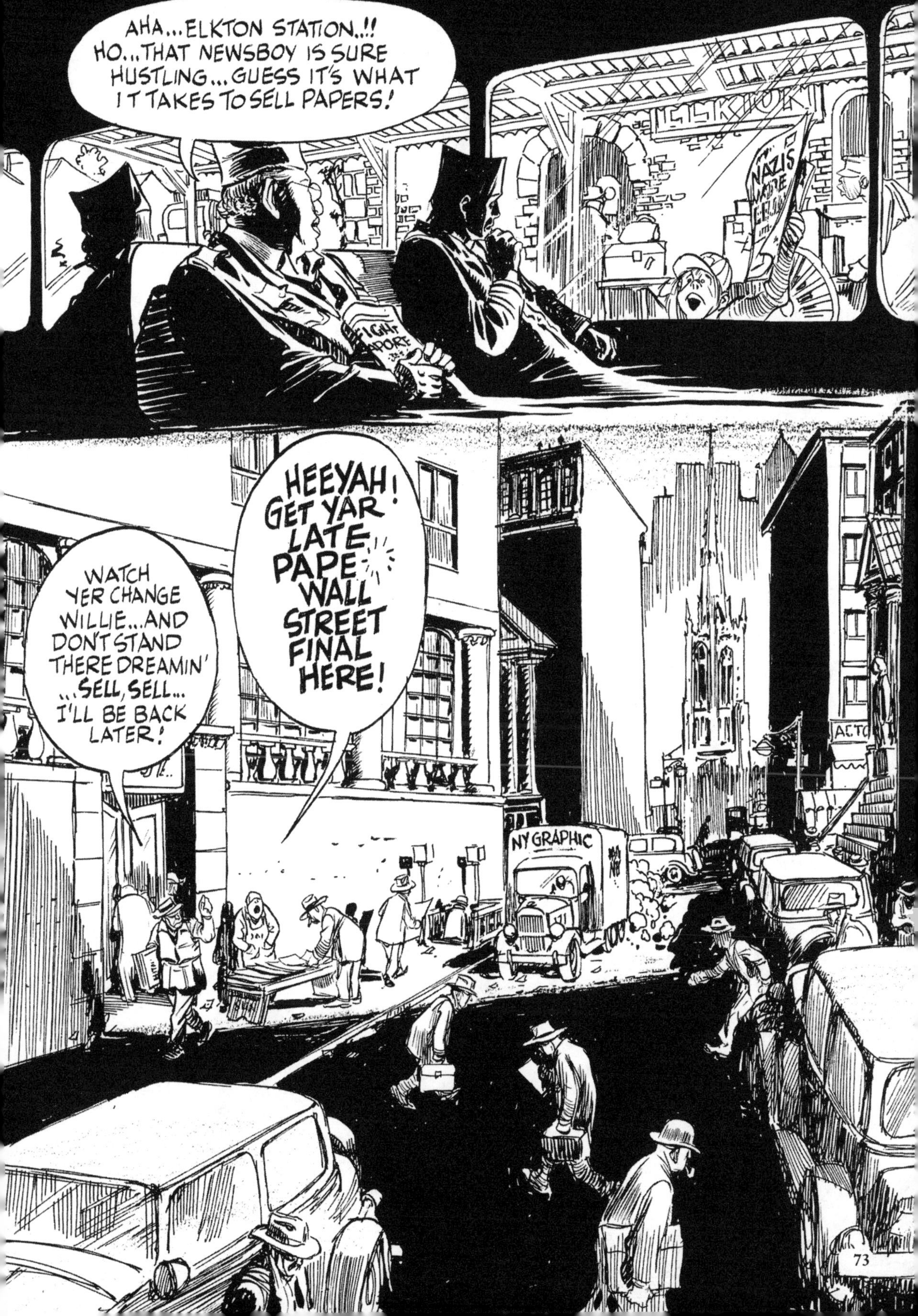
AHA...ELKTON STATION..!! HO...THAT NEWSBOY IS SURE HUSTLING...GUESS IT'S WHAT IT TAKES TO SELL PAPERS!
WATCH YER CHANGE WILLIE...AND DON'T STAND THERE DREAMIN' ...SELL, SELL... I'LL BE BACK LATER!
HEEYAH! GET YAR LATE PAPE WALL STREET FINAL HERE!
NY GRAPHIC

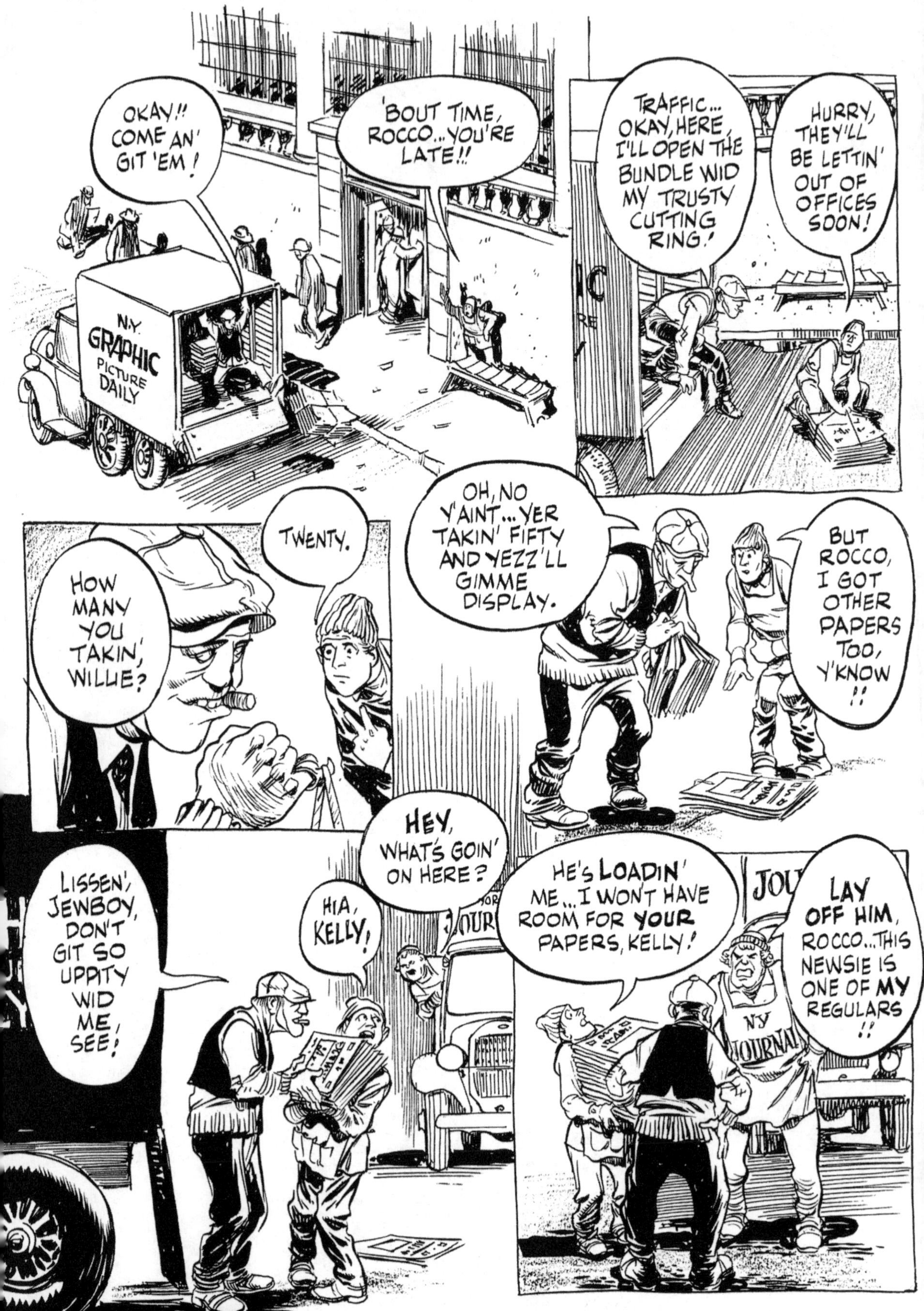
N.Y. GRAPHIC PICTURE DAILY
OKAY!! COME AN' GIT 'EM!
'BOUT TIME, ROCCO... YOU'RE LATE!!
TRAFFIC... OKAY, HERE, I'LL OPEN THE BUNDLE WID MY TRUSTY CUTTING RING!
HURRY, THEY'LL BE LETTIN' OUT OF OFFICES SOON!
HOW MANY YOU TAKIN', WILLIE?
TWENTY.
OH, NO Y'AINT... YER TAKIN' FIFTY AND YEZZ'LL GIMME DISPLAY.
BUT ROCCO, I GOT OTHER PAPERS TOO, Y'KNOW!!
LISSEN', JEWBOY, DON'T GIT SO UPPITY WID ME, SEE!
HIA, KELLY!
HEY, WHAT'S GOIN' ON HERE?
HE'S LOADIN' ME... I WON'T HAVE ROOM FOR YOUR PAPERS, KELLY!
LAY OFF HIM, ROCCO... THIS NEWSIE IS ONE OF MY REGULARS!!
NY JOURNAL

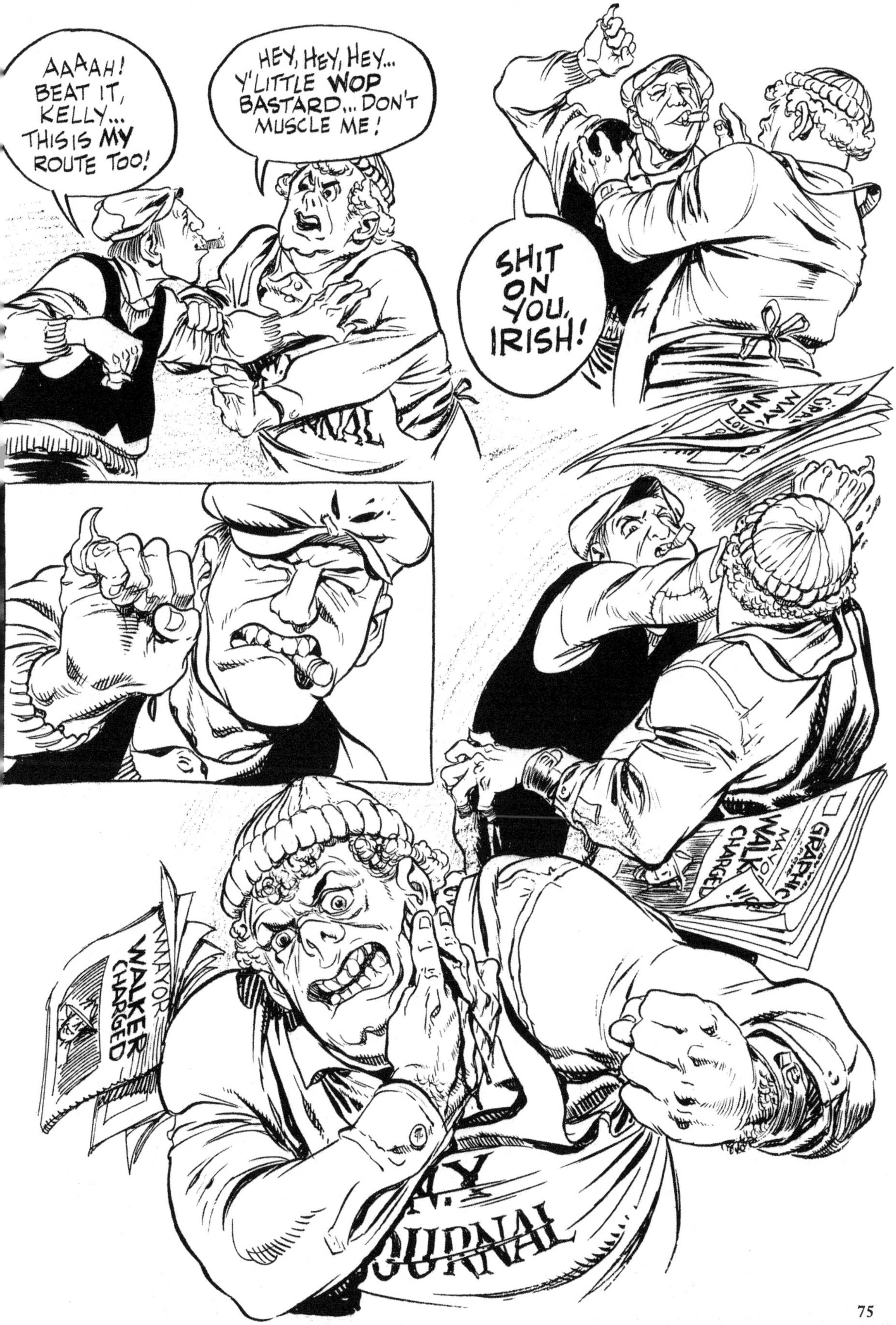
AAAAH! BEAT IT, KELLY... THIS IS MY ROUTE TOO!
HEY, HEY, HEY... Y'LITTLE WOP BASTARD... DON'T MUSCLE ME!
SHIT ON YOU, IRISH!
GRAPHIC
MAYOR WALKER CHARGED
MAYOR WALKER CHARGED
N.Y. JOURNAL

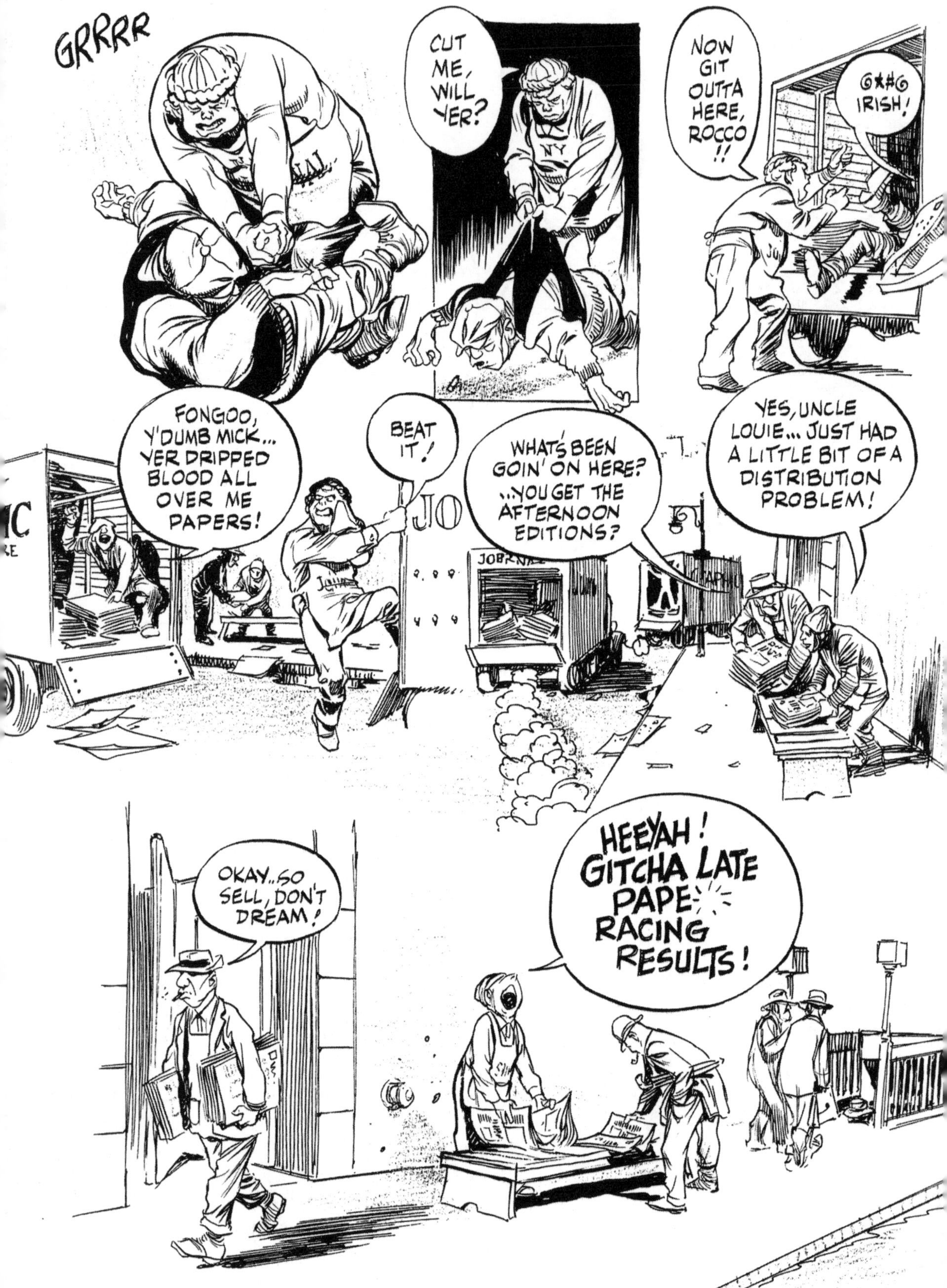
GRRRR
CUT ME, WILL YER?
NOW GIT OUTTA HERE, ROCCO !!
@*#@ IRISH!
FONGOO, Y'DUMB MICK... YER DRIPPED BLOOD ALL OVER ME PAPERS!
BEAT IT!
WHAT'S BEEN GOIN' ON HERE? ..YOU GET THE AFTERNOON EDITIONS?
YES, UNCLE LOUIE... JUST HAD A LITTLE BIT OF A DISTRIBUTION PROBLEM!
OKAY..SO SELL, DON'T DREAM!
HEEYAH! GITCHA LATE PAPE RACING RESULTS!

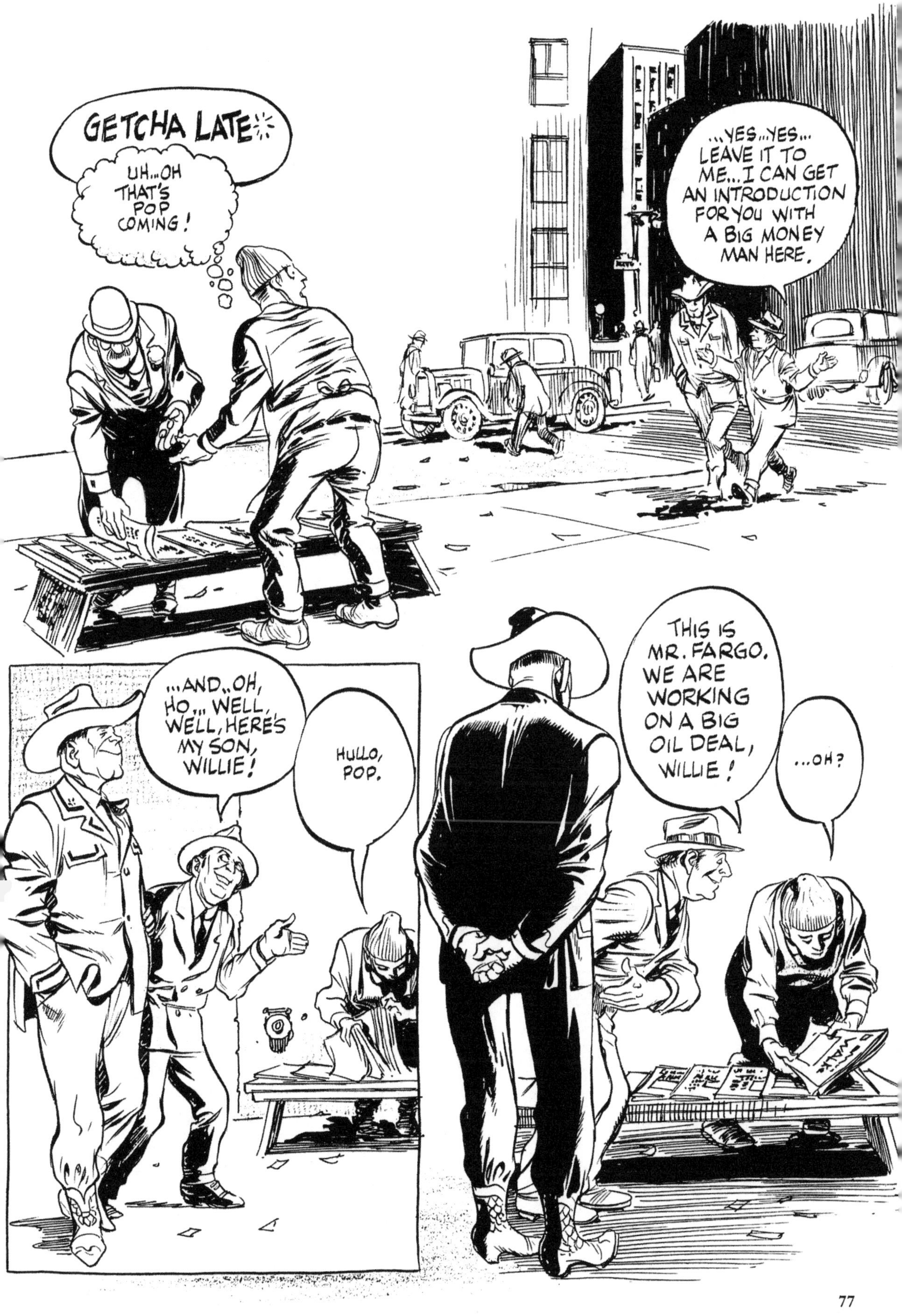
GETCHA LATE
UH...OH THAT'S POP COMING!
...YES...YES... LEAVE IT TO ME...I CAN GET AN INTRODUCTION FOR YOU WITH A BIG MONEY MAN HERE.
...AND..OH, HO... WELL, WELL, HERE'S MY SON, WILLIE!
HULLO, POP.
THIS IS MR. FARGO. WE ARE WORKING ON A BIG OIL DEAL, WILLIE!
...OH?

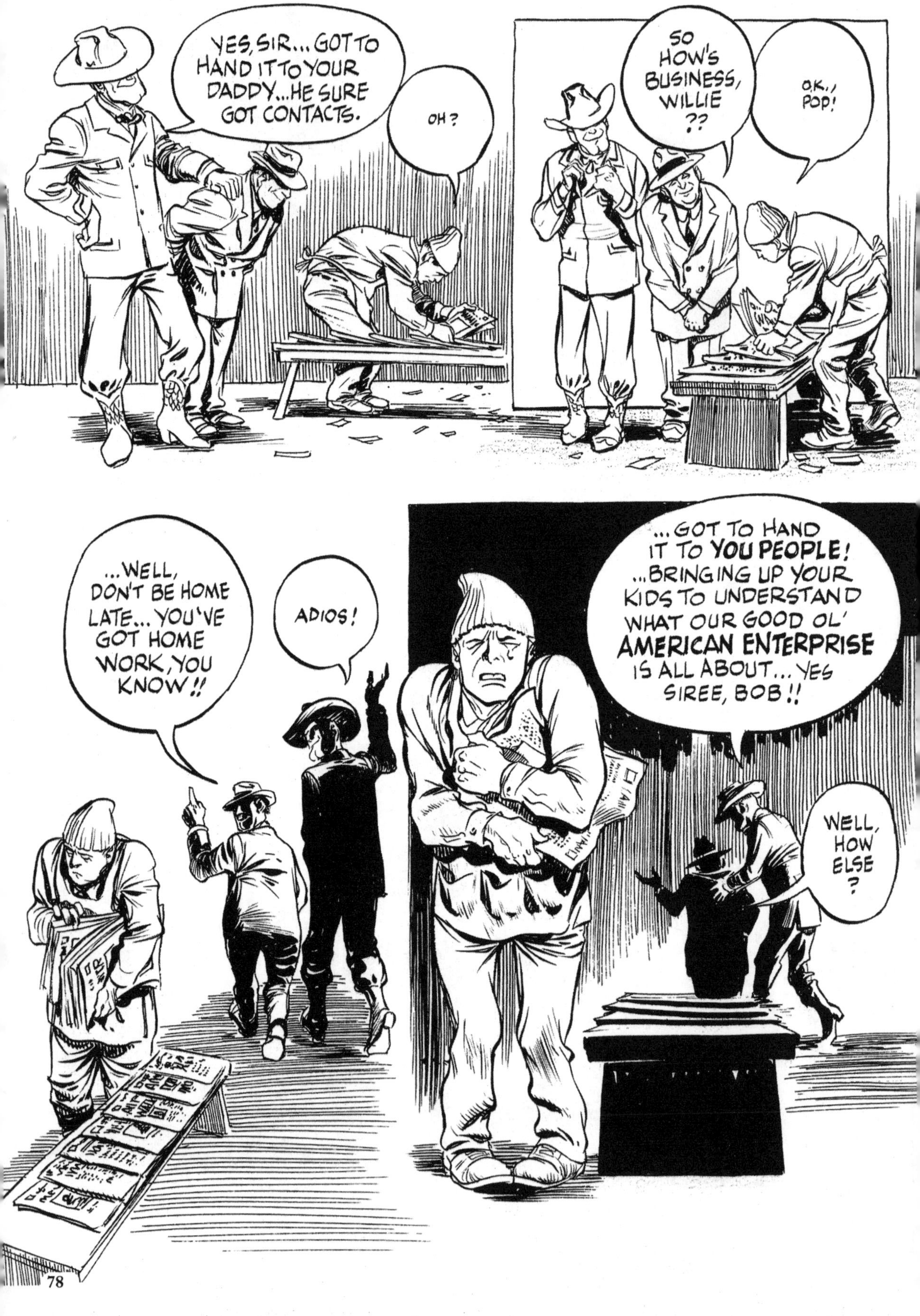
YES, SIR... GOT TO HAND IT TO YOUR DADDY...HE SURE GOT CONTACTS.
OH?
SO HOW'S BUSINESS, WILLIE ??
O.K., POP!
...WELL, DON'T BE HOME LATE... YOU'VE GOT HOME WORK, YOU KNOW!!
ADIOS!
...GOT TO HAND IT TO YOU PEOPLE! ...BRINGING UP YOUR KIDS TO UNDERSTAND WHAT OUR GOOD OL' AMERICAN ENTERPRISE IS ALL ABOUT... YES SIREE, BOB!!
WELL, HOW ELSE ?

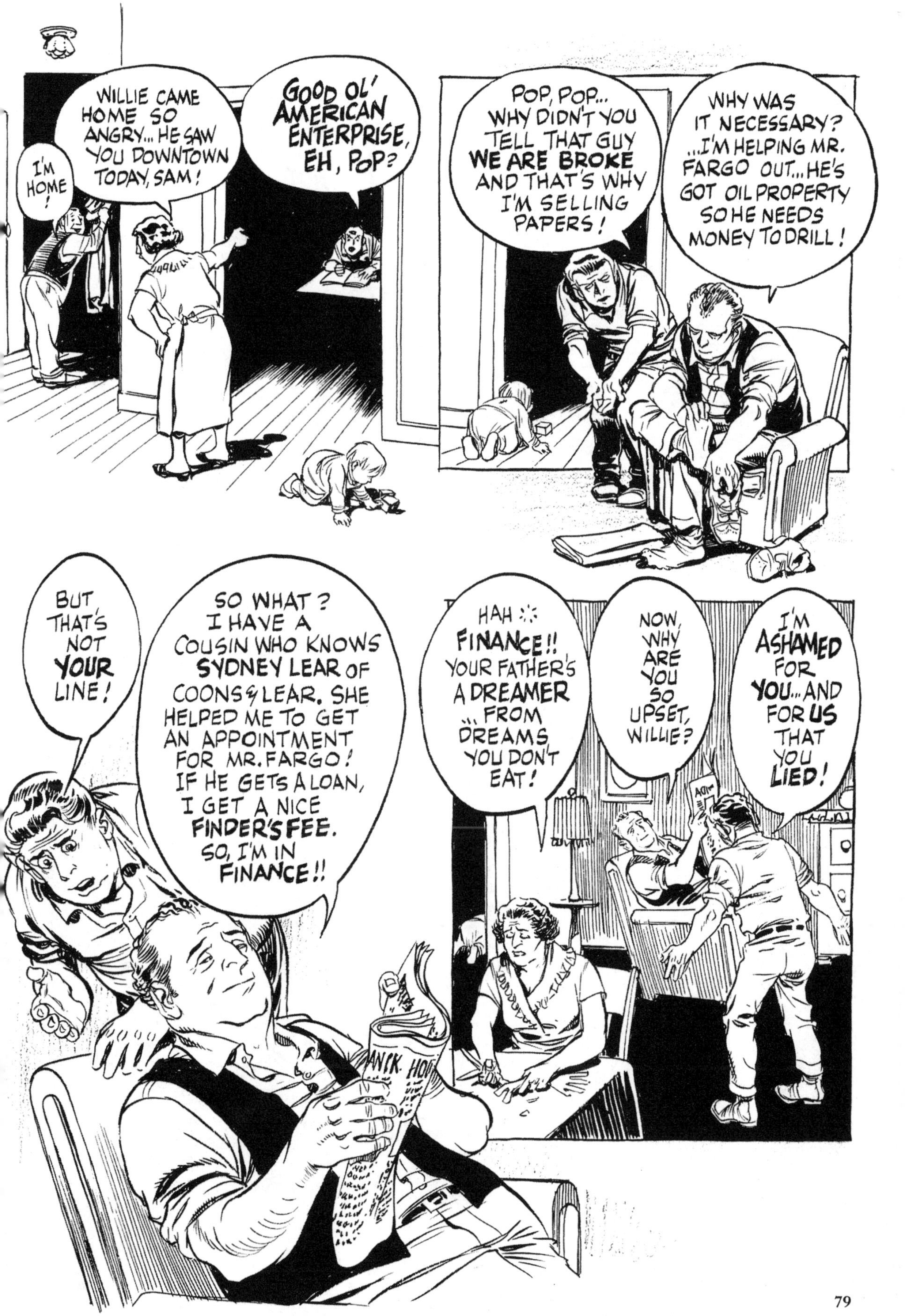
I'M HOME!
WILLIE CAME HOME SO ANGRY... HE SAW YOU DOWNTOWN TODAY, SAM!
GOOD OL' AMERICAN ENTERPRISE, EH, POP?
POP, POP... WHY DIDN'T YOU TELL THAT GUY **WE ARE BROKE** AND THAT'S WHY I'M SELLING PAPERS!
WHY WAS IT NECESSARY? ...I'M HELPING MR. FARGO OUT... HE'S GOT OIL PROPERTY SO HE NEEDS MONEY TO DRILL!
BUT THAT'S NOT **YOUR** LINE!
SO WHAT? I HAVE A COUSIN WHO KNOWS **SYDNEY LEAR** OF COONS & LEAR. SHE HELPED ME TO GET AN APPOINTMENT FOR MR. FARGO! IF HE GETS A LOAN, I GET A NICE **FINDER'S FEE.** SO, I'M IN **FINANCE**!!
HAH :: **FINANCE**!! YOUR FATHER'S A **DREAMER** ... FROM DREAMS YOU DON'T EAT!
NOW, WHY ARE YOU SO UPSET, WILLIE?
I'M **ASHAMED** FOR **YOU**... AND FOR **US** THAT YOU **LIED**!

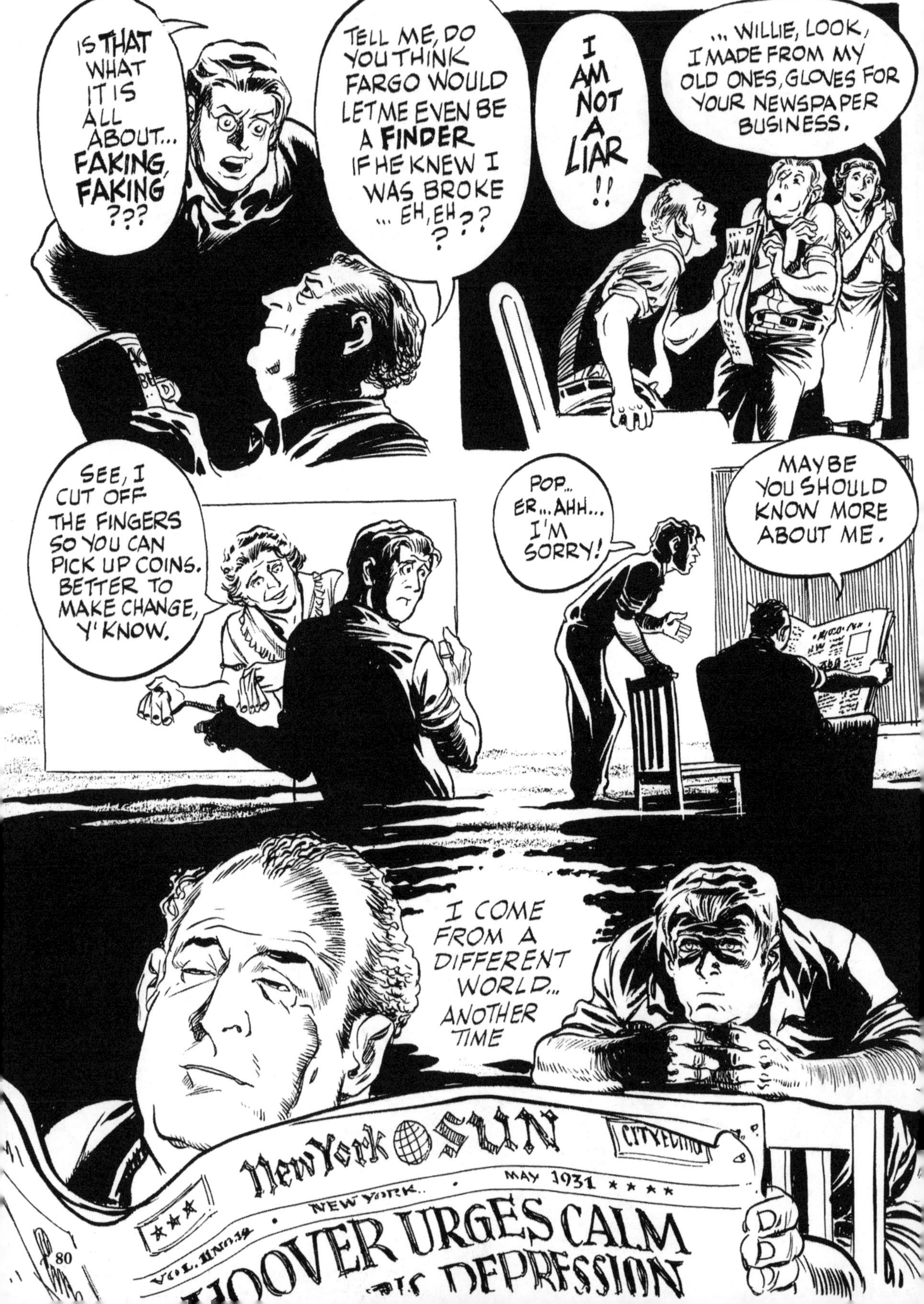
IS THAT WHAT IT IS ALL ABOUT... FAKING, FAKING ???
TELL ME, DO YOU THINK FARGO WOULD LET ME EVEN BE A FINDER IF HE KNEW I WAS BROKE ... EH, EH ???
I AM NOT A LIAR !!
... WILLIE, LOOK, I MADE FROM MY OLD ONES, GLOVES FOR YOUR NEWSPAPER BUSINESS.
SEE, I CUT OFF THE FINGERS SO YOU CAN PICK UP COINS. BETTER TO MAKE CHANGE, Y'KNOW.
POP... ER... AHH... I'M SORRY!
MAYBE YOU SHOULD KNOW MORE ABOUT ME.
I COME FROM A DIFFERENT WORLD... ANOTHER TIME
New York SUN
MAY 1931
NEW YORK
VOL. II NO.14
HOOVER URGES CALM
DEPRESSION

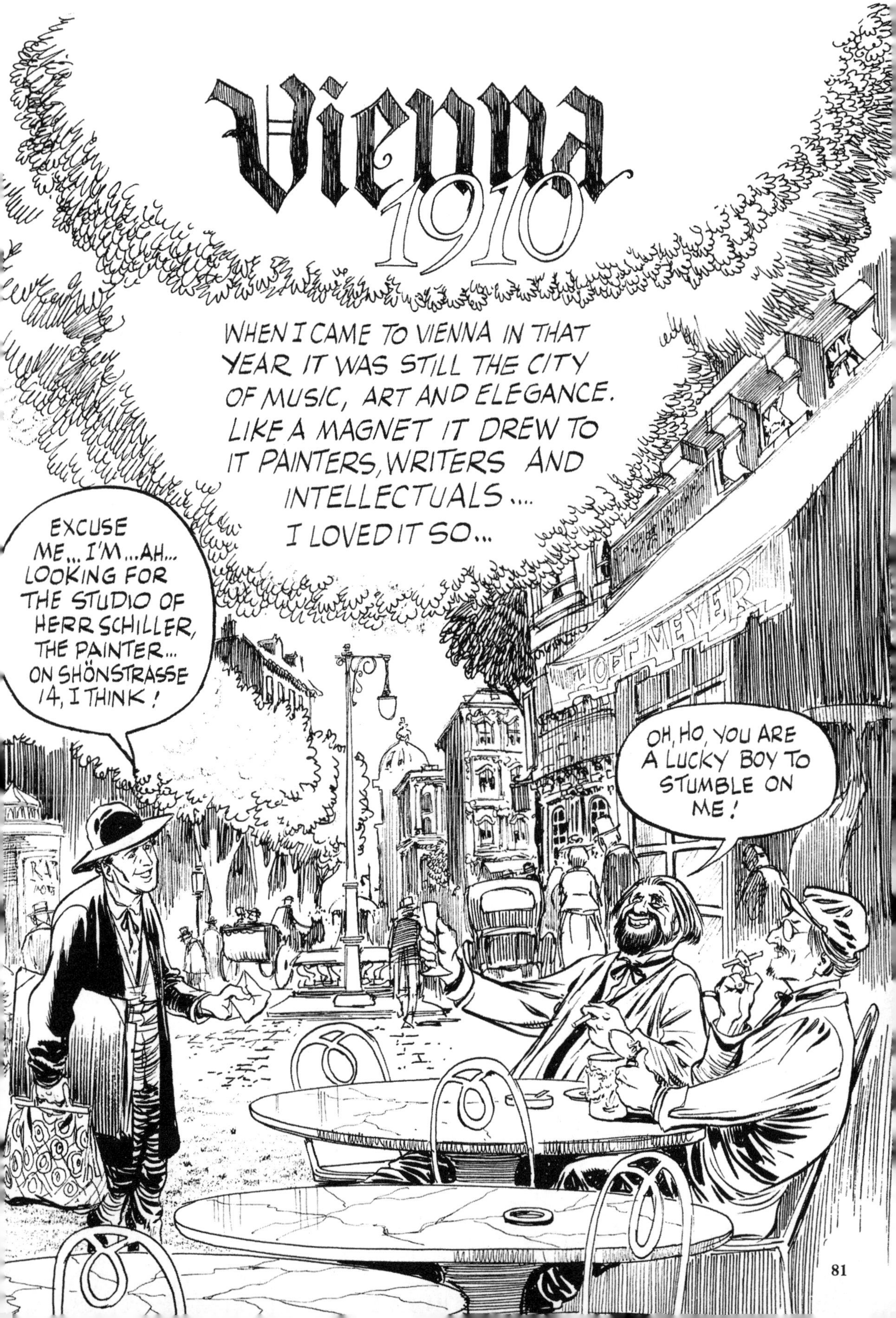

VIENNA 1910
WHEN I CAME TO VIENNA IN THAT YEAR IT WAS STILL THE CITY OF MUSIC, ART AND ELEGANCE. LIKE A MAGNET IT DREW TO IT PAINTERS, WRITERS AND INTELLECTUALS.... I LOVED IT SO...
EXCUSE ME... I'M...AH... LOOKING FOR THE STUDIO OF HERR SCHILLER, THE PAINTER... ON SHÖNSTRASSE 14, I THINK!
OH, HO, YOU ARE A LUCKY BOY TO STUMBLE ON ME!
HOFFMEYER

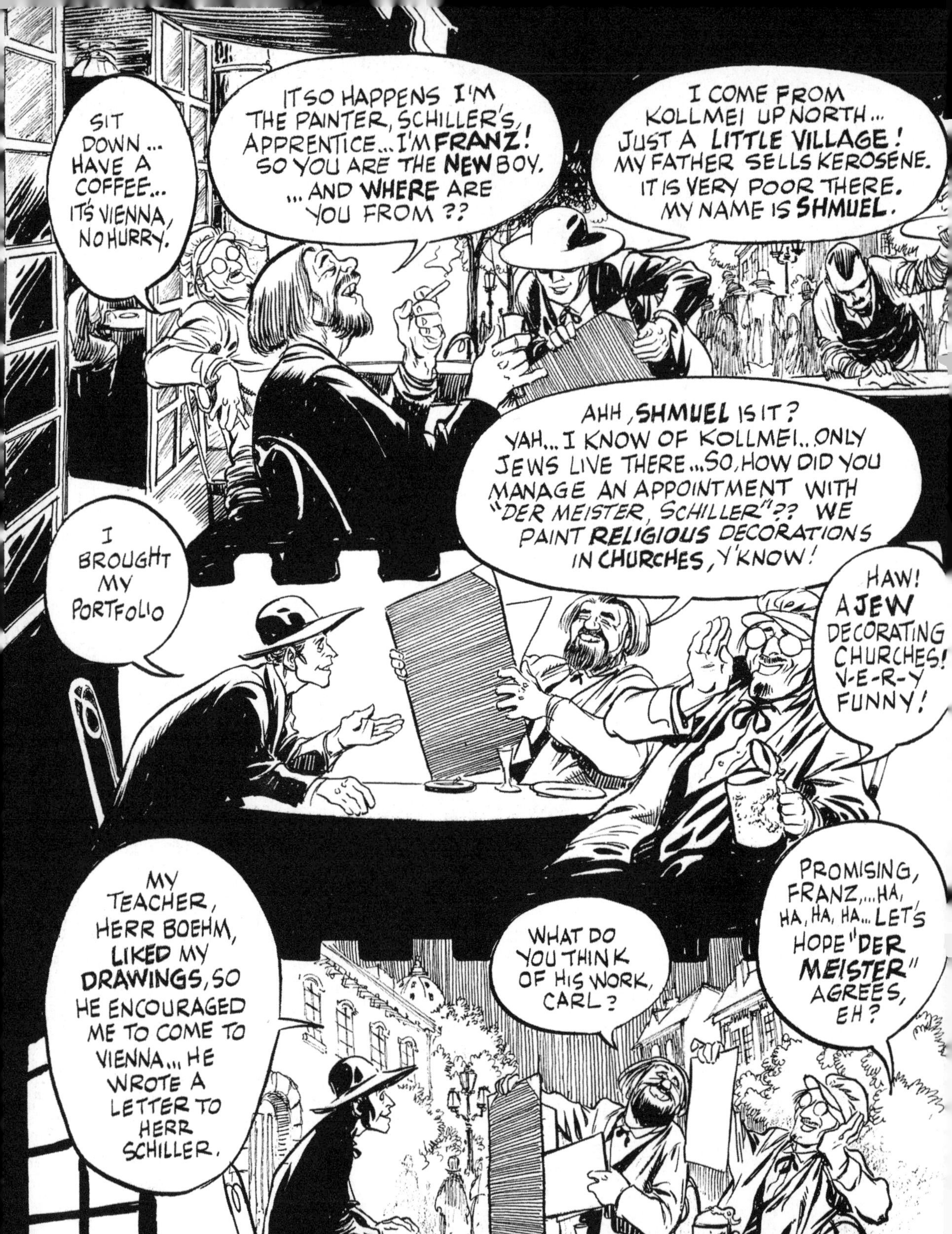
SIT DOWN... HAVE A COFFEE... IT'S VIENNA, NO HURRY.
IT SO HAPPENS I'M THE PAINTER, SCHILLER'S, APPRENTICE... I'M FRANZ! SO YOU ARE THE NEW BOY. ... AND WHERE ARE YOU FROM ??
I COME FROM KOLLMEI UP NORTH... JUST A LITTLE VILLAGE! MY FATHER SELLS KEROSENE. IT IS VERY POOR THERE. MY NAME IS SHMUEL.
AHH, SHMUEL IS IT? YAH... I KNOW OF KOLLMEI.. ONLY JEWS LIVE THERE... SO, HOW DID YOU MANAGE AN APPOINTMENT WITH "DER MEISTER, SCHILLER"?? WE PAINT RELIGIOUS DECORATIONS IN CHURCHES, Y'KNOW!
I BROUGHT MY PORTFOLIO
HAW! A JEW DECORATING CHURCHES! V-E-R-Y FUNNY!
MY TEACHER, HERR BOEHM, LIKED MY DRAWINGS, SO HE ENCOURAGED ME TO COME TO VIENNA... HE WROTE A LETTER TO HERR SCHILLER.
WHAT DO YOU THINK OF HIS WORK, CARL?
PROMISING, FRANZ,... HA, HA, HA, HA... LET'S HOPE "DER MEISTER" AGREES, EH?

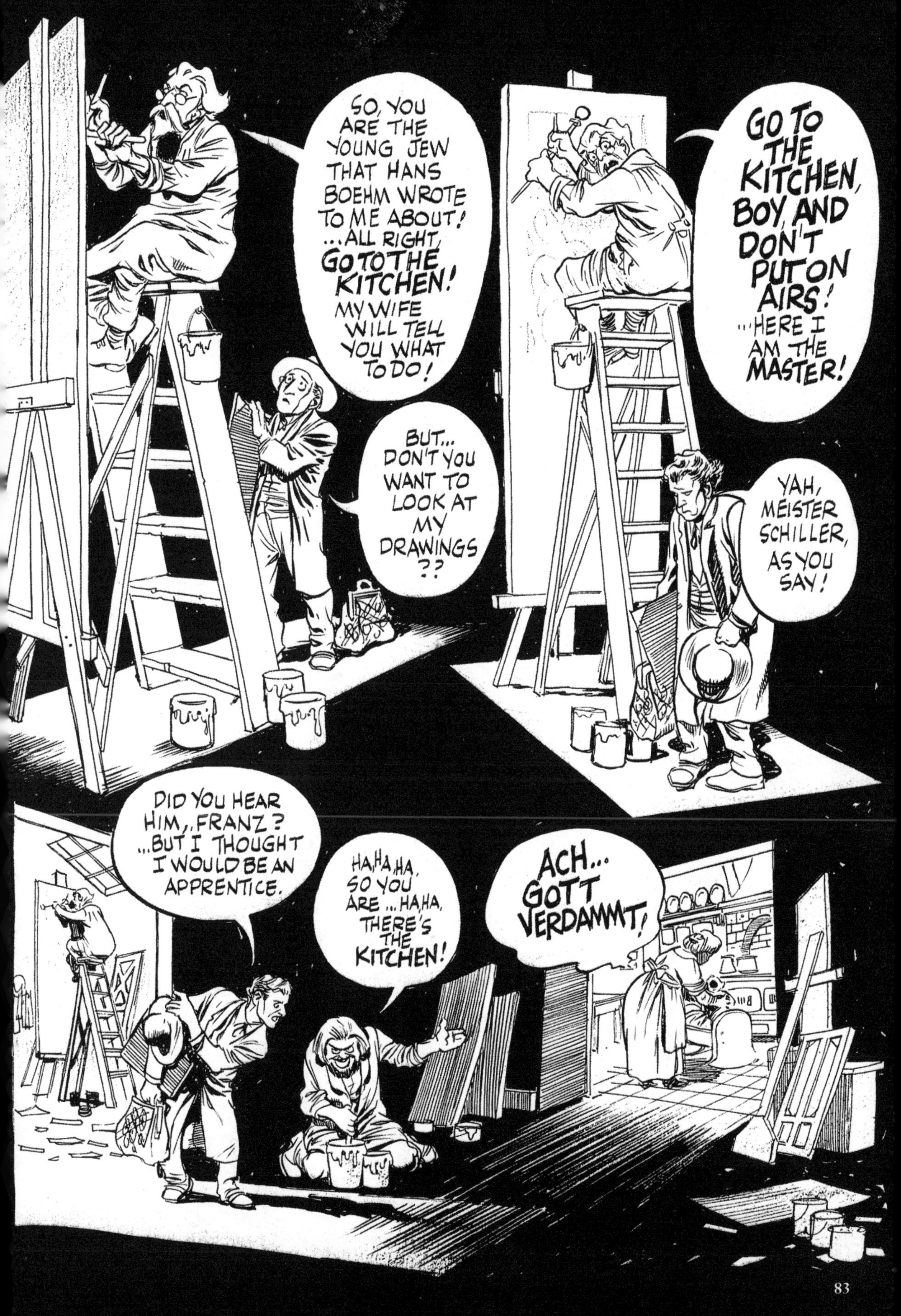
SO, YOU ARE THE YOUNG JEW THAT HANS BOEHM WROTE TO ME ABOUT! ...ALL RIGHT, GO TO THE KITCHEN! MY WIFE WILL TELL YOU WHAT TO DO!
BUT... DON'T YOU WANT TO LOOK AT MY DRAWINGS??
GO TO THE KITCHEN, BOY, AND DON'T PUT ON AIRS! ...HERE I AM THE MASTER!
YAH, MEISTER SCHILLER, AS YOU SAY!
DID YOU HEAR HIM, FRANZ? ...BUT I THOUGHT I WOULD BE AN APPRENTICE.
HA,HA,HA, SO YOU ARE ...HA,HA, THERE'S THE KITCHEN!
ACH... GOTT VERDAMMT!

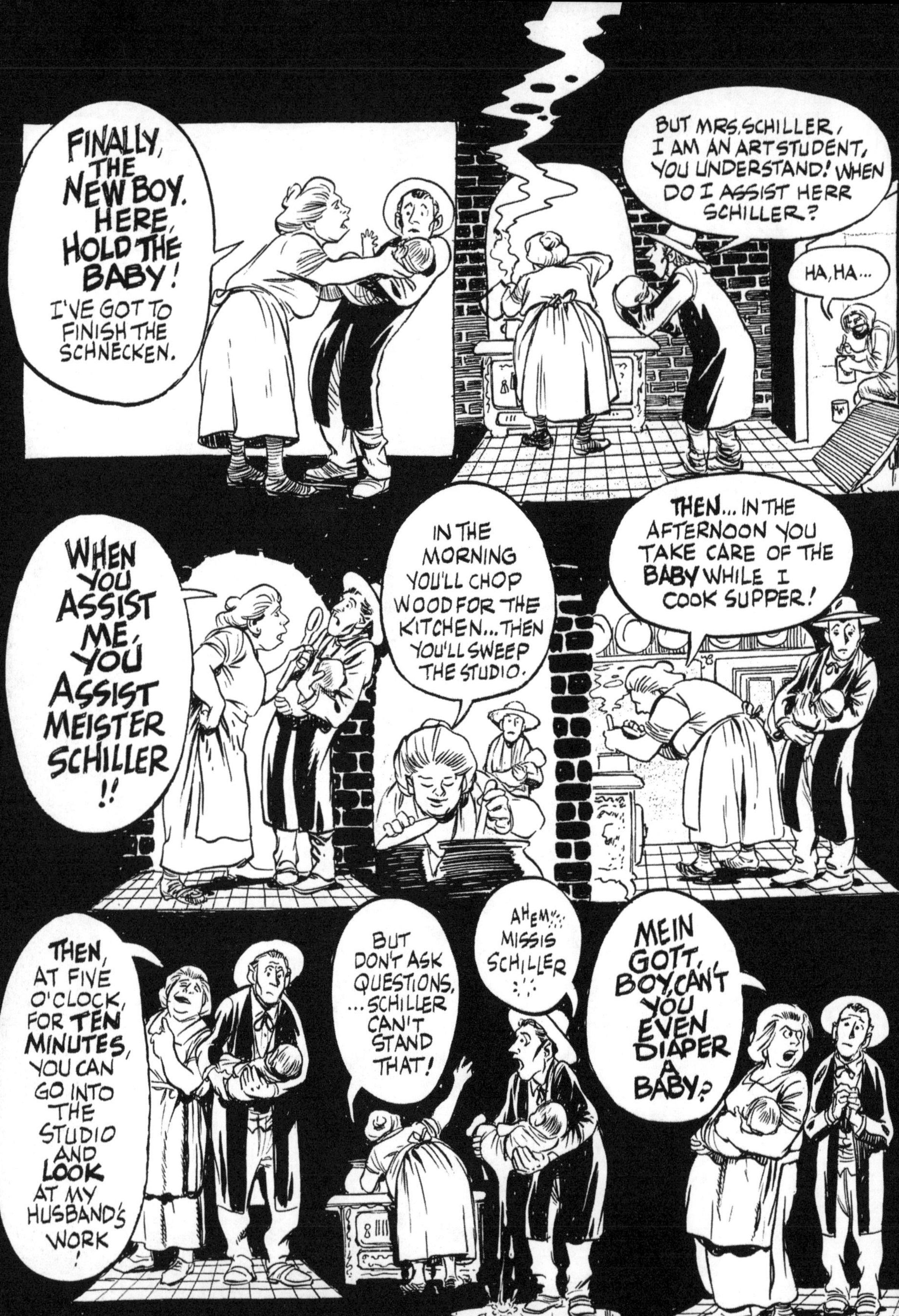
FINALLY, THE NEW BOY. HERE, HOLD THE BABY! I'VE GOT TO FINISH THE SCHNECKEN.
BUT MRS. SCHILLER, I AM AN ART STUDENT, YOU UNDERSTAND! WHEN DO I ASSIST HERR SCHILLER?
HA, HA...
WHEN YOU ASSIST ME, YOU ASSIST MEISTER SCHILLER!!
IN THE MORNING YOU'LL CHOP WOOD FOR THE KITCHEN... THEN YOU'LL SWEEP THE STUDIO.
THEN... IN THE AFTERNOON YOU TAKE CARE OF THE BABY WHILE I COOK SUPPER!
THEN, AT FIVE O'CLOCK, FOR TEN MINUTES, YOU CAN GO INTO THE STUDIO AND LOOK AT MY HUSBAND'S WORK!
BUT DON'T ASK QUESTIONS. ...SCHILLER CAN'T STAND THAT!
AHEM... MISSIS SCHILLER
MEIN GOTT, BOY, CAN'T YOU EVEN DIAPER A BABY?

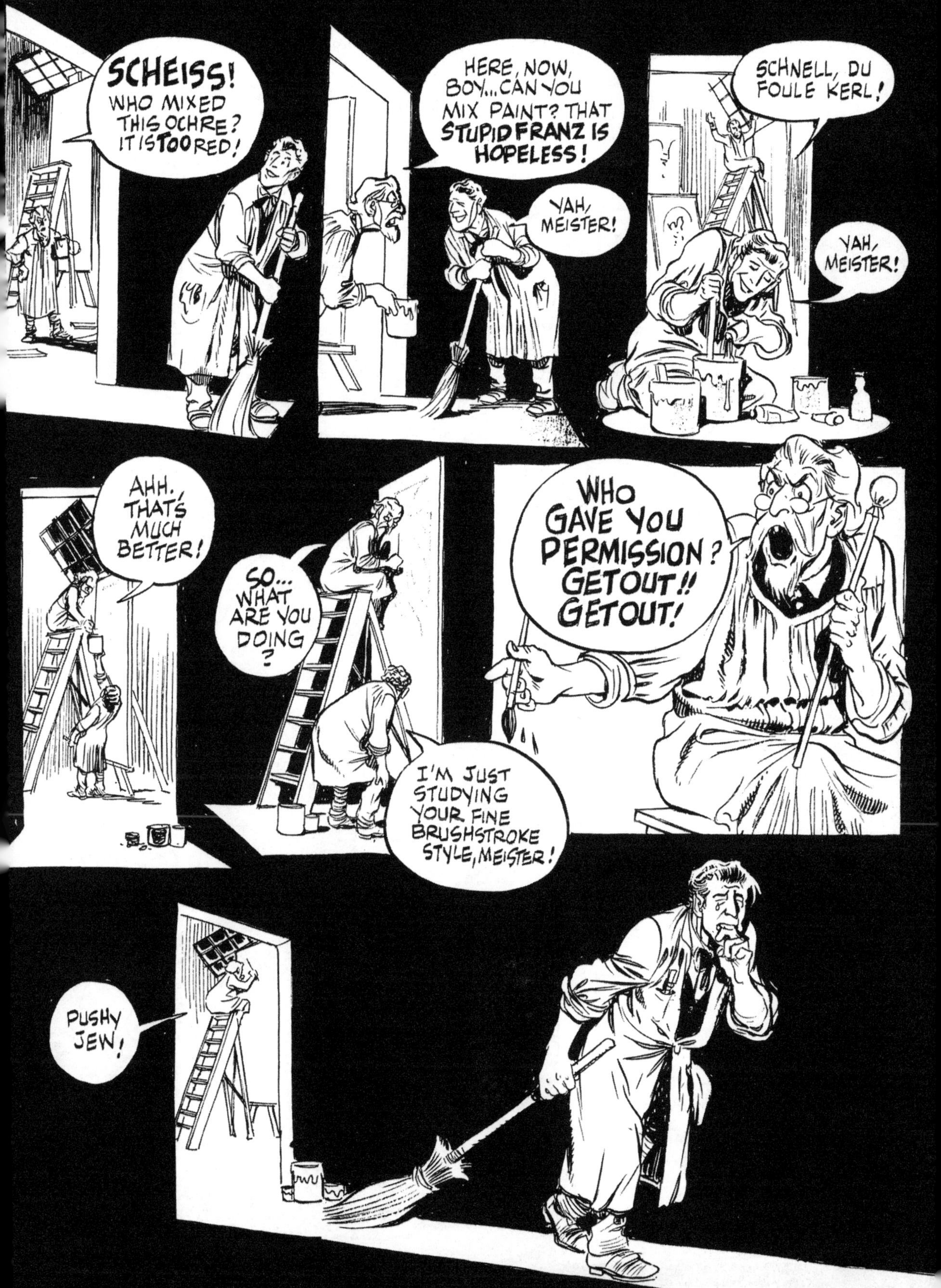
SCHEISS! WHO MIXED THIS OCHRE? IT IS TOO RED!
HERE, NOW, BOY... CAN YOU MIX PAINT? THAT STUPID FRANZ IS HOPELESS!
YAH, MEISTER!
SCHNELL, DU FOULE KERL!
YAH, MEISTER!
AHH, THAT'S MUCH BETTER!
SO... WHAT ARE YOU DOING?
I'M JUST STUDYING YOUR FINE BRUSHSTROKE STYLE, MEISTER!
WHO GAVE YOU PERMISSION? GETOUT!! GETOUT!
PUSHY JEW!

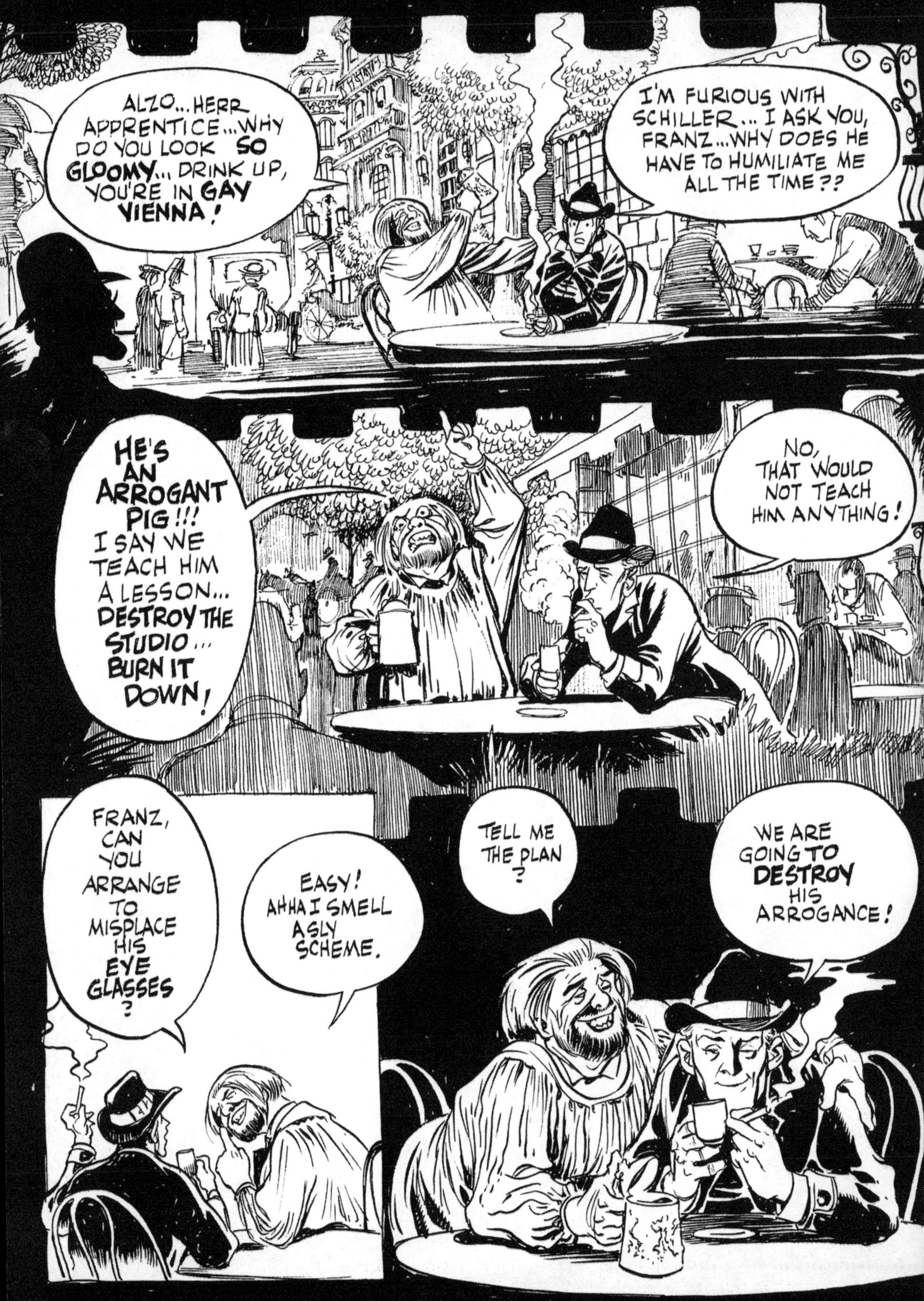

ALZO... HERR APPRENTICE... WHY DO YOU LOOK **SO GLOOMY**... DRINK UP, YOU'RE IN **GAY VIENNA**!
I'M FURIOUS WITH SCHILLER... I ASK YOU, FRANZ... WHY DOES HE HAVE TO HUMILIATE ME ALL THE TIME??
HE'S AN ARROGANT PIG!!! I SAY WE TEACH HIM A LESSON... **DESTROY** THE **STUDIO... BURN IT DOWN!**
NO, THAT WOULD NOT TEACH HIM ANYTHING!
FRANZ, CAN YOU ARRANGE TO MISPLACE HIS **EYE GLASSES**?
EASY! AHHA I SMELL A SLY SCHEME.
TELL ME THE PLAN?
WE ARE GOING TO **DESTROY** HIS ARROGANCE!

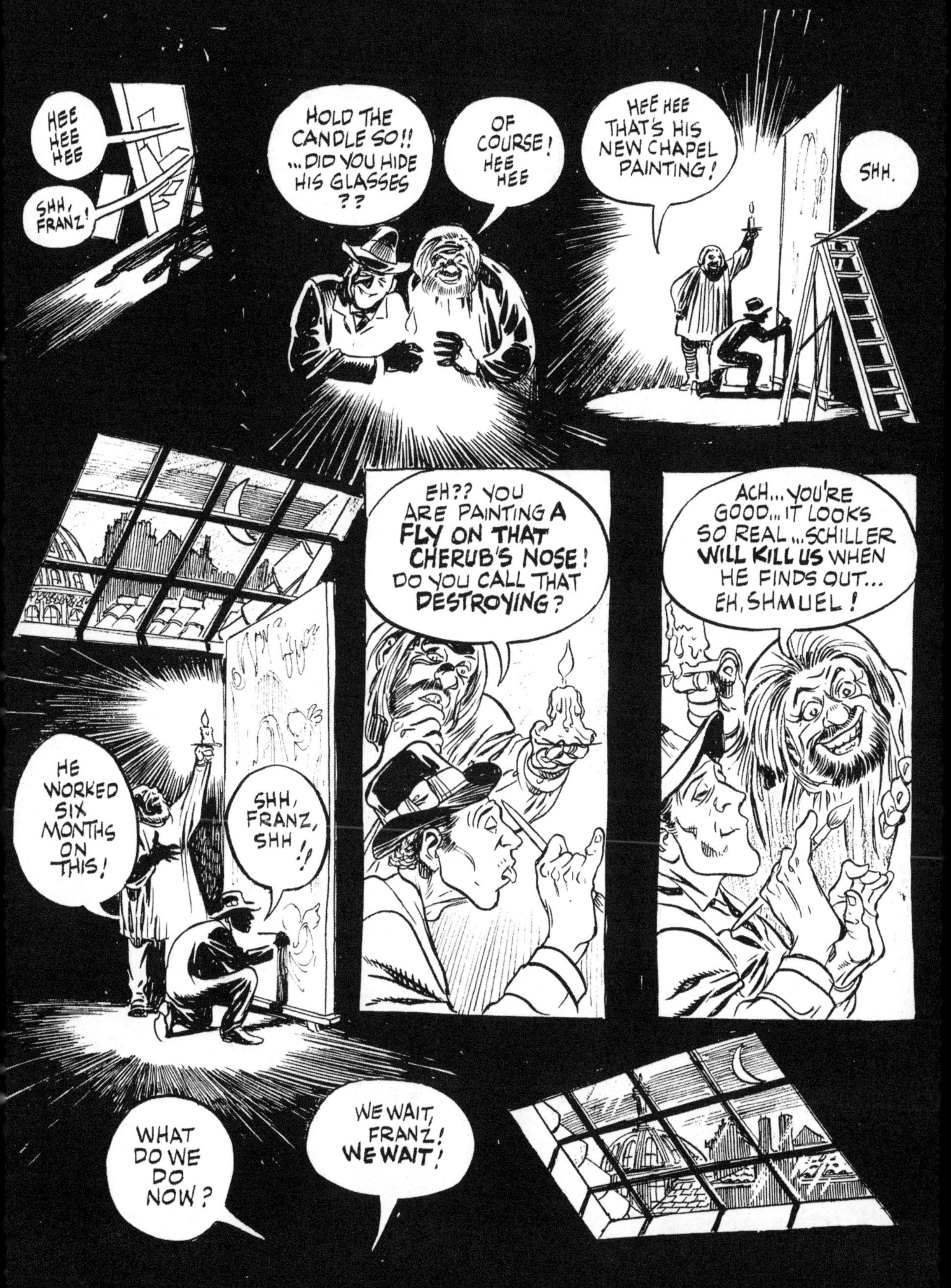
HEE HEE HEE
SHH, FRANZ!
HOLD THE CANDLE SO!! ...DID YOU HIDE HIS GLASSES ??
OF COURSE! HEE HEE
HEE HEE THAT'S HIS NEW CHAPEL PAINTING!
SHH.
HE WORKED SIX MONTHS ON THIS!
SHH, FRANZ, SHH !!
EH?? YOU ARE PAINTING A FLY ON THAT CHERUB'S NOSE! DO YOU CALL THAT DESTROYING?
ACH... YOU'RE GOOD... IT LOOKS SO REAL... SCHILLER WILL KILL US WHEN HE FINDS OUT... EH, SHMUEL!
WHAT DO WE DO NOW?
WE WAIT, FRANZ! WE WAIT!

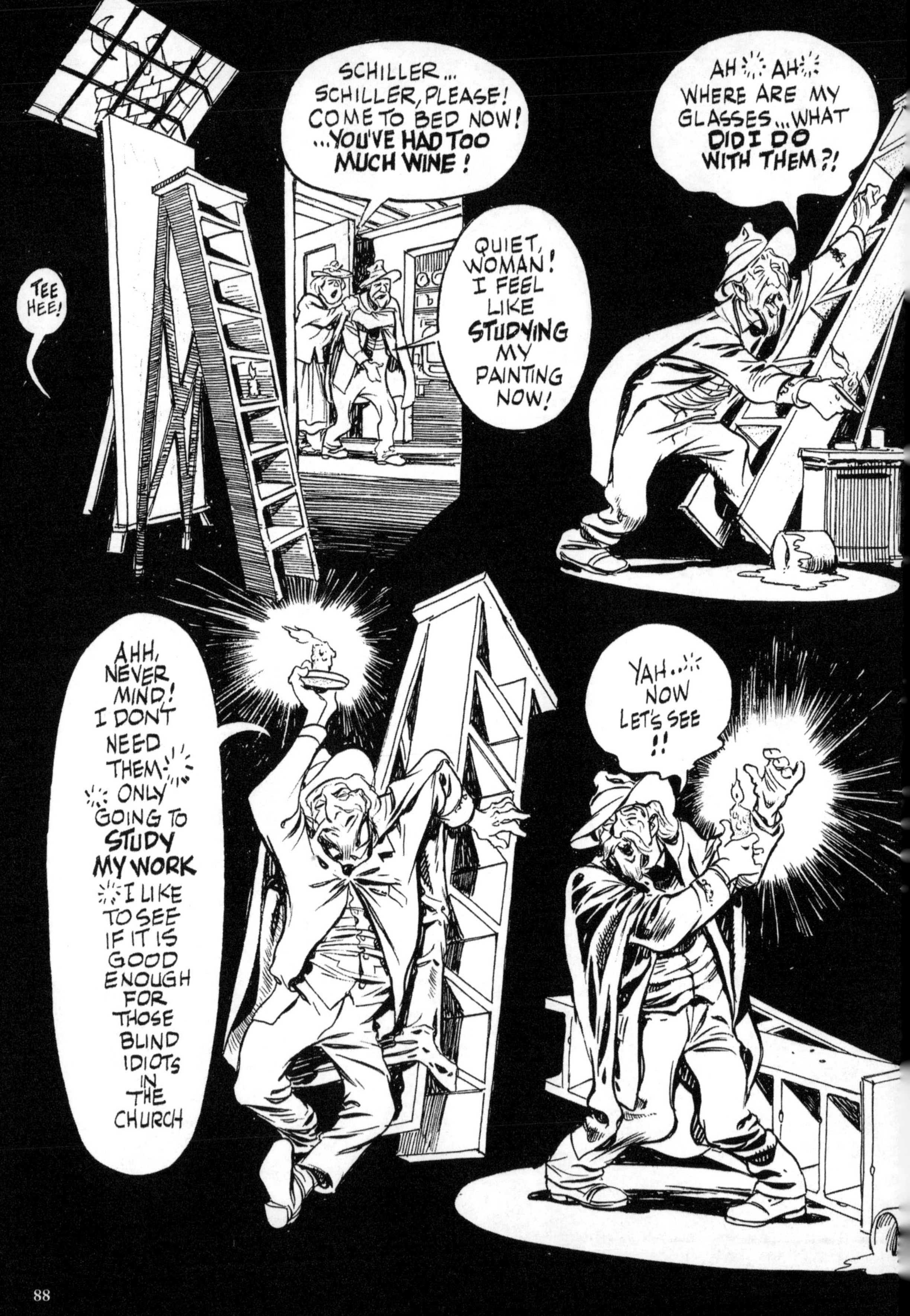

TEE HEE!
SCHILLER... SCHILLER, PLEASE! COME TO BED NOW! ...YOU'VE HAD TOO MUCH WINE!
QUIET, WOMAN! I FEEL LIKE STUDYING MY PAINTING NOW!
AH... AH... WHERE ARE MY GLASSES... WHAT DID I DO WITH THEM?!
AHH, NEVER MIND! I DON'T NEED THEM... ONLY GOING TO STUDY MY WORK... I LIKE TO SEE IF IT IS GOOD ENOUGH FOR THOSE BLIND IDIOTS IN THE CHURCH
YAH... NOW LET'S SEE!!

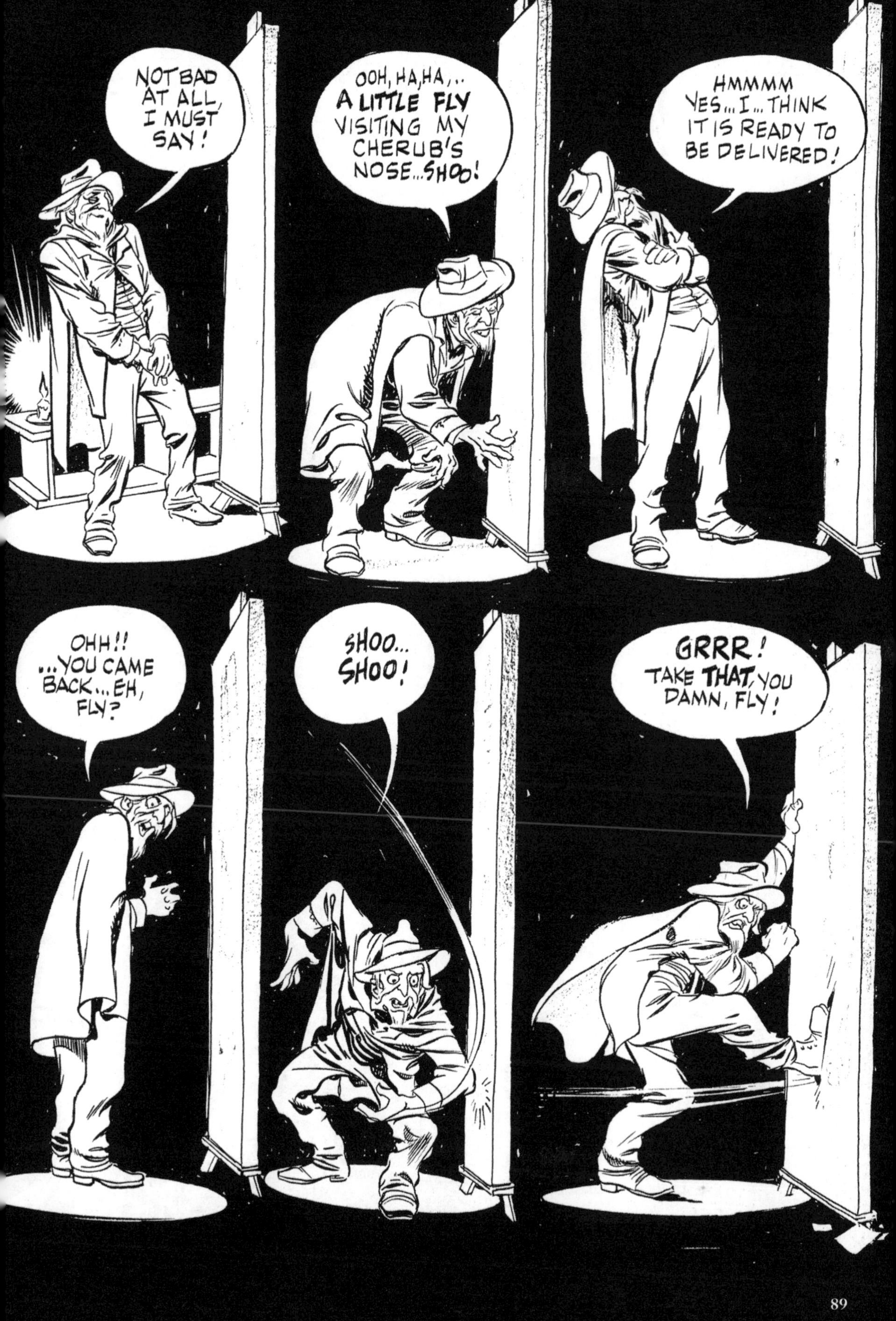
NOT BAD AT ALL, I MUST SAY!
OOH, HA, HA, .. A LITTLE FLY VISITING MY CHERUB'S NOSE...SHOO!
HMMMM YES... I... THINK IT IS READY TO BE DELIVERED!
OHH!! ...YOU CAME BACK... EH, FLY?
SHOO... SHOO!
GRRR! TAKE THAT, YOU DAMN, FLY!

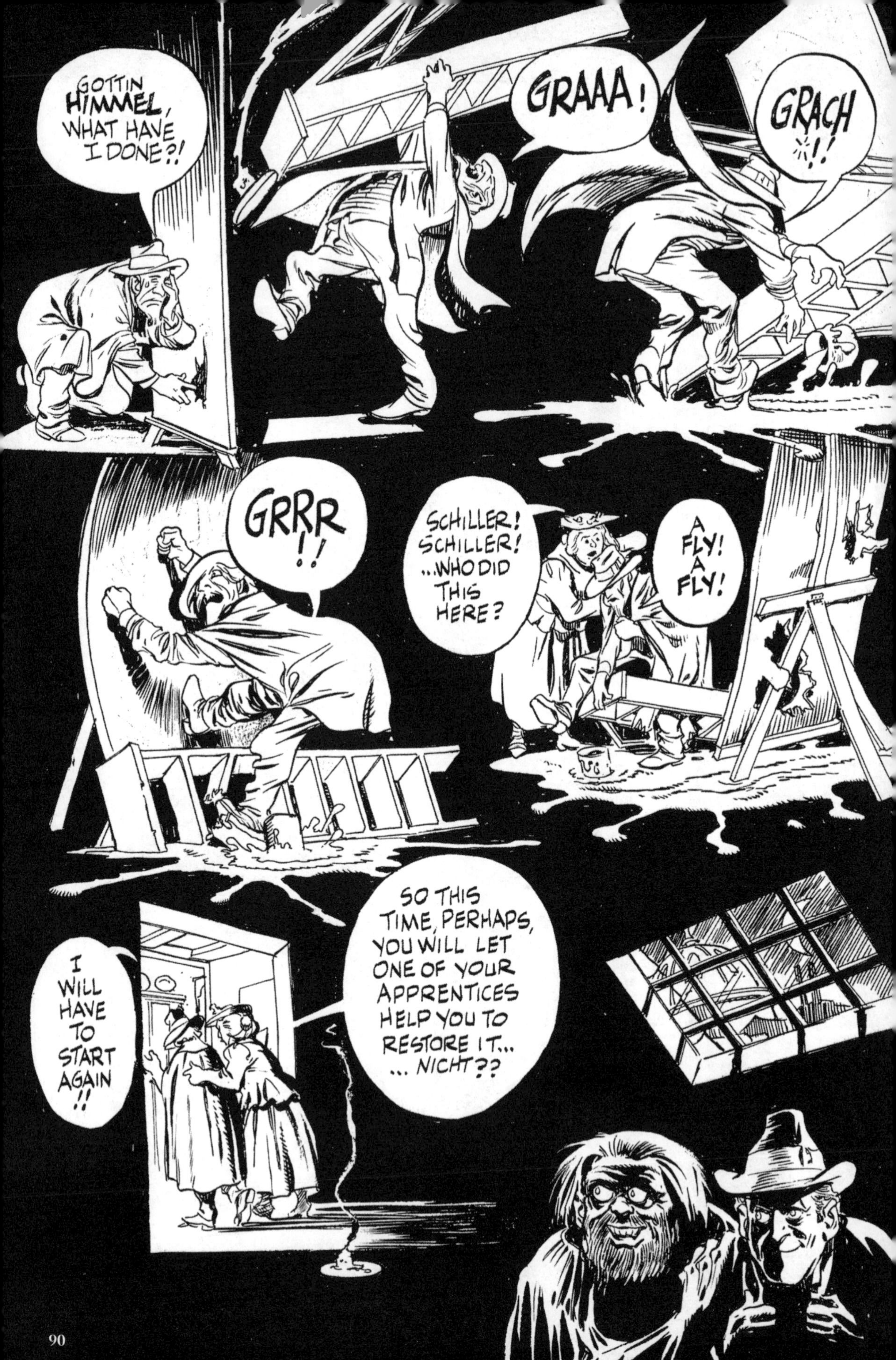
GOTTIN HIMMEL, WHAT HAVE I DONE?!
GRAAA!
GRACH !!
GRRR !!
SCHILLER! SCHILLER! ...WHO DID THIS HERE?
A FLY! A FLY!
I WILL HAVE TO START AGAIN !!
SO THIS TIME, PERHAPS, YOU WILL LET ONE OF YOUR APPRENTICES HELP YOU TO RESTORE IT... ... NICHT??

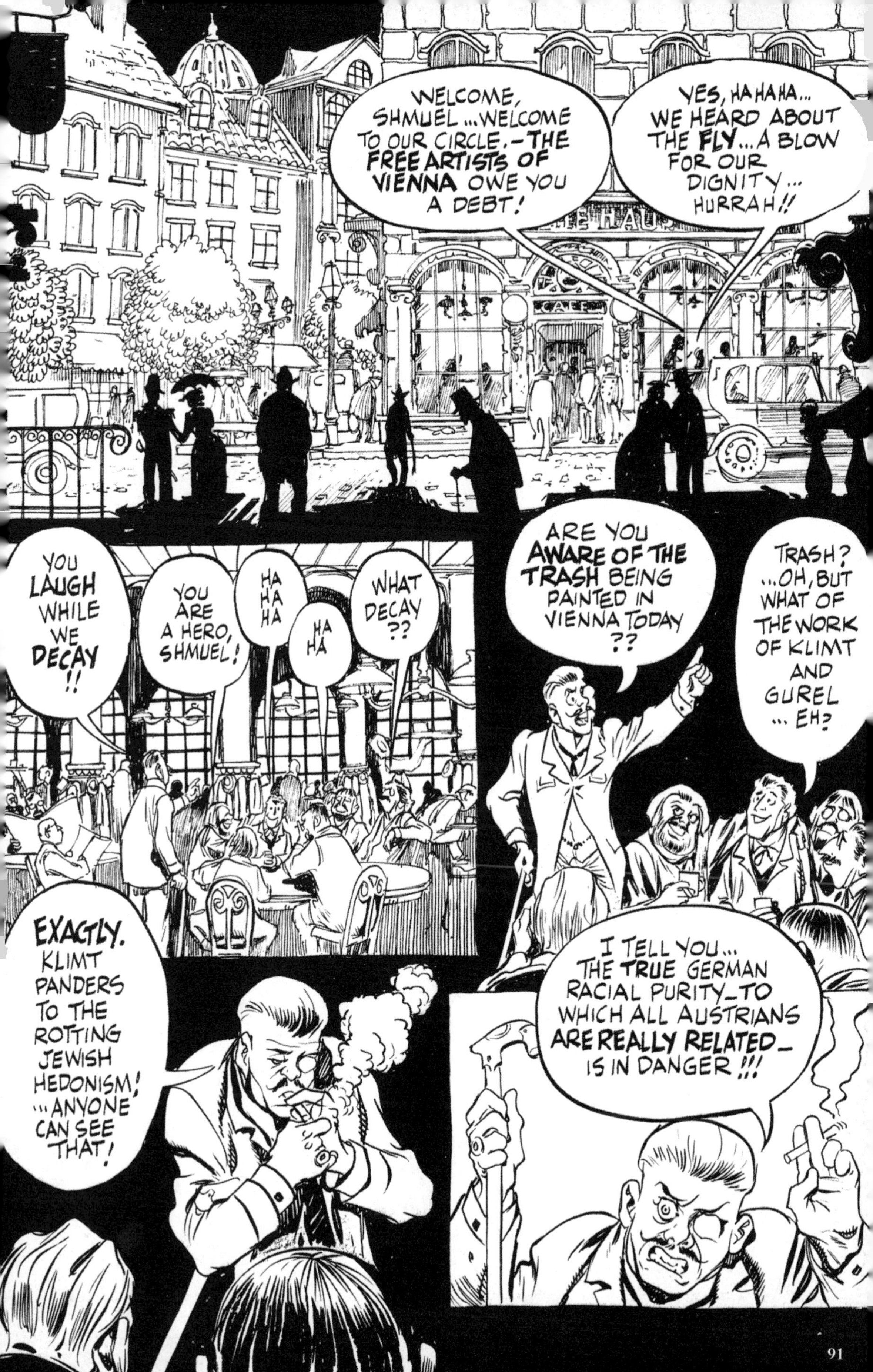
WELCOME, SHMUEL ... WELCOME TO OUR CIRCLE. – THE FREE ARTISTS OF VIENNA OWE YOU A DEBT!
YES, HA HA HA... WE HEARD ABOUT THE FLY... A BLOW FOR OUR DIGNITY... HURRAH!!
YOU LAUGH WHILE WE DECAY!!
YOU ARE A HERO, SHMUEL!
HA HA HA
HA HA
WHAT DECAY??
ARE YOU AWARE OF THE TRASH BEING PAINTED IN VIENNA TODAY??
TRASH? ...OH, BUT WHAT OF THE WORK OF KLIMT AND GUREL ... EH?
EXACTLY. KLIMT PANDERS TO THE ROTTING JEWISH HEDONISM! ...ANYONE CAN SEE THAT!
I TELL YOU... THE TRUE GERMAN RACIAL PURITY – TO WHICH ALL AUSTRIANS ARE REALLY RELATED – IS IN DANGER!!!

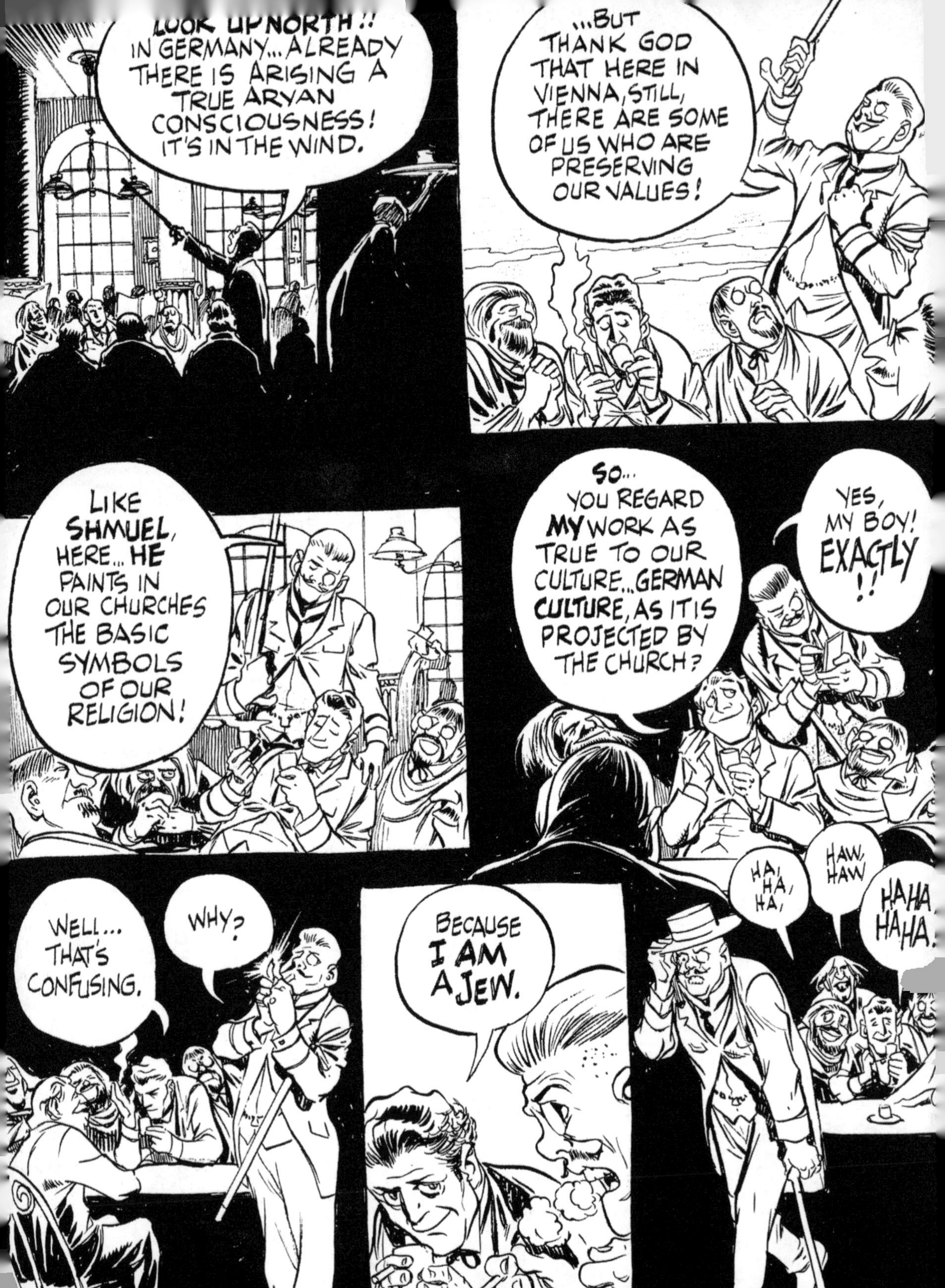
LOOK UP NORTH!! IN GERMANY... ALREADY THERE IS ARISING A TRUE ARYAN CONSCIOUSNESS! IT'S IN THE WIND.
...BUT THANK GOD THAT HERE IN VIENNA, STILL, THERE ARE SOME OF US WHO ARE PRESERVING OUR VALUES!
LIKE SHMUEL, HERE... HE PAINTS IN OUR CHURCHES THE BASIC SYMBOLS OF OUR RELIGION!
SO... YOU REGARD MY WORK AS TRUE TO OUR CULTURE... GERMAN CULTURE, AS IT IS PROJECTED BY THE CHURCH?
YES, MY BOY! EXACTLY!!
WELL... THAT'S CONFUSING.
WHY?
BECAUSE I AM A JEW.
HA, HA, HA,
HAW, HAW
HAHA HAHA!

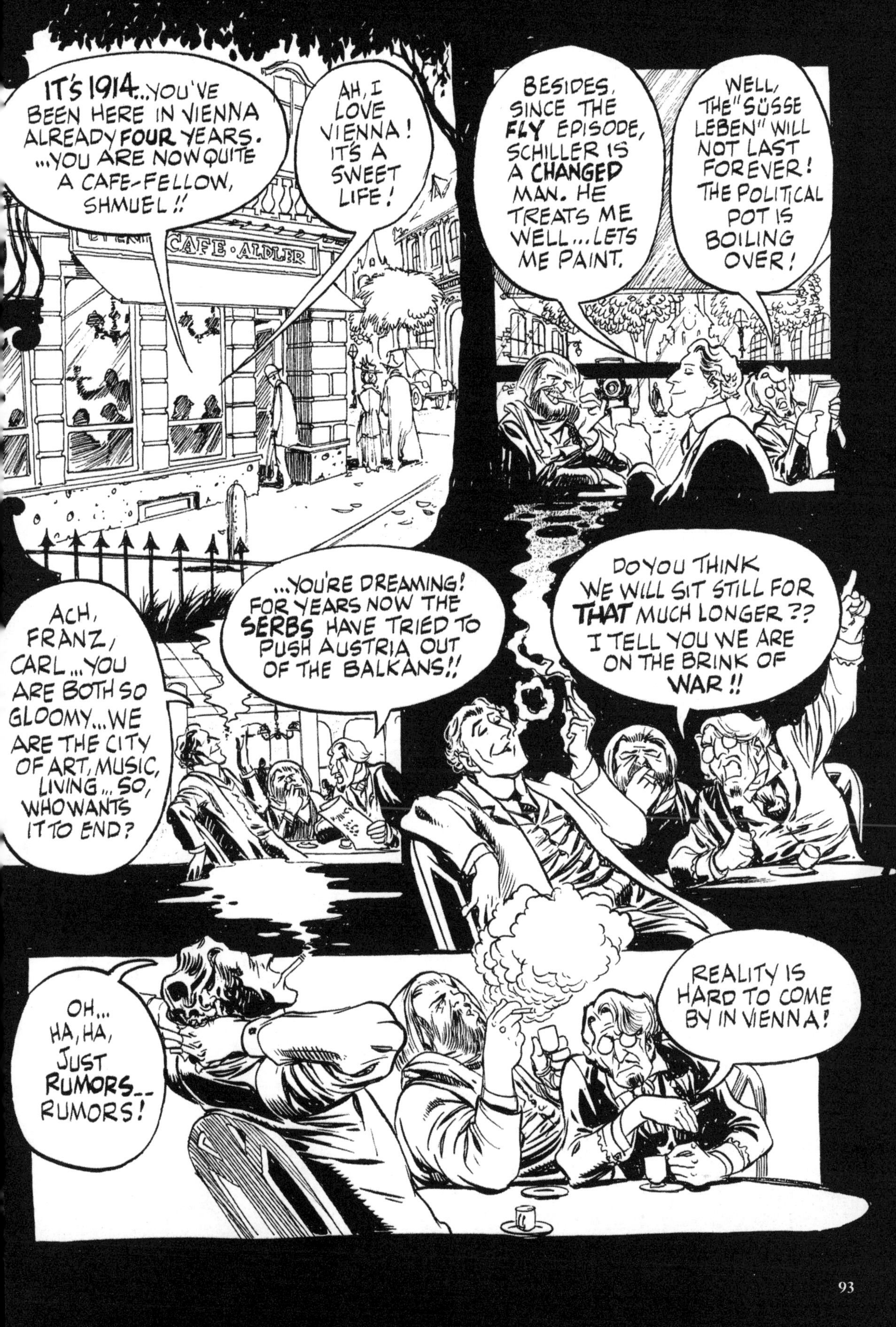
IT'S 1914...YOU'VE BEEN HERE IN VIENNA ALREADY FOUR YEARS. ...YOU ARE NOW QUITE A CAFE-FELLOW, SHMUEL!!
AH, I LOVE VIENNA! IT'S A SWEET LIFE!
CAFE · ALDLER
BESIDES, SINCE THE FLY EPISODE, SCHILLER IS A CHANGED MAN. HE TREATS ME WELL...LETS ME PAINT.
WELL, THE "SÜSSE LEBEN" WILL NOT LAST FOREVER! THE POLITICAL POT IS BOILING OVER!
ACH, FRANZ, CARL...YOU ARE BOTH SO GLOOMY...WE ARE THE CITY OF ART, MUSIC, LIVING... SO, WHO WANTS IT TO END?
...YOU'RE DREAMING! FOR YEARS NOW THE SERBS HAVE TRIED TO PUSH AUSTRIA OUT OF THE BALKANS!!
DO YOU THINK WE WILL SIT STILL FOR THAT MUCH LONGER?? I TELL YOU WE ARE ON THE BRINK OF WAR!!
OH... HA, HA, JUST RUMORS-- RUMORS!
REALITY IS HARD TO COME BY IN VIENNA!

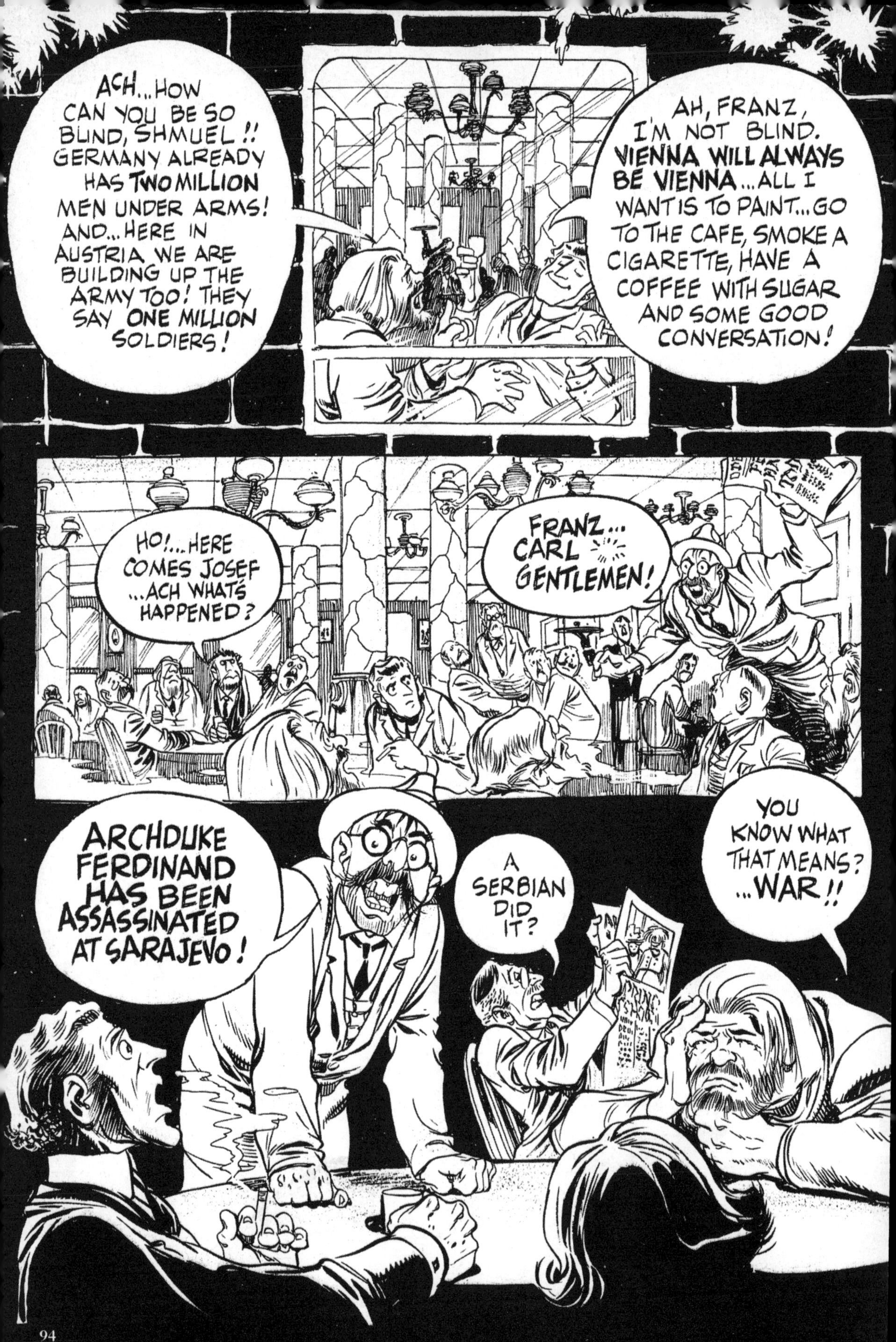
ACH...HOW CAN YOU BE SO BLIND, SHMUEL!! GERMANY ALREADY HAS TWO MILLION MEN UNDER ARMS! AND...HERE IN AUSTRIA WE ARE BUILDING UP THE ARMY TOO! THEY SAY ONE MILLION SOLDIERS!
AH, FRANZ, I'M NOT BLIND. VIENNA WILL ALWAYS BE VIENNA...ALL I WANT IS TO PAINT...GO TO THE CAFE, SMOKE A CIGARETTE, HAVE A COFFEE WITH SUGAR AND SOME GOOD CONVERSATION!
HO!...HERE COMES JOSEF ...ACH WHAT'S HAPPENED?
FRANZ... CARL GENTLEMEN!
ARCHDUKE FERDINAND HAS BEEN ASSASSINATED AT SARAJEVO!
A SERBIAN DID IT?
YOU KNOW WHAT THAT MEANS? ...WAR!!

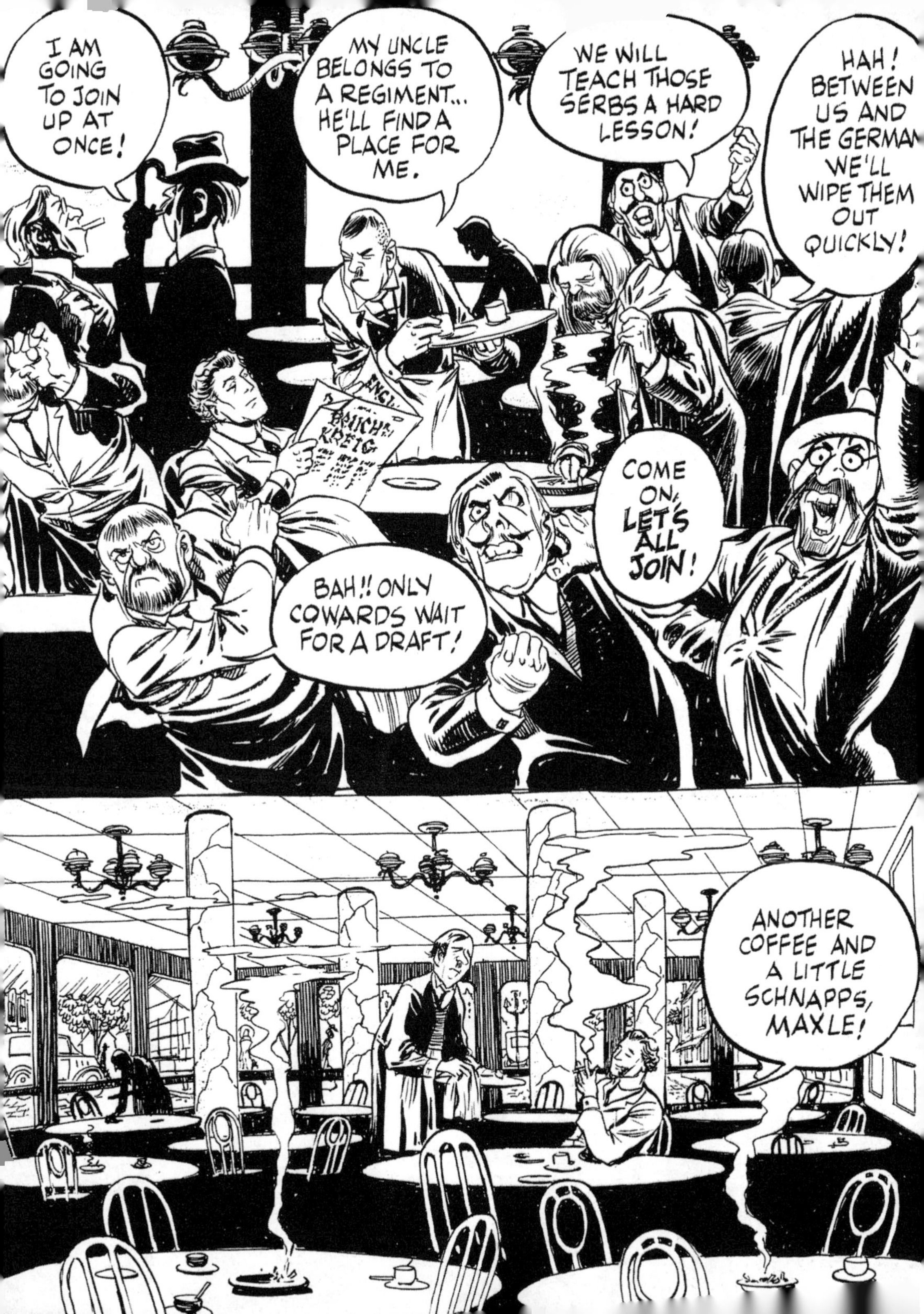
I AM GOING TO JOIN UP AT ONCE!
MY UNCLE BELONGS TO A REGIMENT... HE'LL FIND A PLACE FOR ME.
WE WILL TEACH THOSE SERBS A HARD LESSON!
HAH! BETWEEN US AND THE GERMAN WE'LL WIPE THEM OUT QUICKLY!
COME ON, LET'S ALL JOIN!
BAH!! ONLY COWARDS WAIT FOR A DRAFT!
ANOTHER COFFEE AND A LITTLE SCHNAPPS, MAXLE!

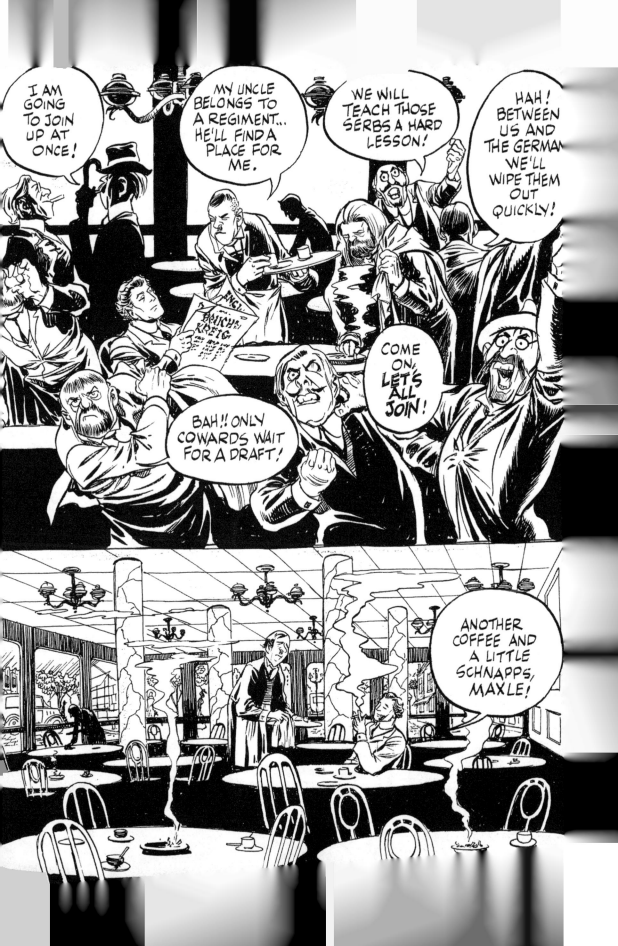

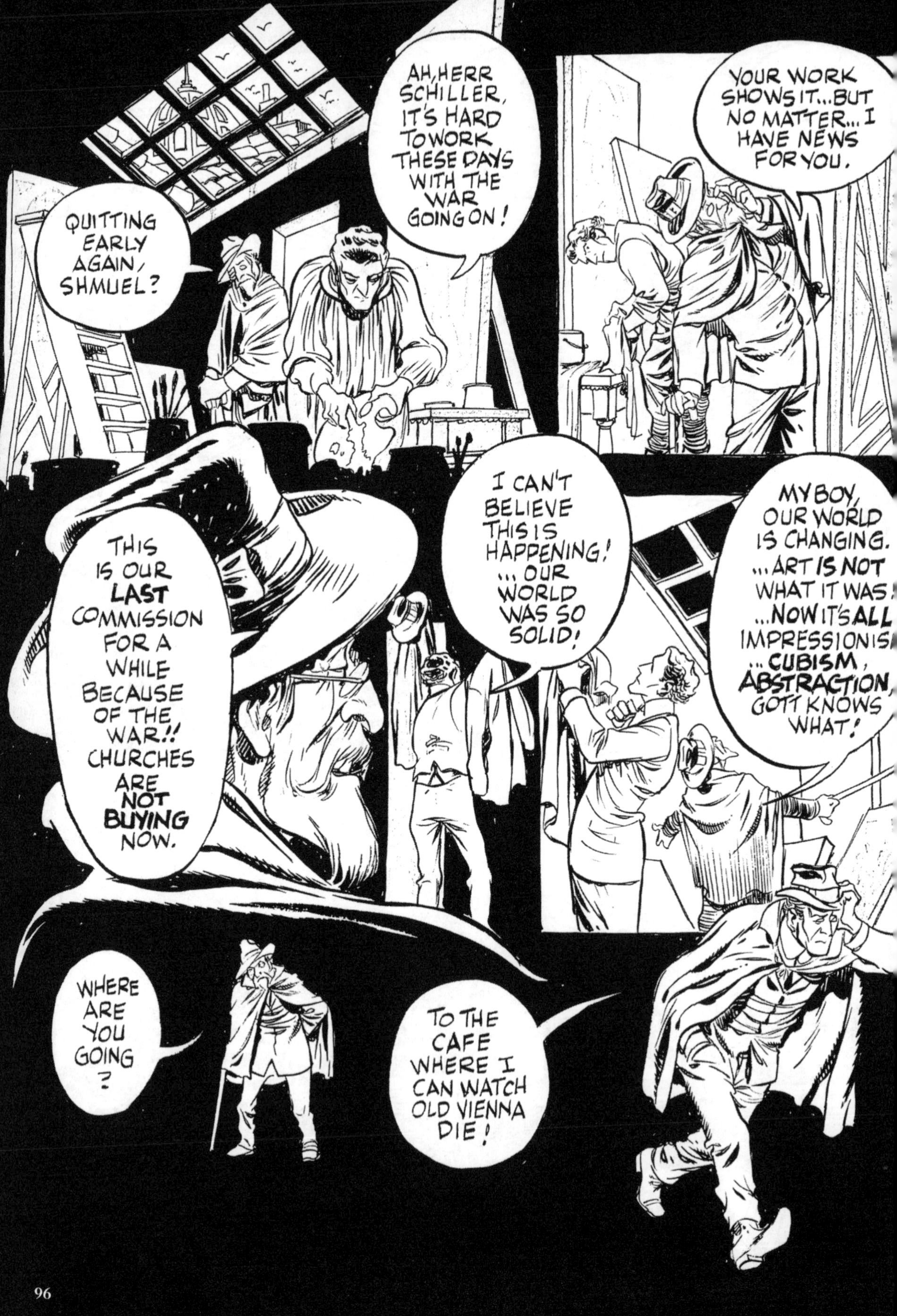
QUITTING EARLY AGAIN, SHMUEL?
AH, HERR SCHILLER, IT'S HARD TO WORK THESE DAYS WITH THE WAR GOING ON!
YOUR WORK SHOWS IT... BUT NO MATTER... I HAVE NEWS FOR YOU.
THIS IS OUR **LAST** COMMISSION FOR A WHILE BECAUSE OF THE WAR!! CHURCHES ARE **NOT BUYING** NOW.
I CAN'T BELIEVE THIS IS HAPPENING! ...OUR WORLD WAS SO SOLID!
MY BOY, OUR WORLD IS CHANGING. ...ART **IS NOT** WHAT IT WAS! ...**NOW** IT'S **ALL** IMPRESSIONIS ...**CUBISM**, **ABSTRACTION**, GOTT KNOWS WHAT!
WHERE ARE YOU GOING?
TO THE CAFE WHERE I CAN WATCH OLD VIENNA DIE!

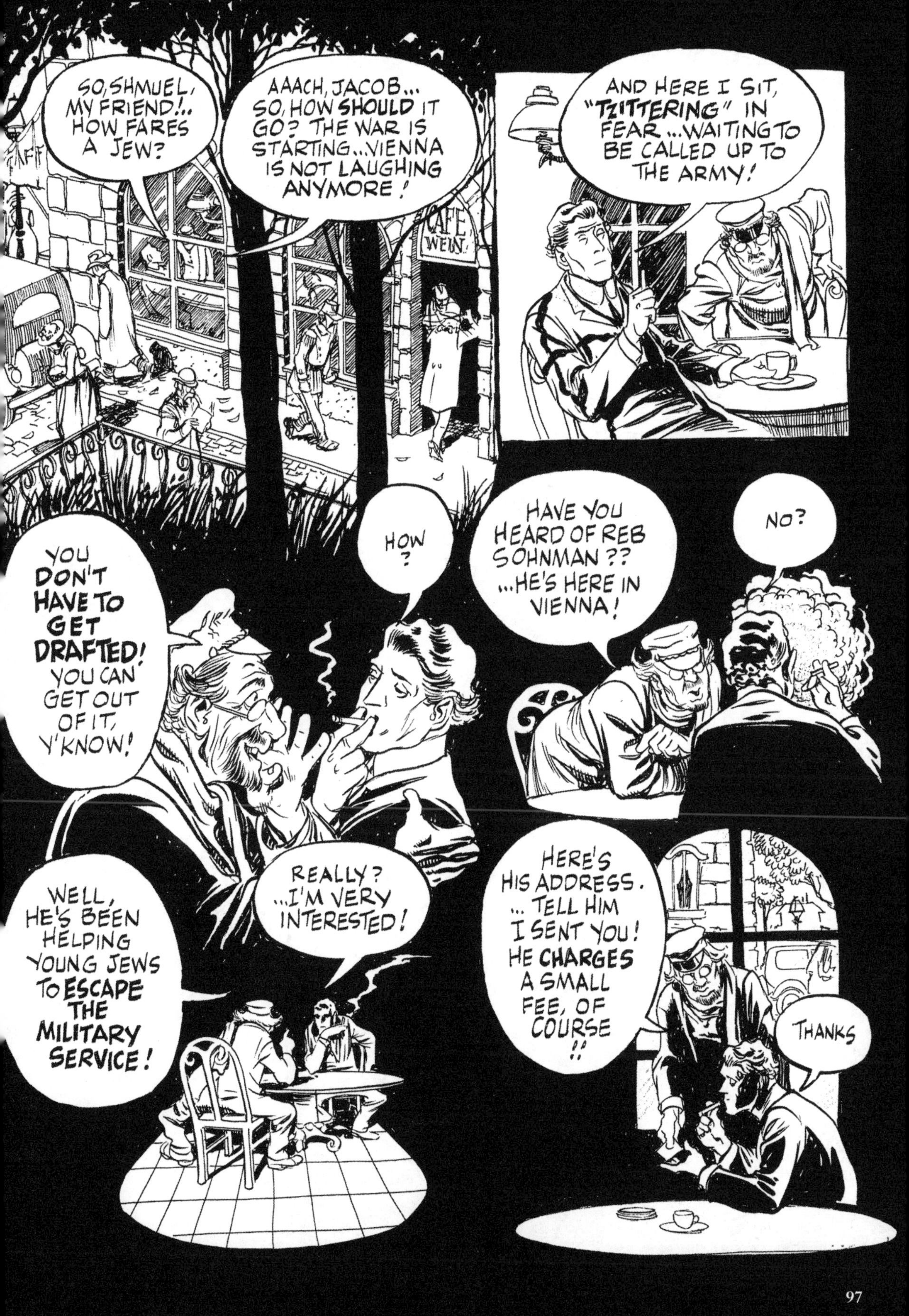
SO, SHMUEL, MY FRIEND!.. HOW FARES A JEW?
AAACH, JACOB... SO, HOW SHOULD IT GO? THE WAR IS STARTING...VIENNA IS NOT LAUGHING ANYMORE!
CAFE WEIN
AND HERE I SIT, "TZITTERING" IN FEAR...WAITING TO BE CALLED UP TO THE ARMY!
YOU DON'T HAVE TO GET DRAFTED! YOU CAN GET OUT OF IT, Y'KNOW!
HOW?
HAVE YOU HEARD OF REB SOHNMAN?? ...HE'S HERE IN VIENNA!
NO?
WELL, HE'S BEEN HELPING YOUNG JEWS TO ESCAPE THE MILITARY SERVICE!
REALLY? ...I'M VERY INTERESTED!
HERE'S HIS ADDRESS. ... TELL HIM I SENT YOU! HE CHARGES A SMALL FEE, OF COURSE!!
THANKS

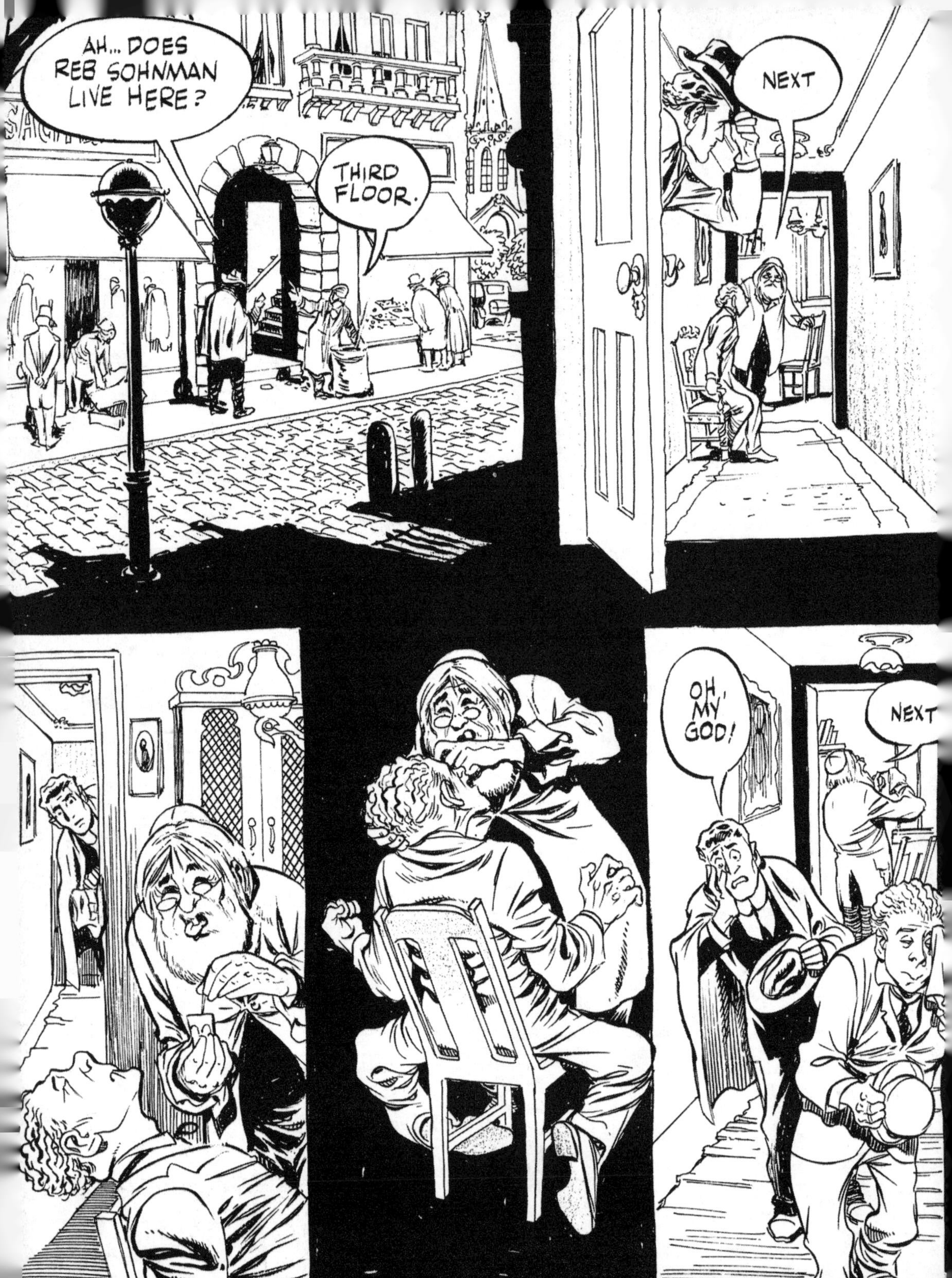
AH... DOES REB SOHNMAN LIVE HERE?
THIRD FLOOR.
NEXT
OH, MY GOD!
NEXT

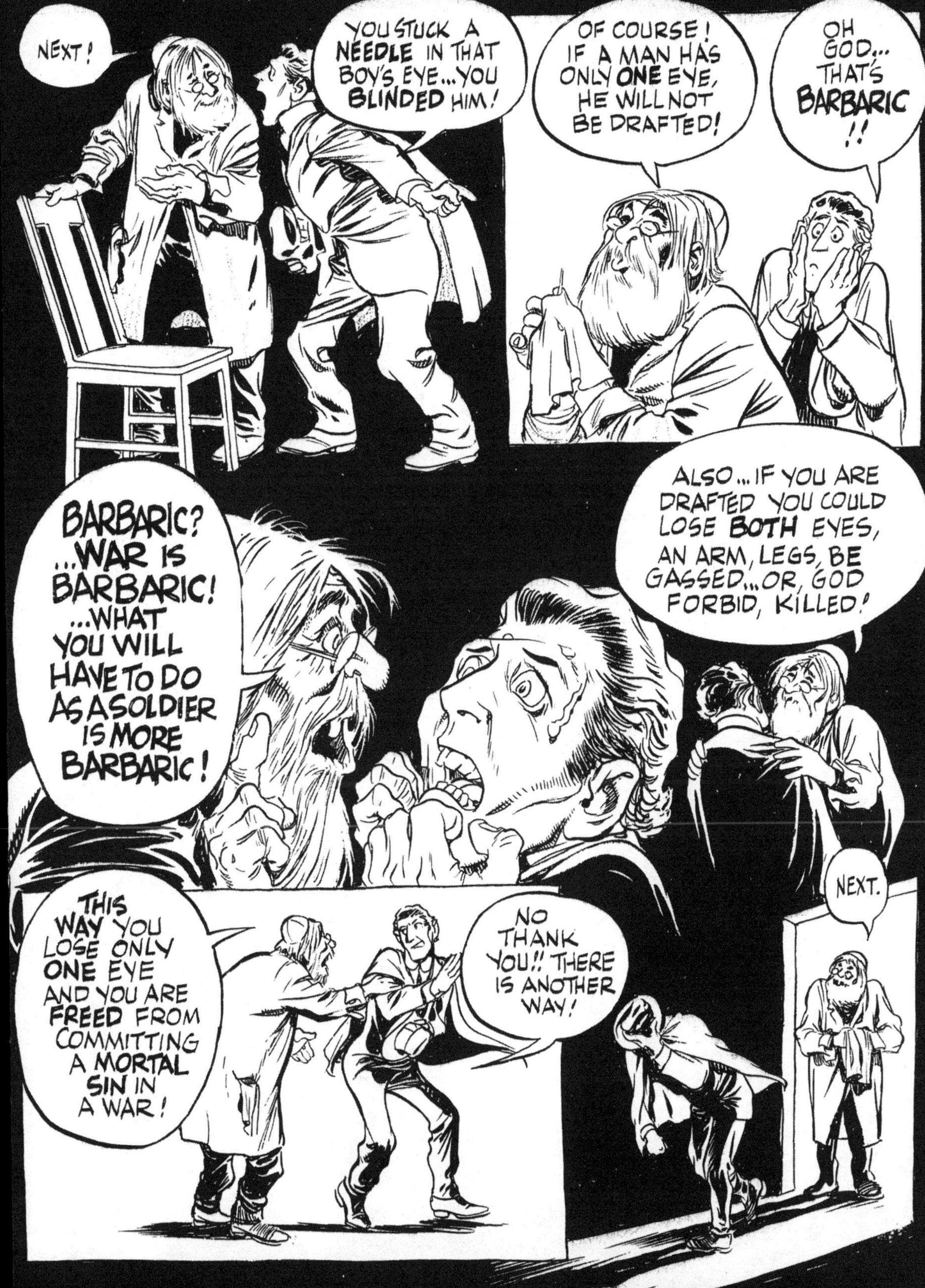
NEXT!
YOU STUCK A NEEDLE IN THAT BOY'S EYE...YOU BLINDED HIM!
OF COURSE! IF A MAN HAS ONLY ONE EYE, HE WILL NOT BE DRAFTED!
OH GOD... THAT'S BARBARIC!!
BARBARIC? ...WAR IS BARBARIC! ...WHAT YOU WILL HAVE TO DO AS A SOLDIER IS MORE BARBARIC!
ALSO... IF YOU ARE DRAFTED YOU COULD LOSE BOTH EYES, AN ARM, LEGS, BE GASSED...OR, GOD FORBID, KILLED!
THIS WAY YOU LOSE ONLY ONE EYE AND YOU ARE FREED FROM COMMITTING A MORTAL SIN IN A WAR!
NO THANK YOU!! THERE IS ANOTHER WAY!
NEXT.

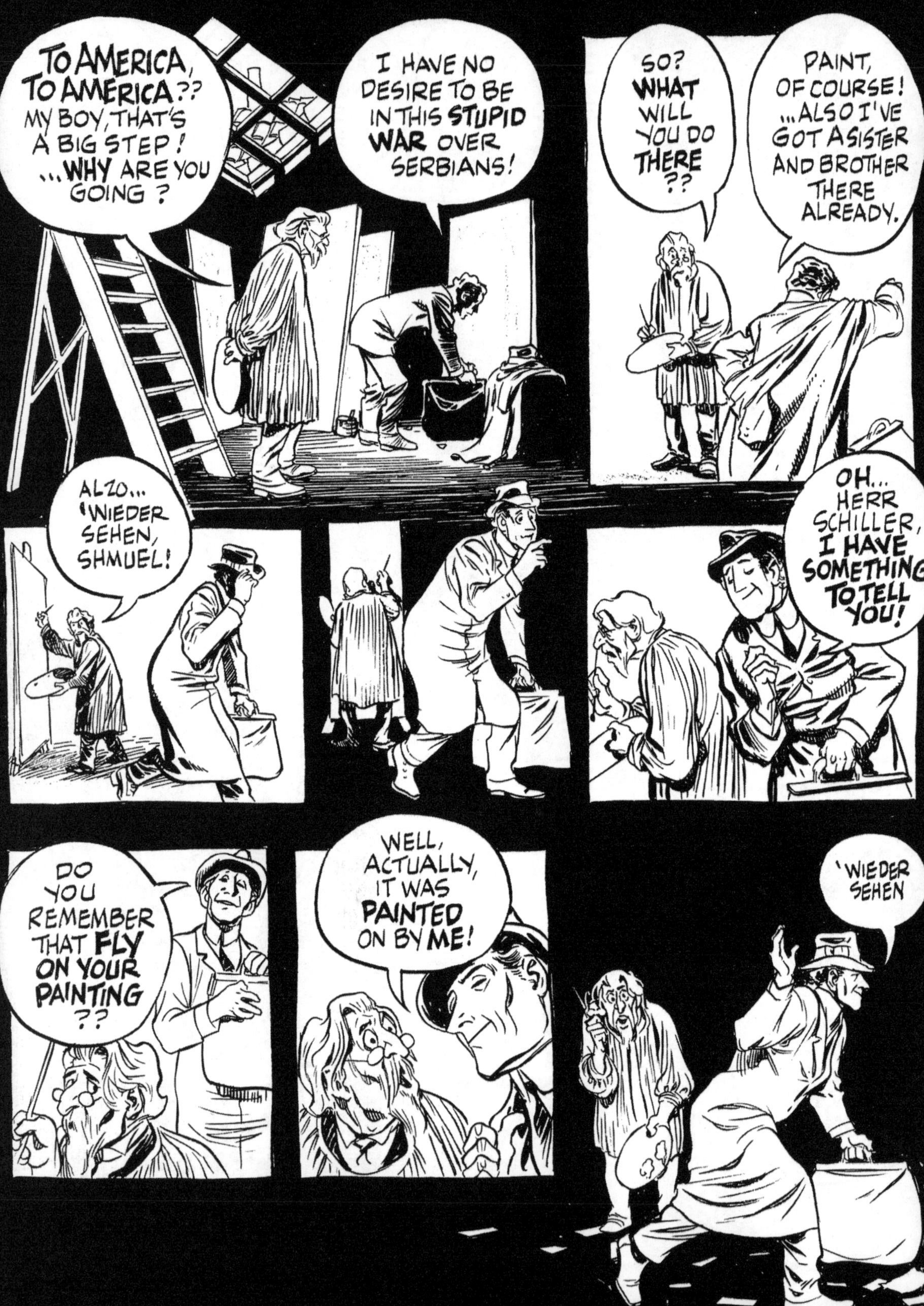
TO AMERICA, TO AMERICA?? MY BOY, THAT'S A BIG STEP! ...WHY ARE YOU GOING?
I HAVE NO DESIRE TO BE IN THIS STUPID WAR OVER SERBIANS!
SO? WHAT WILL YOU DO THERE??
PAINT, OF COURSE! ...ALSO I'VE GOT A SISTER AND BROTHER THERE ALREADY.
ALZO... 'WIEDER SEHEN, SHMUEL!
OH... HERR SCHILLER, I HAVE SOMETHING TO TELL YOU!
DO YOU REMEMBER THAT FLY ON YOUR PAINTING??
WELL, ACTUALLY, IT WAS PAINTED ON BY ME!
'WIEDER SEHEN

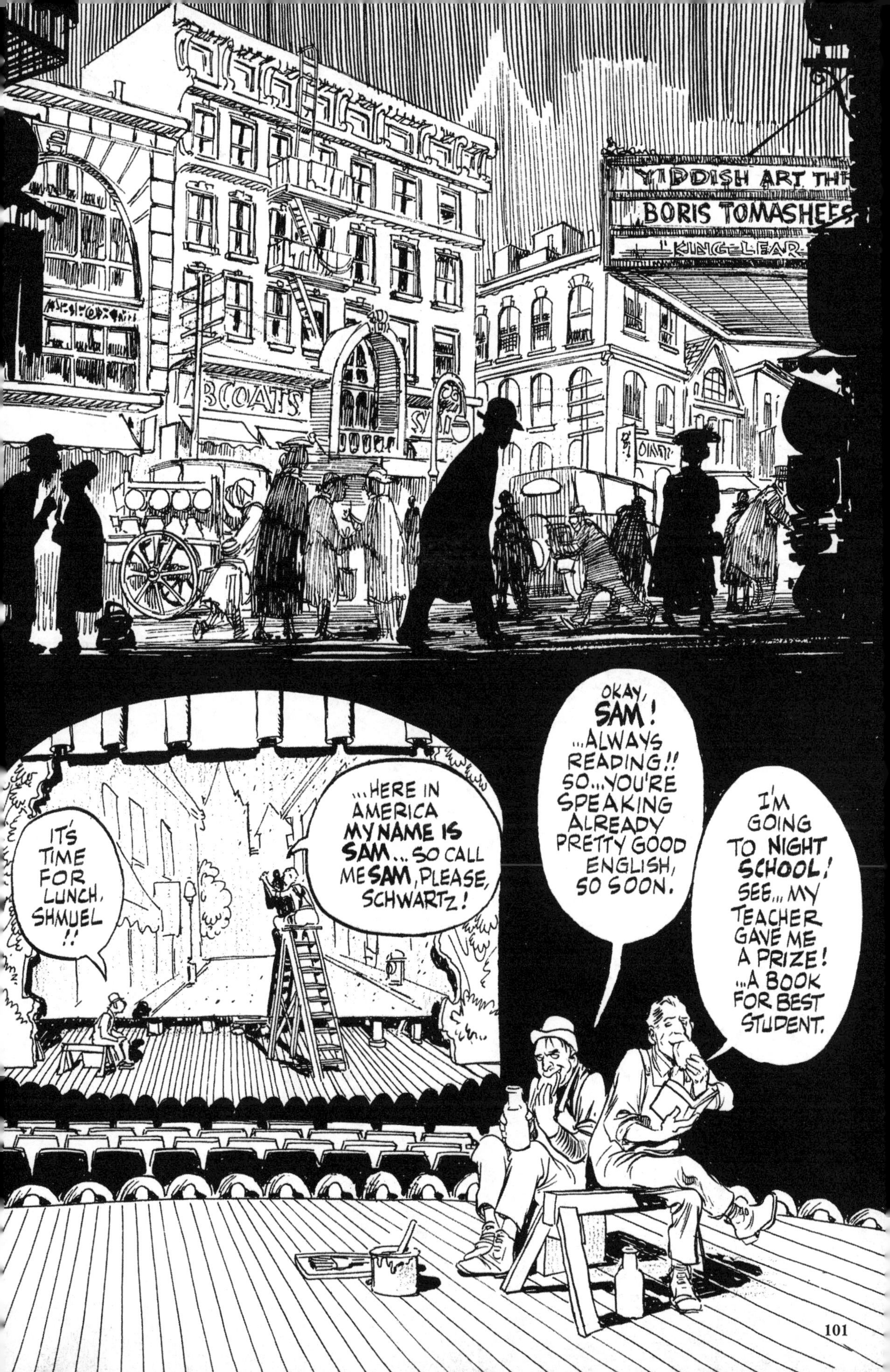
YIDDISH ART TH
BORIS TOMASHEFS
KING LEAR
BCOATS
IT'S TIME FOR LUNCH, SHMUEL!!
...HERE IN AMERICA MY NAME IS SAM... SO CALL ME SAM, PLEASE, SCHWARTZ!
OKAY, SAM! ...ALWAYS READING!! SO... YOU'RE SPEAKING ALREADY PRETTY GOOD ENGLISH, SO SOON.
I'M GOING TO NIGHT SCHOOL! SEE... MY TEACHER GAVE ME A PRIZE! ...A BOOK FOR BEST STUDENT.

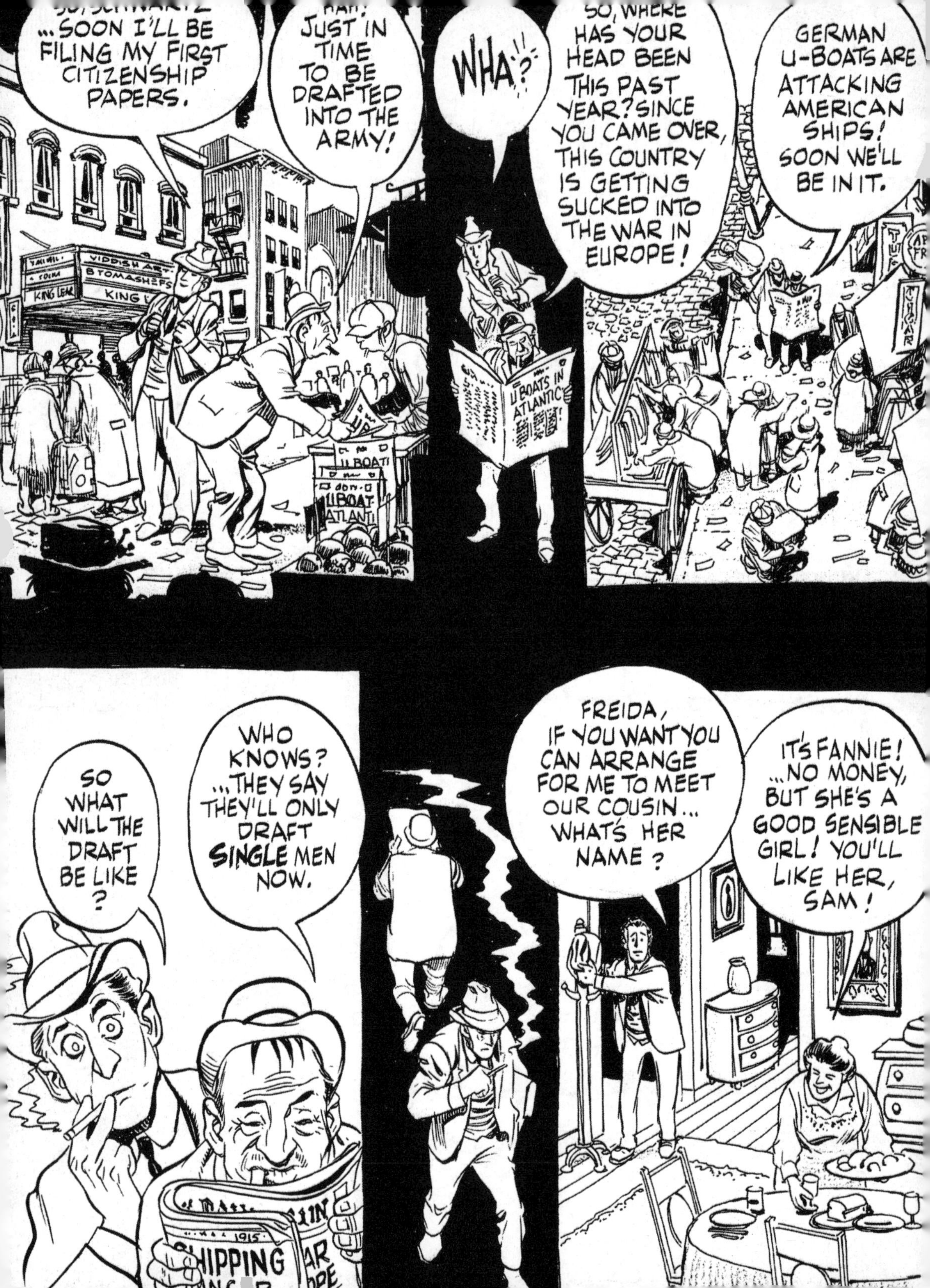
...SOON I'LL BE FILING MY FIRST CITIZENSHIP PAPERS.
JUST IN TIME TO BE DRAFTED INTO THE ARMY!
YIDDISH ART
TOMASHEFS
KING LEAR
U BOATS
WHA?
SO, WHERE HAS YOUR HEAD BEEN THIS PAST YEAR? SINCE YOU CAME OVER, THIS COUNTRY IS GETTING SUCKED INTO THE WAR IN EUROPE!
U BOATS IN ATLANTIC
GERMAN U-BOATS ARE ATTACKING AMERICAN SHIPS! SOON WE'LL BE IN IT.
SO WHAT WILL THE DRAFT BE LIKE?
WHO KNOWS? ...THEY SAY THEY'LL ONLY DRAFT **SINGLE** MEN NOW.
1915
SHIPPING
FREIDA, IF YOU WANT YOU CAN ARRANGE FOR ME TO MEET OUR COUSIN... WHAT'S HER NAME?
IT'S FANNIE! ...NO MONEY, BUT SHE'S A GOOD SENSIBLE GIRL! YOU'LL LIKE HER, SAM!

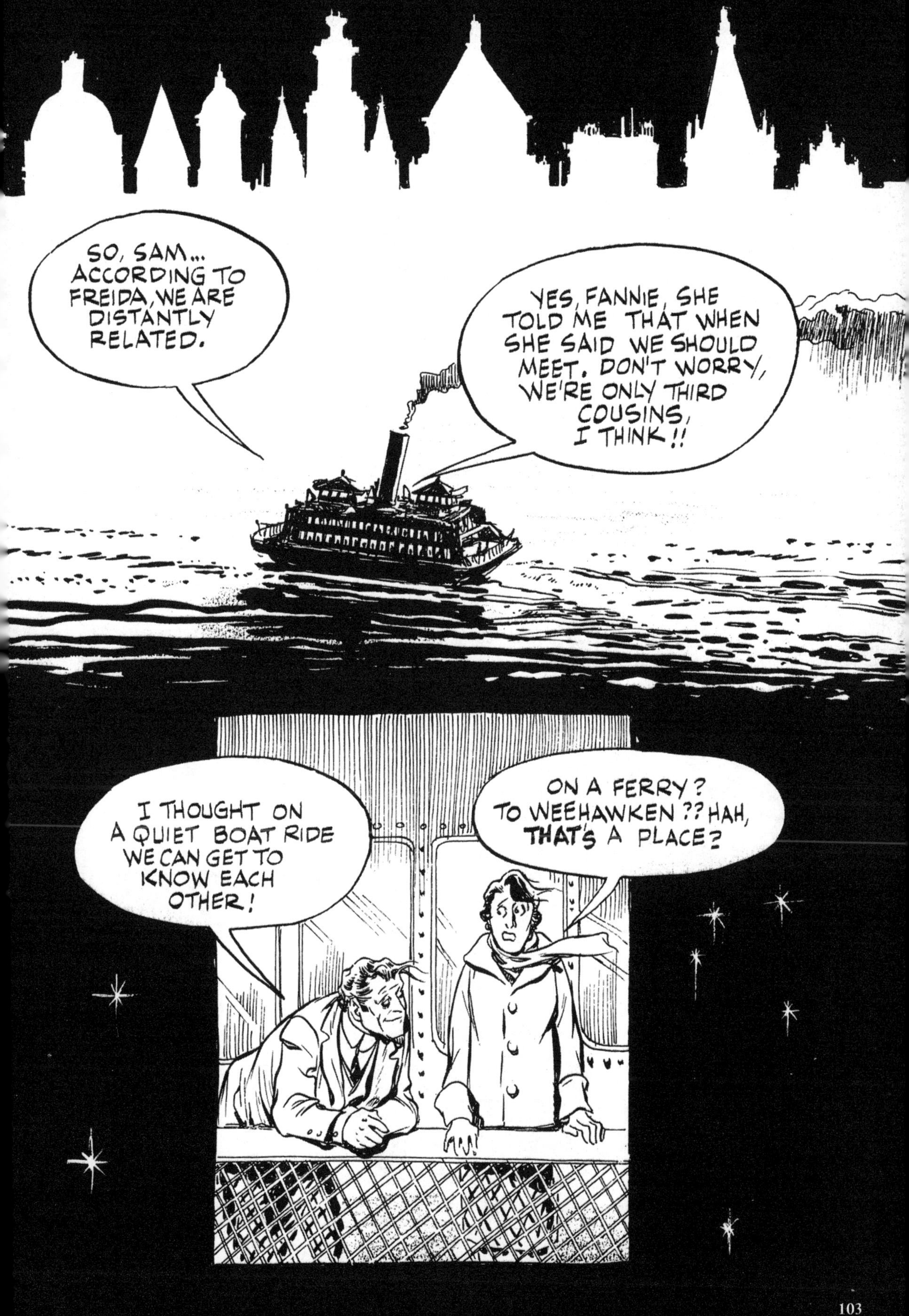
SO, SAM... ACCORDING TO FREIDA, WE ARE DISTANTLY RELATED.
YES, FANNIE, SHE TOLD ME THAT WHEN SHE SAID WE SHOULD MEET. DON'T WORRY, WE'RE ONLY THIRD COUSINS, I THINK!!
I THOUGHT ON A QUIET BOAT RIDE WE CAN GET TO KNOW EACH OTHER!
ON A FERRY? TO WEEHAWKEN?? HAH, THAT'S A PLACE?

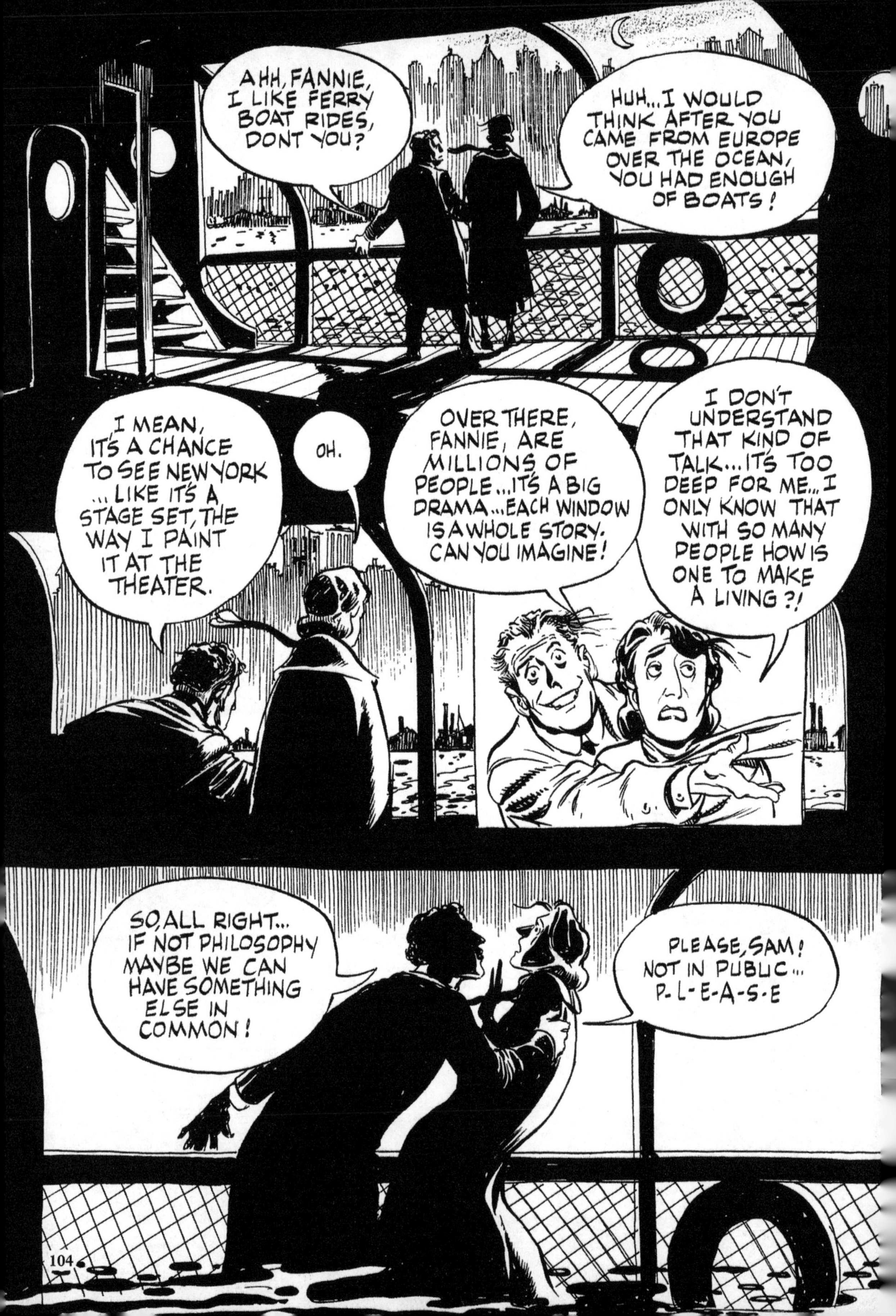
AHH, FANNIE, I LIKE FERRY BOAT RIDES, DONT YOU?
HUH... I WOULD THINK AFTER YOU CAME FROM EUROPE OVER THE OCEAN, YOU HAD ENOUGH OF BOATS!
I MEAN, IT'S A CHANCE TO SEE NEW YORK ... LIKE IT'S A STAGE SET, THE WAY I PAINT IT AT THE THEATER.
OH.
OVER THERE, FANNIE, ARE MILLIONS OF PEOPLE... IT'S A BIG DRAMA... EACH WINDOW IS A WHOLE STORY. CAN YOU IMAGINE!
I DON'T UNDERSTAND THAT KIND OF TALK... IT'S TOO DEEP FOR ME... I ONLY KNOW THAT WITH SO MANY PEOPLE HOW IS ONE TO MAKE A LIVING?!
SO, ALL RIGHT... IF NOT PHILOSOPHY MAYBE WE CAN HAVE SOMETHING ELSE IN COMMON!
PLEASE, SAM! NOT IN PUBLIC... P-L-E-A-S-E

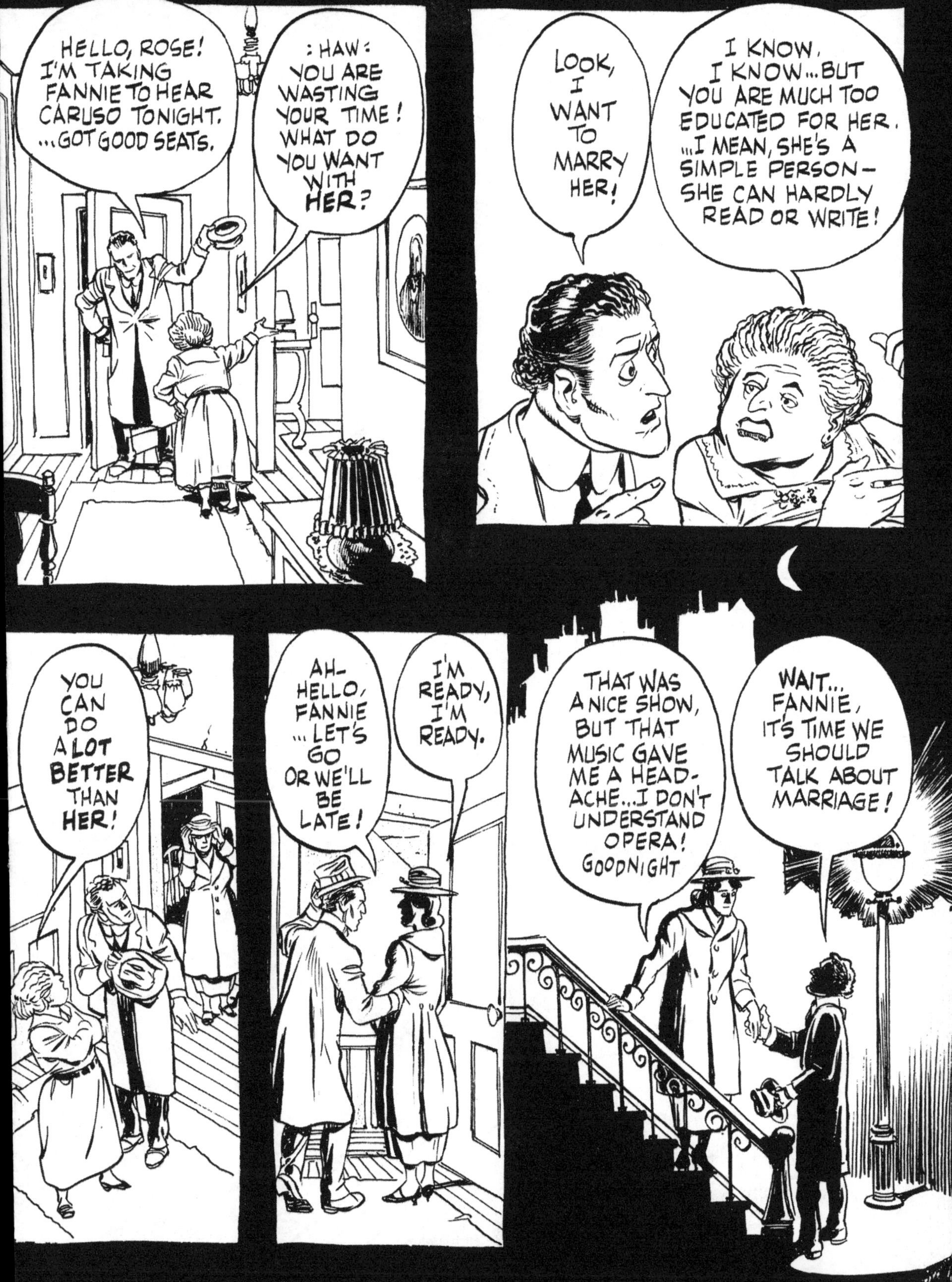
HELLO, ROSE! I'M TAKING FANNIE TO HEAR CARUSO TONIGHT. ...GOT GOOD SEATS.
: HAW : YOU ARE WASTING YOUR TIME! WHAT DO YOU WANT WITH **HER**?
LOOK, I WANT TO MARRY HER!
I KNOW, I KNOW... BUT YOU ARE MUCH TOO EDUCATED FOR HER. ...I MEAN, SHE'S A SIMPLE PERSON – SHE CAN HARDLY READ OR WRITE!
YOU CAN DO A **LOT BETTER** THAN **HER**!
AH– HELLO, FANNIE ...LET'S GO OR WE'LL BE LATE!
I'M READY, I'M READY.
THAT WAS A NICE SHOW, BUT THAT MUSIC GAVE ME A HEAD-ACHE... I DON'T UNDERSTAND OPERA! GOODNIGHT
WAIT... FANNIE, IT'S TIME WE SHOULD TALK ABOUT MARRIAGE!

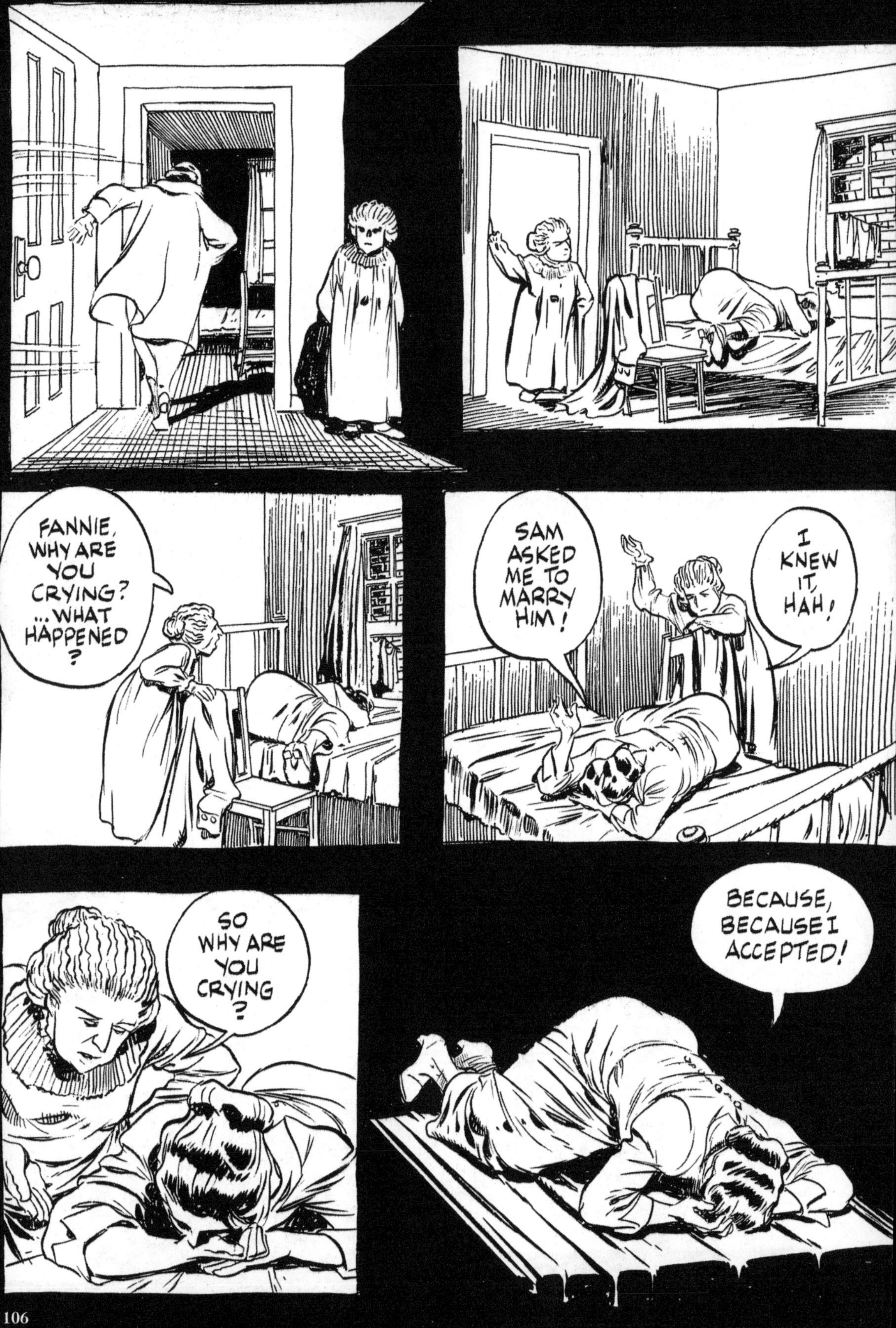
FANNIE, WHY ARE YOU CRYING? ...WHAT HAPPENED?
SAM ASKED ME TO MARRY HIM!
I KNEW IT, HAH!
SO WHY ARE YOU CRYING?
BECAUSE, BECAUSE I ACCEPTED!

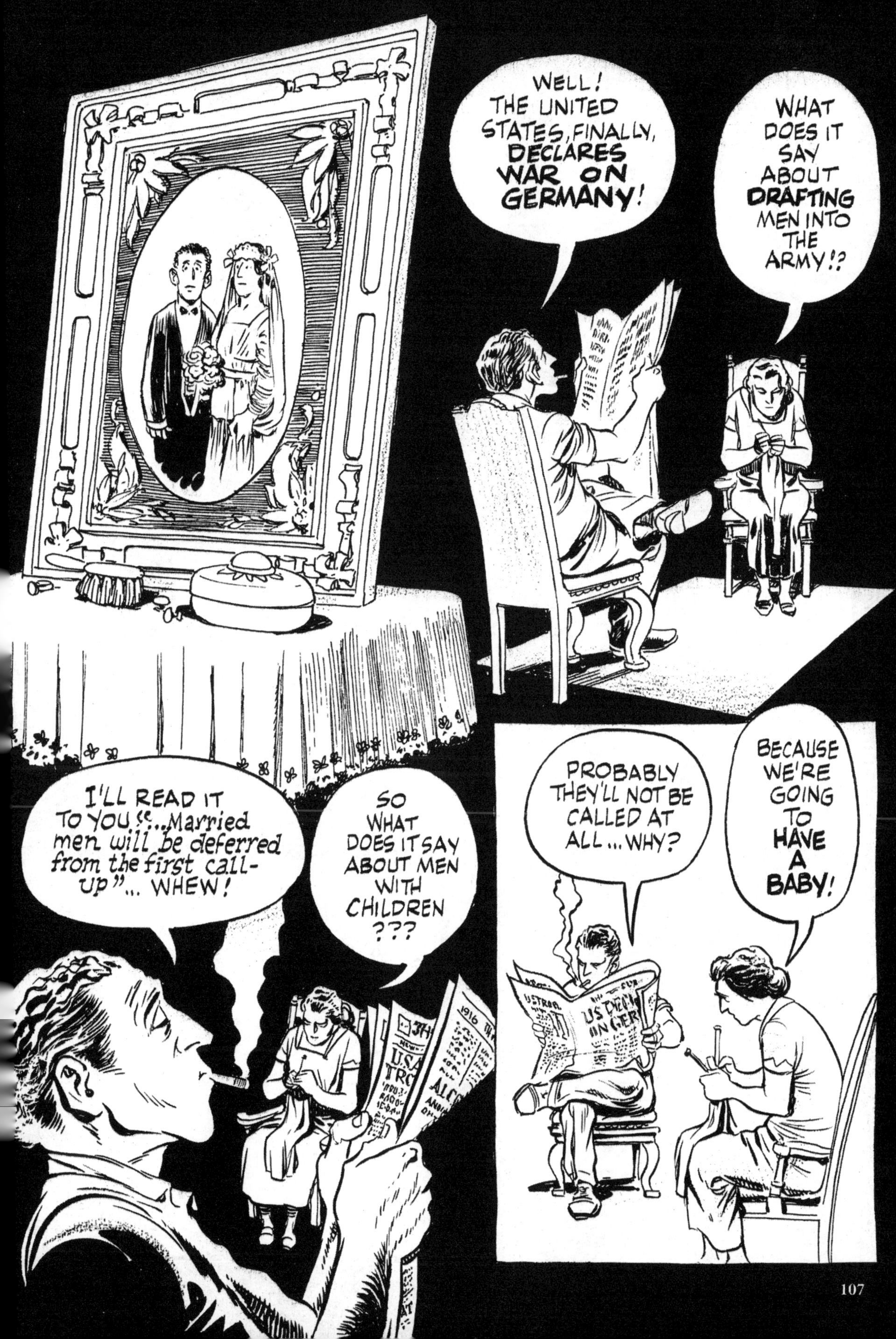
WELL! THE UNITED STATES, FINALLY, DECLARES WAR ON GERMANY!
WHAT DOES IT SAY ABOUT DRAFTING MEN INTO THE ARMY!?
I'LL READ IT TO YOU "...Married men will be deferred from the first call-up"... WHEW!
SO WHAT DOES IT SAY ABOUT MEN WITH CHILDREN ???
PROBABLY THEY'LL NOT BE CALLED AT ALL... WHY?
BECAUSE WE'RE GOING TO HAVE A BABY!

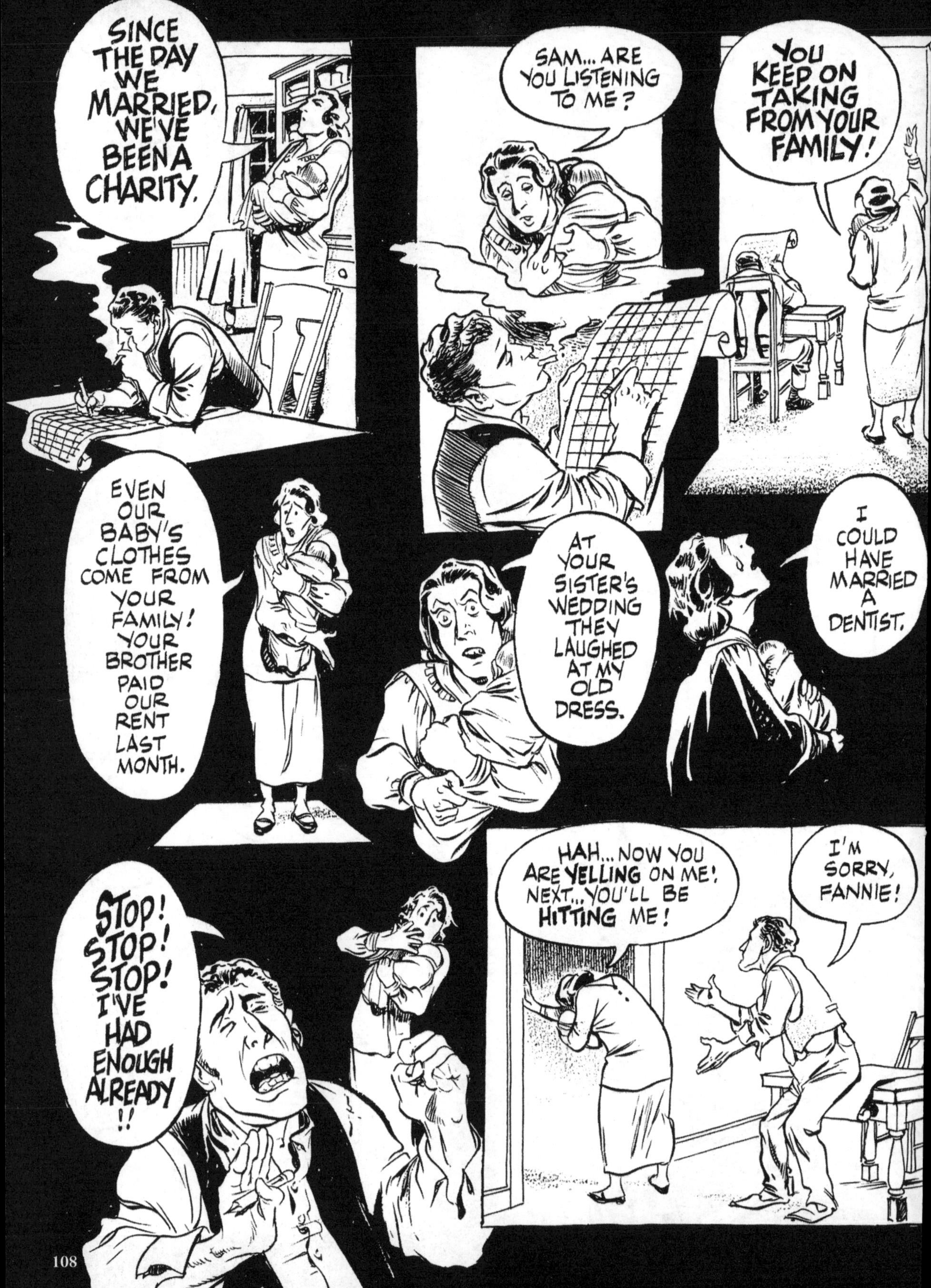
SINCE THE DAY WE MARRIED, WE'VE BEEN A CHARITY.
SAM... ARE YOU LISTENING TO ME?
YOU KEEP ON TAKING FROM YOUR FAMILY!
EVEN OUR BABY'S CLOTHES COME FROM YOUR FAMILY! YOUR BROTHER PAID OUR RENT LAST MONTH.
AT YOUR SISTER'S WEDDING THEY LAUGHED AT MY OLD DRESS.
I COULD HAVE MARRIED A DENTIST.
STOP! STOP! STOP! I'VE HAD ENOUGH ALREADY!!
HAH... NOW YOU ARE YELLING ON ME! NEXT... YOU'LL BE HITTING ME!
I'M SORRY, FANNIE!

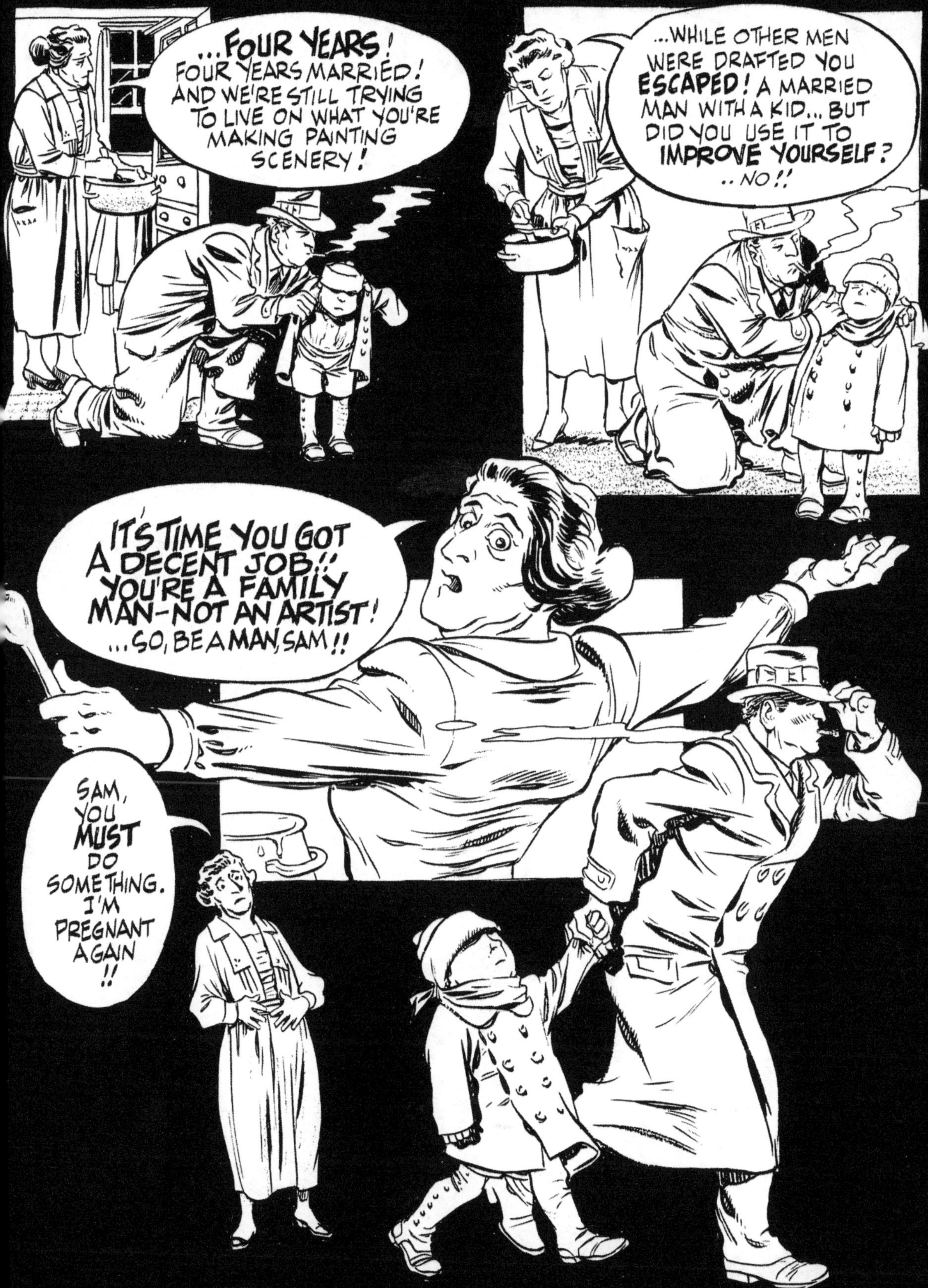
...FOUR YEARS! FOUR YEARS MARRIED! AND WE'RE STILL TRYING TO LIVE ON WHAT YOU'RE MAKING PAINTING SCENERY!
...WHILE OTHER MEN WERE DRAFTED YOU ESCAPED! A MARRIED MAN WITH A KID... BUT DID YOU USE IT TO IMPROVE YOURSELF? ..NO!!
IT'S TIME YOU GOT A DECENT JOB!! YOU'RE A FAMILY MAN-NOT AN ARTIST! ...SO, BE A MAN, SAM!!
SAM, YOU MUST DO SOMETHING. I'M PREGNANT AGAIN!!

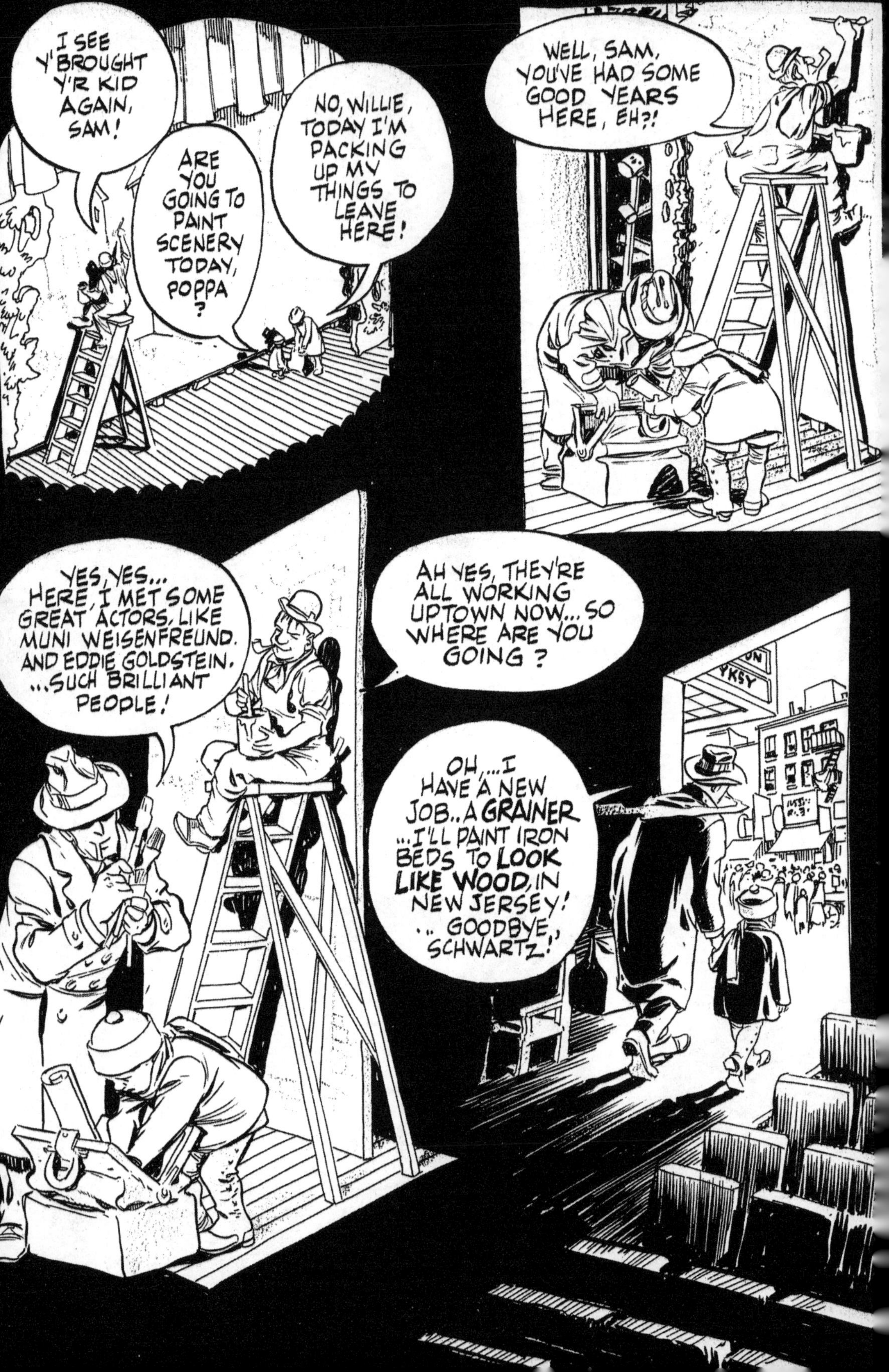
I SEE Y'BROUGHT Y'R KID AGAIN, SAM!
ARE YOU GOING TO PAINT SCENERY TODAY, POPPA ?
NO, WILLIE, TODAY I'M PACKING UP MY THINGS TO LEAVE HERE!
WELL, SAM, YOU'VE HAD SOME GOOD YEARS HERE, EH?!
YES, YES... HERE, I MET SOME GREAT ACTORS, LIKE MUNI WEISENFREUND. AND EDDIE GOLDSTEIN. ...SUCH BRILLIANT PEOPLE!
AH YES, THEY'RE ALL WORKING UPTOWN NOW... SO WHERE ARE YOU GOING ?
OH, ...I HAVE A NEW JOB.. A **GRAINER** ...I'LL PAINT IRON BEDS TO **LOOK LIKE WOOD**, IN NEW JERSEY! ... GOODBYE SCHWARTZ!

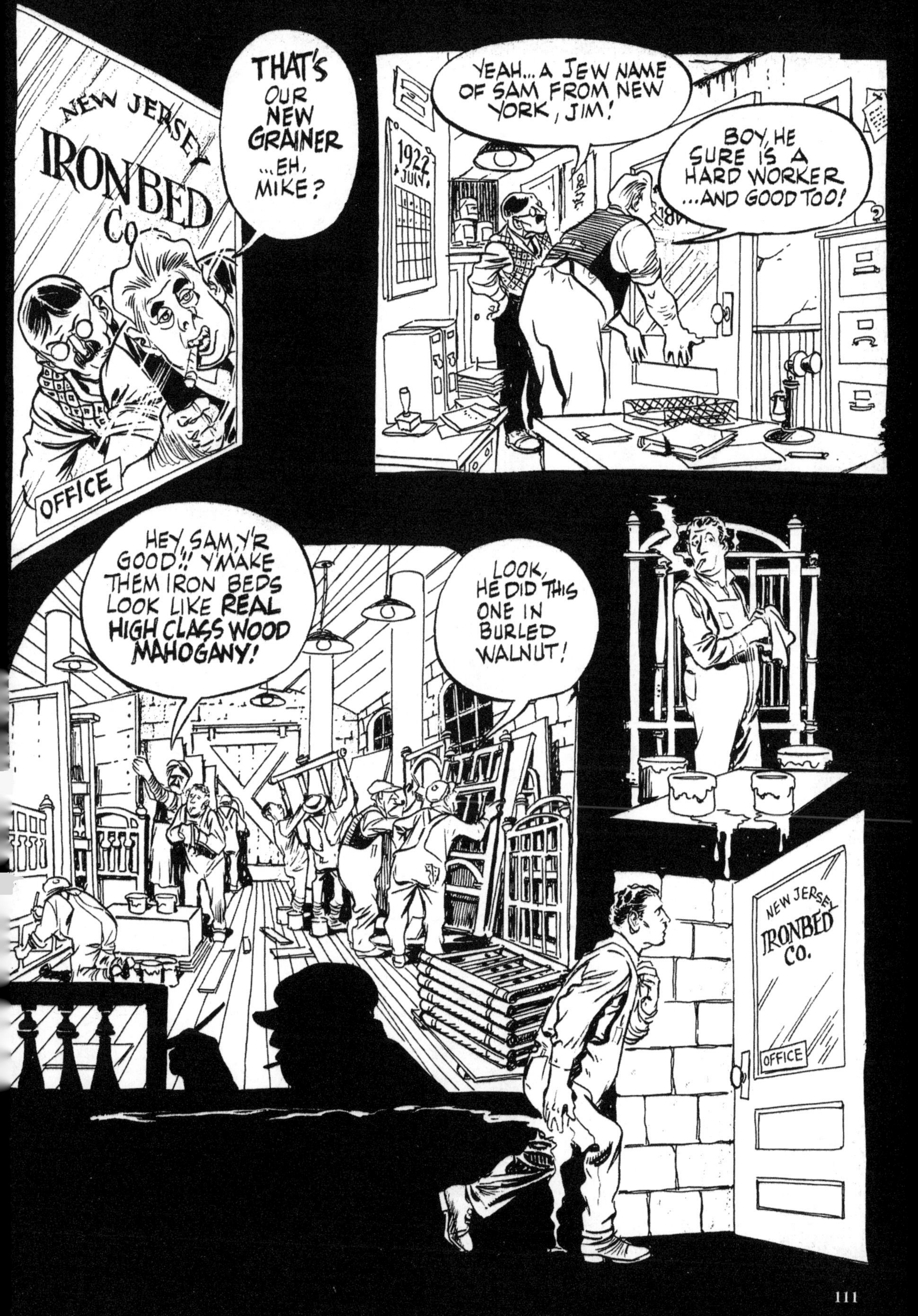
NEW JERSEY
IRONBED
Co.
OFFICE
THAT'S OUR NEW GRAINER ...EH, MIKE?
YEAH... A JEW NAME OF SAM FROM NEW YORK, JIM!
1922
JULY
BOY, HE SURE IS A HARD WORKER ...AND GOOD TOO!
HEY, SAM, Y'R GOOD!! Y'MAKE THEM IRON BEDS LOOK LIKE REAL HIGH CLASS WOOD MAHOGANY!
LOOK, HE DID THIS ONE IN BURLED WALNUT!
NEW JERSEY
IRONBED
Co.
OFFICE

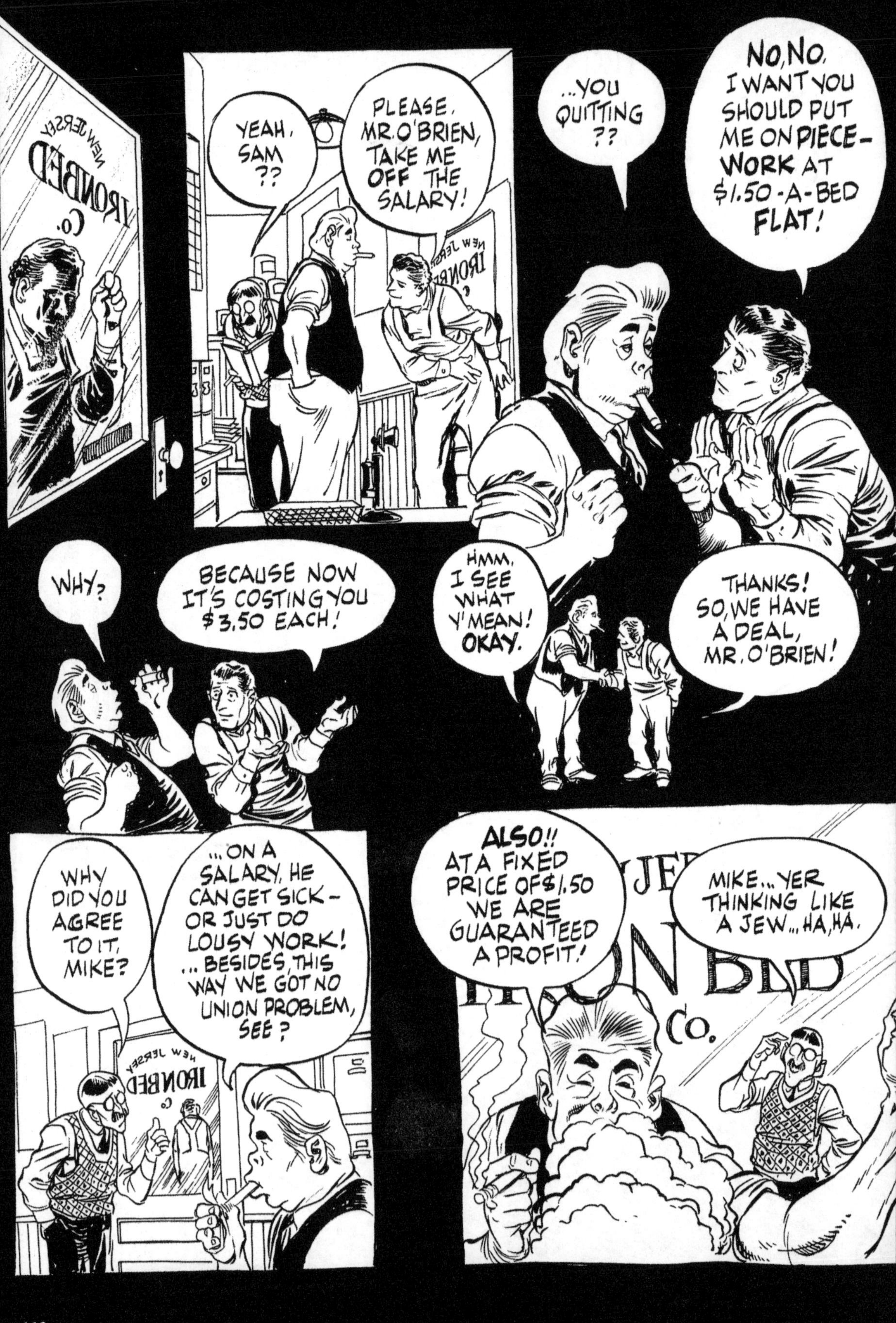
YEAH, SAM ??
PLEASE, MR. O'BRIEN, TAKE ME OFF THE SALARY!
...YOU QUITTING ??
NO, NO. I WANT YOU SHOULD PUT ME ON PIECE-WORK AT $1.50-A-BED FLAT!
WHY?
BECAUSE NOW IT'S COSTING YOU $3.50 EACH!
HMM, I SEE WHAT Y'MEAN! OKAY.
THANKS! SO, WE HAVE A DEAL, MR. O'BRIEN!
WHY DID YOU AGREE TO IT, MIKE?
...ON A SALARY, HE CAN GET SICK - OR JUST DO LOUSY WORK! ...BESIDES, THIS WAY WE GOT NO UNION PROBLEM, SEE?
ALSO!! AT A FIXED PRICE OF $1.50 WE ARE GUARANTEED A PROFIT!
MIKE... YER THINKING LIKE A JEW... HA, HA.

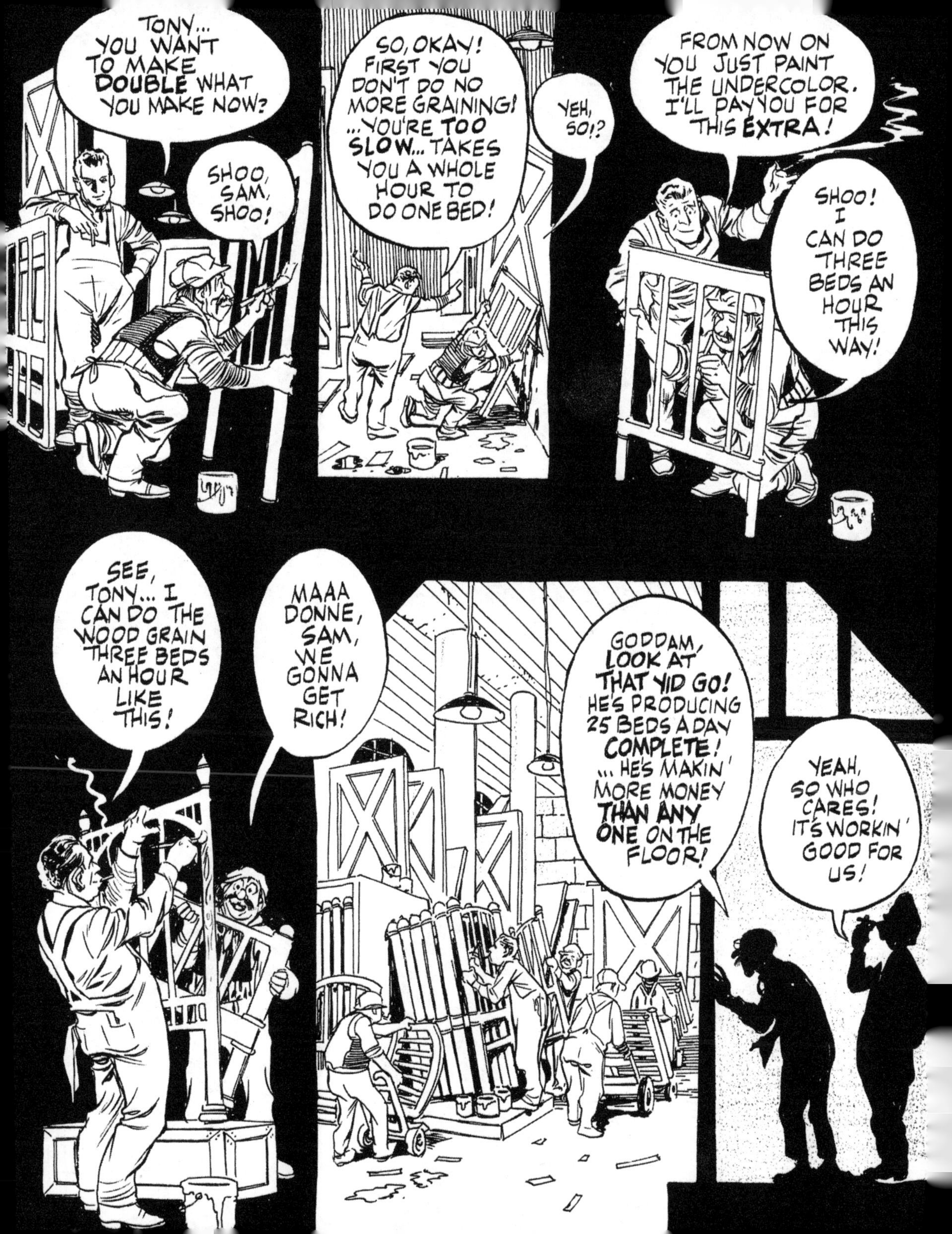
TONY... YOU WANT TO MAKE **DOUBLE** WHAT YOU MAKE NOW?
SHOO, SAM, SHOO!
SO, OKAY! FIRST YOU DON'T DO NO MORE GRAINING! ...YOU'RE **TOO SLOW**... TAKES YOU A WHOLE HOUR TO DO ONE BED!
YEH, SO!?
FROM NOW ON YOU JUST PAINT THE UNDERCOLOR. I'LL PAY YOU FOR THIS **EXTRA**!
SHOO! I CAN DO THREE BEDS AN HOUR THIS WAY!
SEE, TONY... I CAN DO THE WOOD GRAIN THREE BEDS AN HOUR LIKE THIS!
MAAA DONNE, SAM, WE GONNA GET RICH!
GODDAM, **LOOK AT THAT YID GO!** HE'S PRODUCING 25 BEDS A DAY **COMPLETE**! ... HE'S MAKIN' MORE MONEY **THAN ANY ONE** ON THE FLOOR!
YEAH, SO WHO CARES! IT'S WORKIN' GOOD FOR US!

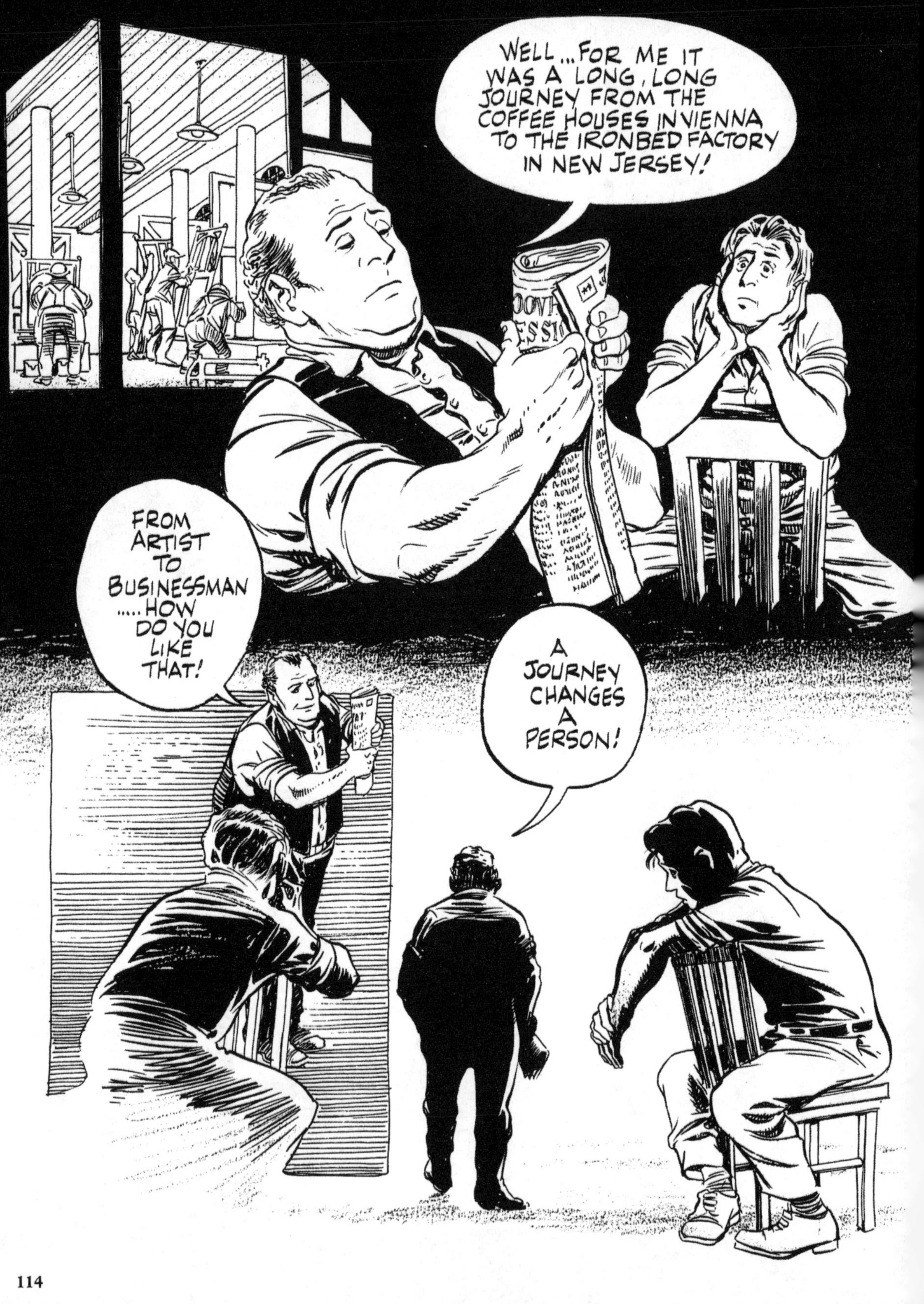
WELL ... FOR ME IT WAS A LONG, LONG JOURNEY FROM THE COFFEE HOUSES IN VIENNA TO THE IRONBED FACTORY IN NEW JERSEY!
FROM ARTIST TO BUSINESSMAN ..... HOW DO YOU LIKE THAT!
A JOURNEY CHANGES A PERSON!

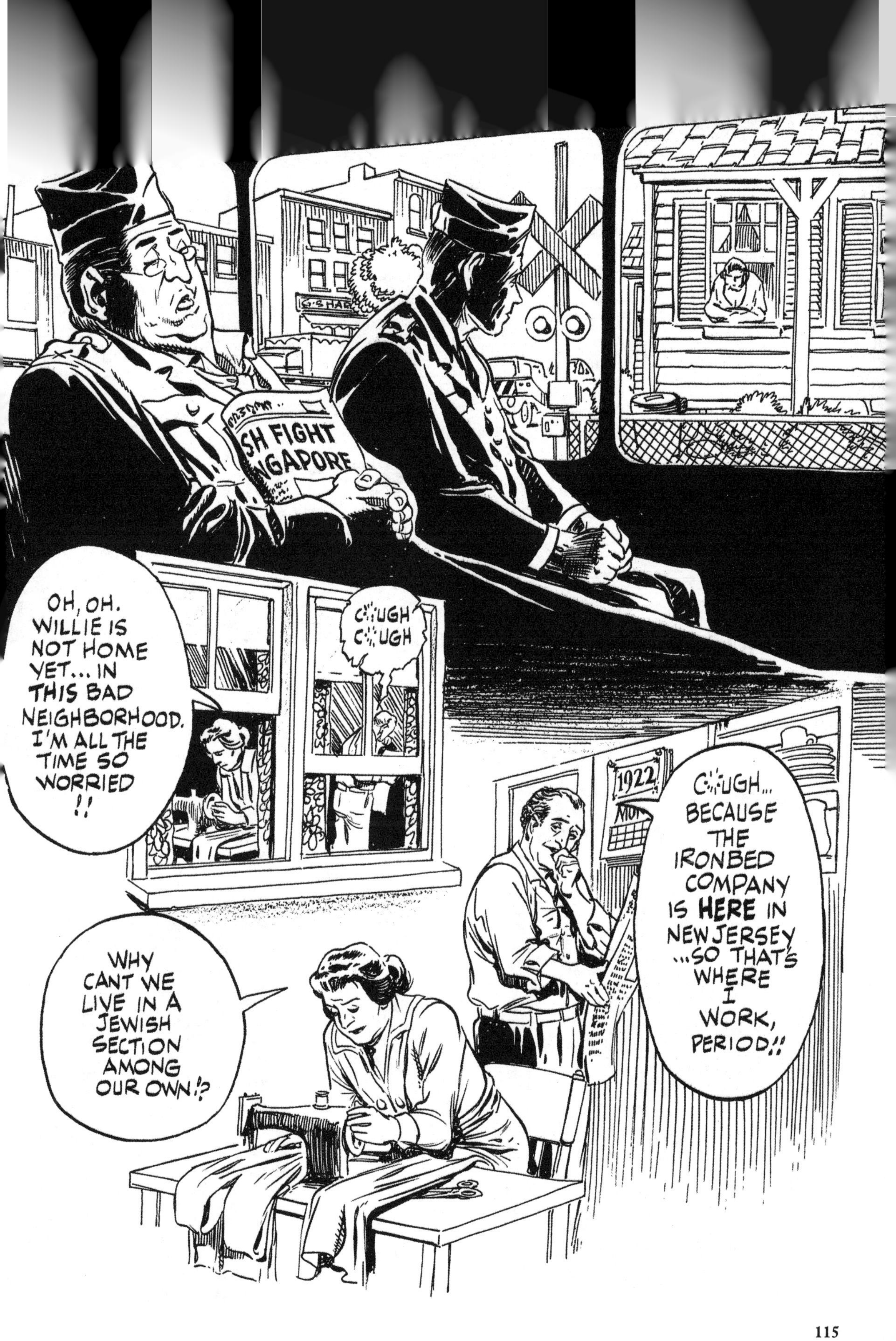
SH FIGHT
NGAPORE
OH, OH. WILLIE IS NOT HOME YET... IN THIS BAD NEIGHBORHOOD. I'M ALL THE TIME SO WORRIED!!
COUGH COUGH
1922
COUGH... BECAUSE THE IRONBED COMPANY IS HERE IN NEW JERSEY ...SO THAT'S WHERE I WORK, PERIOD!!
WHY CANT WE LIVE IN A JEWISH SECTION AMONG OUR OWN!?

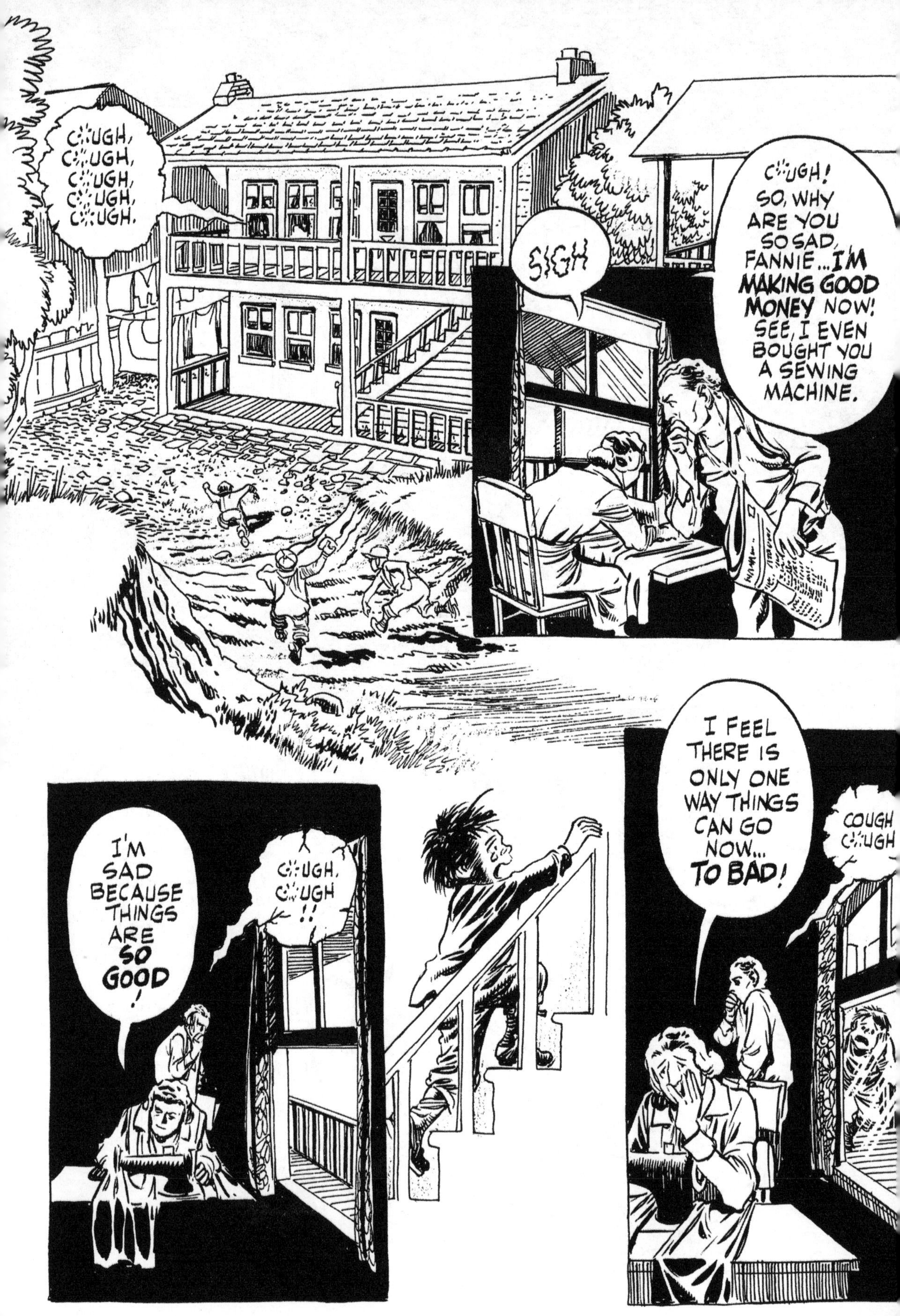
COUGH, COUGH, COUGH, COUGH, COUGH.
SIGH
COUGH! SO, WHY ARE YOU SO SAD, FANNIE... **I'M MAKING GOOD MONEY** NOW! SEE, I EVEN BOUGHT YOU A SEWING MACHINE.
I'M SAD BECAUSE THINGS ARE **SO GOOD**!
COUGH, COUGH!!
I FEEL THERE IS ONLY ONE WAY THINGS CAN GO NOW... **TO BAD**!
COUGH COUGH

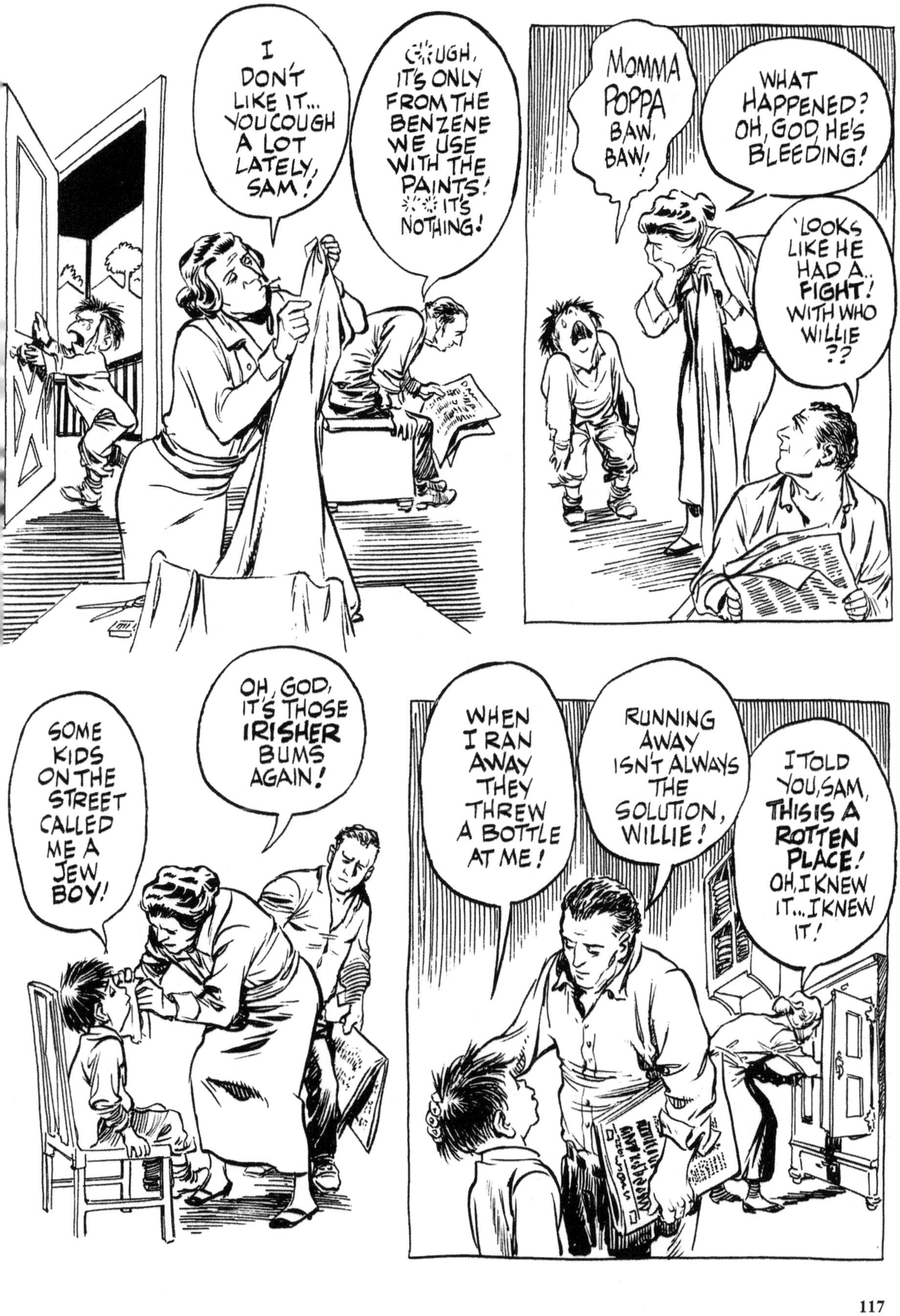
I DON'T LIKE IT... YOU COUGH A LOT LATELY, SAM!
COUGH, IT'S ONLY FROM THE BENZENE WE USE WITH THE PAINTS! IT'S NOTHING!
MOMMA POPPA BAW, BAW!
WHAT HAPPENED? OH, GOD, HE'S BLEEDING!
LOOKS LIKE HE HAD A FIGHT! WITH WHO WILLIE??
SOME KIDS ON THE STREET CALLED ME A JEW BOY!
OH, GOD, IT'S THOSE IRISHER BUMS AGAIN!
WHEN I RAN AWAY THEY THREW A BOTTLE AT ME!
RUNNING AWAY ISN'T ALWAYS THE SOLUTION, WILLIE!
I TOLD YOU, SAM, THIS IS A ROTTEN PLACE! OH, I KNEW IT... I KNEW IT!

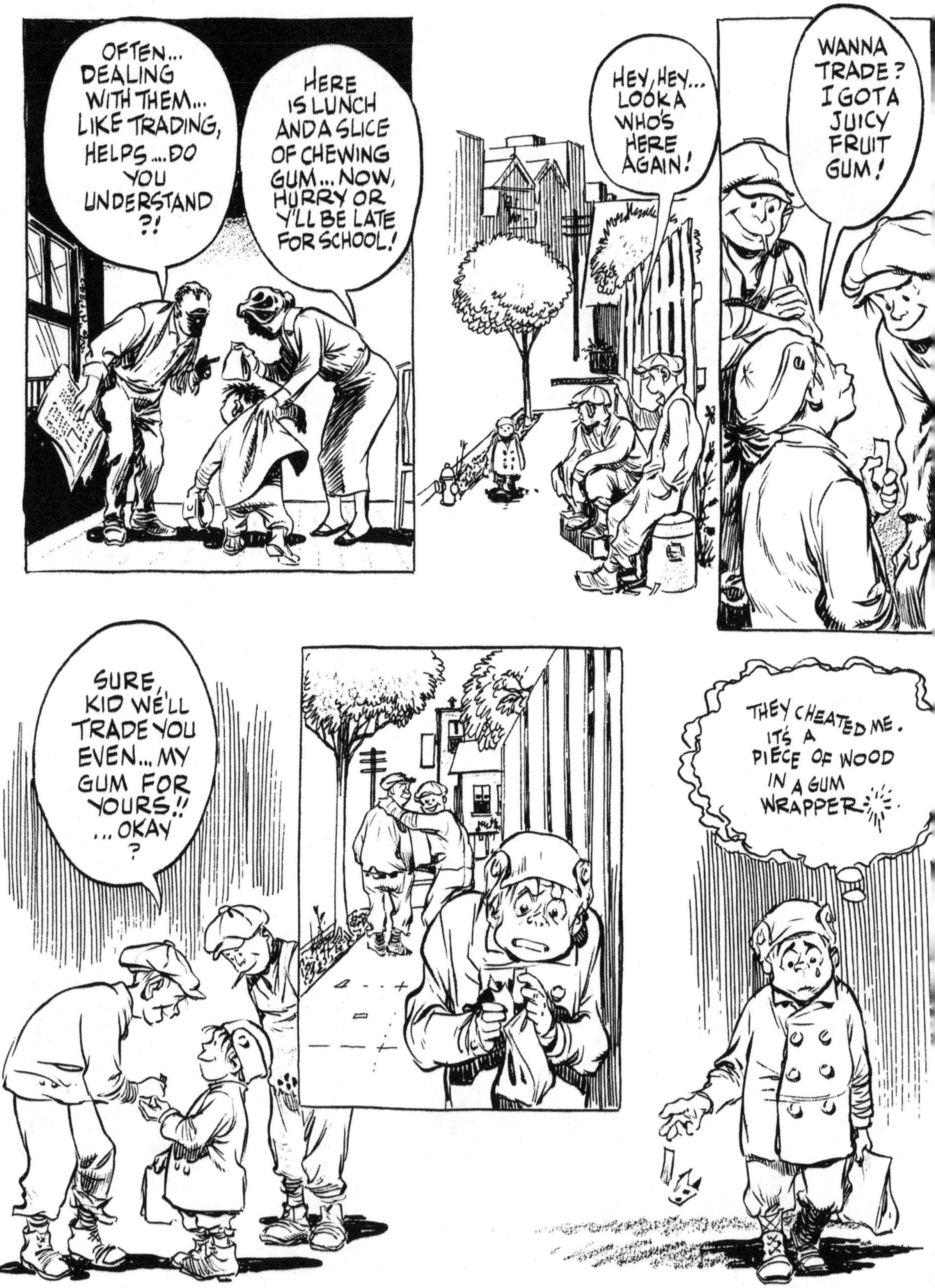
OFTEN... DEALING WITH THEM... LIKE TRADING, HELPS....DO YOU UNDERSTAND ?!
HERE IS LUNCH AND A SLICE OF CHEWING GUM... NOW, HURRY OR Y'LL BE LATE FOR SCHOOL!
HEY, HEY... LOOKA WHO'S HERE AGAIN!
WANNA TRADE? I GOTA JUICY FRUIT GUM!
SURE, KID WE'LL TRADE YOU EVEN... MY GUM FOR YOURS!! ...OKAY ?
THEY CHEATED ME. IT'S A PIECE OF WOOD IN A GUM WRAPPER

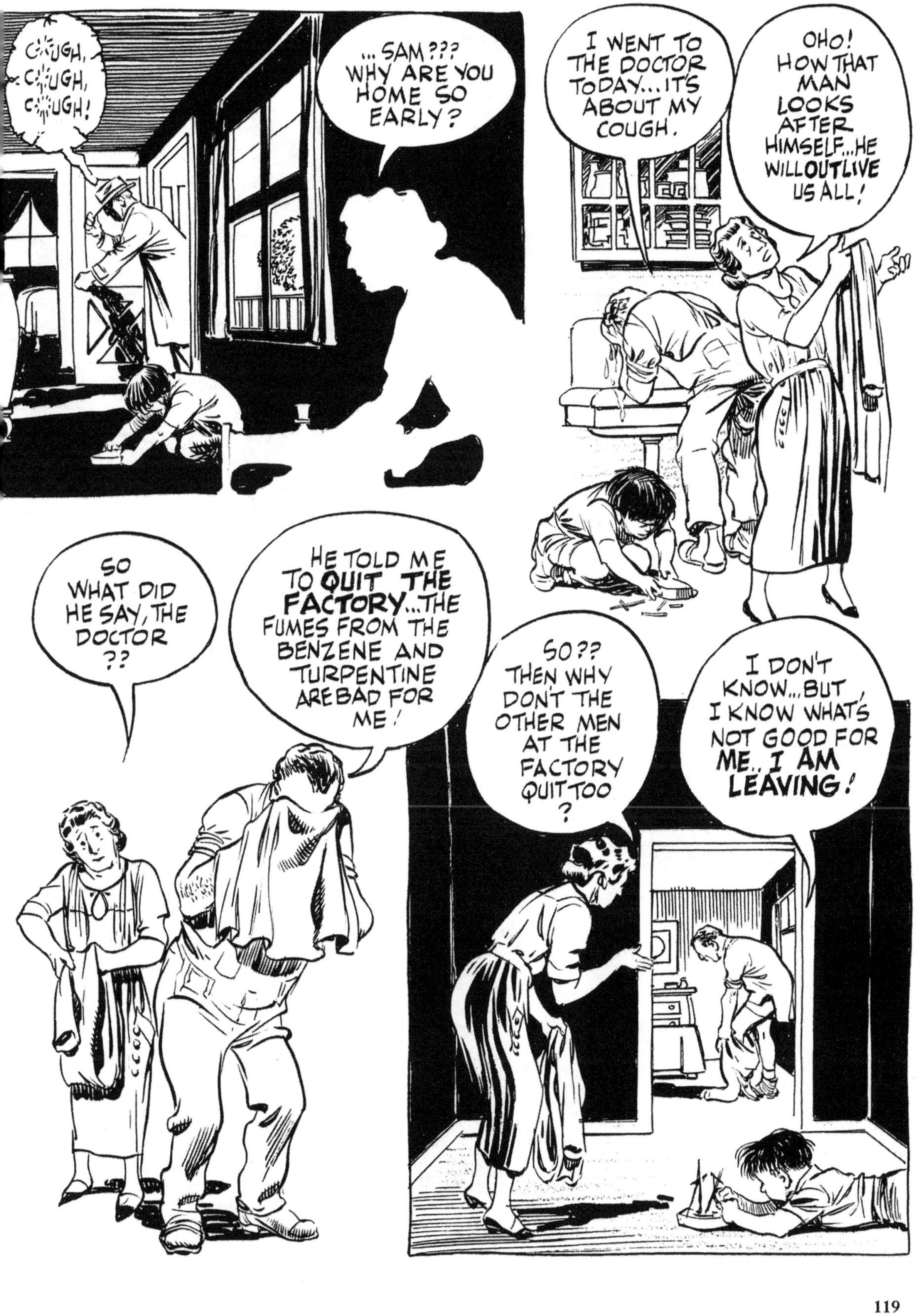
COUGH, COUGH, COUGH!
... SAM??? WHY ARE YOU HOME SO EARLY?
I WENT TO THE DOCTOR TODAY... IT'S ABOUT MY COUGH.
OHO! HOW THAT MAN LOOKS AFTER HIMSELF... HE WILL OUTLIVE US ALL!
SO WHAT DID HE SAY, THE DOCTOR ??
HE TOLD ME TO QUIT THE FACTORY... THE FUMES FROM THE BENZENE AND TURPENTINE ARE BAD FOR ME!
SO?? THEN WHY DON'T THE OTHER MEN AT THE FACTORY QUIT TOO ?
I DON'T KNOW... BUT I KNOW WHAT'S NOT GOOD FOR ME.. I AM LEAVING!

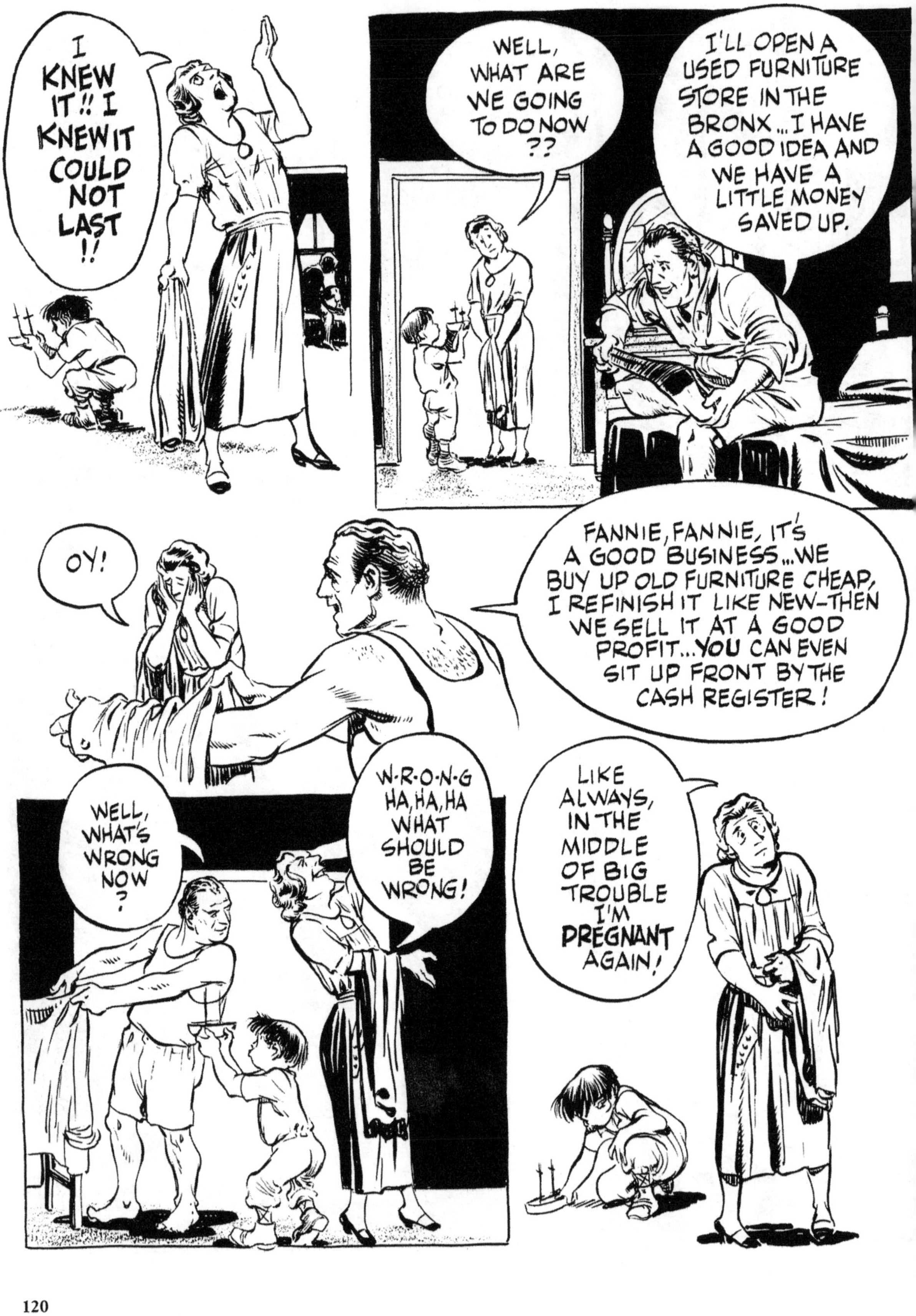
I KNEW IT!! I KNEW IT COULD NOT LAST!!
WELL, WHAT ARE WE GOING TO DO NOW??
I'LL OPEN A USED FURNITURE STORE IN THE BRONX... I HAVE A GOOD IDEA AND WE HAVE A LITTLE MONEY SAVED UP.
OY!
FANNIE, FANNIE, IT'S A GOOD BUSINESS... WE BUY UP OLD FURNITURE CHEAP, I REFINISH IT LIKE NEW–THEN WE SELL IT AT A GOOD PROFIT... YOU CAN EVEN SIT UP FRONT BY THE CASH REGISTER!
WELL, WHAT'S WRONG NOW?
W-R-O-N-G HA, HA, HA WHAT SHOULD BE WRONG!
LIKE ALWAYS, IN THE MIDDLE OF BIG TROUBLE I'M PREGNANT AGAIN!

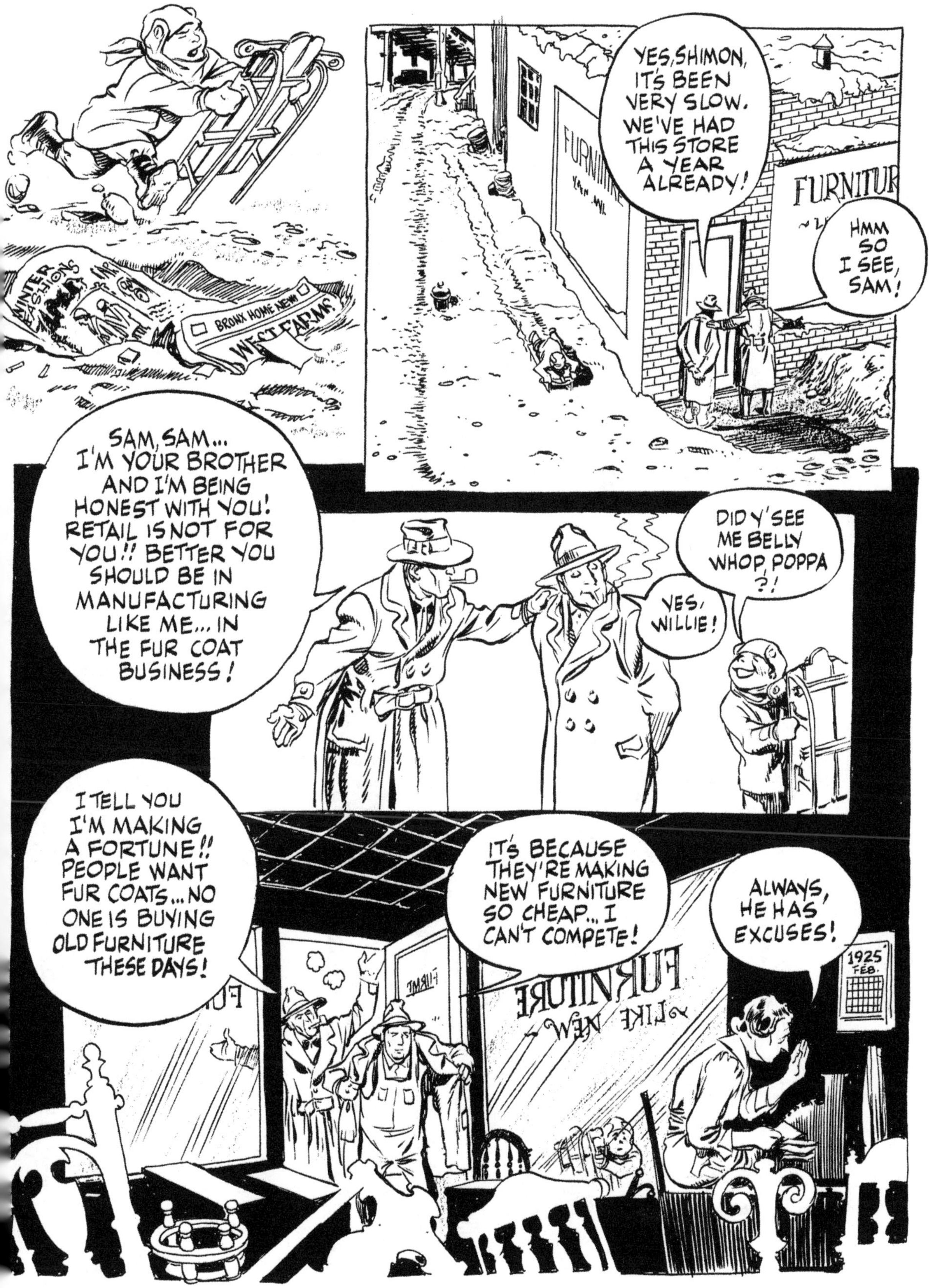
WINTER FASHIONS
BRONX HOME NEWS
WEST FARMS
YES, SHIMON, IT'S BEEN VERY SLOW. WE'VE HAD THIS STORE A YEAR ALREADY!
FURNITURE
HMM SO I SEE, SAM!
SAM, SAM... I'M YOUR BROTHER AND I'M BEING HONEST WITH YOU! RETAIL IS NOT FOR YOU!! BETTER YOU SHOULD BE IN MANUFACTURING LIKE ME... IN THE FUR COAT BUSINESS!
YES, WILLIE!
DID Y'SEE ME BELLY WHOP, POPPA ?!
I TELL YOU I'M MAKING A FORTUNE!! PEOPLE WANT FUR COATS... NO ONE IS BUYING OLD FURNITURE THESE DAYS!
IT'S BECAUSE THEY'RE MAKING NEW FURNITURE SO CHEAP... I CAN'T COMPETE!
ALWAYS, HE HAS EXCUSES!
1925 FEB.
FURNITURE LIKE NEW

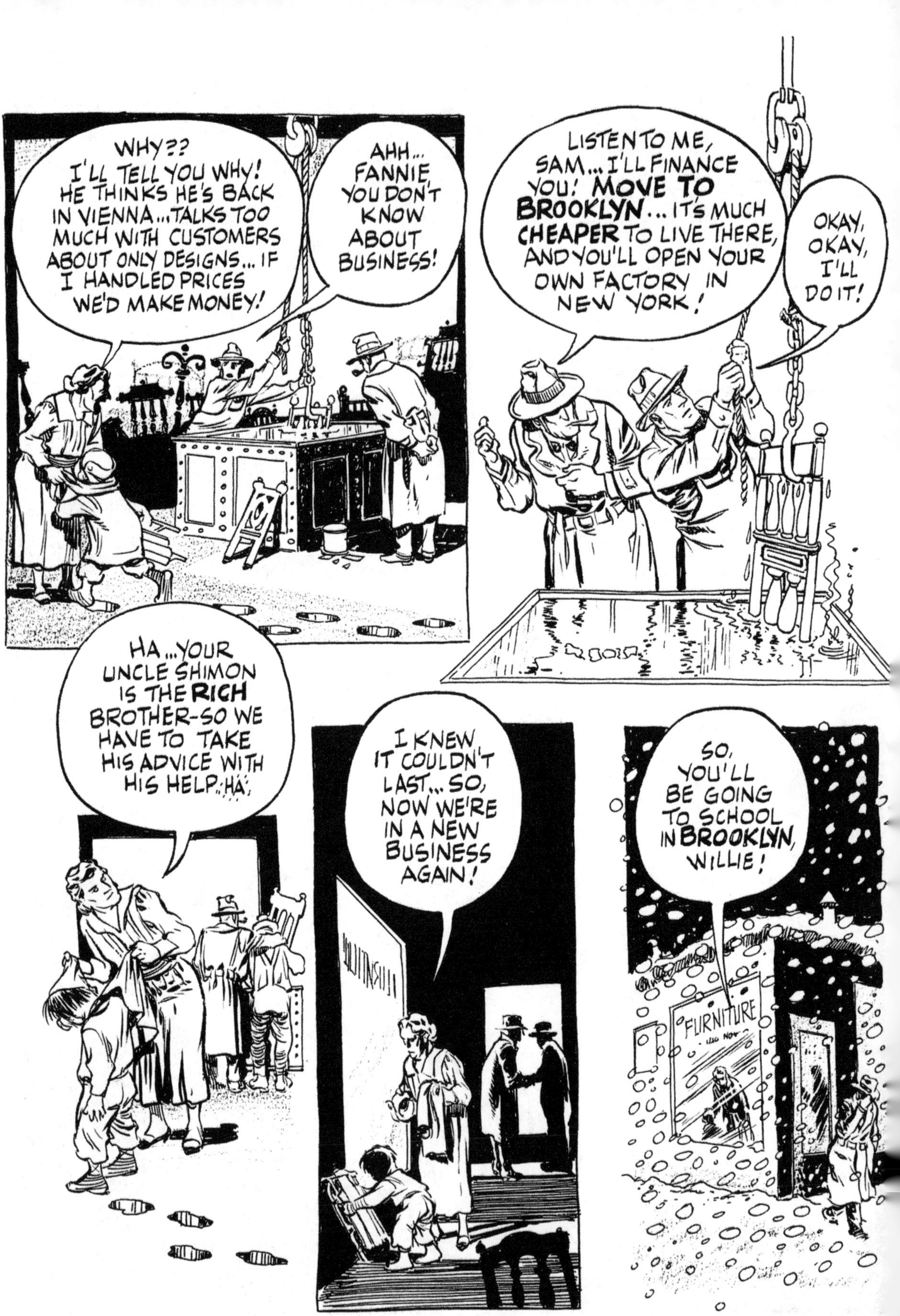

WHY?? I'LL TELL YOU WHY! HE THINKS HE'S BACK IN VIENNA...TALKS TOO MUCH WITH CUSTOMERS ABOUT ONLY DESIGNS... IF I HANDLED PRICES WE'D MAKE MONEY!
AHH... FANNIE, YOU DON'T KNOW ABOUT BUSINESS!
LISTEN TO ME, SAM... I'LL FINANCE YOU! MOVE TO BROOKLYN... IT'S MUCH CHEAPER TO LIVE THERE, AND YOU'LL OPEN YOUR OWN FACTORY IN NEW YORK!
OKAY, OKAY, I'LL DO IT!
HA...YOUR UNCLE SHIMON IS THE RICH BROTHER-SO WE HAVE TO TAKE HIS ADVICE WITH HIS HELP...HA
I KNEW IT COULDN'T LAST... SO, NOW WE'RE IN A NEW BUSINESS AGAIN!
SO, YOU'LL BE GOING TO SCHOOL IN BROOKLYN, WILLIE!
FURNITURE

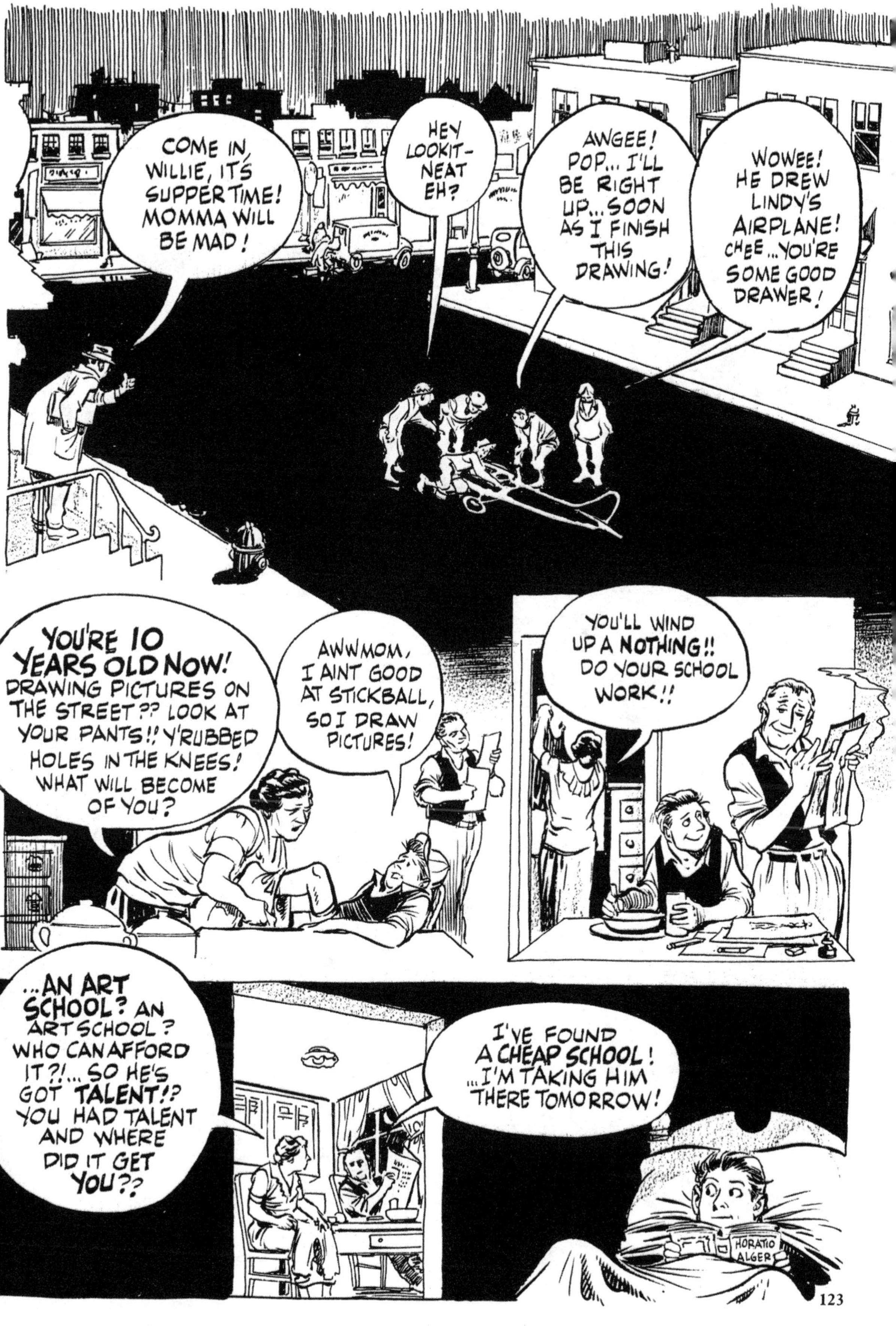
COME IN, WILLIE, IT'S SUPPERTIME! MOMMA WILL BE MAD!
HEY LOOKIT- NEAT EH?
AWGEE! POP... I'LL BE RIGHT UP... SOON AS I FINISH THIS DRAWING!
WOWEE! HE DREW LINDY'S AIRPLANE! CHEE...YOU'RE SOME GOOD DRAWER!
YOU'RE 10 YEARS OLD NOW! DRAWING PICTURES ON THE STREET?? LOOK AT YOUR PANTS!! Y'RUBBED HOLES IN THE KNEES! WHAT WILL BECOME OF YOU?
AWWMOM, I AINT GOOD AT STICKBALL, SO I DRAW PICTURES!
YOU'LL WIND UP A NOTHING!! DO YOUR SCHOOL WORK!!
...AN ART SCHOOL? AN ART SCHOOL? WHO CAN AFFORD IT?!... SO HE'S GOT TALENT!? YOU HAD TALENT AND WHERE DID IT GET YOU??
I'VE FOUND A CHEAP SCHOOL! ...I'M TAKING HIM THERE TOMORROW!
HORATIO ALGER

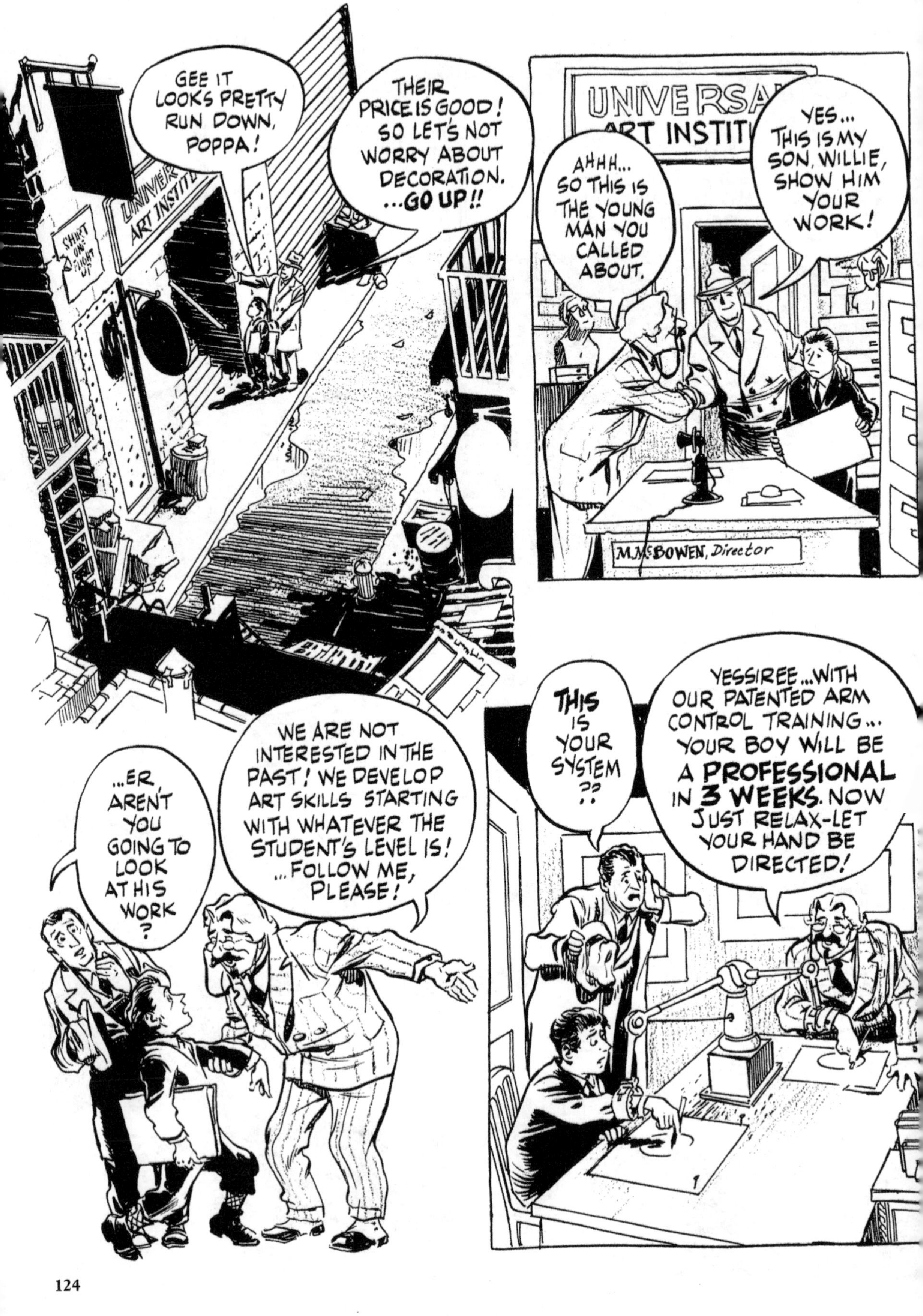
GEE IT LOOKS PRETTY RUN DOWN, POPPA!
THEIR PRICE IS GOOD! SO LET'S NOT WORRY ABOUT DECORATION. ...**GO UP!!**
UNIVERSA
ART INSTIT
AHHH... SO THIS IS THE YOUNG MAN YOU CALLED ABOUT.
YES... THIS IS MY SON, WILLIE, SHOW HIM YOUR WORK!
M.M. McBOWEN, Director
...ER, AREN'T YOU GOING TO LOOK AT HIS WORK?
WE ARE NOT INTERESTED IN THE PAST! WE DEVELOP ART SKILLS STARTING WITH WHATEVER THE STUDENT'S LEVEL IS! ...FOLLOW ME, PLEASE!
THIS IS YOUR SYSTEM??
YESSIREE...WITH OUR PATENTED ARM CONTROL TRAINING... YOUR BOY WILL BE A **PROFESSIONAL** IN **3 WEEKS**. NOW JUST RELAX-LET YOUR HAND BE DIRECTED!

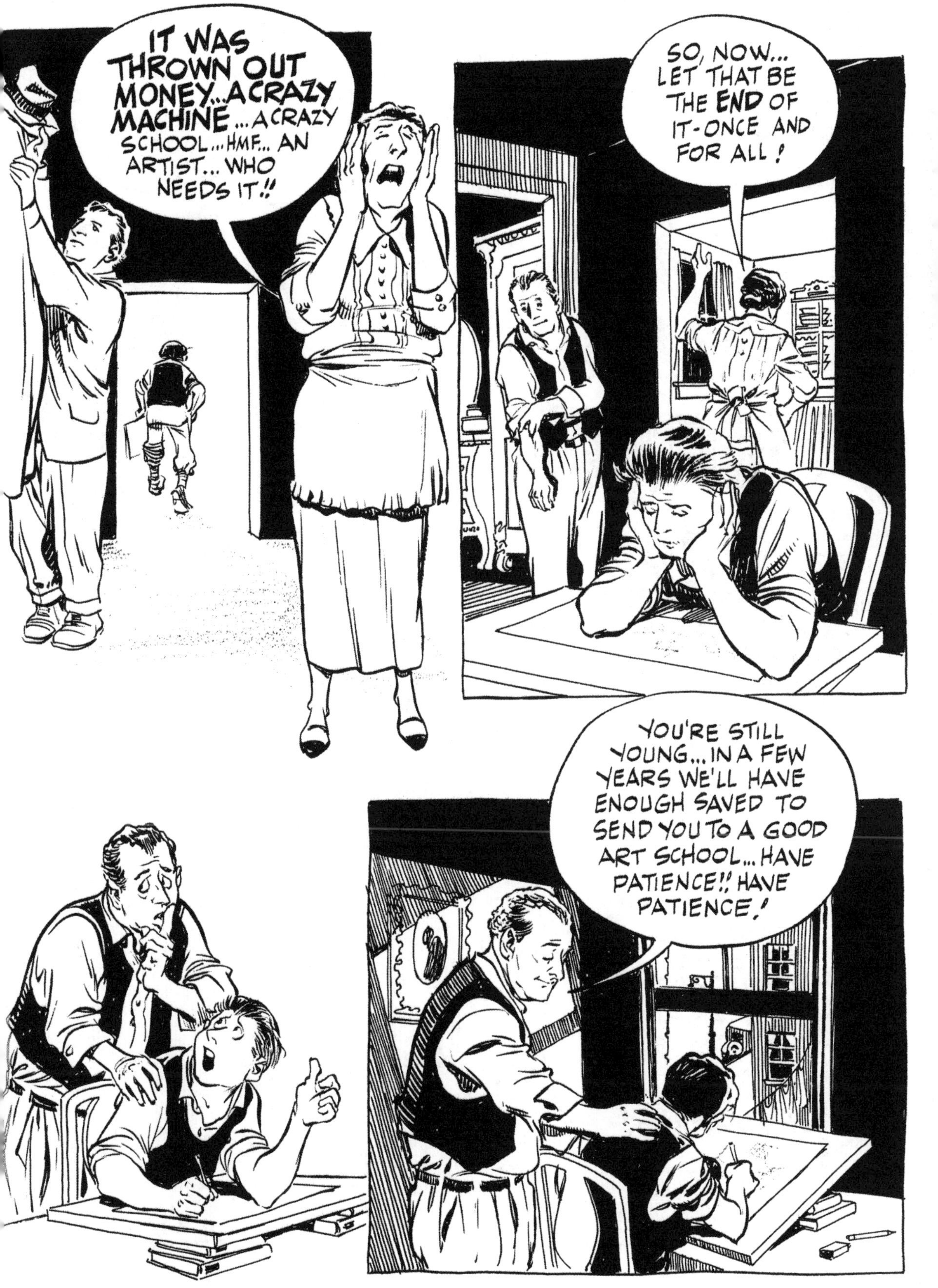
IT WAS THROWN OUT MONEY...A CRAZY MACHINE ...A CRAZY SCHOOL...HMF... AN ARTIST... WHO NEEDS IT!!
SO, NOW... LET THAT BE THE END OF IT-ONCE AND FOR ALL!
YOU'RE STILL YOUNG...IN A FEW YEARS WE'LL HAVE ENOUGH SAVED TO SEND YOU TO A GOOD ART SCHOOL... HAVE PATIENCE!! HAVE PATIENCE!

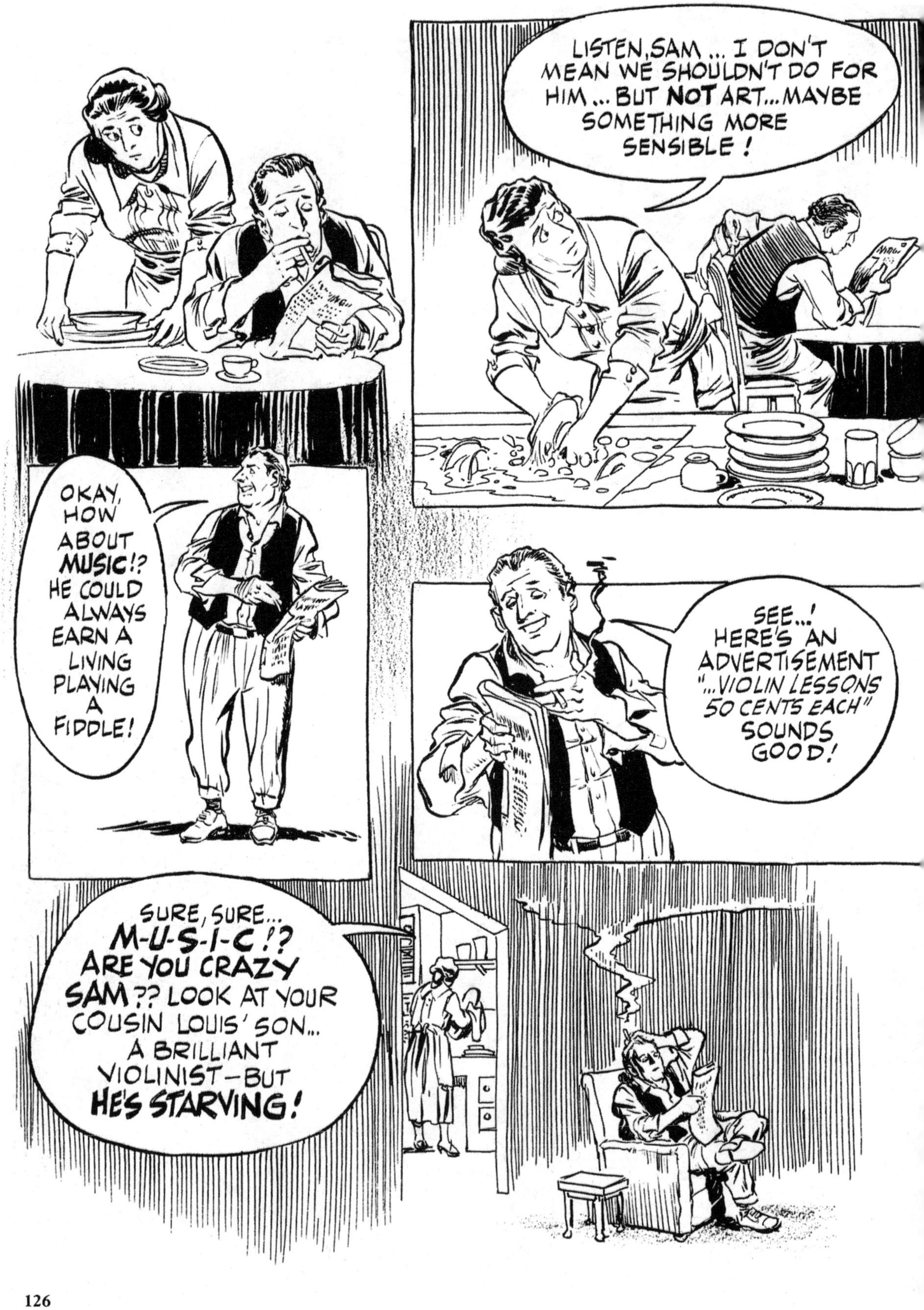
LISTEN, SAM ... I DON'T MEAN WE SHOULDN'T DO FOR HIM ... BUT NOT ART... MAYBE SOMETHING MORE SENSIBLE!
OKAY, HOW ABOUT MUSIC!? HE COULD ALWAYS EARN A LIVING PLAYING A FIDDLE!
SEE..! HERE'S AN ADVERTISEMENT "...VIOLIN LESSONS 50 CENTS EACH" SOUNDS GOOD!
SURE, SURE... M-U-S-I-C!? ARE YOU CRAZY SAM?? LOOK AT YOUR COUSIN LOUIS' SON... A BRILLIANT VIOLINIST—BUT HE'S STARVING!

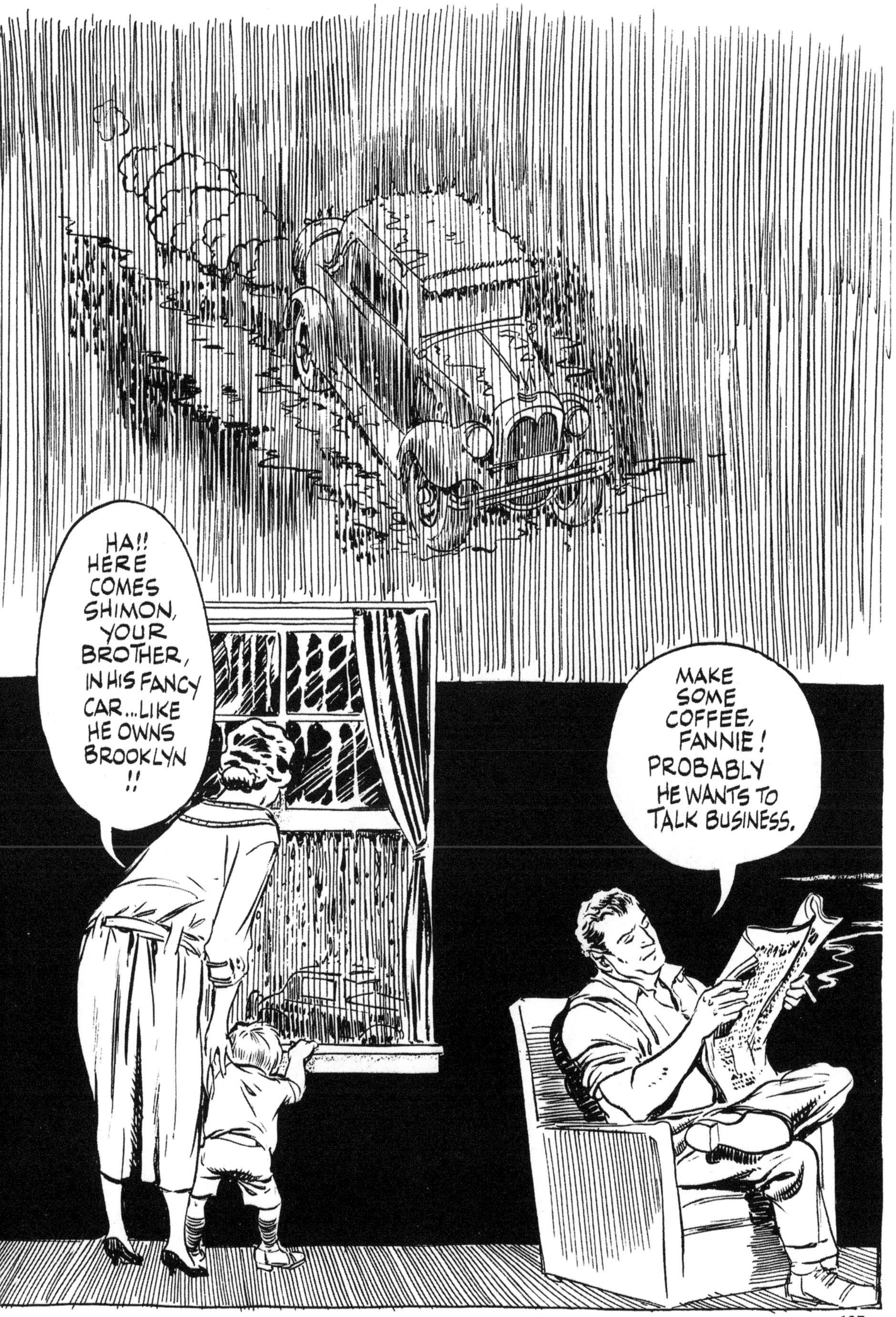
HA!! HERE COMES SHIMON, YOUR BROTHER, IN HIS FANCY CAR...LIKE HE OWNS BROOKLYN !!
MAKE SOME COFFEE, FANNIE! PROBABLY HE WANTS TO TALK BUSINESS.

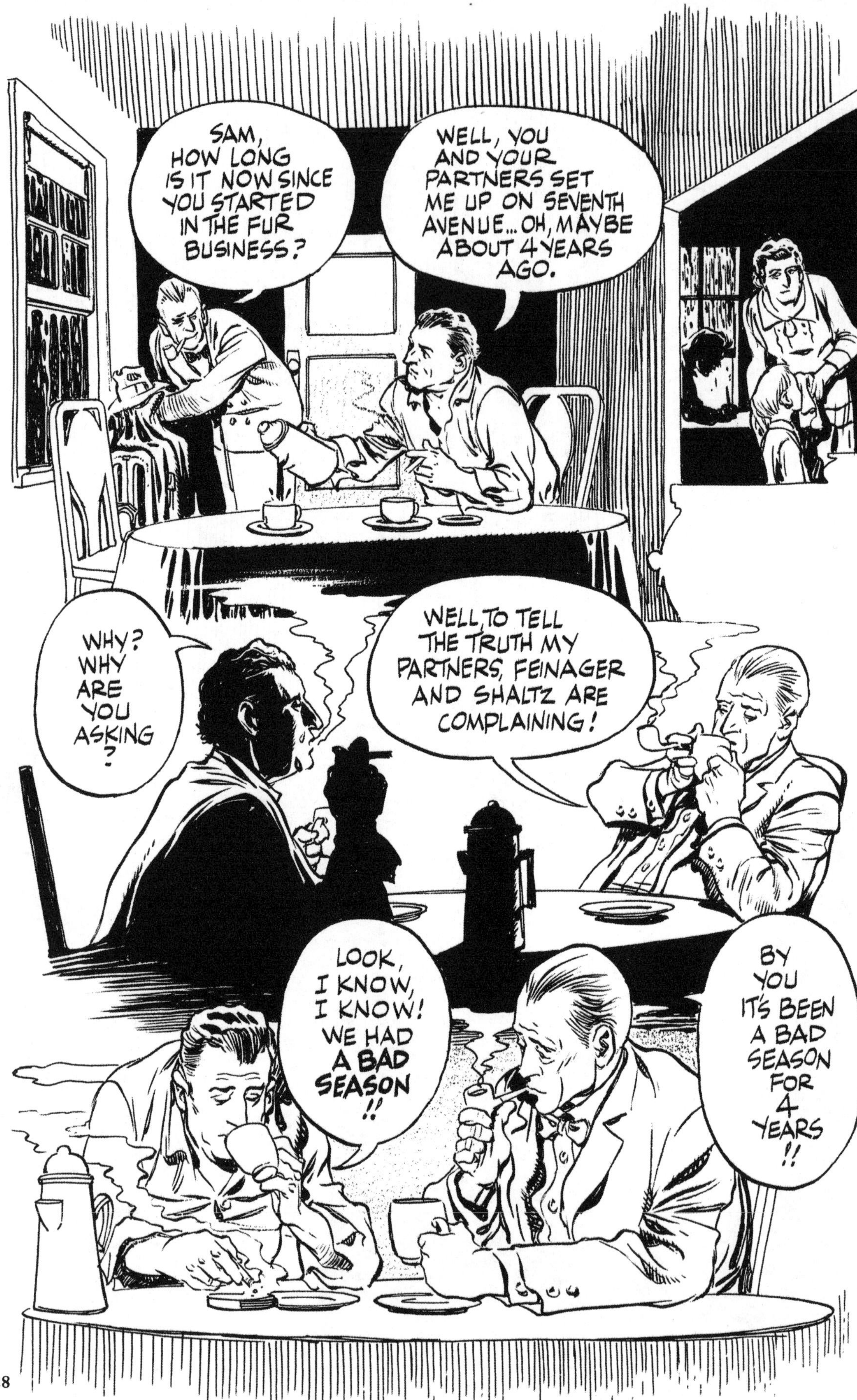
SAM, HOW LONG IS IT NOW SINCE YOU STARTED IN THE FUR BUSINESS?
WELL, YOU AND YOUR PARTNERS SET ME UP ON SEVENTH AVENUE... OH, MAYBE ABOUT 4 YEARS AGO.
WHY? WHY ARE YOU ASKING?
WELL, TO TELL THE TRUTH MY PARTNERS, FEINAGER AND SHALTZ ARE COMPLAINING!
LOOK, I KNOW, I KNOW! WE HAD **A BAD SEASON**!!
BY YOU IT'S BEEN A BAD SEASON FOR 4 YEARS!!

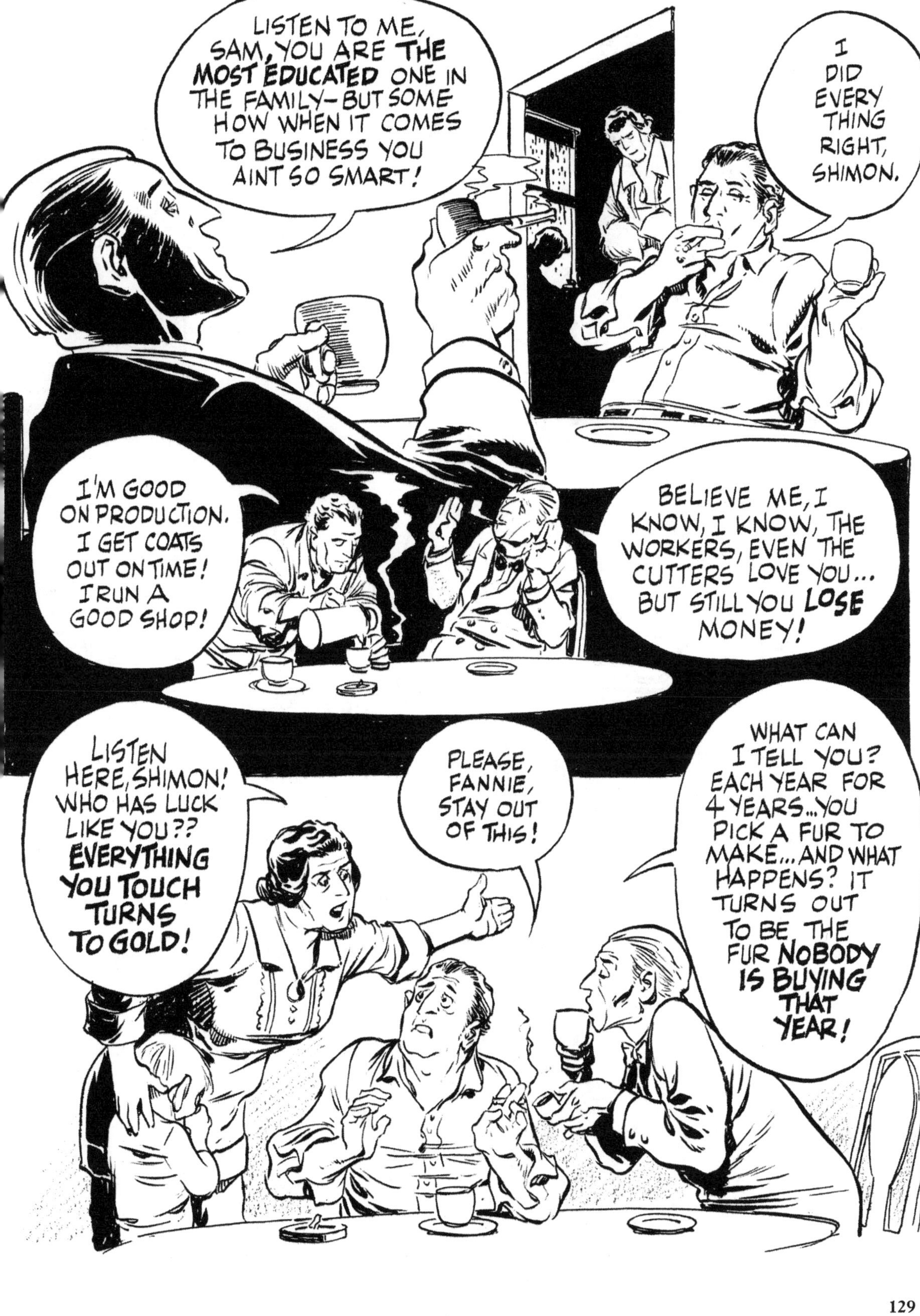
LISTEN TO ME, SAM, YOU ARE **THE MOST EDUCATED** ONE IN THE FAMILY—BUT SOME HOW WHEN IT COMES TO BUSINESS YOU AINT SO SMART!
I DID EVERY THING RIGHT, SHIMON.
I'M GOOD ON PRODUCTION. I GET COATS OUT ON TIME! I RUN A GOOD SHOP!
BELIEVE ME, I KNOW, I KNOW, THE WORKERS, EVEN THE CUTTERS LOVE YOU... BUT STILL YOU **LOSE** MONEY!
LISTEN HERE, SHIMON! WHO HAS LUCK LIKE YOU?? **EVERYTHING YOU TOUCH TURNS TO GOLD!**
PLEASE, FANNIE, STAY OUT OF THIS!
WHAT CAN I TELL YOU? EACH YEAR FOR 4 YEARS... YOU PICK A FUR TO MAKE... AND WHAT HAPPENS? IT TURNS OUT TO BE THE FUR **NOBODY IS BUYING THAT YEAR!**

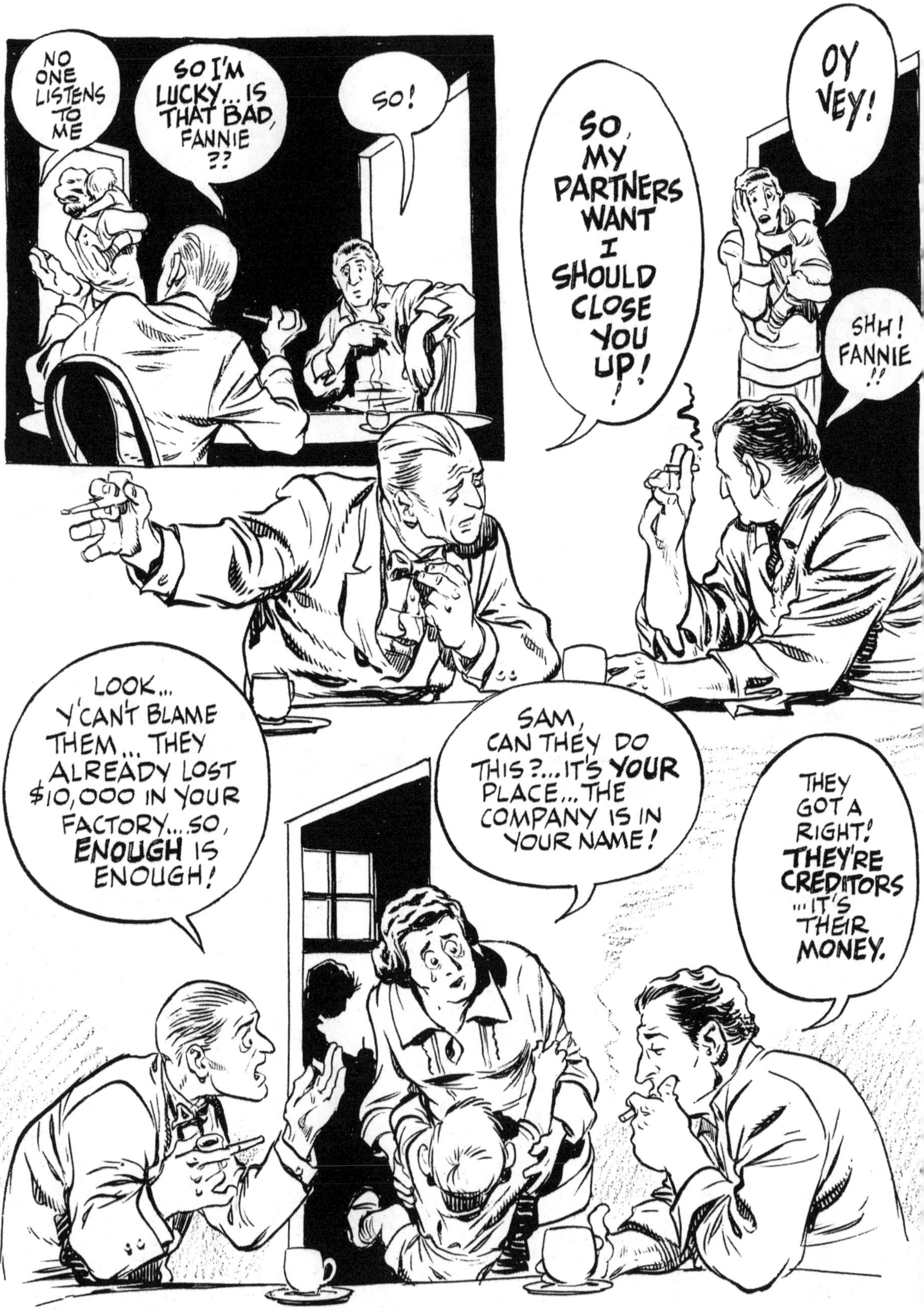
NO ONE LISTENS TO ME
SO I'M LUCKY... IS THAT BAD, FANNIE ??
SO!
SO, MY PARTNERS WANT I SHOULD CLOSE YOU UP!
OY VEY!
SHH! FANNIE !!
LOOK... Y'CAN'T BLAME THEM... THEY ALREADY LOST $10,000 IN YOUR FACTORY... SO, ENOUGH IS ENOUGH!
SAM, CAN THEY DO THIS?... IT'S YOUR PLACE... THE COMPANY IS IN YOUR NAME!
THEY GOT A RIGHT! THEY'RE CREDITORS ... IT'S THEIR MONEY.

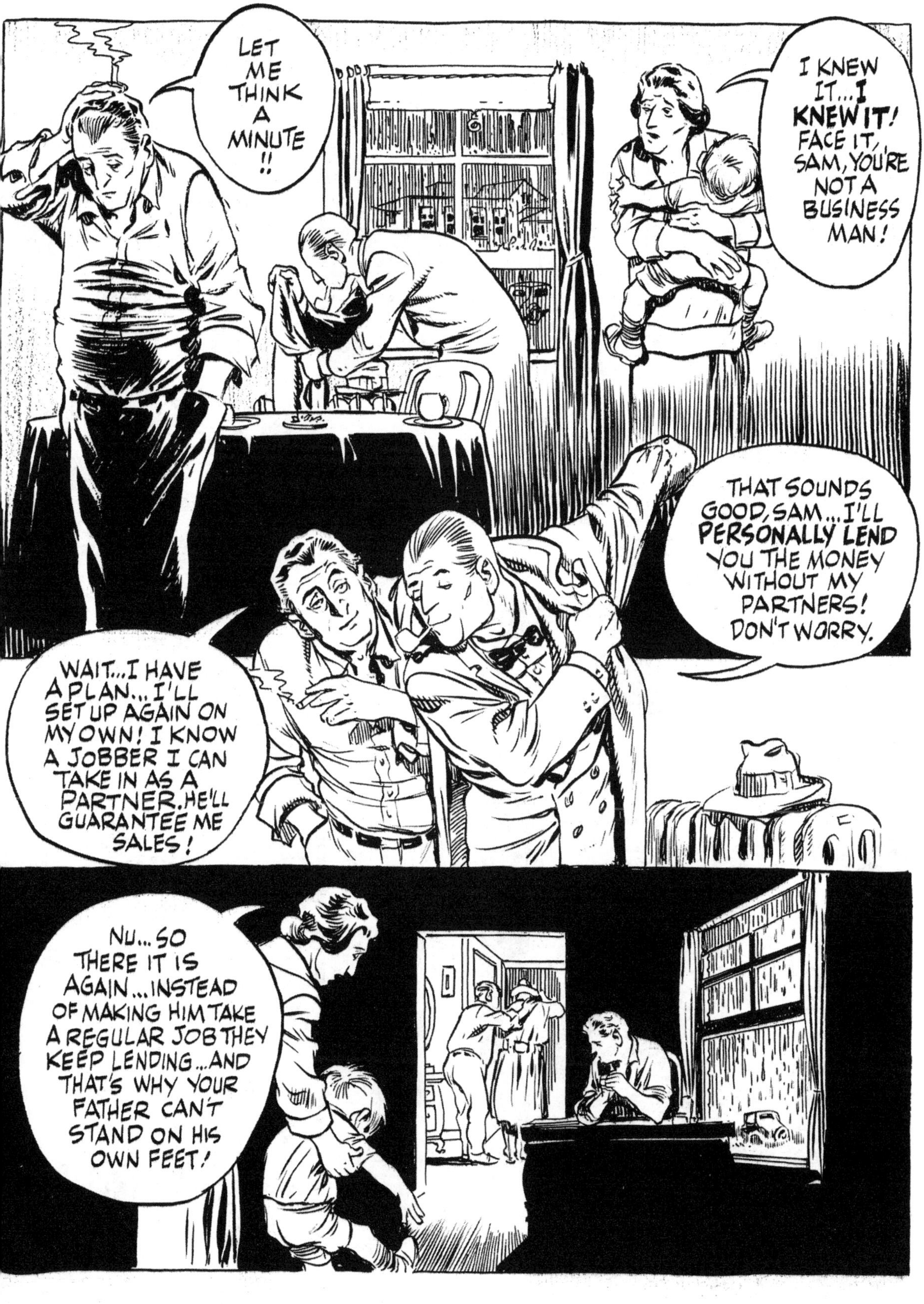
LET ME THINK A MINUTE !!
I KNEW IT... I KNEW IT! FACE IT, SAM, YOU'RE NOT A BUSINESS MAN!
WAIT... I HAVE A PLAN... I'LL SET UP AGAIN ON MY OWN! I KNOW A JOBBER I CAN TAKE IN AS A PARTNER. HE'LL GUARANTEE ME SALES!
THAT SOUNDS GOOD, SAM... I'LL PERSONALLY LEND YOU THE MONEY WITHOUT MY PARTNERS! DON'T WORRY.
NU... SO THERE IT IS AGAIN... INSTEAD OF MAKING HIM TAKE A REGULAR JOB THEY KEEP LENDING... AND THAT'S WHY YOUR FATHER CAN'T STAND ON HIS OWN FEET!

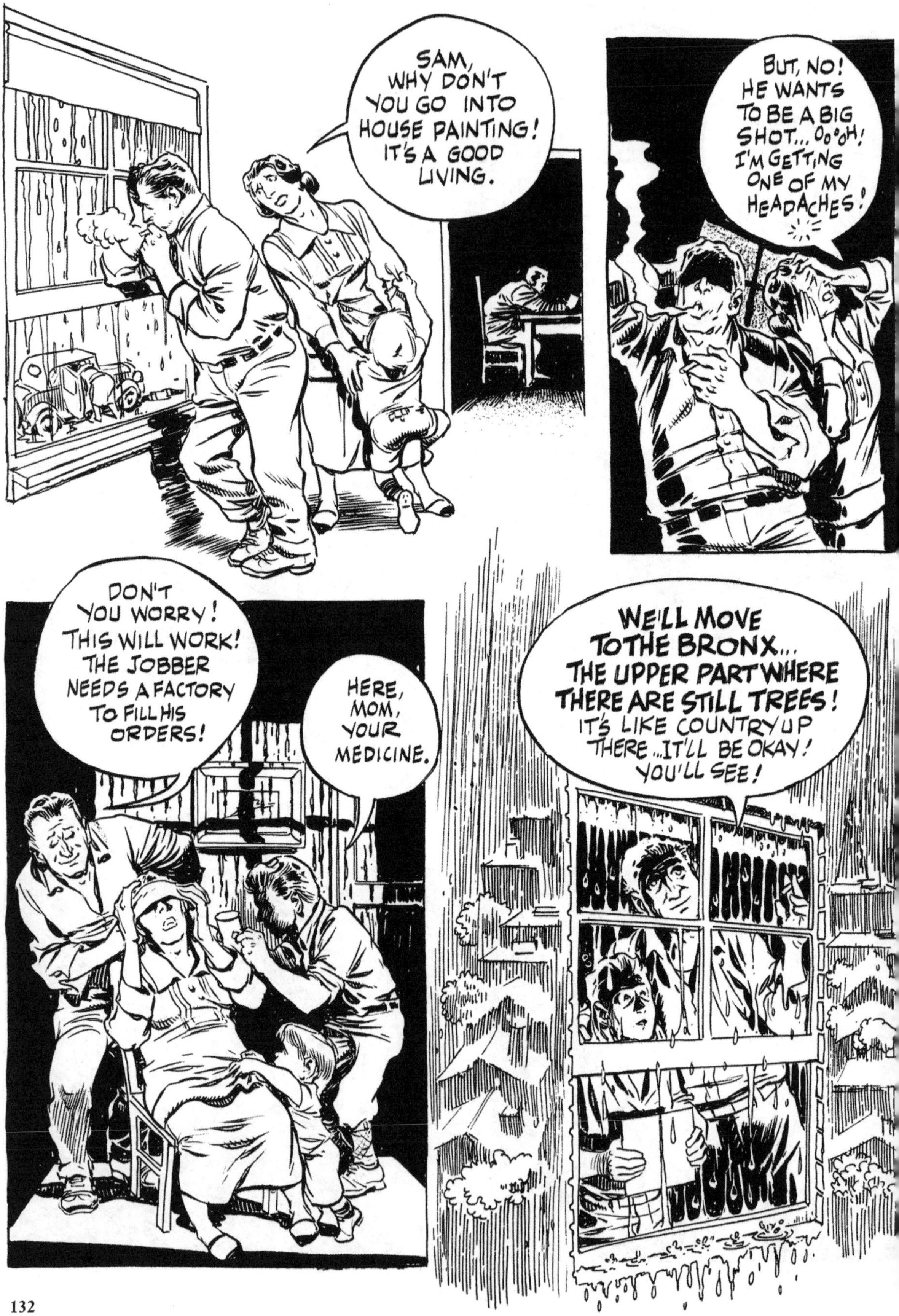
SAM, WHY DON'T YOU GO INTO HOUSE PAINTING! IT'S A GOOD LIVING.
BUT, NO! HE WANTS TO BE A BIG SHOT... OoooH! I'M GETTING ONE OF MY HEADACHES!
DON'T YOU WORRY! THIS WILL WORK! THE JOBBER NEEDS A FACTORY TO FILL HIS ORDERS!
HERE, MOM, YOUR MEDICINE.
WE'LL MOVE TO THE BRONX... THE UPPER PART WHERE THERE ARE STILL TREES! IT'S LIKE COUNTRY UP THERE ...IT'LL BE OKAY! YOU'LL SEE!

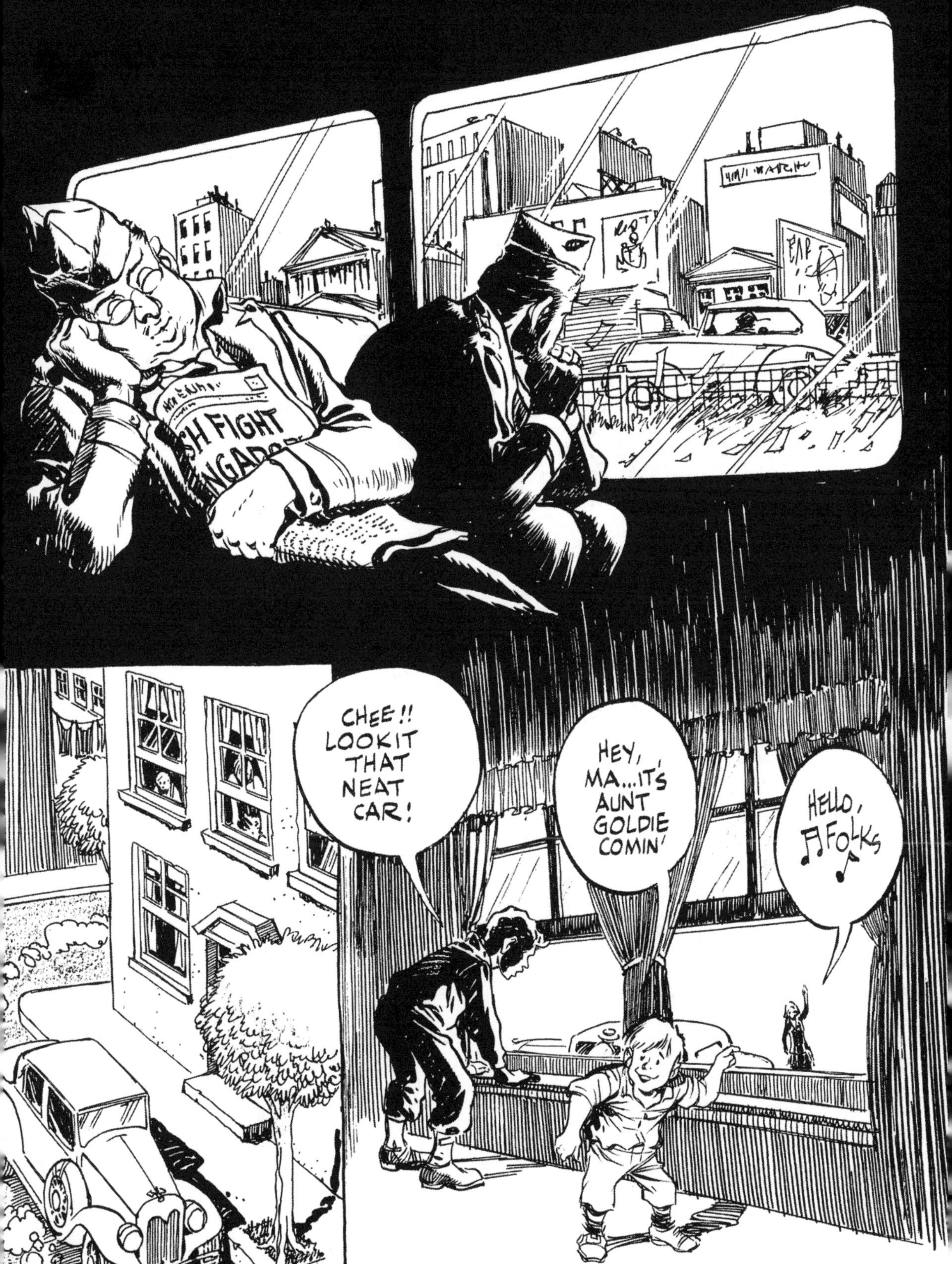
CHEE!! LOOKIT THAT NEAT CAR!
HEY, MA...IT'S AUNT GOLDIE COMIN'
HELLO, FOLKS

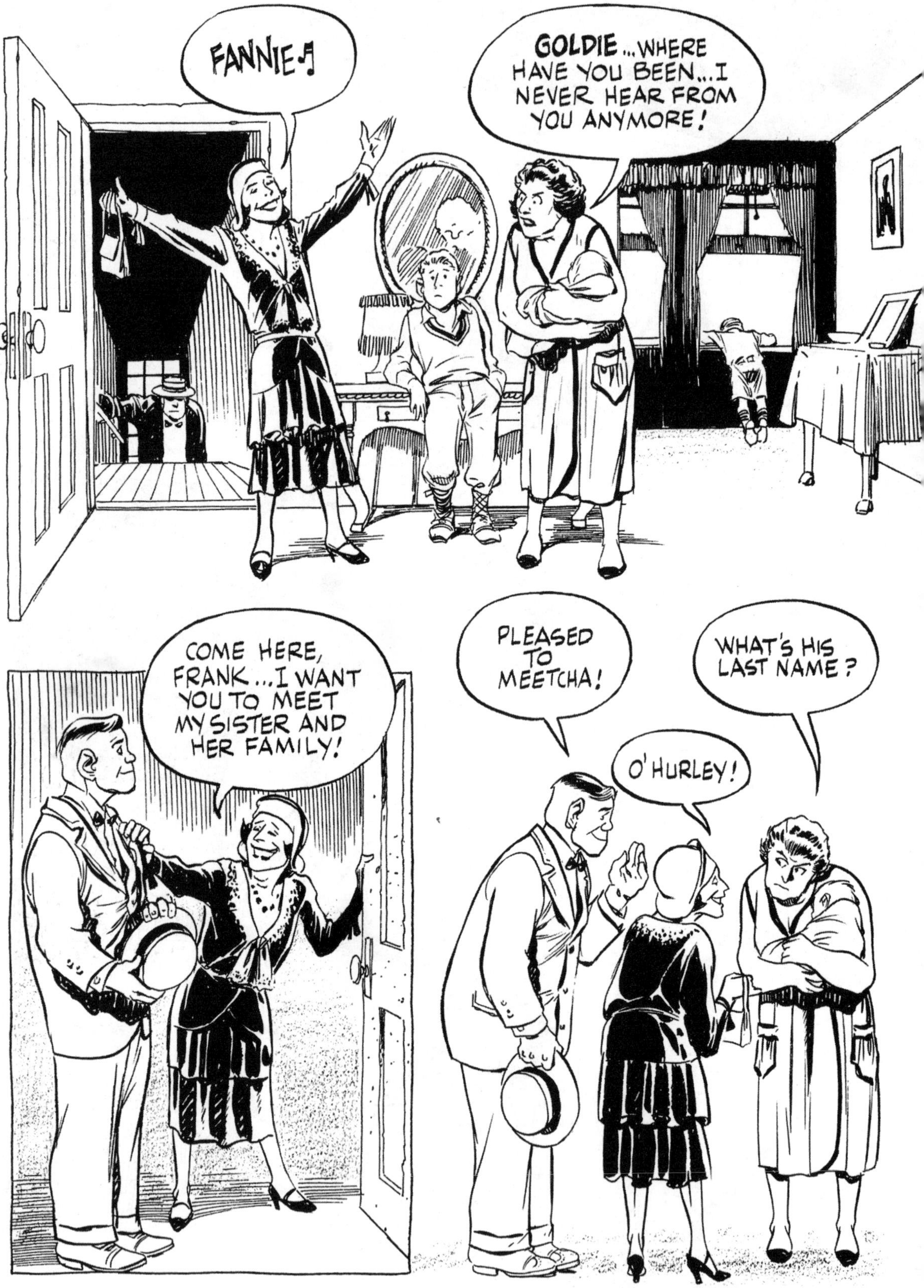
FANNIE!
GOLDIE...WHERE HAVE YOU BEEN...I NEVER HEAR FROM YOU ANYMORE!
COME HERE, FRANK...I WANT YOU TO MEET MY SISTER AND HER FAMILY!
PLEASED TO MEETCHA!
WHAT'S HIS LAST NAME?
O'HURLEY!

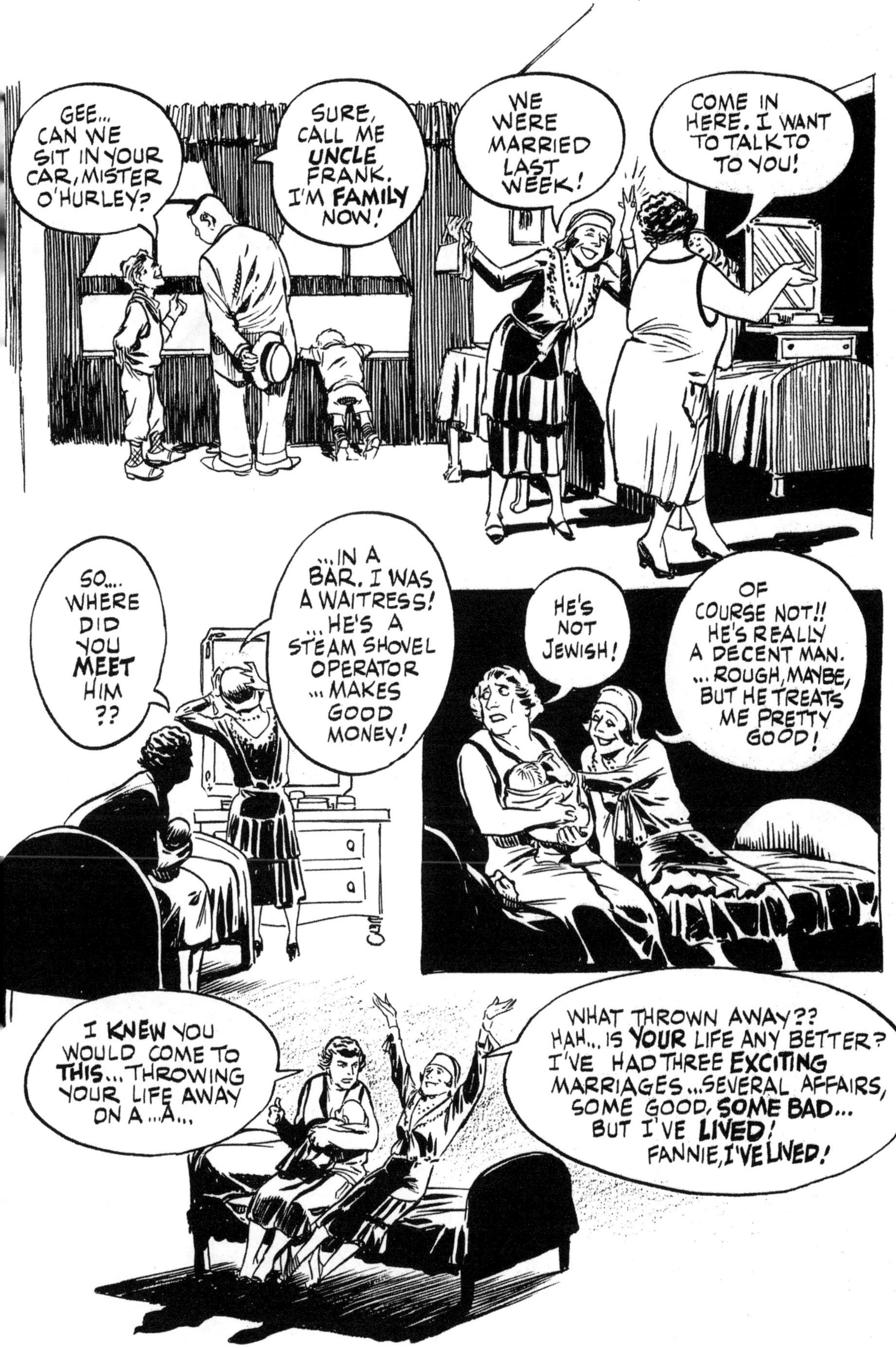
GEE... CAN WE SIT IN YOUR CAR, MISTER O'HURLEY?
SURE, CALL ME UNCLE FRANK. I'M FAMILY NOW!
WE WERE MARRIED LAST WEEK!
COME IN HERE. I WANT TO TALK TO TO YOU!
SO.... WHERE DID YOU MEET HIM ??
...IN A BAR. I WAS A WAITRESS! ...HE'S A STEAM SHOVEL OPERATOR ...MAKES GOOD MONEY!
HE'S NOT JEWISH!
OF COURSE NOT!! HE'S REALLY A DECENT MAN. ...ROUGH, MAYBE, BUT HE TREATS ME PRETTY GOOD!
I KNEW YOU WOULD COME TO THIS... THROWING YOUR LIFE AWAY ON A...A...
WHAT THROWN AWAY?? HAH... IS YOUR LIFE ANY BETTER? I'VE HAD THREE EXCITING MARRIAGES...SEVERAL AFFAIRS, SOME GOOD, SOME BAD... BUT I'VE LIVED! FANNIE, I'VE LIVED!

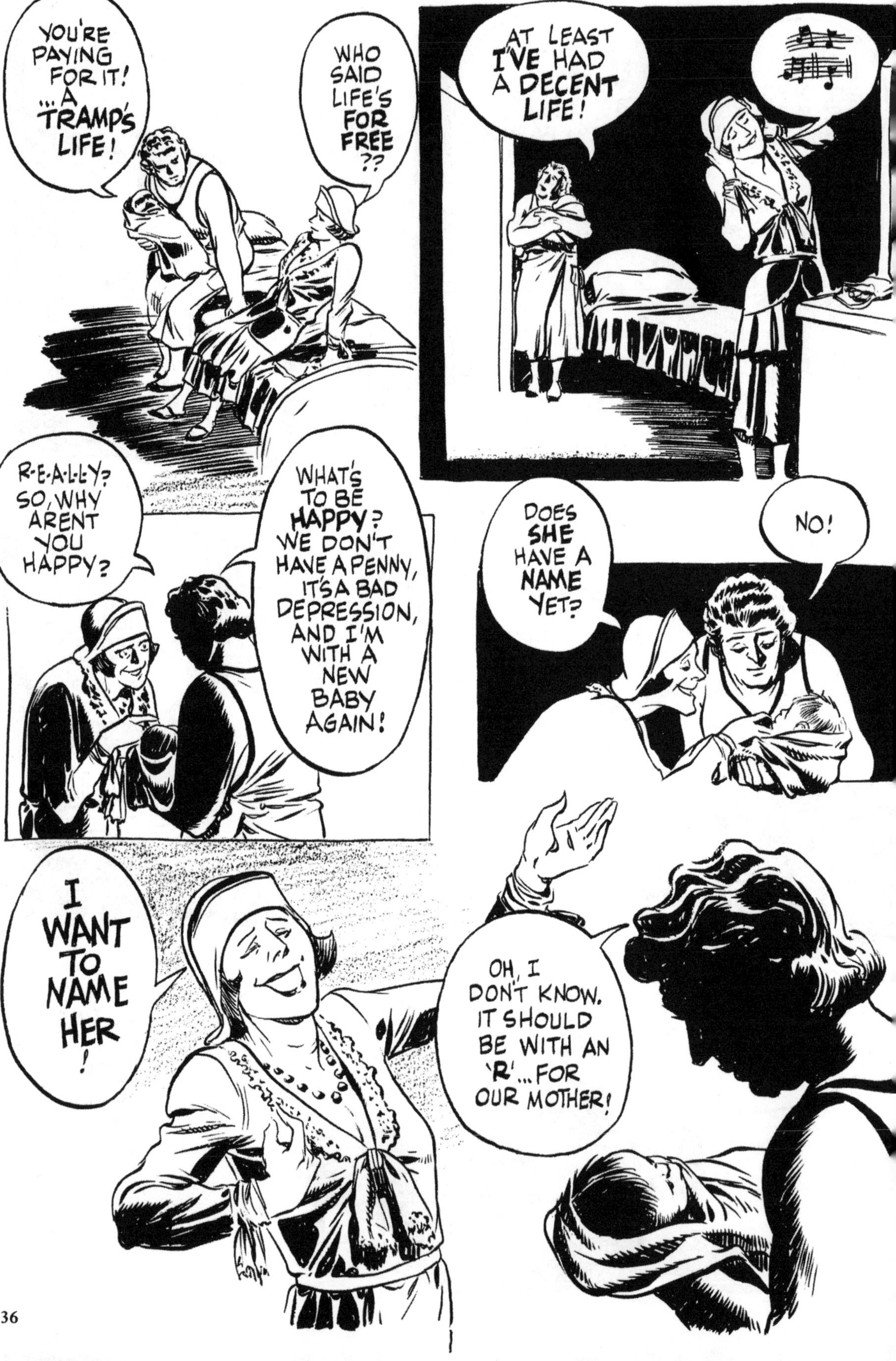
YOU'RE PAYING FOR IT! ...A TRAMP'S LIFE!
WHO SAID LIFE'S FOR FREE??
AT LEAST I'VE HAD A DECENT LIFE!
R-E-A-L-L-Y? SO, WHY AREN'T YOU HAPPY?
WHAT'S TO BE HAPPY? WE DON'T HAVE A PENNY, IT'S A BAD DEPRESSION, AND I'M WITH A NEW BABY AGAIN!
DOES SHE HAVE A NAME YET?
NO!
I WANT TO NAME HER!
OH, I DON'T KNOW. IT SHOULD BE WITH AN 'R'...FOR OUR MOTHER!

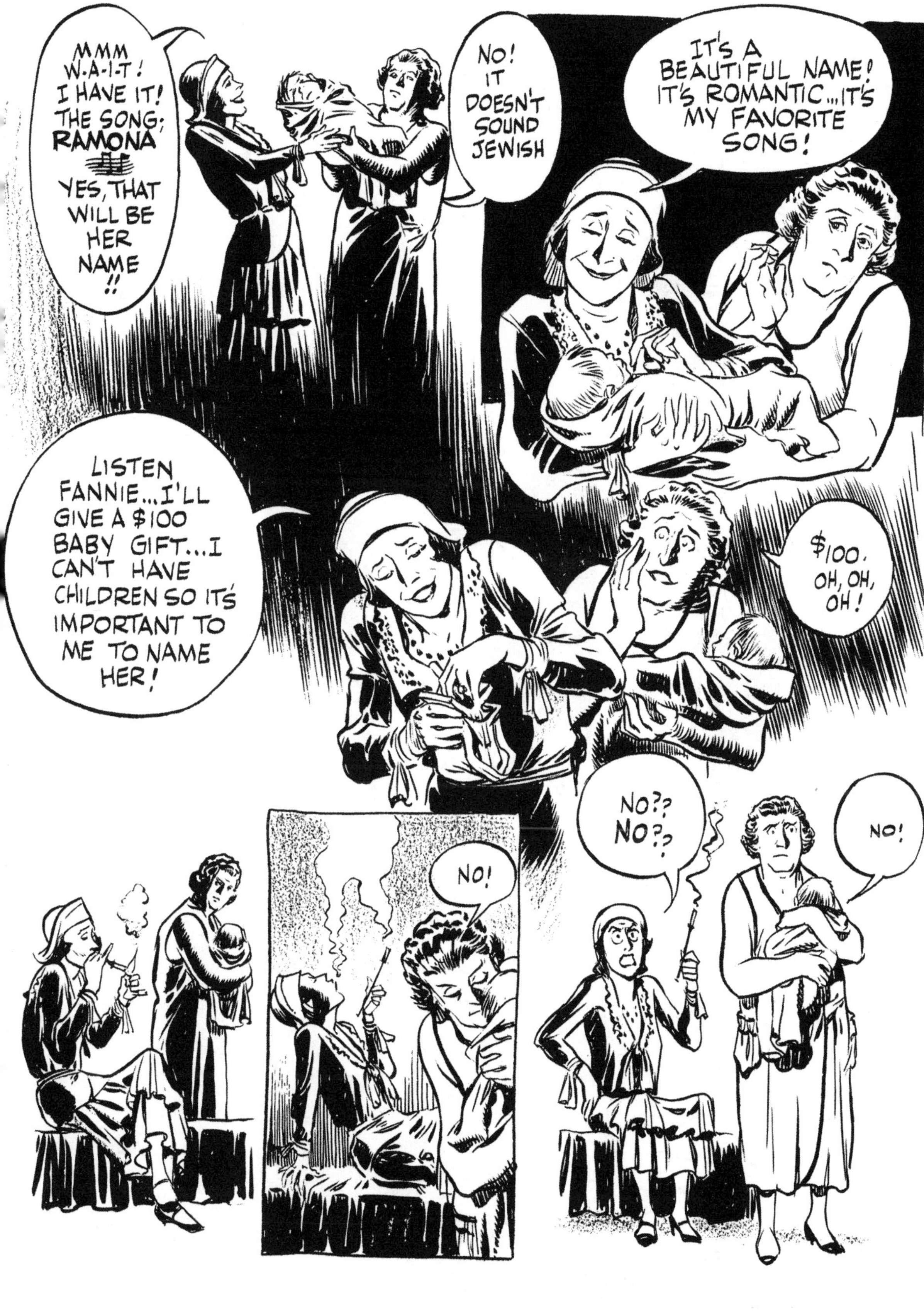
MMM W-A-I-T! I HAVE IT! THE SONG: RAMONA YES, THAT WILL BE HER NAME!!
NO! IT DOESN'T SOUND JEWISH
IT'S A BEAUTIFUL NAME! IT'S ROMANTIC... IT'S MY FAVORITE SONG!
LISTEN FANNIE... I'LL GIVE A $100 BABY GIFT... I CAN'T HAVE CHILDREN SO IT'S IMPORTANT TO ME TO NAME HER!
$100. OH, OH, OH!
NO!
NO?? NO??
NO!

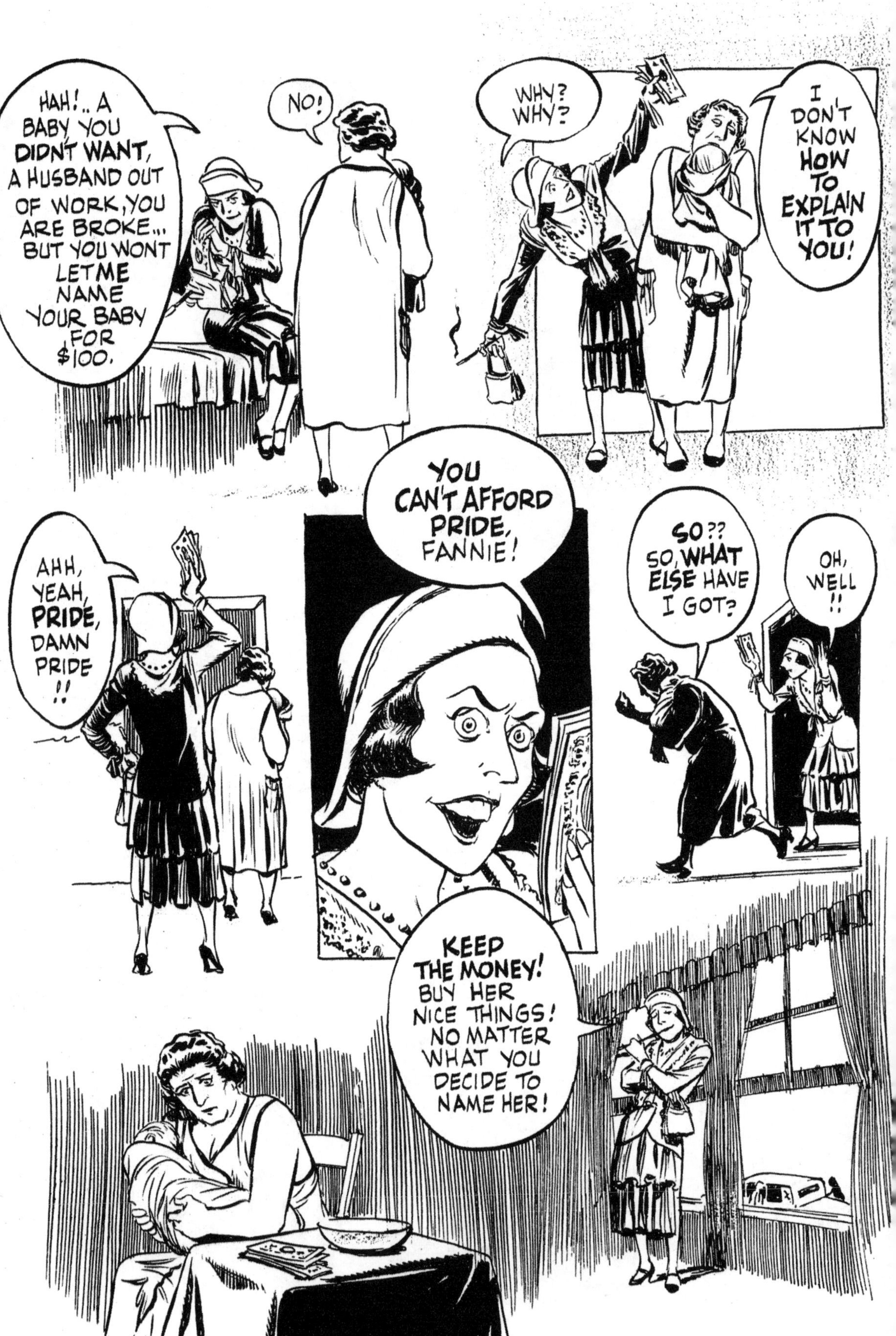
HAH!.. A BABY YOU DIDN'T WANT, A HUSBAND OUT OF WORK, YOU ARE BROKE... BUT YOU WONT LET ME NAME YOUR BABY FOR $100.
NO!
WHY? WHY?
I DON'T KNOW HOW TO EXPLAIN IT TO YOU!
AHH, YEAH, PRIDE, DAMN PRIDE !!
YOU CAN'T AFFORD PRIDE, FANNIE!
SO?? SO, WHAT ELSE HAVE I GOT?
OH, WELL !!
KEEP THE MONEY! BUY HER NICE THINGS! NO MATTER WHAT YOU DECIDE TO NAME HER!

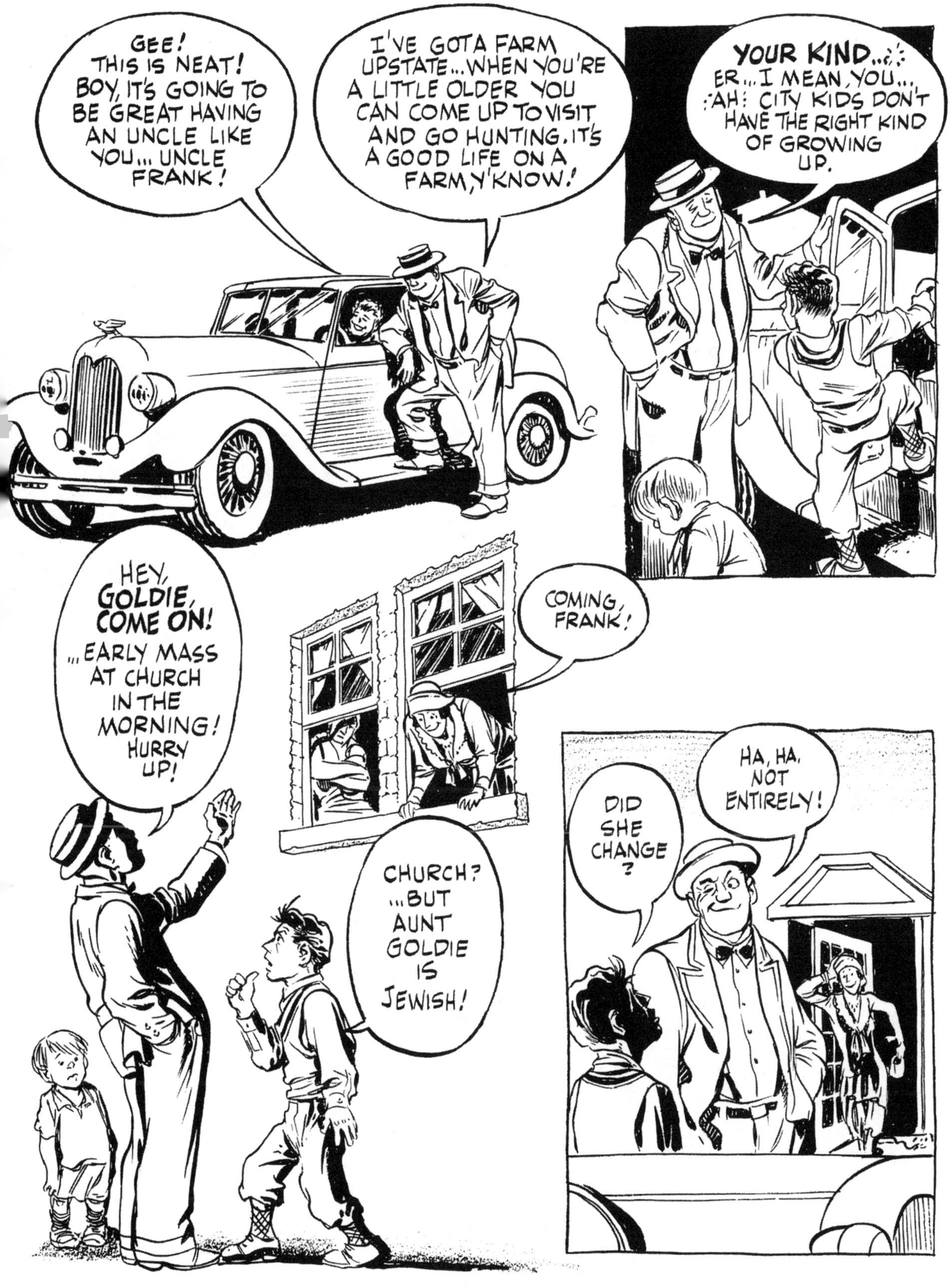
GEE! THIS IS NEAT! BOY, IT'S GOING TO BE GREAT HAVING AN UNCLE LIKE YOU... UNCLE FRANK!
I'VE GOTA FARM UPSTATE... WHEN YOU'RE A LITTLE OLDER YOU CAN COME UP TO VISIT AND GO HUNTING. IT'S A GOOD LIFE ON A FARM, Y'KNOW!
YOUR KIND... ER... I MEAN, YOU... AH: CITY KIDS DON'T HAVE THE RIGHT KIND OF GROWING UP.
HEY, GOLDIE, COME ON! ...EARLY MASS AT CHURCH IN THE MORNING! HURRY UP!
COMING, FRANK!
CHURCH? ...BUT AUNT GOLDIE IS JEWISH!
DID SHE CHANGE?
HA, HA, NOT ENTIRELY!

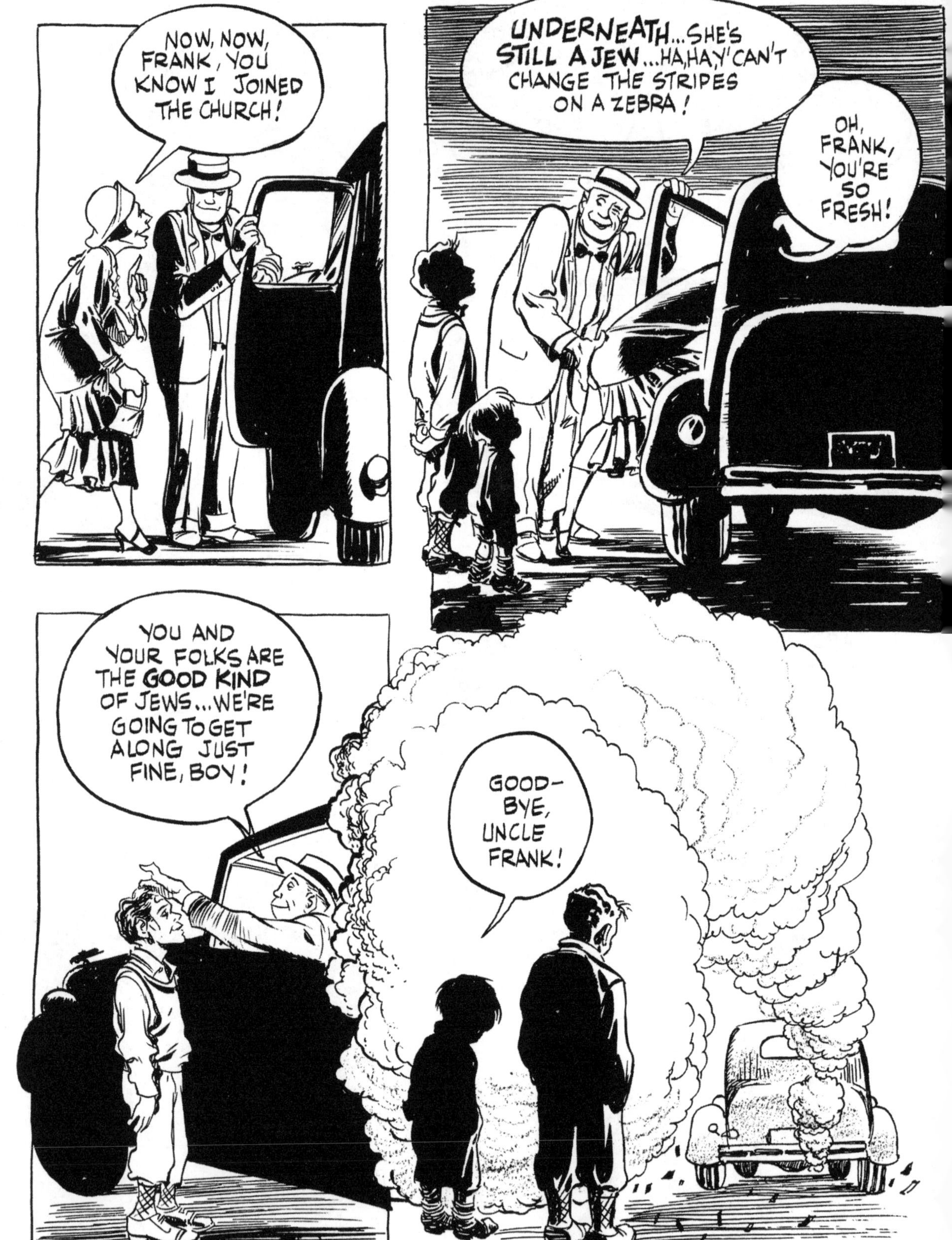
NOW, NOW, FRANK, YOU KNOW I JOINED THE CHURCH!
UNDERNEATH...SHE'S STILL A JEW...HA,HA,Y'CAN'T CHANGE THE STRIPES ON A ZEBRA!
OH, FRANK, YOU'RE SO FRESH!
YOU AND YOUR FOLKS ARE THE GOOD KIND OF JEWS...WE'RE GOING TO GET ALONG JUST FINE, BOY!
GOOD-BYE, UNCLE FRANK!

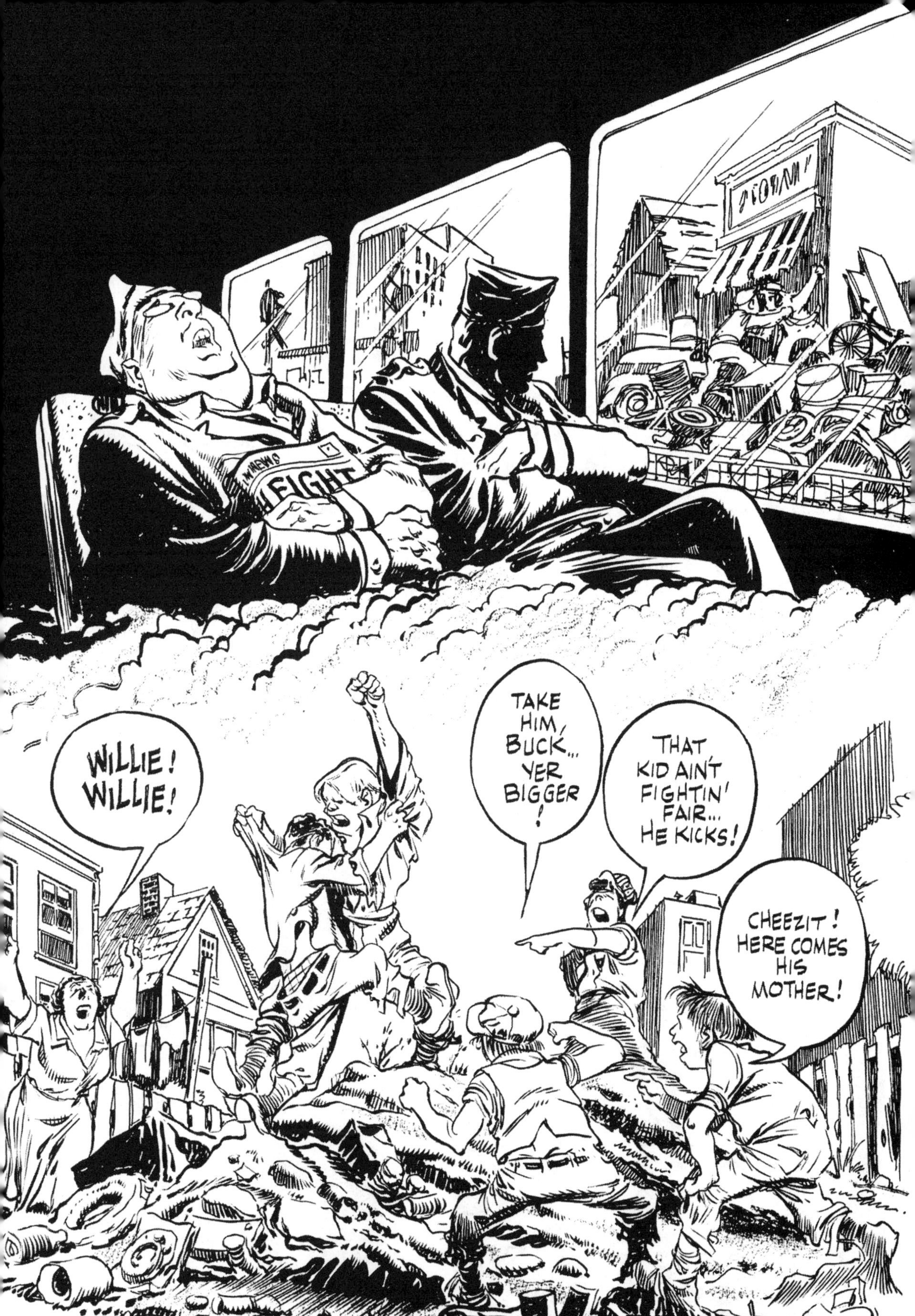

NEWS
FIGHT
WILLIE! WILLIE!
TAKE HIM, BUCK... YER BIGGER!
THAT KID AIN'T FIGHTIN' FAIR... HE KICKS!
CHEEZIT! HERE COMES HIS MOTHER!

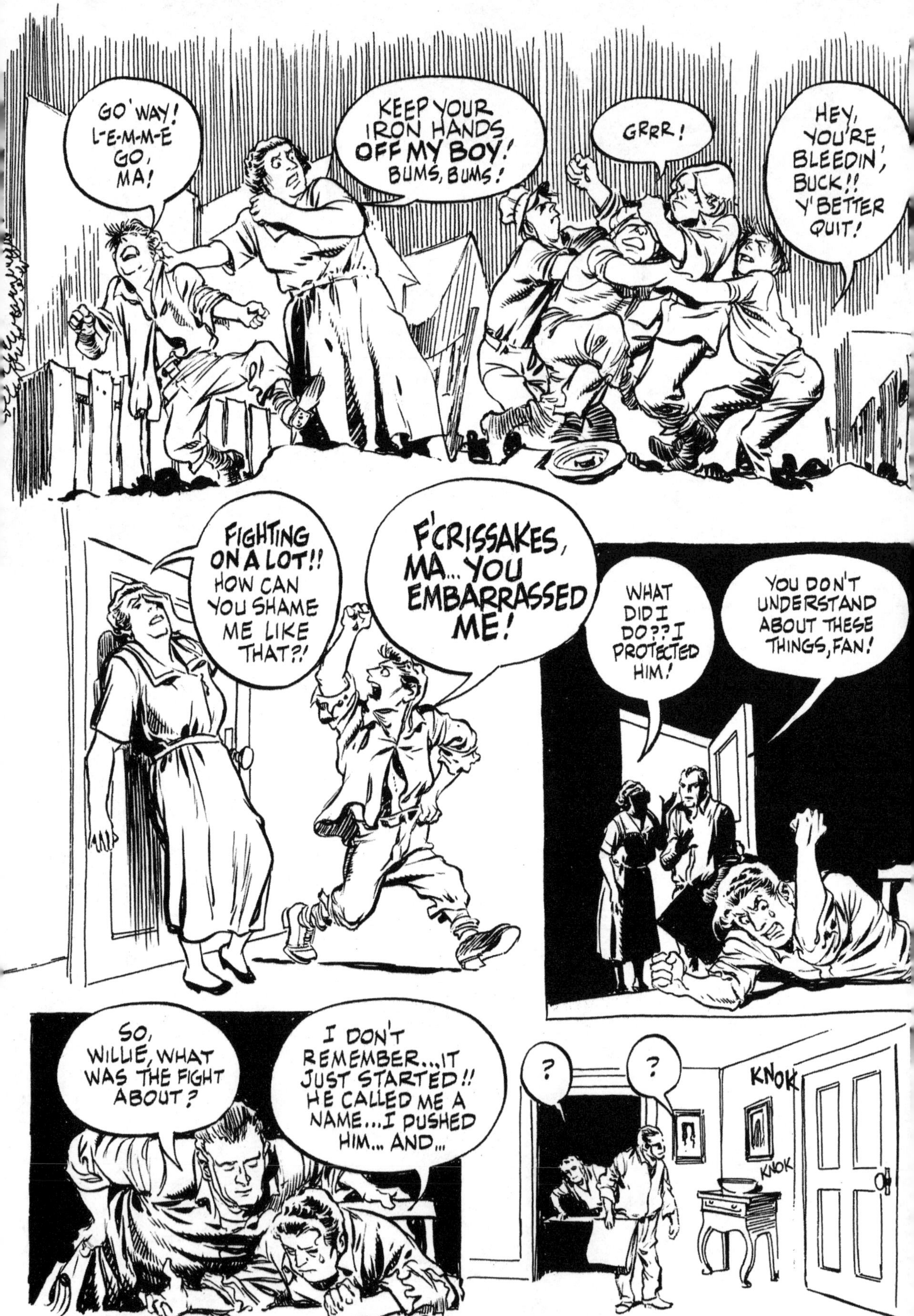
GO' WAY! L-E-M-M-E GO, MA!
KEEP YOUR IRON HANDS OFF MY BOY! BUMS, BUMS!
GRRR!
HEY, YOU'RE BLEEDIN', BUCK!! Y'BETTER QUIT!
FIGHTING ON A LOT!! HOW CAN YOU SHAME ME LIKE THAT?!
F'CRISSAKES, MA... YOU EMBARRASSED ME!
WHAT DID I DO?? I PROTECTED HIM!
YOU DON'T UNDERSTAND ABOUT THESE THINGS, FAN!
SO, WILLIE, WHAT WAS THE FIGHT ABOUT?
I DON'T REMEMBER... IT JUST STARTED!! HE CALLED ME A NAME... I PUSHED HIM... AND...
?
?
KNOK
KNOK

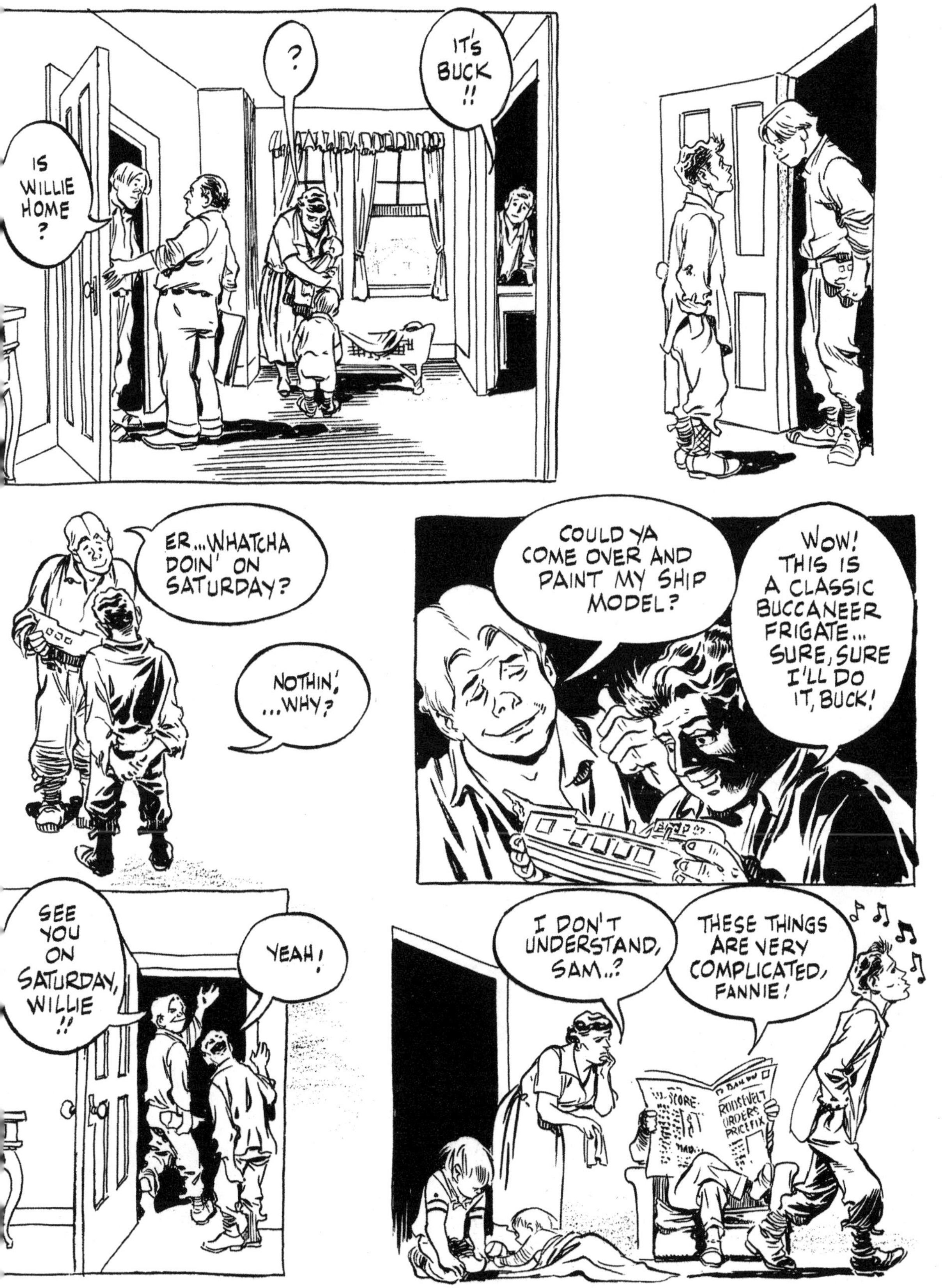

IS WILLIE HOME?
?
IT'S BUCK!!
ER...WHATCHA DOIN' ON SATURDAY?
NOTHIN' ...WHY?
COULD YA COME OVER AND PAINT MY SHIP MODEL?
WOW! THIS IS A CLASSIC BUCCANEER FRIGATE... SURE, SURE I'LL DO IT, BUCK!
SEE YOU ON SATURDAY, WILLIE!!
YEAH!
I DON'T UNDERSTAND, SAM..?
THESE THINGS ARE VERY COMPLICATED, FANNIE!
ROOSEVELT ORDERS PRICE FIX

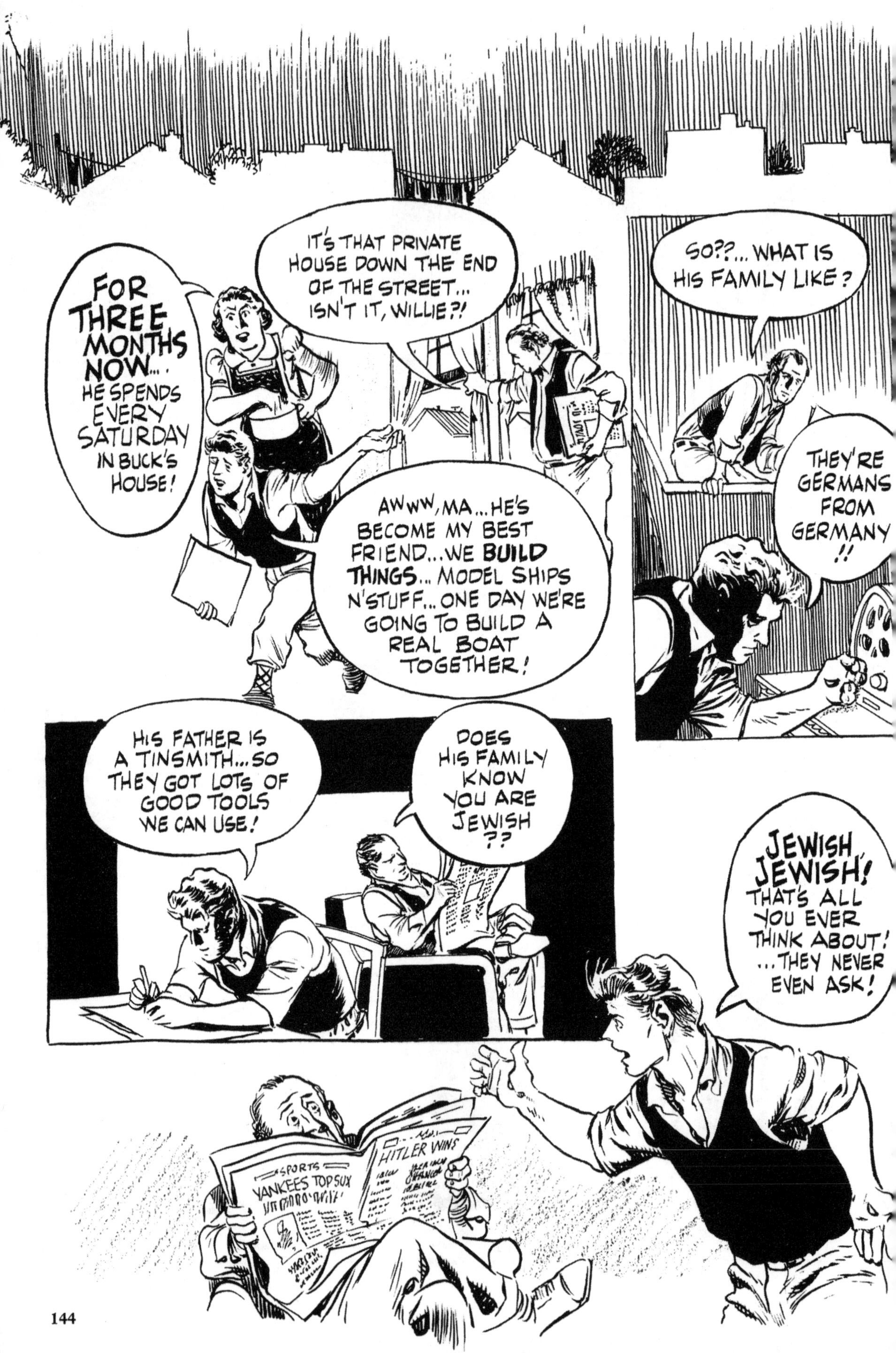
FOR THREE MONTHS NOW... HE SPENDS EVERY SATURDAY IN BUCK'S HOUSE!
IT'S THAT PRIVATE HOUSE DOWN THE END OF THE STREET... ISN'T IT, WILLIE?!
AWWW, MA... HE'S BECOME MY BEST FRIEND... WE BUILD THINGS... MODEL SHIPS N'STUFF... ONE DAY WE'RE GOING TO BUILD A REAL BOAT TOGETHER!
SO??... WHAT IS HIS FAMILY LIKE?
THEY'RE GERMANS FROM GERMANY!!
HIS FATHER IS A TINSMITH... SO THEY GOT LOTS OF GOOD TOOLS WE CAN USE!
DOES HIS FAMILY KNOW YOU ARE JEWISH??
JEWISH, JEWISH! THAT'S ALL YOU EVER THINK ABOUT! ...THEY NEVER EVEN ASK!
SPORTS
YANKEES TOP SOX
HITLER WINS

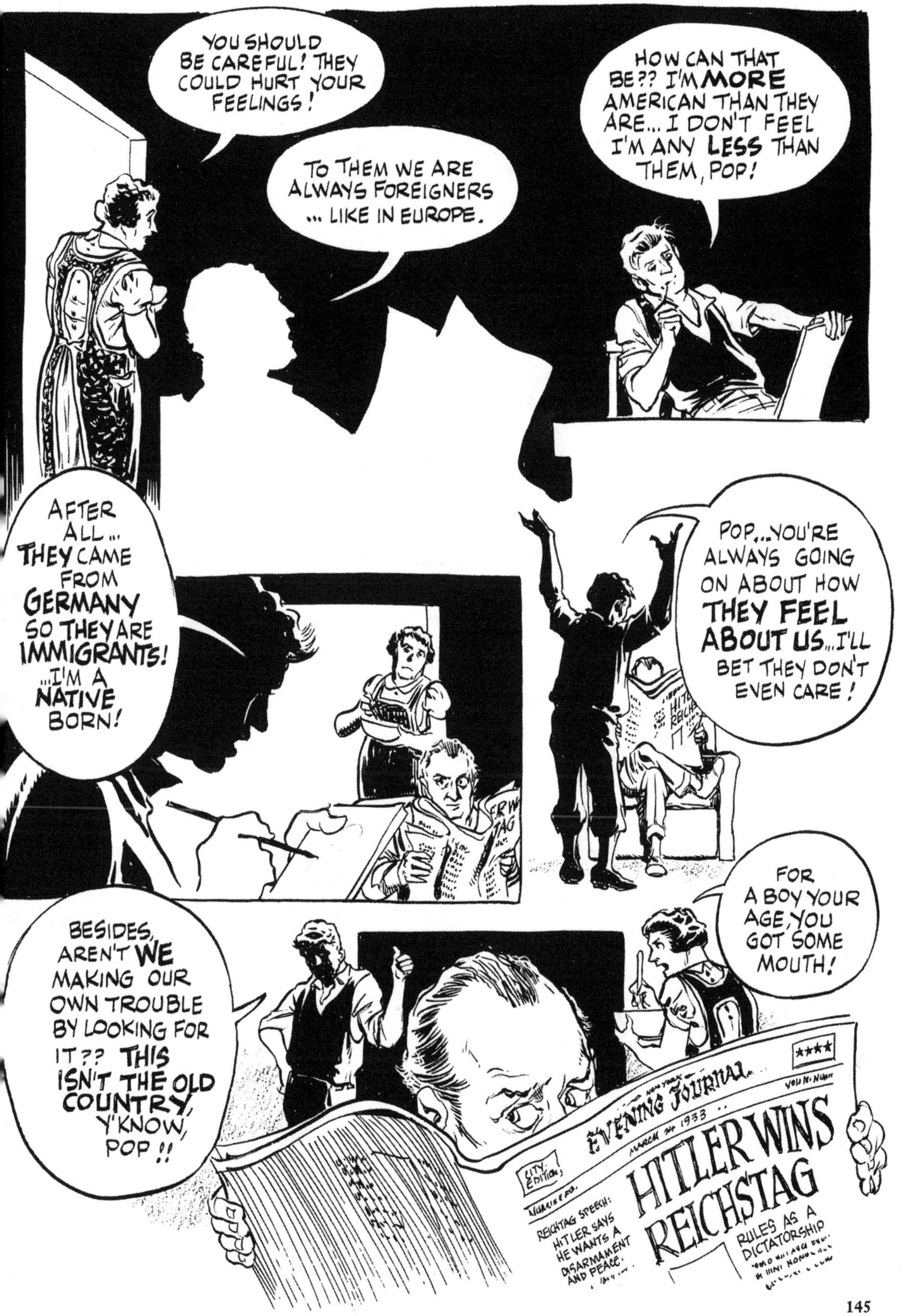
YOU SHOULD BE CAREFUL! THEY COULD HURT YOUR FEELINGS!
TO THEM WE ARE ALWAYS FOREIGNERS ... LIKE IN EUROPE.
HOW CAN THAT BE?? I'M MORE AMERICAN THAN THEY ARE... I DON'T FEEL I'M ANY LESS THAN THEM, POP!
AFTER ALL... THEY CAME FROM GERMANY SO THEY ARE IMMIGRANTS! ...I'M A NATIVE BORN!
POP... YOU'RE ALWAYS GOING ON ABOUT HOW THEY FEEL ABOUT US... I'LL BET THEY DON'T EVEN CARE!
BESIDES, AREN'T WE MAKING OUR OWN TROUBLE BY LOOKING FOR IT?? THIS ISN'T THE OLD COUNTRY, Y'KNOW, POP!!
FOR A BOY YOUR AGE, YOU GOT SOME MOUTH!
EVENING JOURNAL
MARCH 24 1933
CITY EDITION
HITLER WINS REICHSTAG
REICHSTAG SPEECH: HITLER SAYS HE WANTS A DISARMAMENT AND PEACE.
RULES AS A DICTATORSHIP

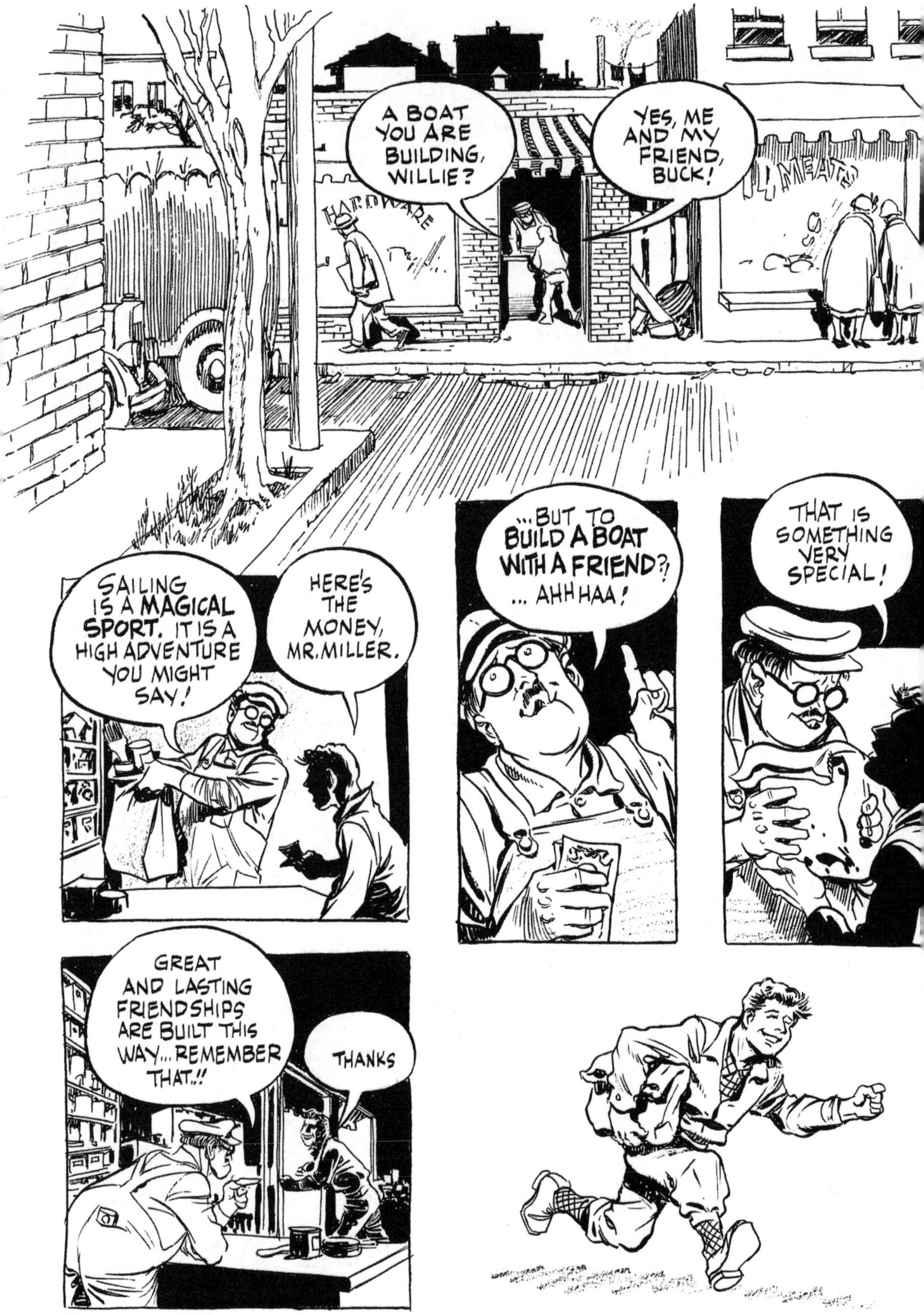
HARDWARE
MEAT
A BOAT YOU ARE BUILDING, WILLIE?
YES, ME AND MY FRIEND, BUCK!
SAILING IS A MAGICAL SPORT. IT IS A HIGH ADVENTURE YOU MIGHT SAY!
HERE'S THE MONEY, MR. MILLER.
...BUT TO BUILD A BOAT WITH A FRIEND?! ... AHHHAA!
THAT IS SOMETHING VERY SPECIAL!
GREAT AND LASTING FRIENDSHIPS ARE BUILT THIS WAY... REMEMBER THAT.!!
THANKS

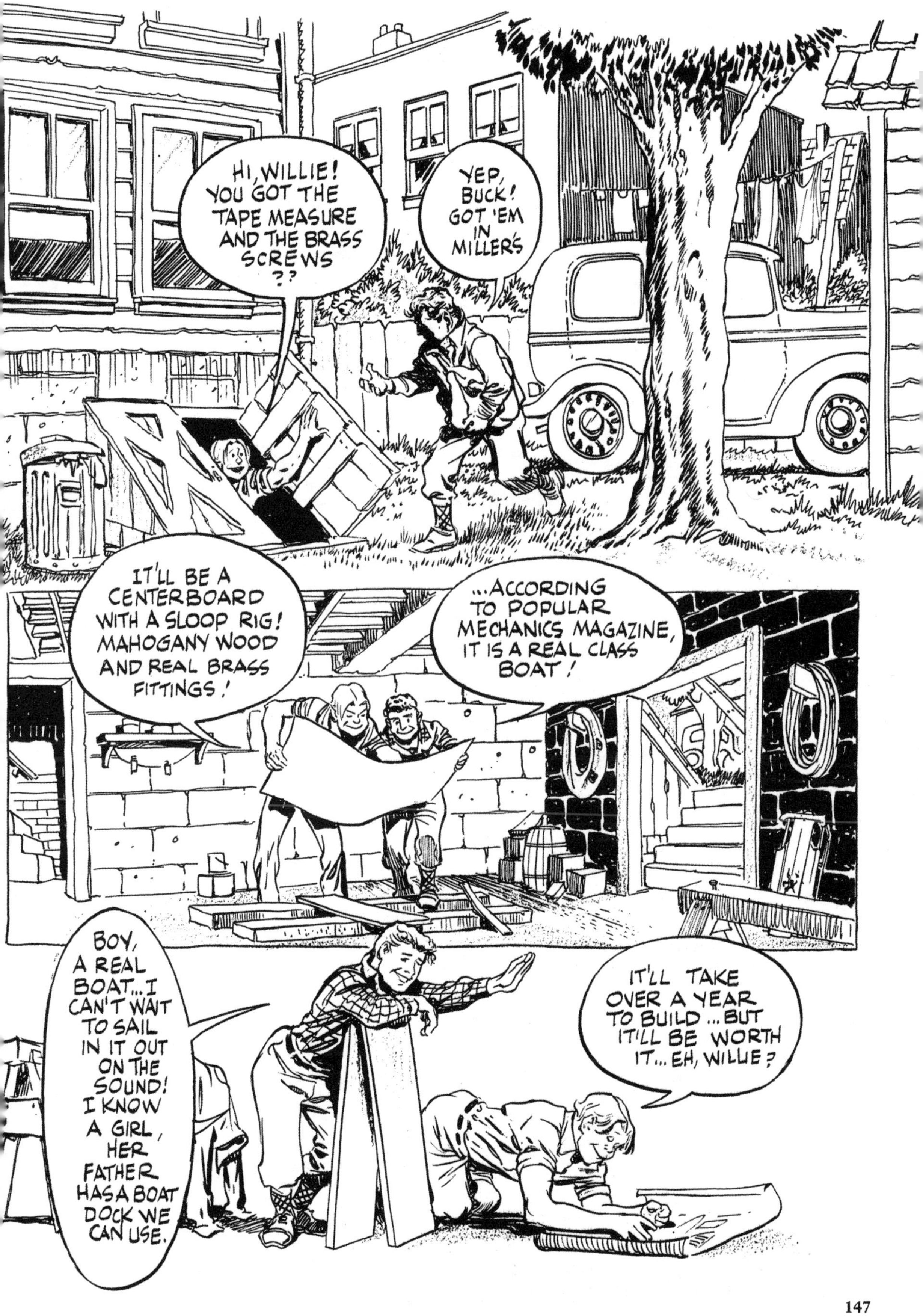
HI, WILLIE! YOU GOT THE TAPE MEASURE AND THE BRASS SCREWS ??
YEP, BUCK! GOT 'EM IN MILLER'S
IT'LL BE A CENTERBOARD WITH A SLOOP RIG! MAHOGANY WOOD AND REAL BRASS FITTINGS!
...ACCORDING TO POPULAR MECHANICS MAGAZINE, IT IS A REAL CLASS BOAT!
BOY, A REAL BOAT...I CAN'T WAIT TO SAIL IN IT OUT ON THE SOUND! I KNOW A GIRL, HER FATHER HAS A BOAT DOCK WE CAN USE.
IT'LL TAKE OVER A YEAR TO BUILD... BUT IT'LL BE WORTH IT... EH, WILLIE?

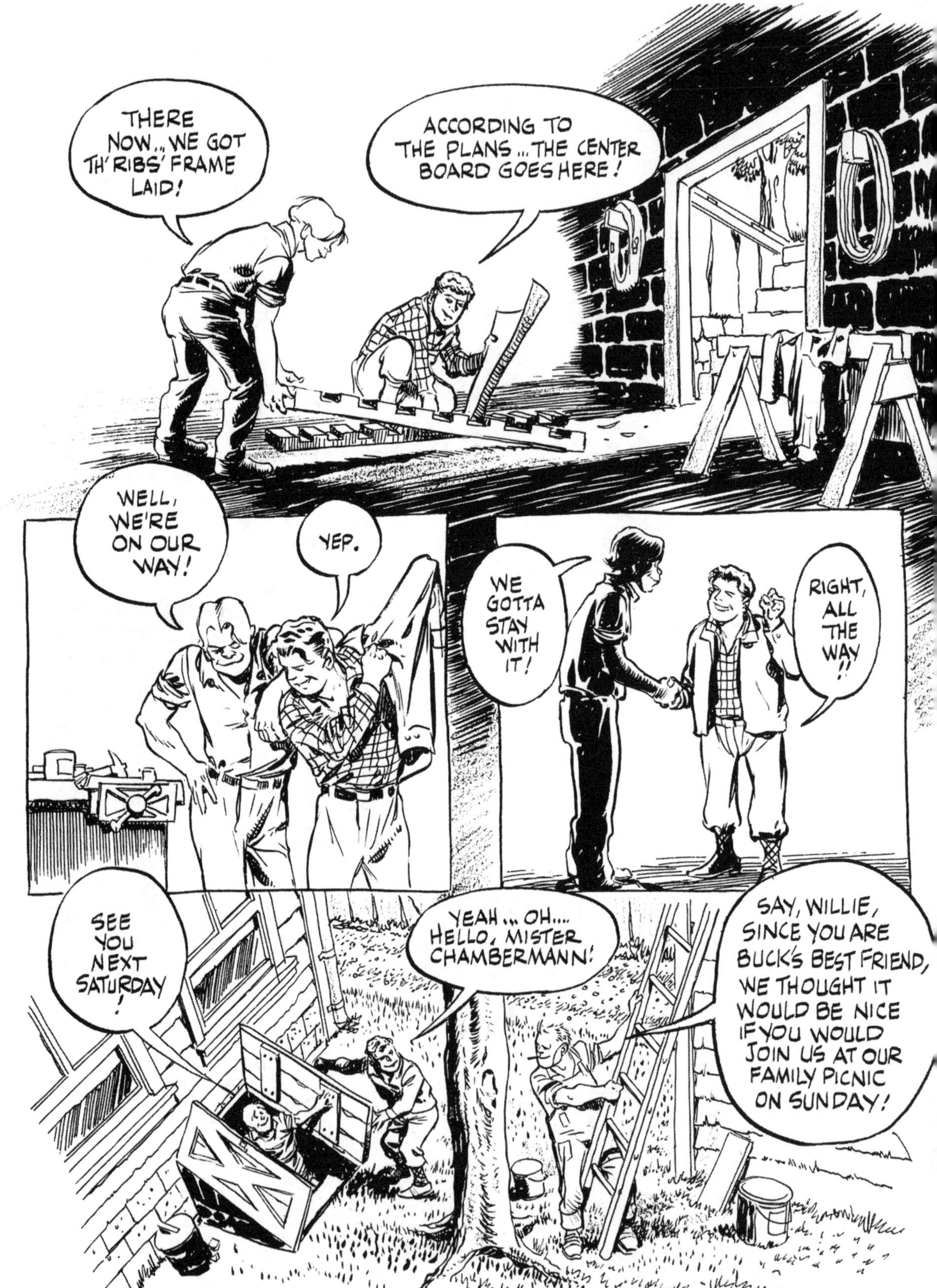
THERE NOW... WE GOT TH' RIBS' FRAME LAID!
ACCORDING TO THE PLANS... THE CENTER BOARD GOES HERE!
WELL, WE'RE ON OUR WAY!
YEP.
WE GOTTA STAY WITH IT!
RIGHT, ALL THE WAY!!
SEE YOU NEXT SATURDAY!
YEAH... OH.... HELLO, MISTER CHAMBERMANN!
SAY, WILLIE, SINCE YOU ARE BUCK'S BEST FRIEND, WE THOUGHT IT WOULD BE NICE IF YOU WOULD JOIN US AT OUR FAMILY PICNIC ON SUNDAY!

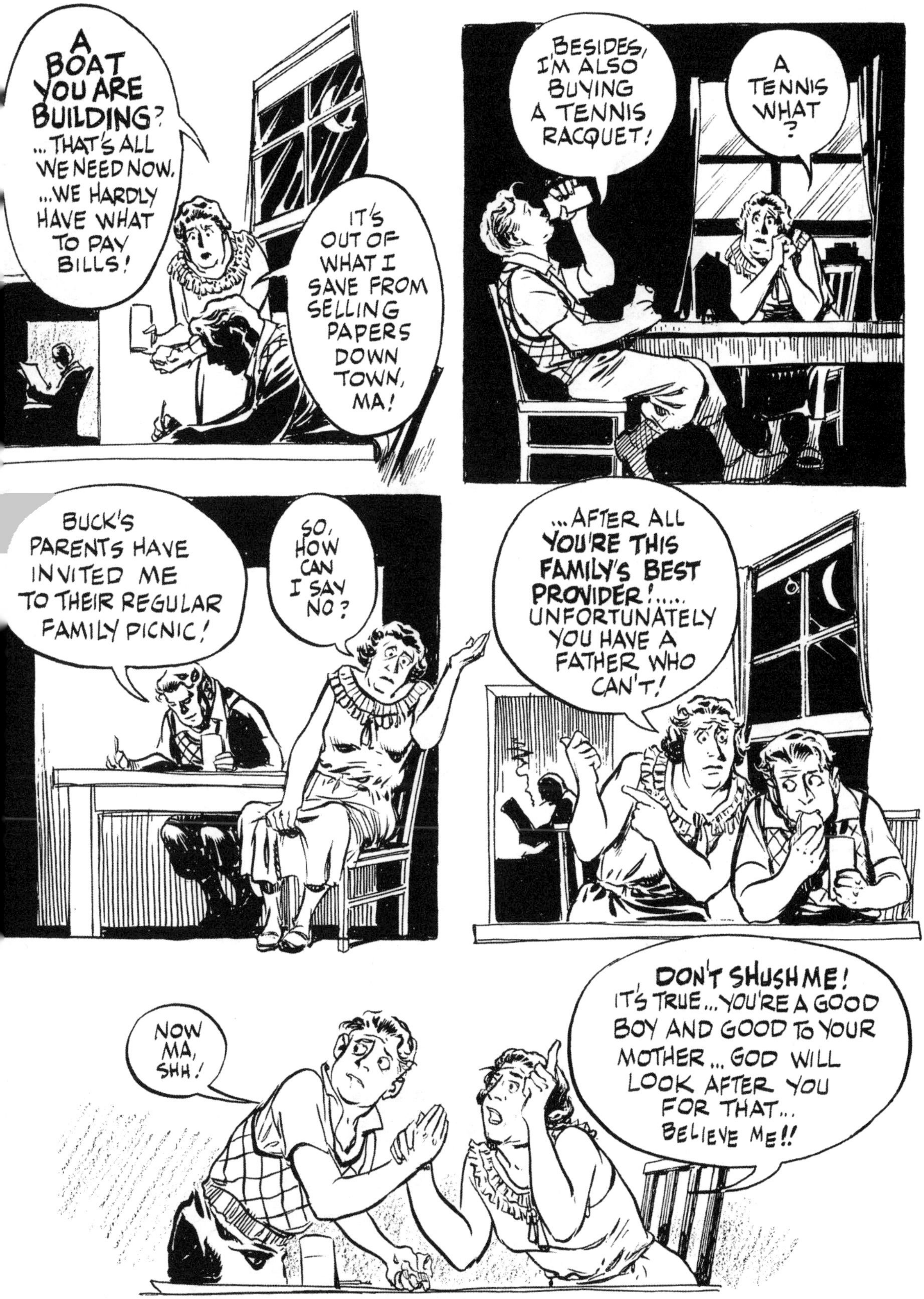

A BOAT YOU ARE BUILDING? ...THAT'S ALL WE NEED NOW. ...WE HARDLY HAVE WHAT TO PAY BILLS!
IT'S OUT OF WHAT I SAVE FROM SELLING PAPERS DOWN TOWN, MA!
BESIDES, I'M ALSO BUYING A TENNIS RACQUET!
A TENNIS WHAT?
BUCK'S PARENTS HAVE INVITED ME TO THEIR REGULAR FAMILY PICNIC!
SO, HOW CAN I SAY NO?
...AFTER ALL YOU'RE THIS FAMILY'S BEST PROVIDER!..... UNFORTUNATELY YOU HAVE A FATHER WHO CAN'T!
NOW MA, SHH!
DON'T SHUSH ME! IT'S TRUE...YOU'RE A GOOD BOY AND GOOD TO YOUR MOTHER... GOD WILL LOOK AFTER YOU FOR THAT... BELIEVE ME!!

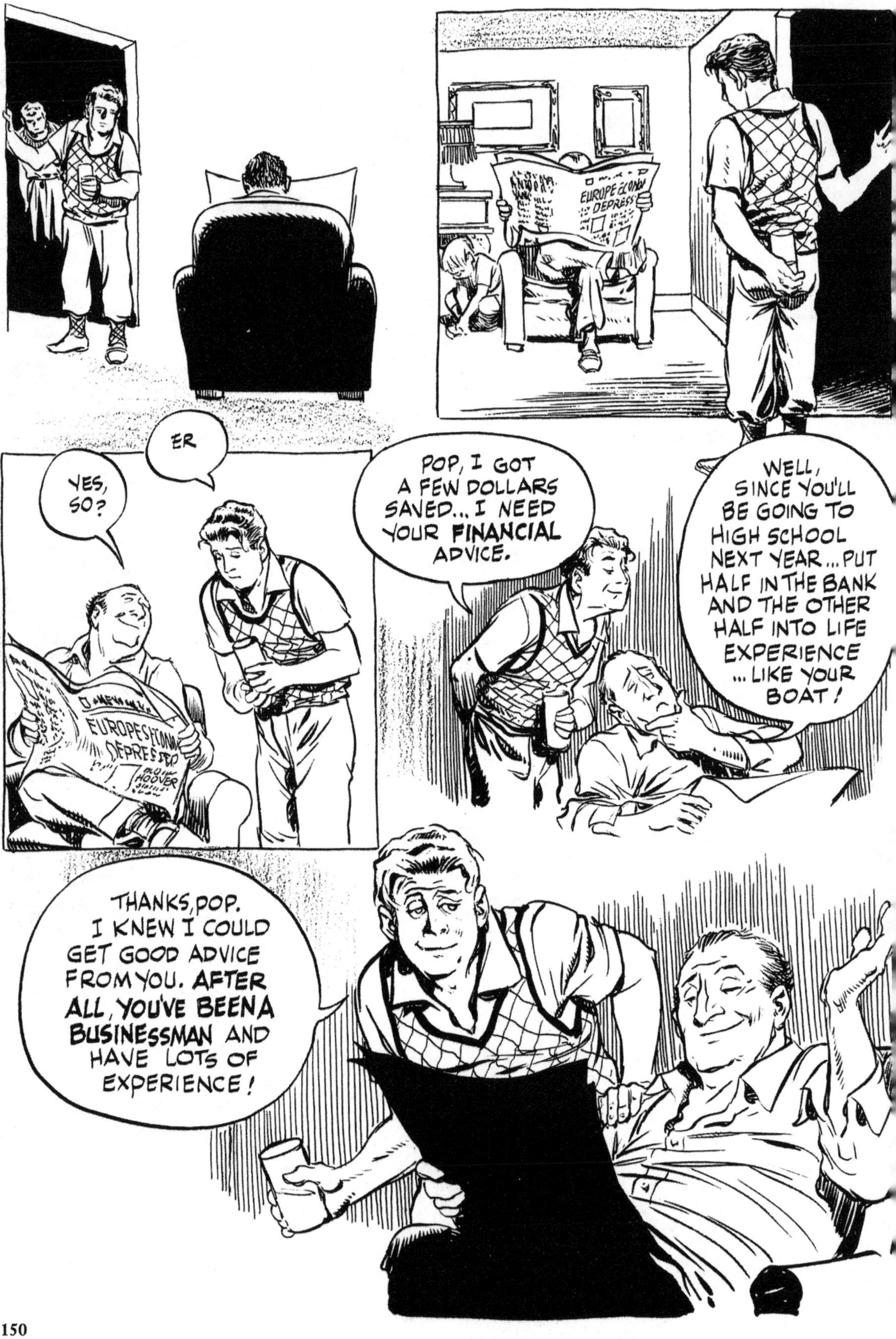
EUROPE ECONO DEPRESS
YES, SO?
ER
EUROPES ECONO DEPRESSED
HOOVER
POP, I GOT A FEW DOLLARS SAVED... I NEED YOUR FINANCIAL ADVICE.
WELL, SINCE YOU'LL BE GOING TO HIGH SCHOOL NEXT YEAR... PUT HALF IN THE BANK AND THE OTHER HALF INTO LIFE EXPERIENCE ... LIKE YOUR BOAT!
THANKS, POP. I KNEW I COULD GET GOOD ADVICE FROM YOU. AFTER ALL, YOU'VE BEEN A BUSINESSMAN AND HAVE LOTS OF EXPERIENCE!

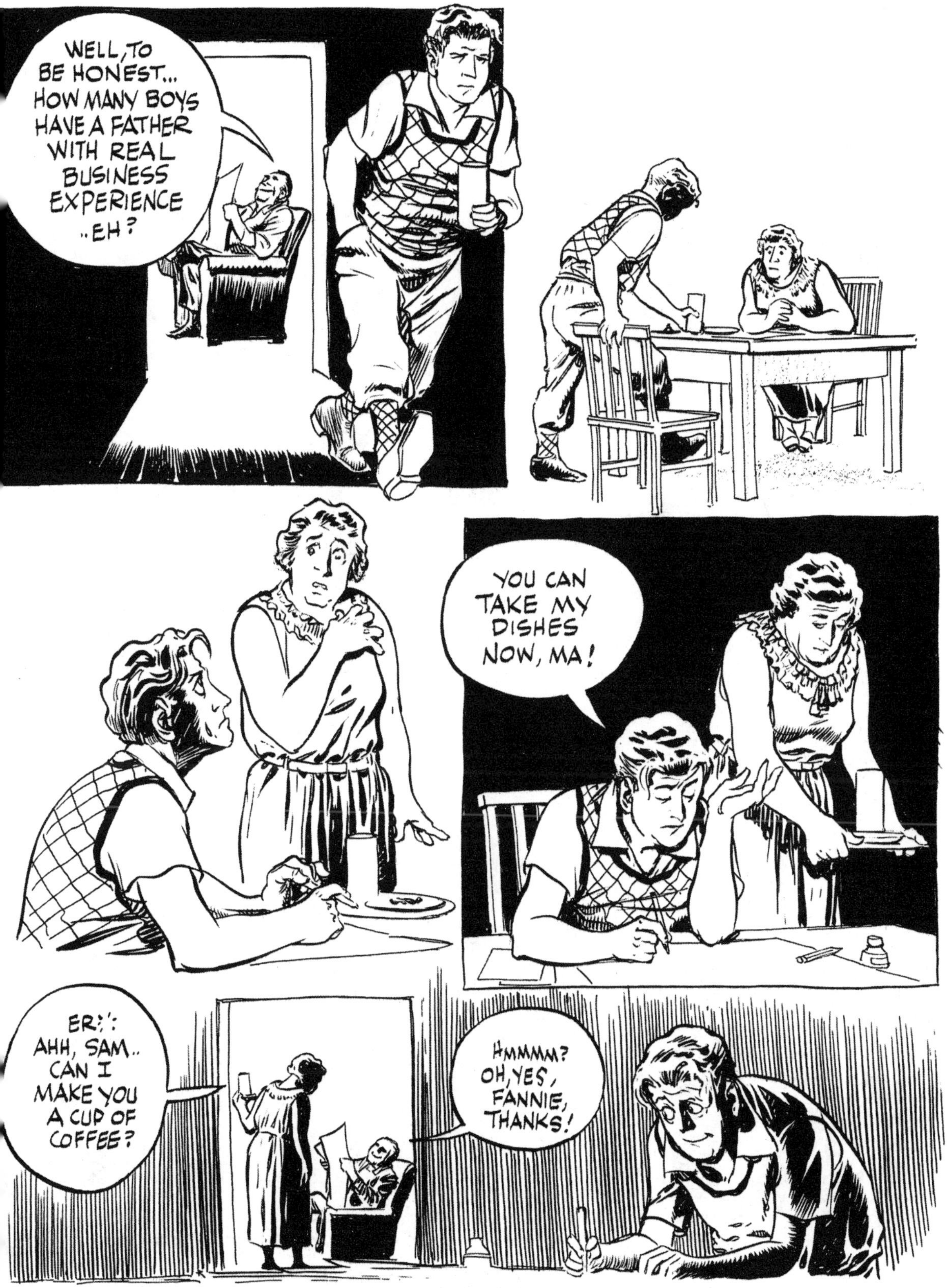
WELL, TO BE HONEST... HOW MANY BOYS HAVE A FATHER WITH REAL BUSINESS EXPERIENCE ..EH?
YOU CAN TAKE MY DISHES NOW, MA!
ER:': AHH, SAM.. CAN I MAKE YOU A CUP OF COFFEE?
HMMMM? OH, YES, FANNIE, THANKS!

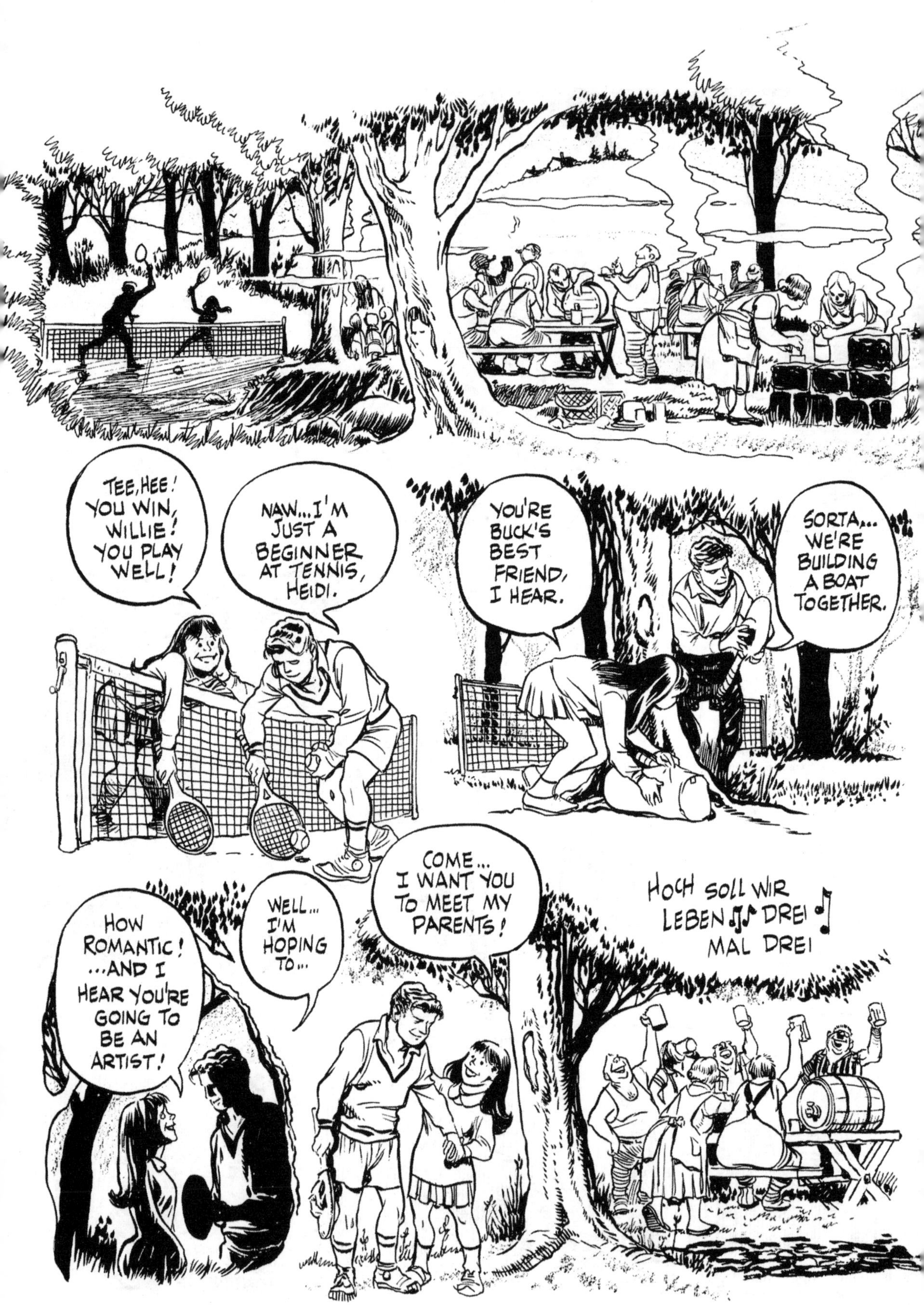
TEE, HEE! YOU WIN, WILLIE! YOU PLAY WELL!
NAW...I'M JUST A BEGINNER AT TENNIS, HEIDI.
YOU'RE BUCK'S BEST FRIEND, I HEAR.
SORTA... WE'RE BUILDING A BOAT TOGETHER.
HOW ROMANTIC! ...AND I HEAR YOU'RE GOING TO BE AN ARTIST!
WELL... I'M HOPING TO...
COME... I WANT YOU TO MEET MY PARENTS!
HOCH SOLL WIR LEBEN DREI MAL DREI

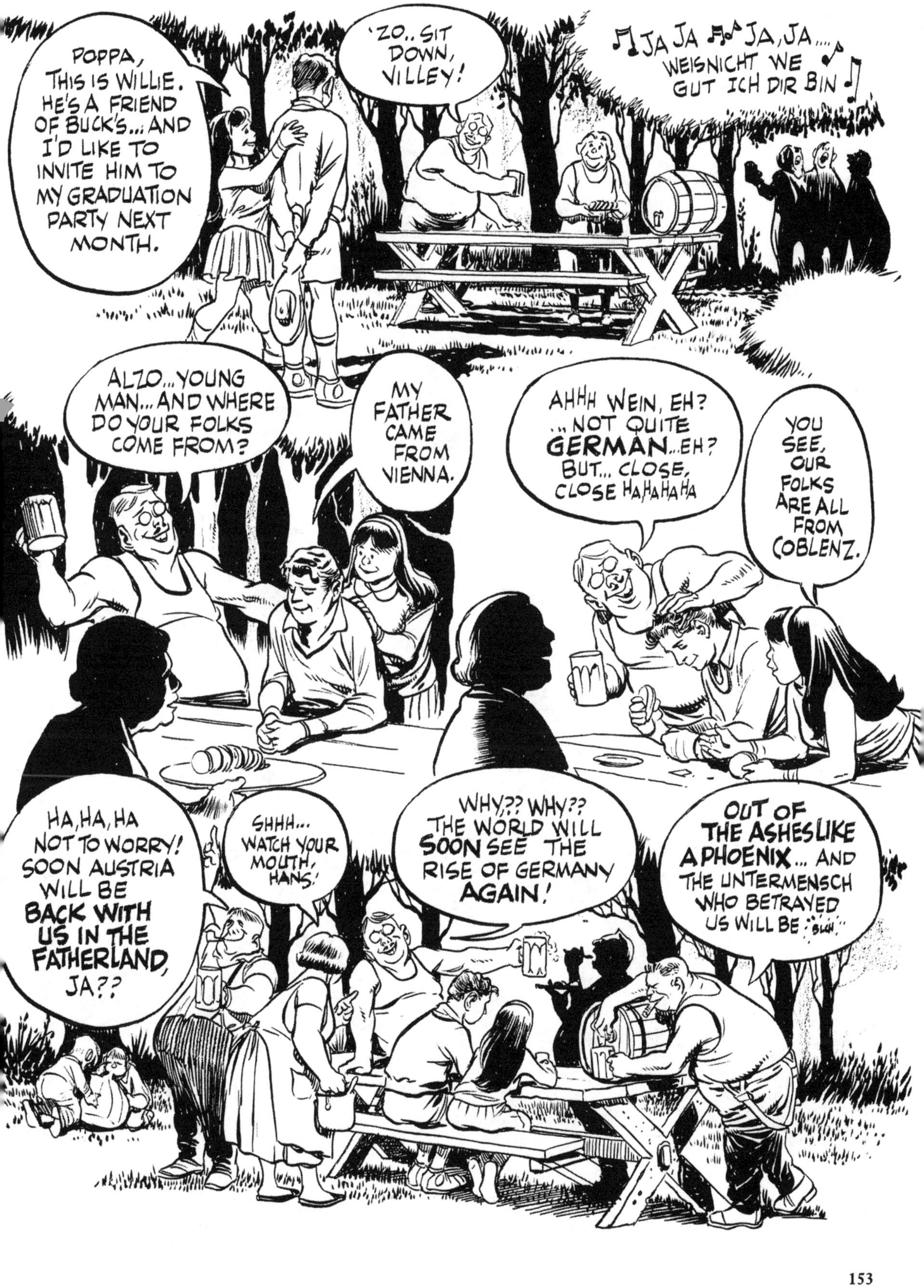

POPPA, THIS IS WILLIE. HE'S A FRIEND OF BUCK'S... AND I'D LIKE TO INVITE HIM TO MY GRADUATION PARTY NEXT MONTH.
'ZO.. SIT DOWN, VILLEY!
JA JA JA, JA.... WEISNICHT WE GUT ICH DIR BIN
ALZO... YOUNG MAN... AND WHERE DO YOUR FOLKS COME FROM?
MY FATHER CAME FROM VIENNA.
AHHH WEIN, EH? ... NOT QUITE GERMAN...EH? BUT... CLOSE, CLOSE HAHAHAHA
YOU SEE, OUR FOLKS ARE ALL FROM COBLENZ.
HA, HA, HA NOT TO WORRY! SOON AUSTRIA WILL BE BACK WITH US IN THE FATHERLAND, JA??
SHHH... WATCH YOUR MOUTH, HANS!
WHY?? WHY?? THE WORLD WILL SOON SEE THE RISE OF GERMANY AGAIN!
OUT OF THE ASHES LIKE A PHOENIX... AND THE UNTERMENSCH WHO BETRAYED US WILL BE

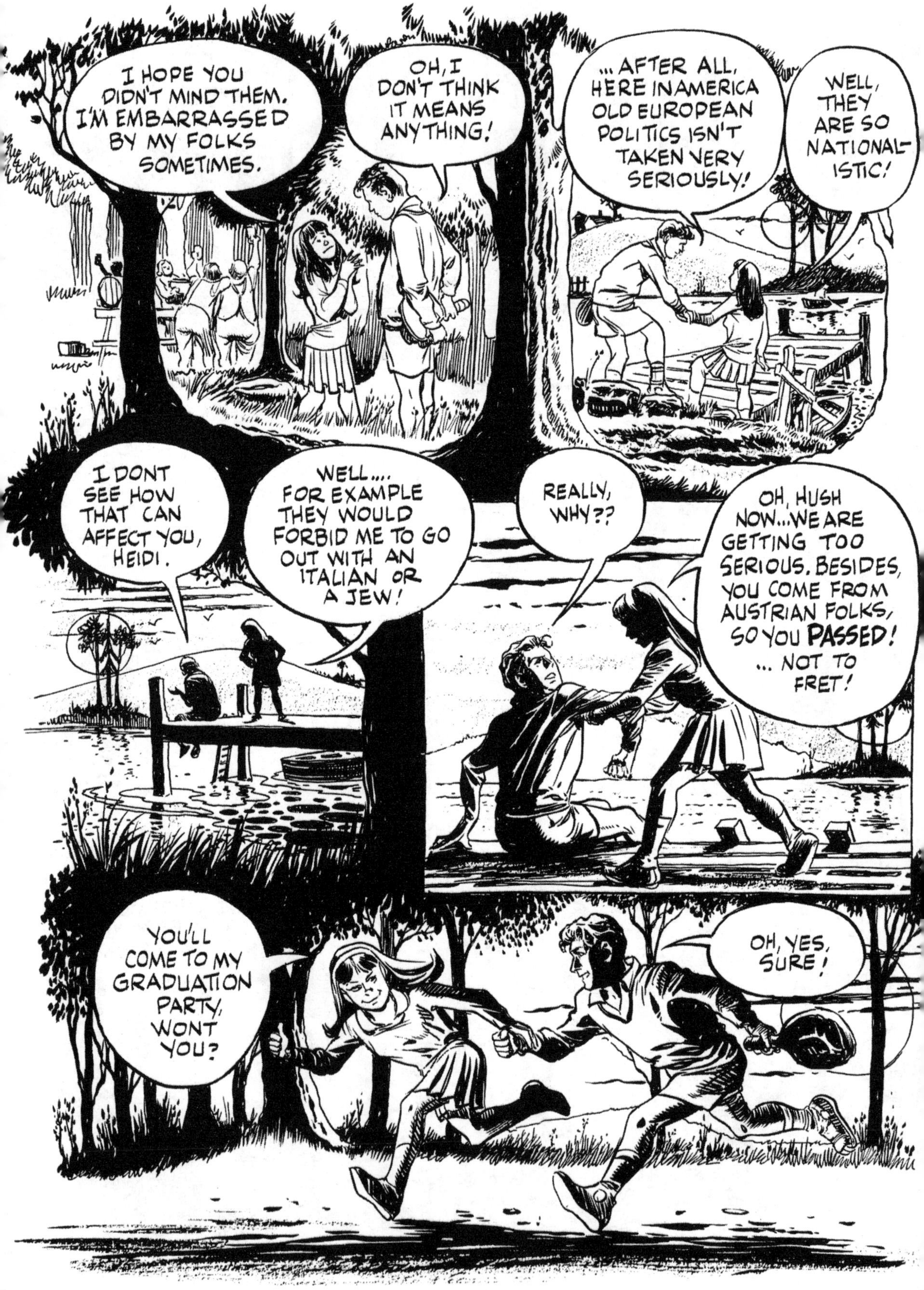
I HOPE YOU DIDN'T MIND THEM. I'M EMBARRASSED BY MY FOLKS SOMETIMES.
OH, I DON'T THINK IT MEANS ANYTHING!
...AFTER ALL, HERE IN AMERICA OLD EUROPEAN POLITICS ISN'T TAKEN VERY SERIOUSLY!
WELL, THEY ARE SO NATIONALISTIC!
I DONT SEE HOW THAT CAN AFFECT YOU, HEIDI.
WELL.... FOR EXAMPLE THEY WOULD FORBID ME TO GO OUT WITH AN ITALIAN OR A JEW!
REALLY, WHY??
OH, HUSH NOW...WE ARE GETTING TOO SERIOUS. BESIDES, YOU COME FROM AUSTRIAN FOLKS, SO YOU **PASSED**! ... NOT TO FRET!
YOU'LL COME TO MY GRADUATION PARTY, WONT YOU?
OH, YES, SURE!

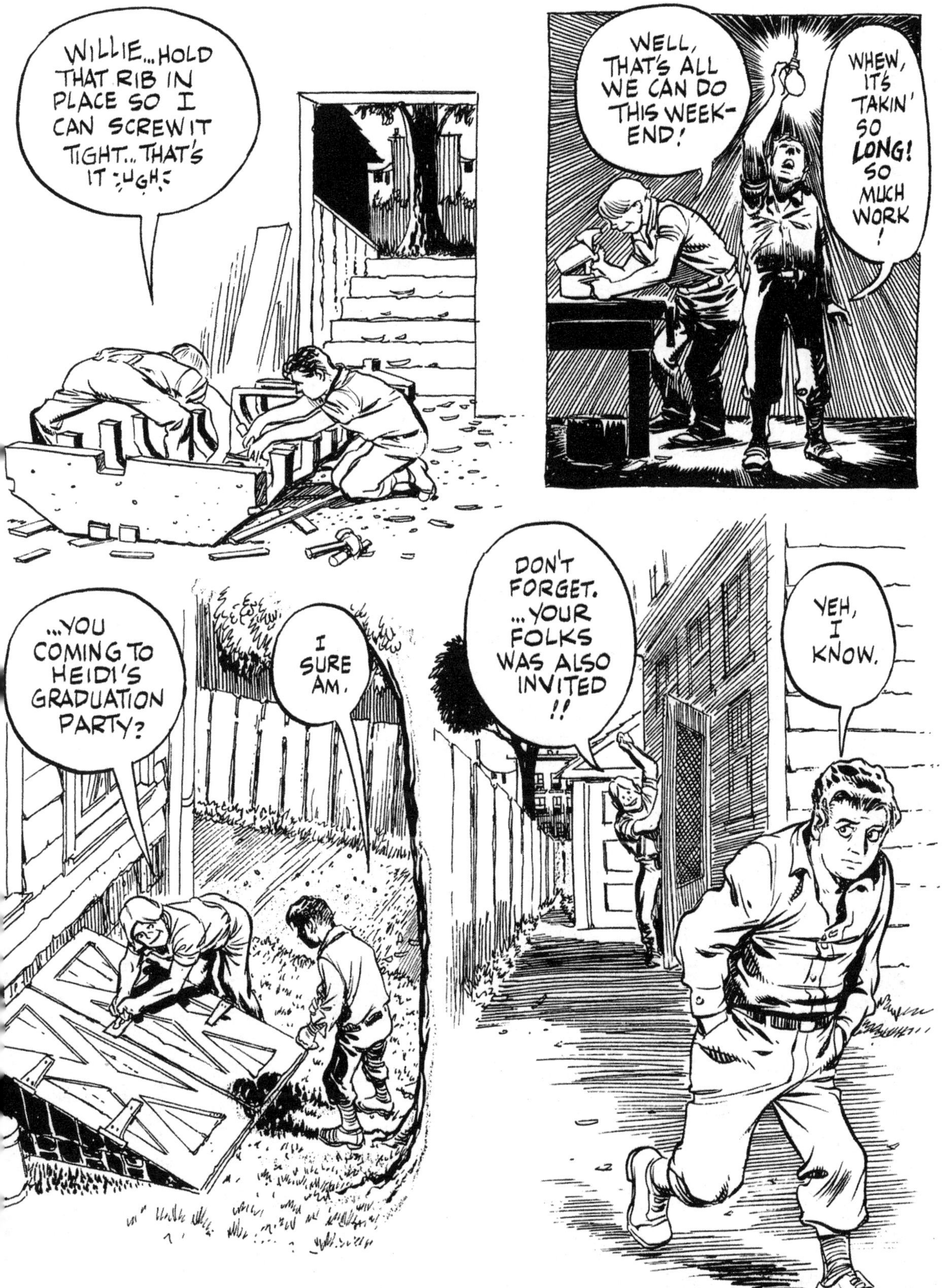
WILLIE...HOLD THAT RIB IN PLACE SO I CAN SCREW IT TIGHT... THAT'S IT UGH
WELL, THAT'S ALL WE CAN DO THIS WEEK-END!
WHEW, IT'S TAKIN' SO LONG! SO MUCH WORK!
...YOU COMING TO HEIDI'S GRADUATION PARTY?
I SURE AM.
DON'T FORGET. ...YOUR FOLKS WAS ALSO INVITED!!
YEH, I KNOW.

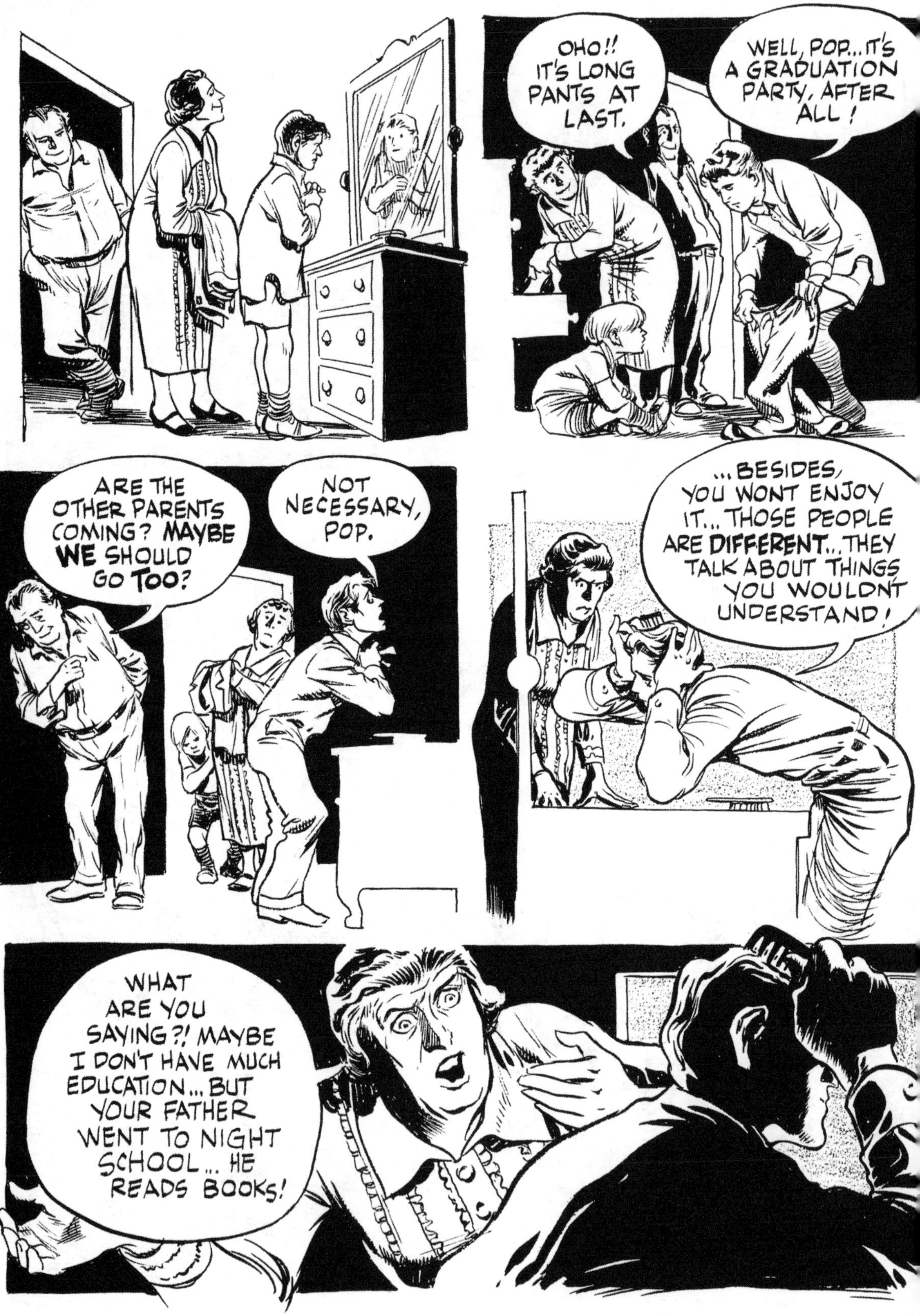
OHO!! IT'S LONG PANTS AT LAST.
WELL, POP... IT'S A GRADUATION PARTY, AFTER ALL!
ARE THE OTHER PARENTS COMING? MAYBE WE SHOULD GO TOO?
NOT NECESSARY, POP.
...BESIDES, YOU WONT ENJOY IT... THOSE PEOPLE ARE DIFFERENT... THEY TALK ABOUT THINGS YOU WOULDN'T UNDERSTAND!
WHAT ARE YOU SAYING?! MAYBE I DON'T HAVE MUCH EDUCATION... BUT YOUR FATHER WENT TO NIGHT SCHOOL... HE READS BOOKS!

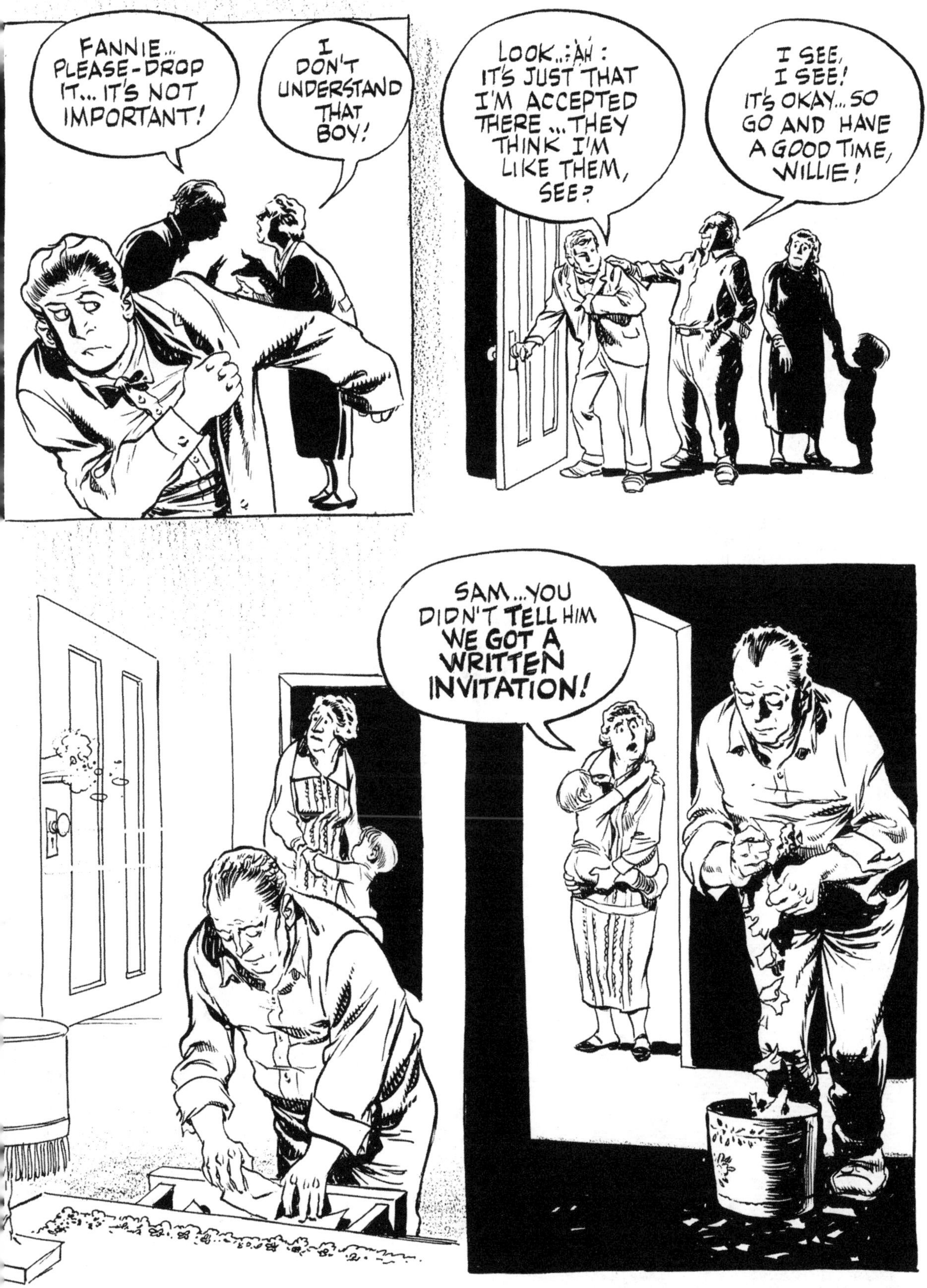
FANNIE... PLEASE-DROP IT... IT'S NOT IMPORTANT!
I DON'T UNDERSTAND THAT BOY!
LOOK..:AH: IT'S JUST THAT I'M ACCEPTED THERE ...THEY THINK I'M LIKE THEM, SEE?
I SEE, I SEE! IT'S OKAY...SO GO AND HAVE A GOOD TIME, WILLIE!
SAM...YOU DIDN'T TELL HIM WE GOT A WRITTEN INVITATION!

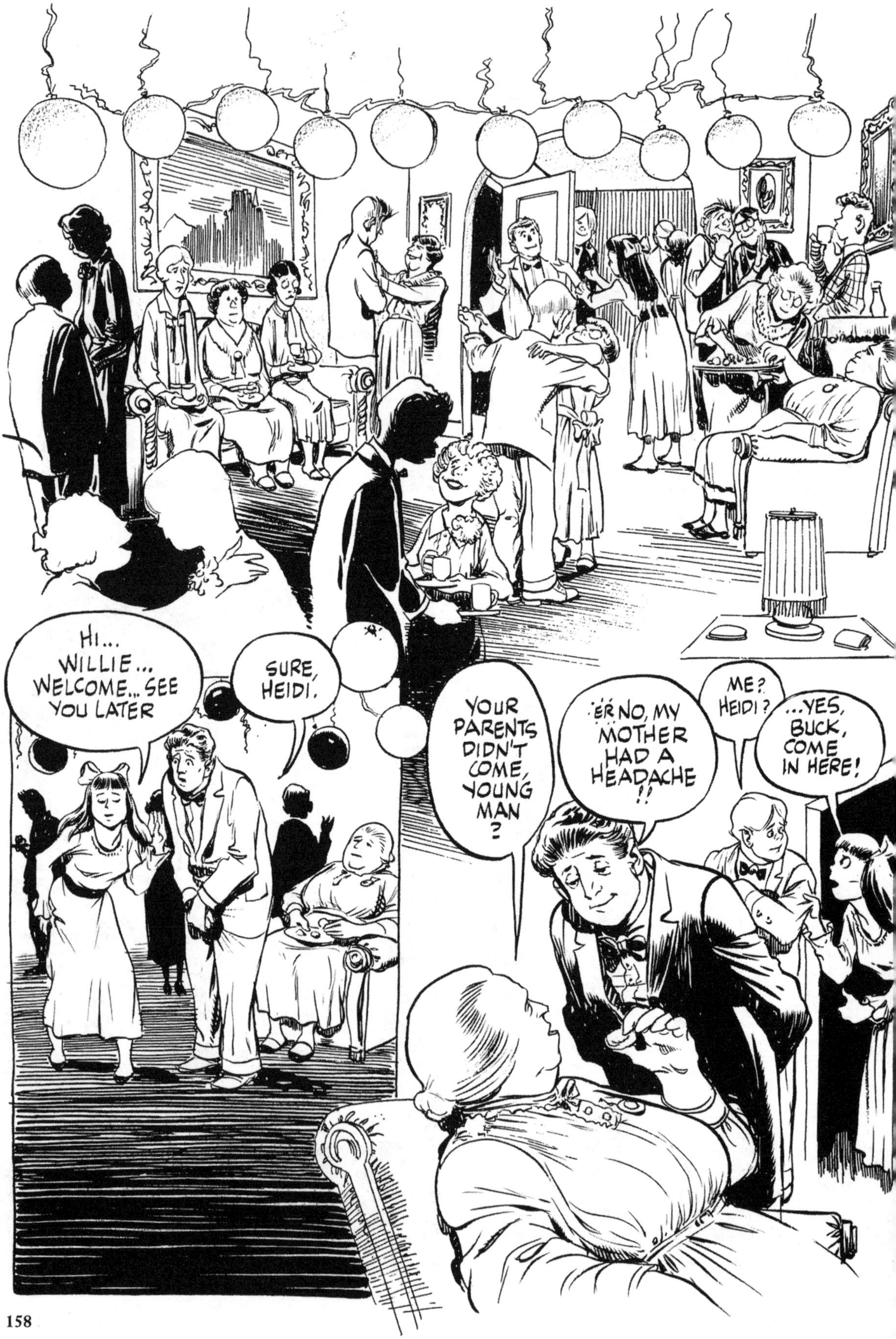
HI... WILLIE... WELCOME... SEE YOU LATER
SURE, HEIDI.
YOUR PARENTS DIDN'T COME, YOUNG MAN ?
ER NO, MY MOTHER HAD A HEADACHE !!
ME? HEIDI?
...YES, BUCK, COME IN HERE!

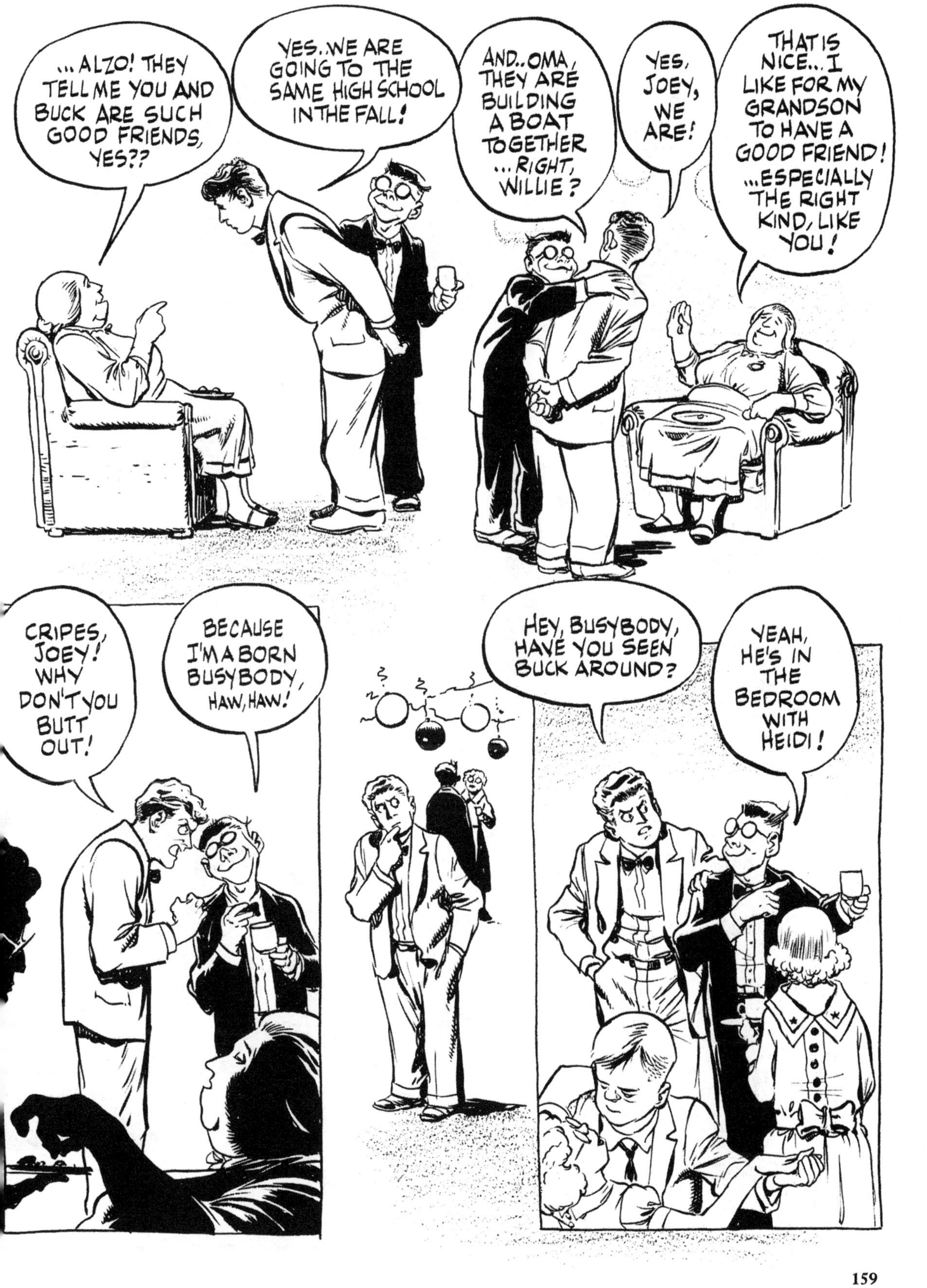
...ALZO! THEY TELL ME YOU AND BUCK ARE SUCH GOOD FRIENDS, YES??
YES..WE ARE GOING TO THE SAME HIGH SCHOOL IN THE FALL!
AND..OMA, THEY ARE BUILDING A BOAT TOGETHER ...RIGHT, WILLIE?
YES, JOEY, WE ARE!
THAT IS NICE... I LIKE FOR MY GRANDSON TO HAVE A GOOD FRIEND! ...ESPECIALLY THE RIGHT KIND, LIKE YOU!
CRIPES, JOEY! WHY DON'T YOU BUTT OUT!
BECAUSE I'M A BORN BUSYBODY, HAW, HAW!
HEY, BUSYBODY, HAVE YOU SEEN BUCK AROUND?
YEAH, HE'S IN THE BEDROOM WITH HEIDI!

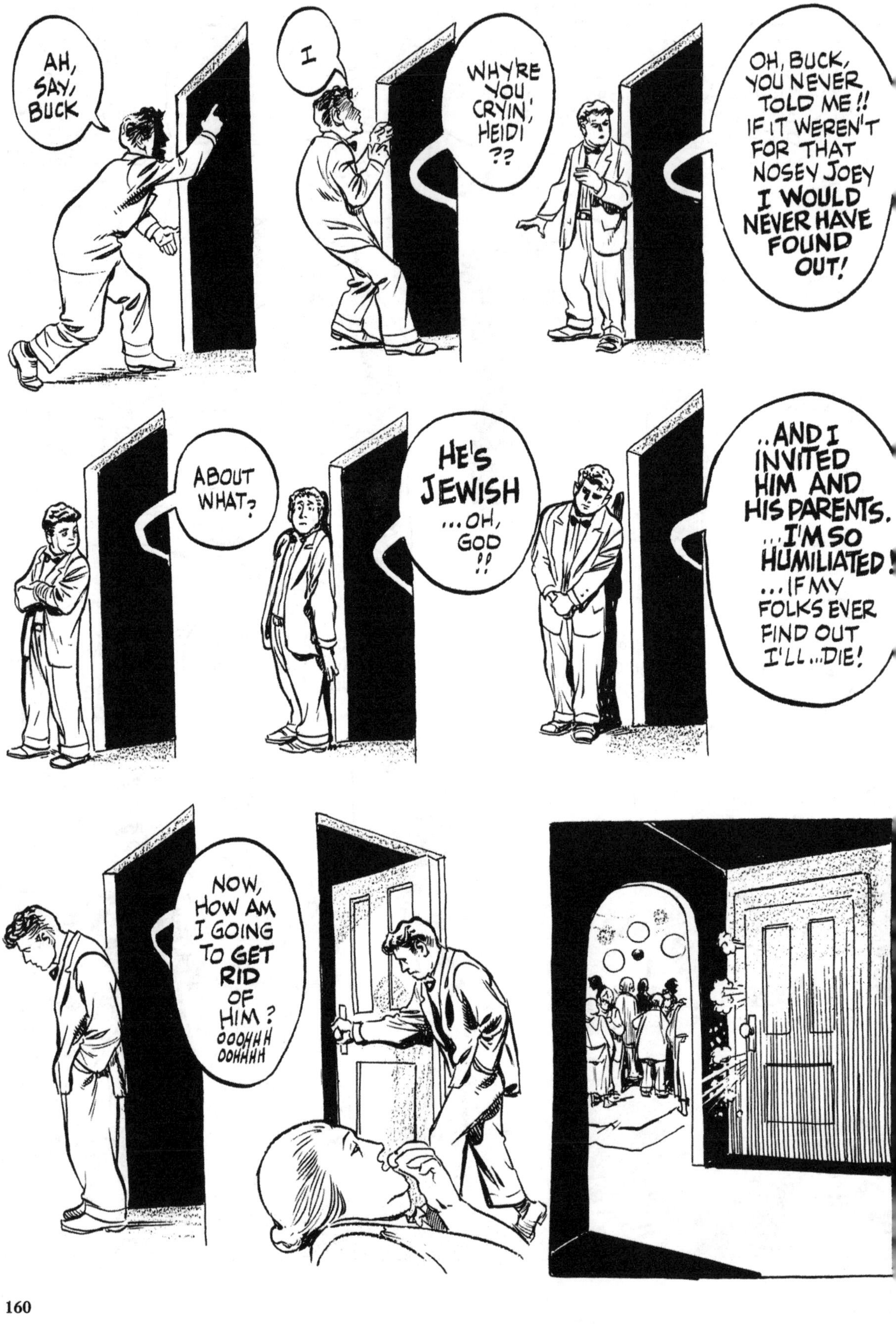
AH, SAY, BUCK
I
WHY'RE YOU CRYIN', HEIDI ??
OH, BUCK, YOU NEVER TOLD ME !! IF IT WEREN'T FOR THAT NOSEY JOEY I WOULD NEVER HAVE FOUND OUT!
ABOUT WHAT?
HE'S JEWISH ...OH, GOD !!
..AND I INVITED HIM AND HIS PARENTS. ...I'M SO HUMILIATED! ...IF MY FOLKS EVER FIND OUT I'LL...DIE!
NOW, HOW AM I GOING TO GET RID OF HIM? OOOHHH OOHHHH

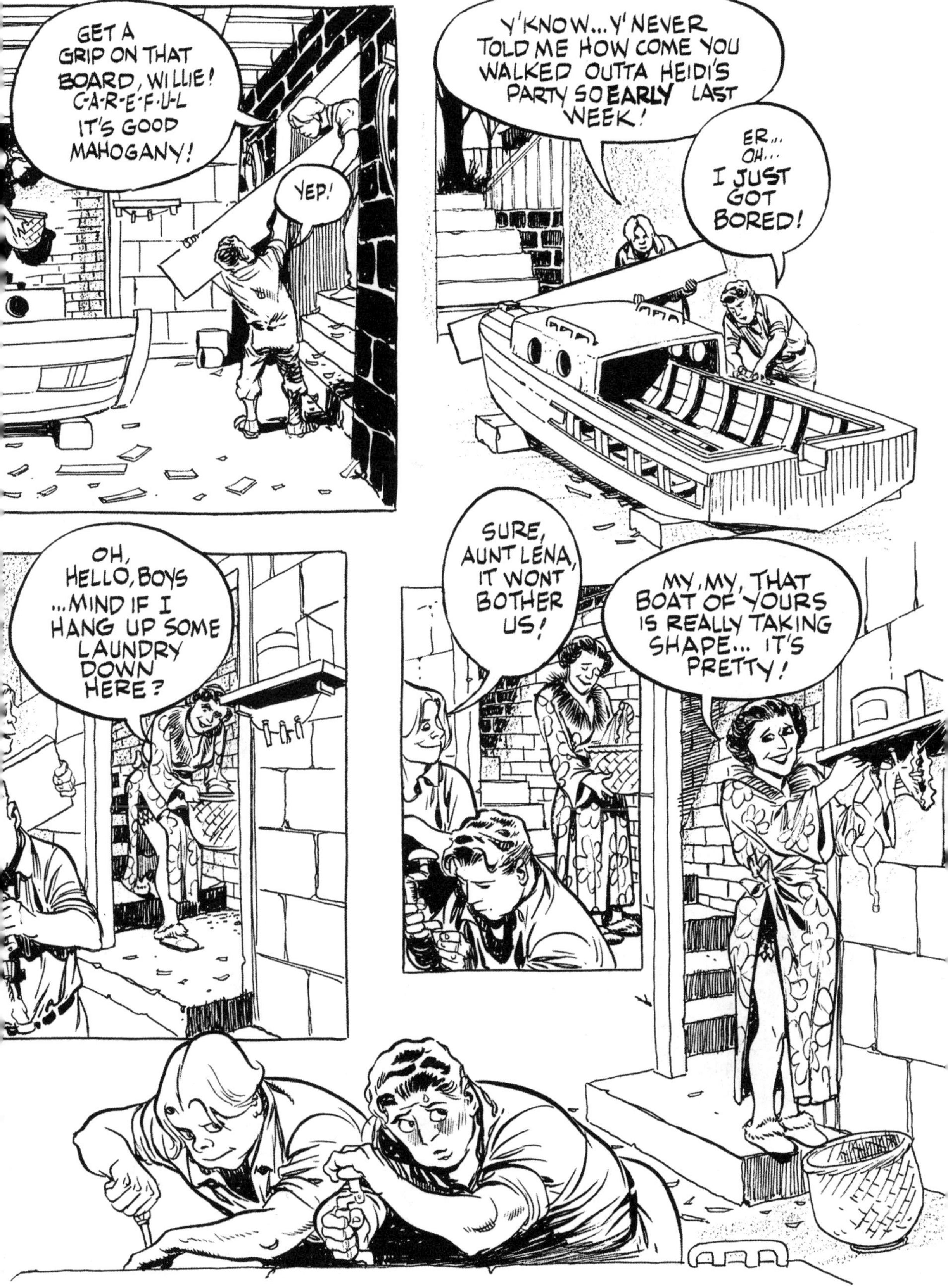
GET A GRIP ON THAT BOARD, WILLIE! C-A-R-E-F-U-L IT'S GOOD MAHOGANY!
YEP!
Y'KNOW... Y'NEVER TOLD ME HOW COME YOU WALKED OUTTA HEIDI'S PARTY SO EARLY LAST WEEK!
ER... OH... I JUST GOT BORED!
OH, HELLO, BOYS ...MIND IF I HANG UP SOME LAUNDRY DOWN HERE?
SURE, AUNT LENA, IT WONT BOTHER US!
MY, MY, THAT BOAT OF YOURS IS REALLY TAKING SHAPE... IT'S PRETTY!

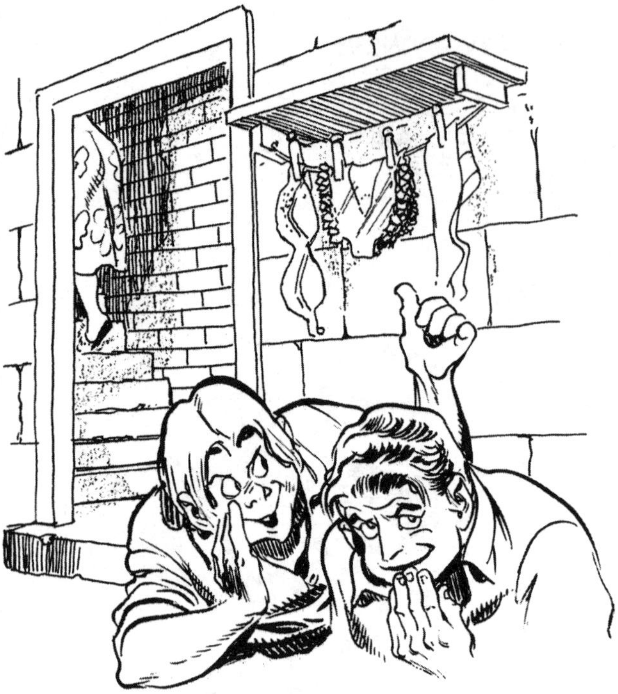
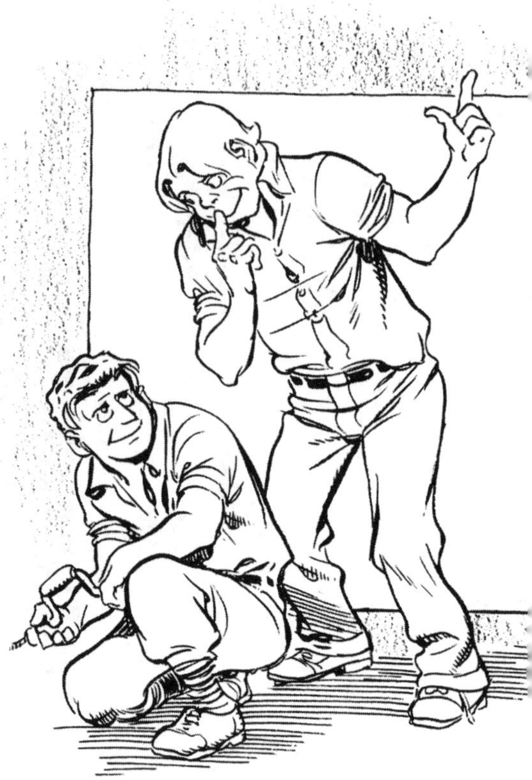
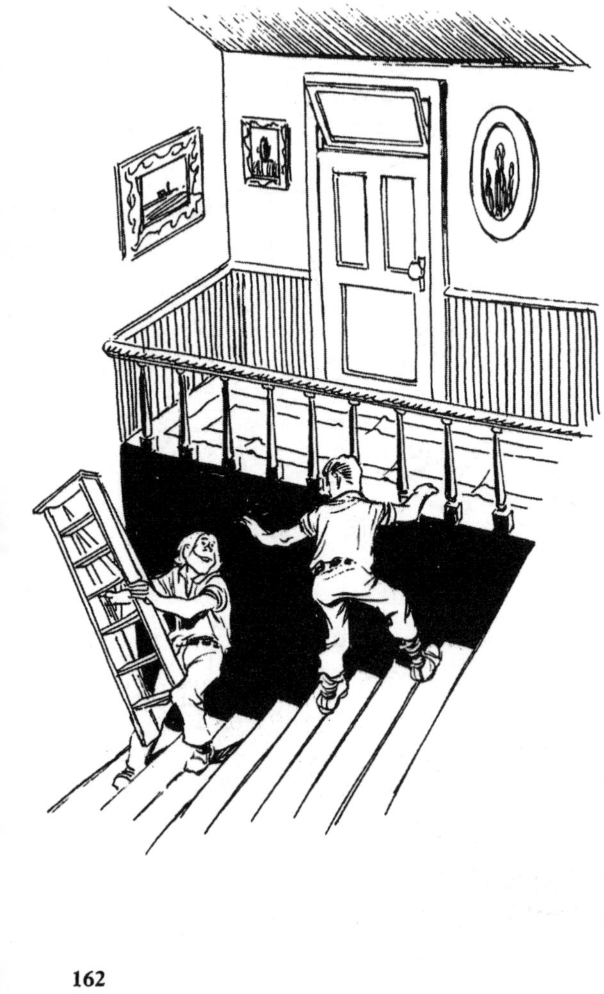
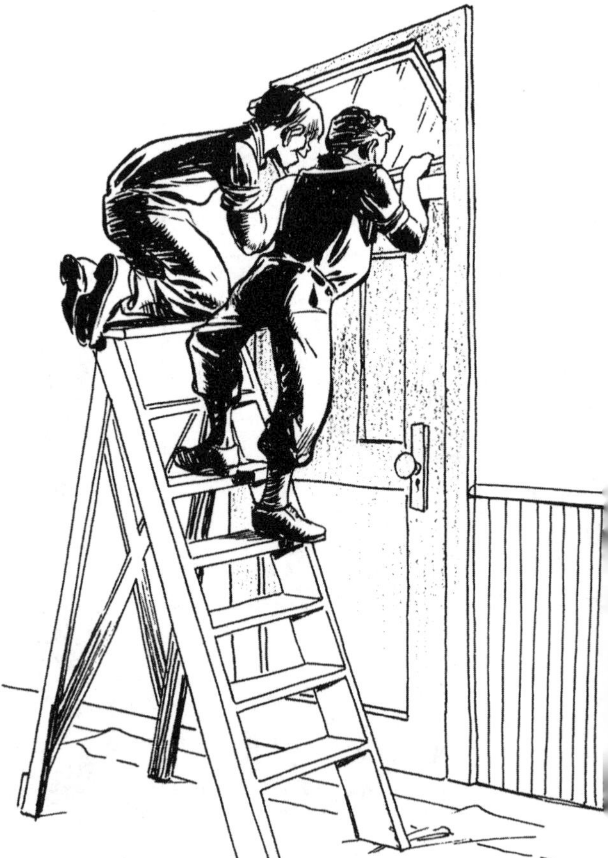

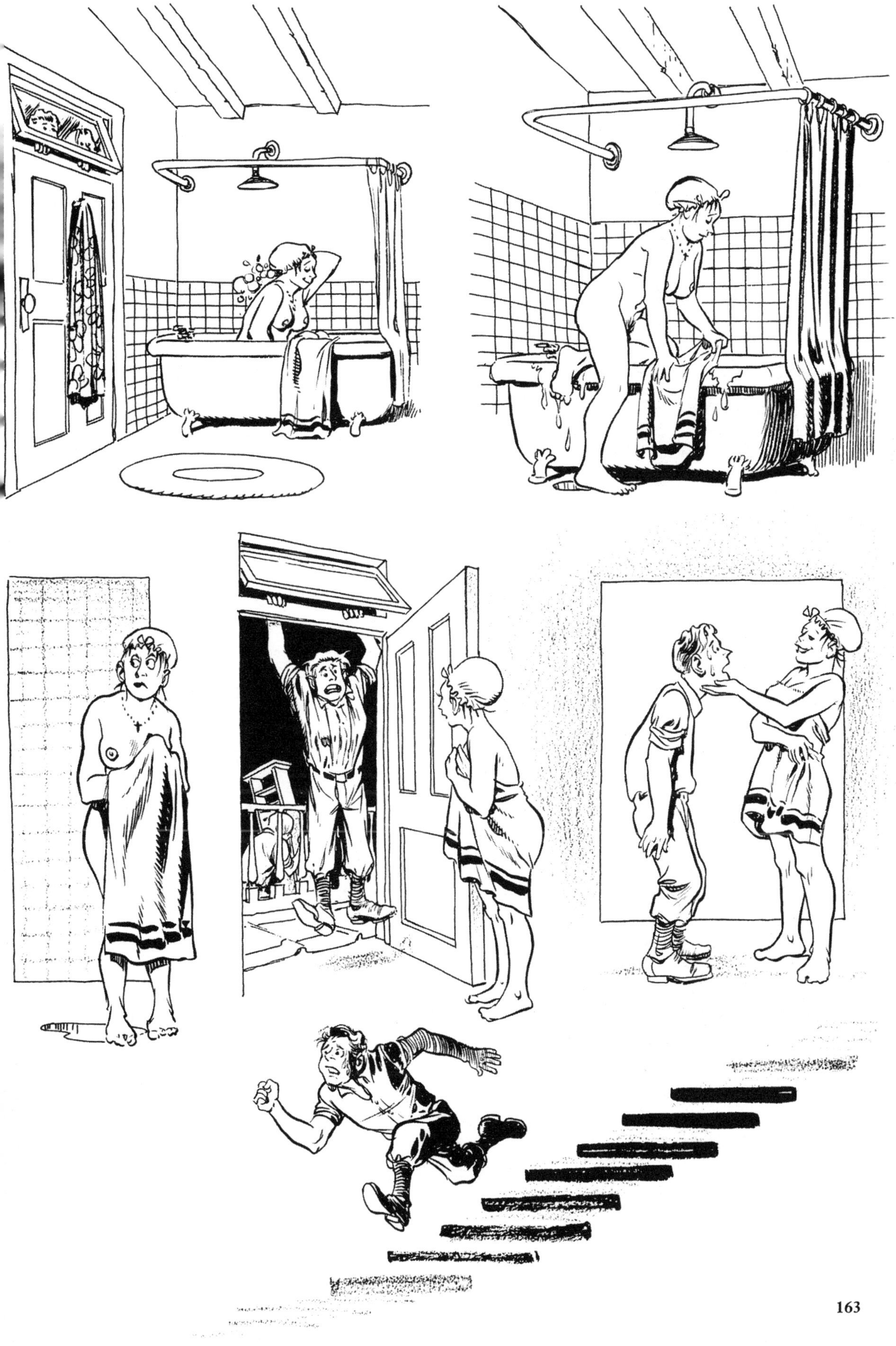

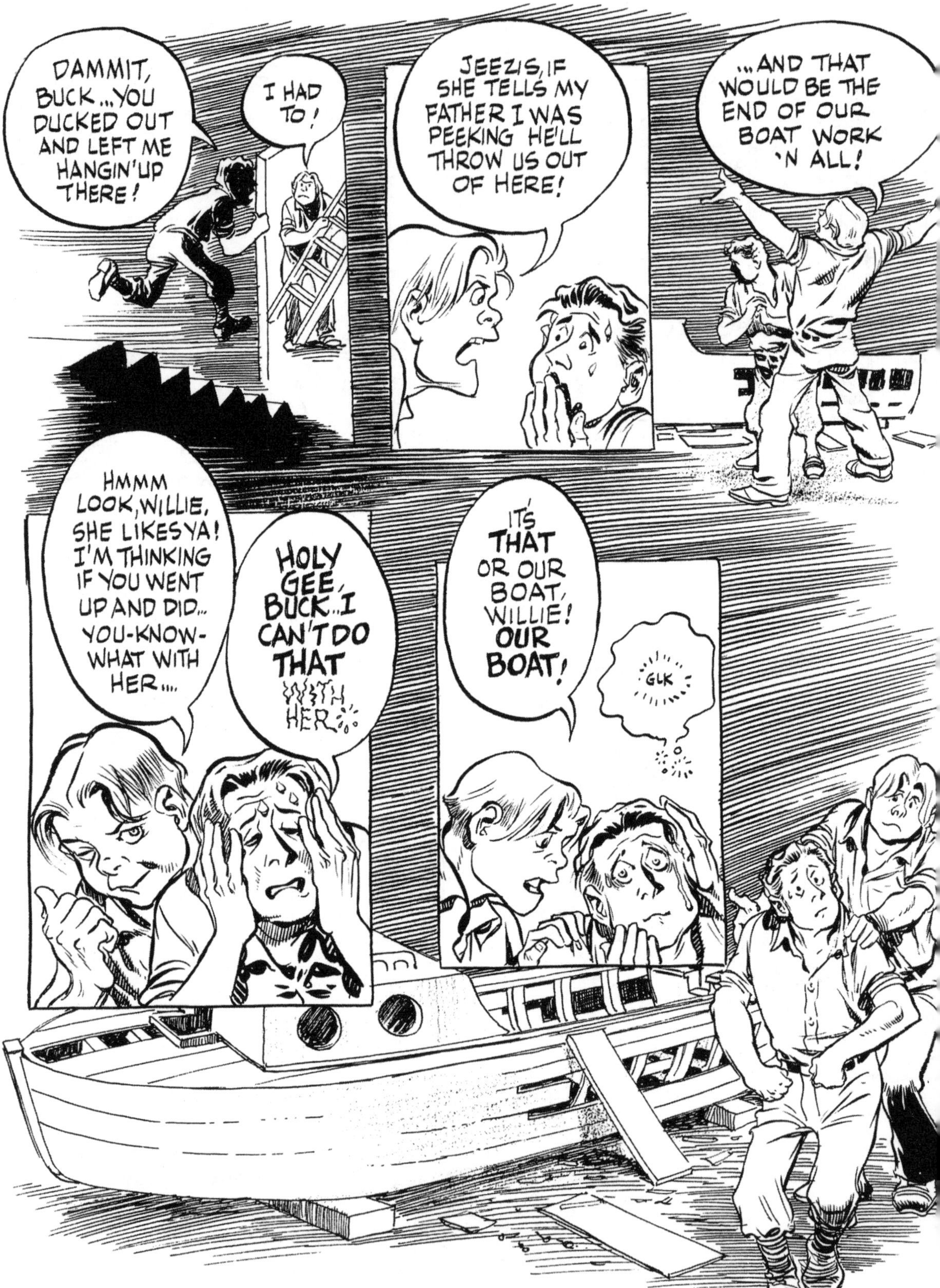
DAMMIT, BUCK...YOU DUCKED OUT AND LEFT ME HANGIN' UP THERE!
I HAD TO!
JEEZIS, IF SHE TELLS MY FATHER I WAS PEEKING HE'LL THROW US OUT OF HERE!
...AND THAT WOULD BE THE END OF OUR BOAT WORK 'N ALL!
HMMM LOOK, WILLIE, SHE LIKES YA! I'M THINKING IF YOU WENT UP AND DID... YOU-KNOW-WHAT WITH HER....
HOLY GEE, BUCK...I CAN'T DO THAT WITH HER
IT'S THAT OR OUR BOAT, WILLIE! OUR BOAT!
GLK

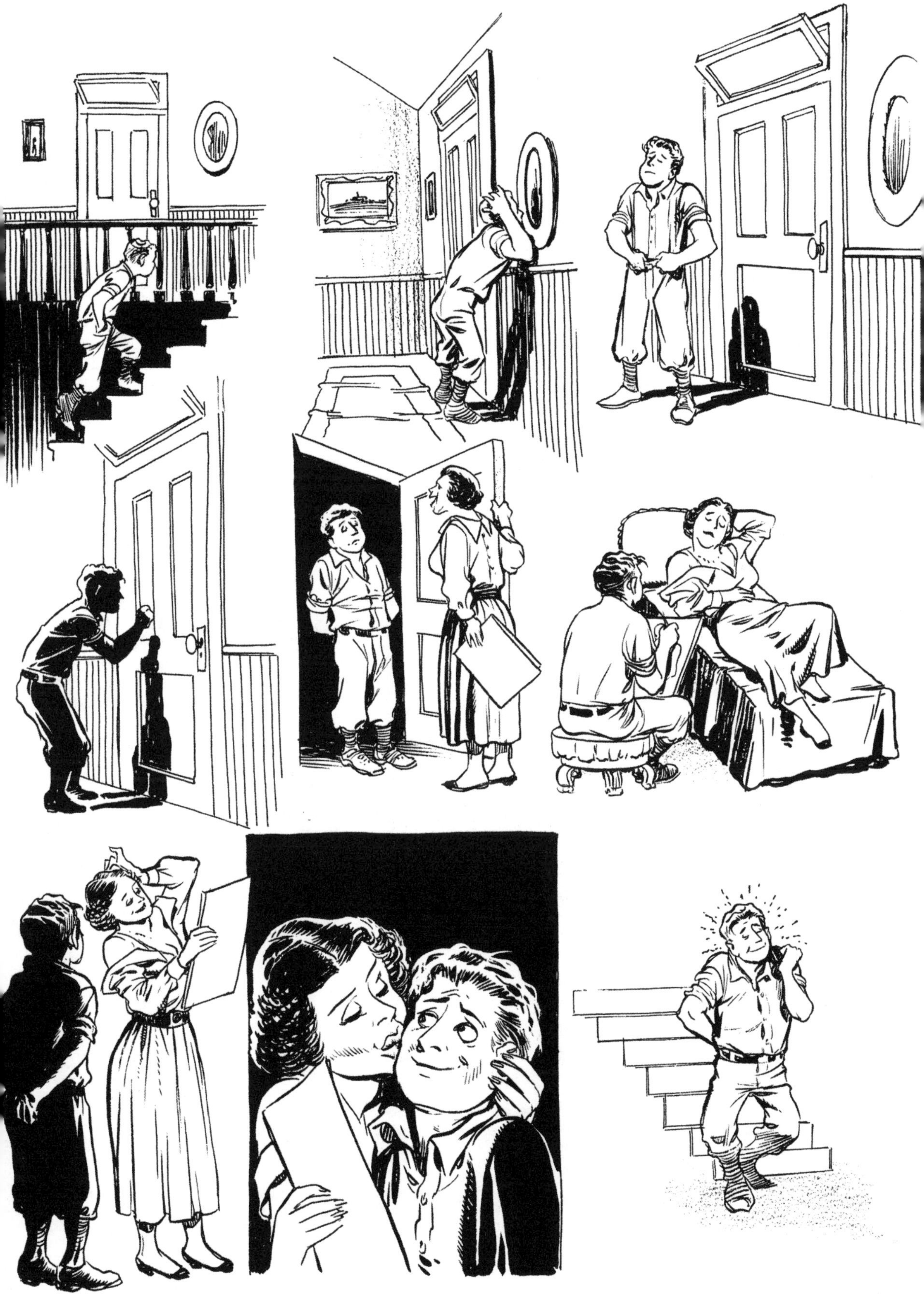

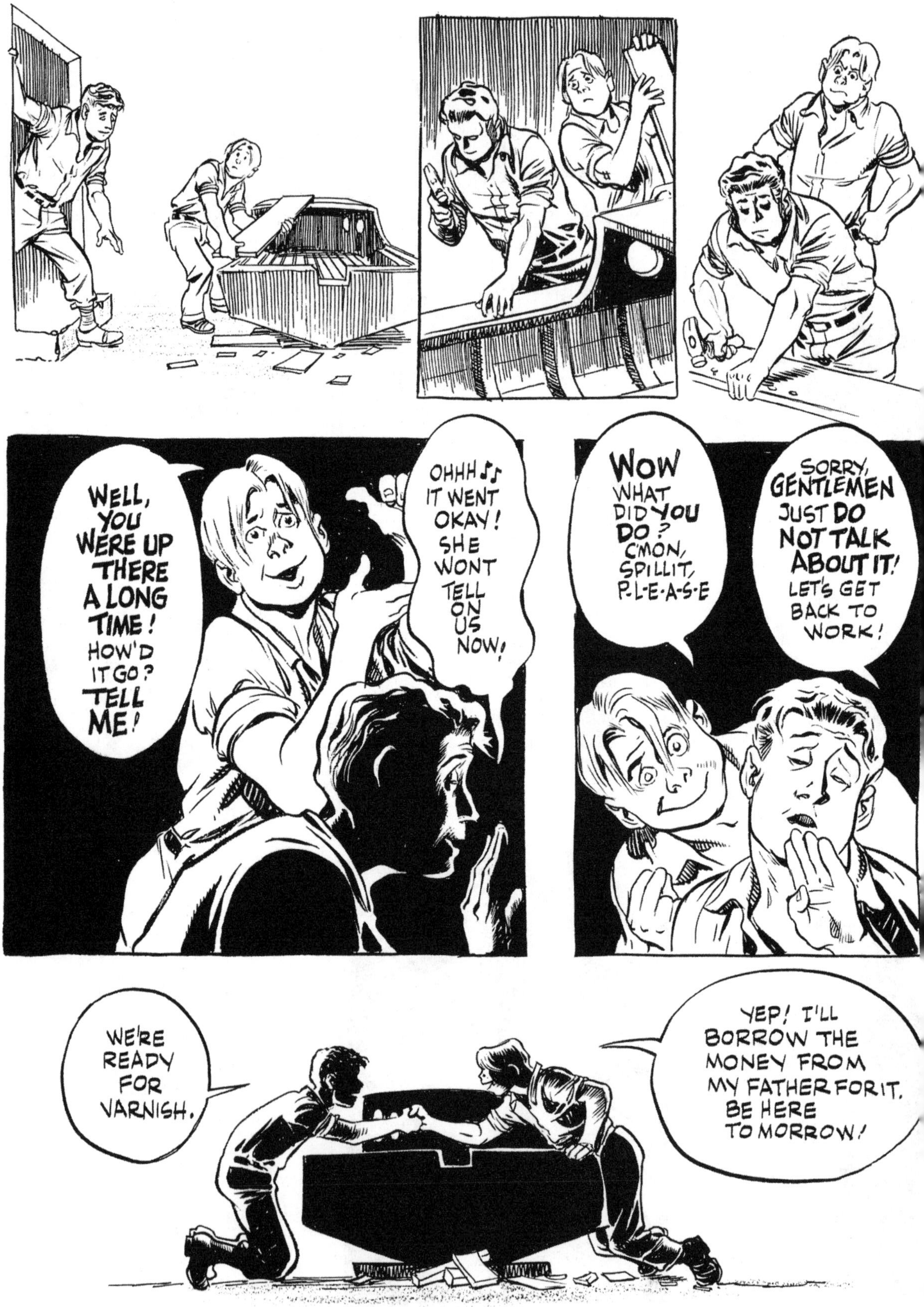
WELL, YOU WERE UP THERE A LONG TIME! HOW'D IT GO? TELL ME!
OHHH♪♪ IT WENT OKAY! SHE WONT TELL ON US NOW!
WOW WHAT DID YOU DO? C'MON, SPILLIT, P-L-E-A-S-E
SORRY, GENTLEMEN JUST DO NOT TALK ABOUT IT! LET'S GET BACK TO WORK!
WE'RE READY FOR VARNISH.
YEP! I'LL BORROW THE MONEY FROM MY FATHER FOR IT. BE HERE TOMORROW!

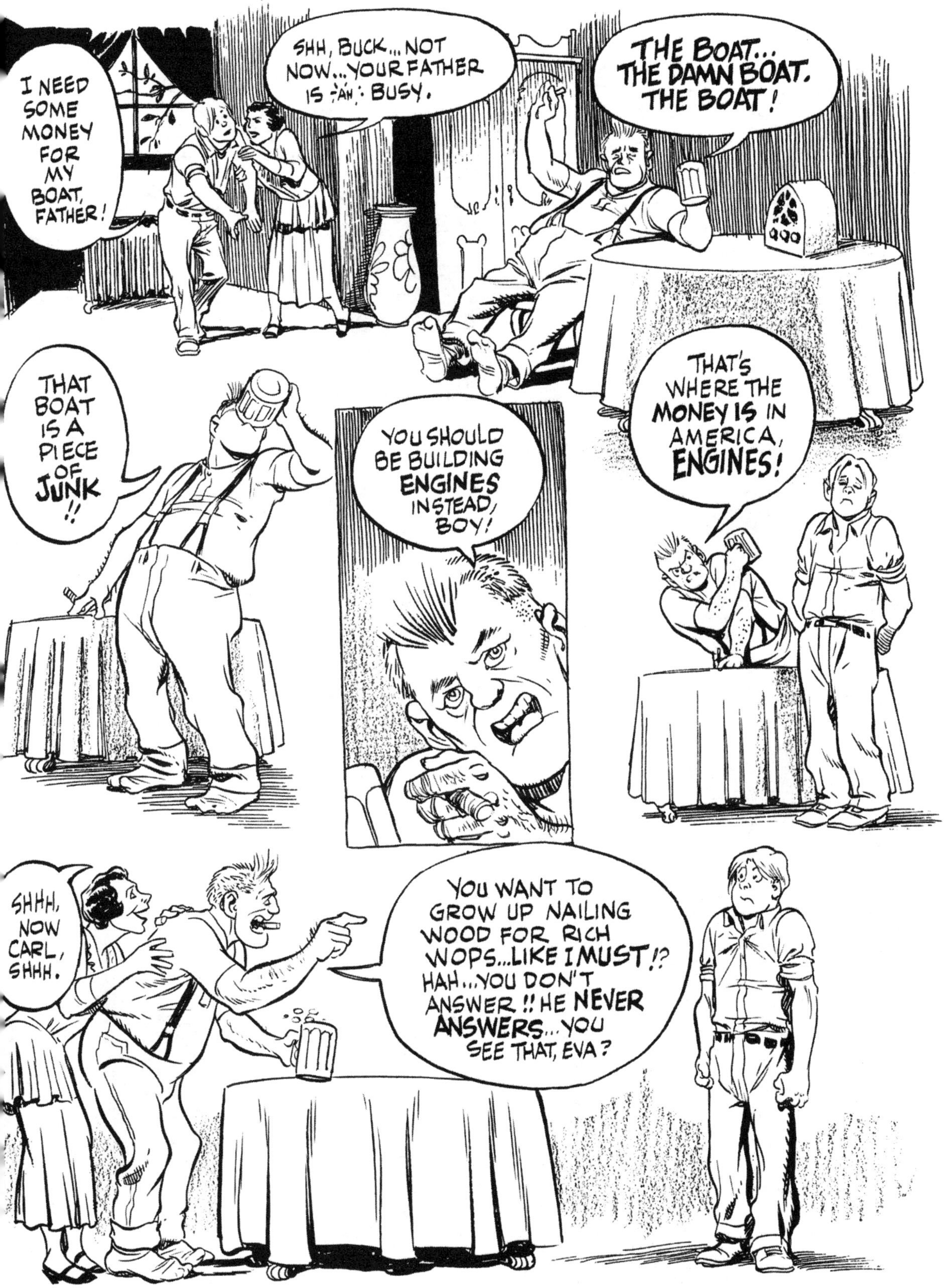
I NEED SOME MONEY FOR MY BOAT, FATHER!
SHH, BUCK... NOT NOW... YOUR FATHER IS -AH- BUSY.
THE BOAT... THE DAMN BOAT. THE BOAT!
THAT BOAT IS A PIECE OF JUNK!!
YOU SHOULD BE BUILDING ENGINES INSTEAD, BOY!
THAT'S WHERE THE MONEY IS IN AMERICA, ENGINES!
SHHH, NOW CARL, SHHH.
YOU WANT TO GROW UP NAILING WOOD FOR RICH WOPS... LIKE I MUST!? HAH... YOU DON'T ANSWER!! HE NEVER ANSWERS... YOU SEE THAT, EVA?

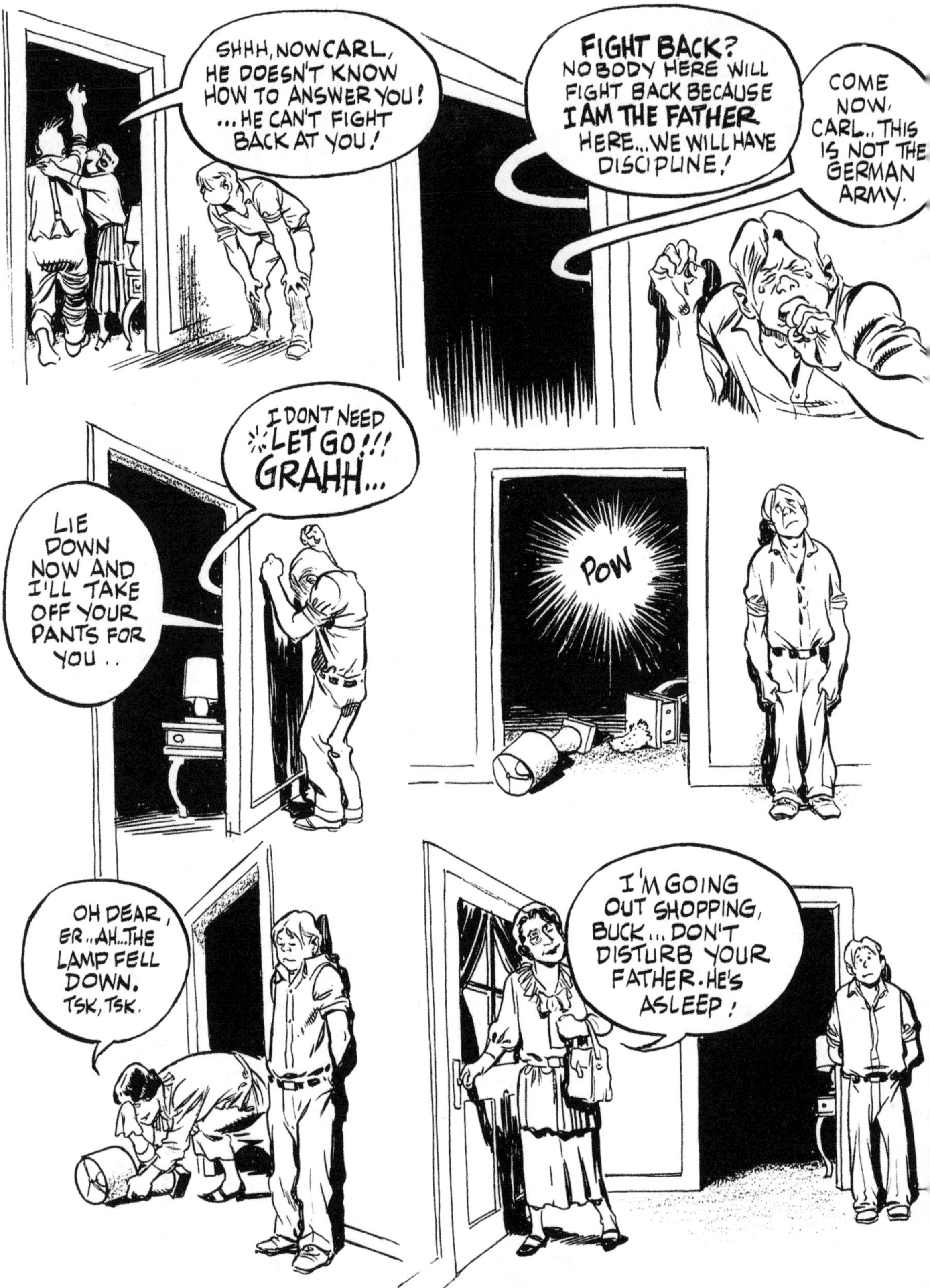
SHHH, NOW CARL, HE DOESN'T KNOW HOW TO ANSWER YOU! ...HE CAN'T FIGHT BACK AT YOU!
FIGHT BACK? NOBODY HERE WILL FIGHT BACK BECAUSE I AM THE FATHER HERE... WE WILL HAVE DISCIPLINE!
COME NOW, CARL.. THIS IS NOT THE GERMAN ARMY.
I DONT NEED LET GO!!! GRAHH...
LIE DOWN NOW AND I'LL TAKE OFF YOUR PANTS FOR YOU..
POW
OH DEAR, ER...AH...THE LAMP FELL DOWN. TSK, TSK.
I'M GOING OUT SHOPPING, BUCK... DON'T DISTURB YOUR FATHER. HE'S ASLEEP!

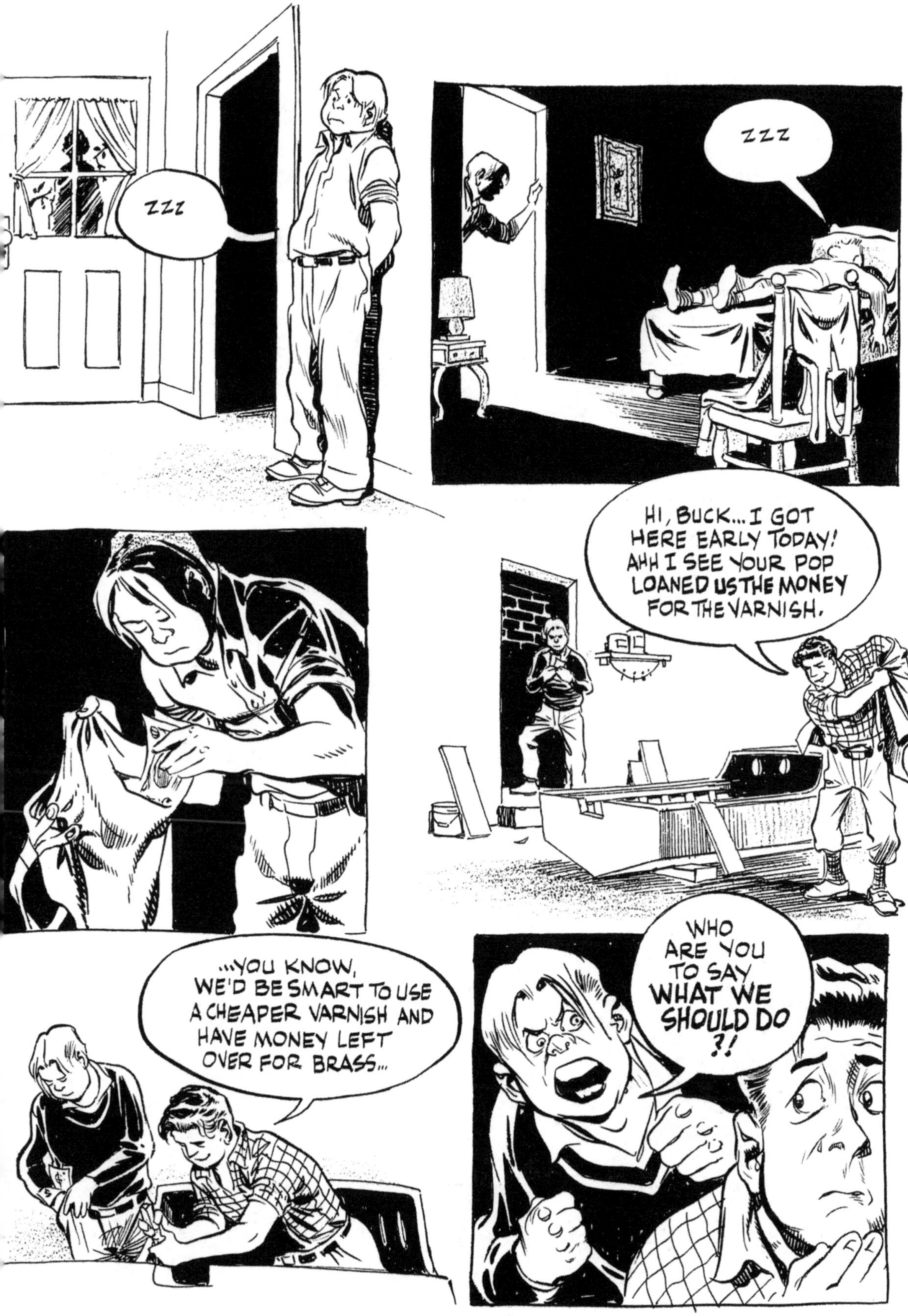
ZZZ
ZZZ
HI, BUCK... I GOT HERE EARLY TODAY! AHH I SEE YOUR POP LOANED US THE MONEY FOR THE VARNISH.
...YOU KNOW, WE'D BE SMART TO USE A CHEAPER VARNISH AND HAVE MONEY LEFT OVER FOR BRASS...
WHO ARE YOU TO SAY WHAT WE SHOULD DO ?!

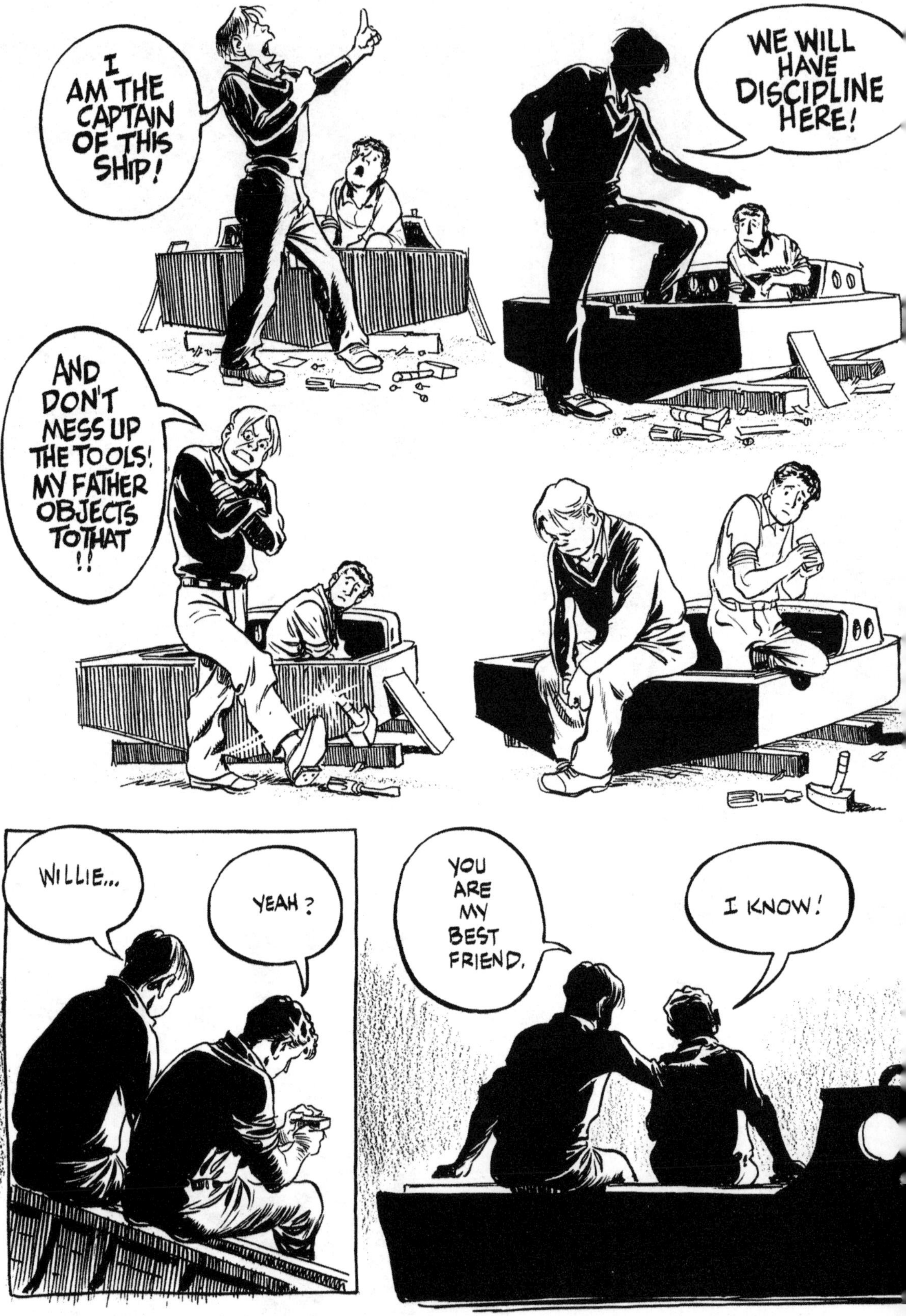
I AM THE CAPTAIN OF THIS SHIP!
WE WILL HAVE DISCIPLINE HERE!
AND DON'T MESS UP THE TOOLS! MY FATHER OBJECTS TO THAT!!
WILLIE...
YEAH?
YOU ARE MY BEST FRIEND.
I KNOW!

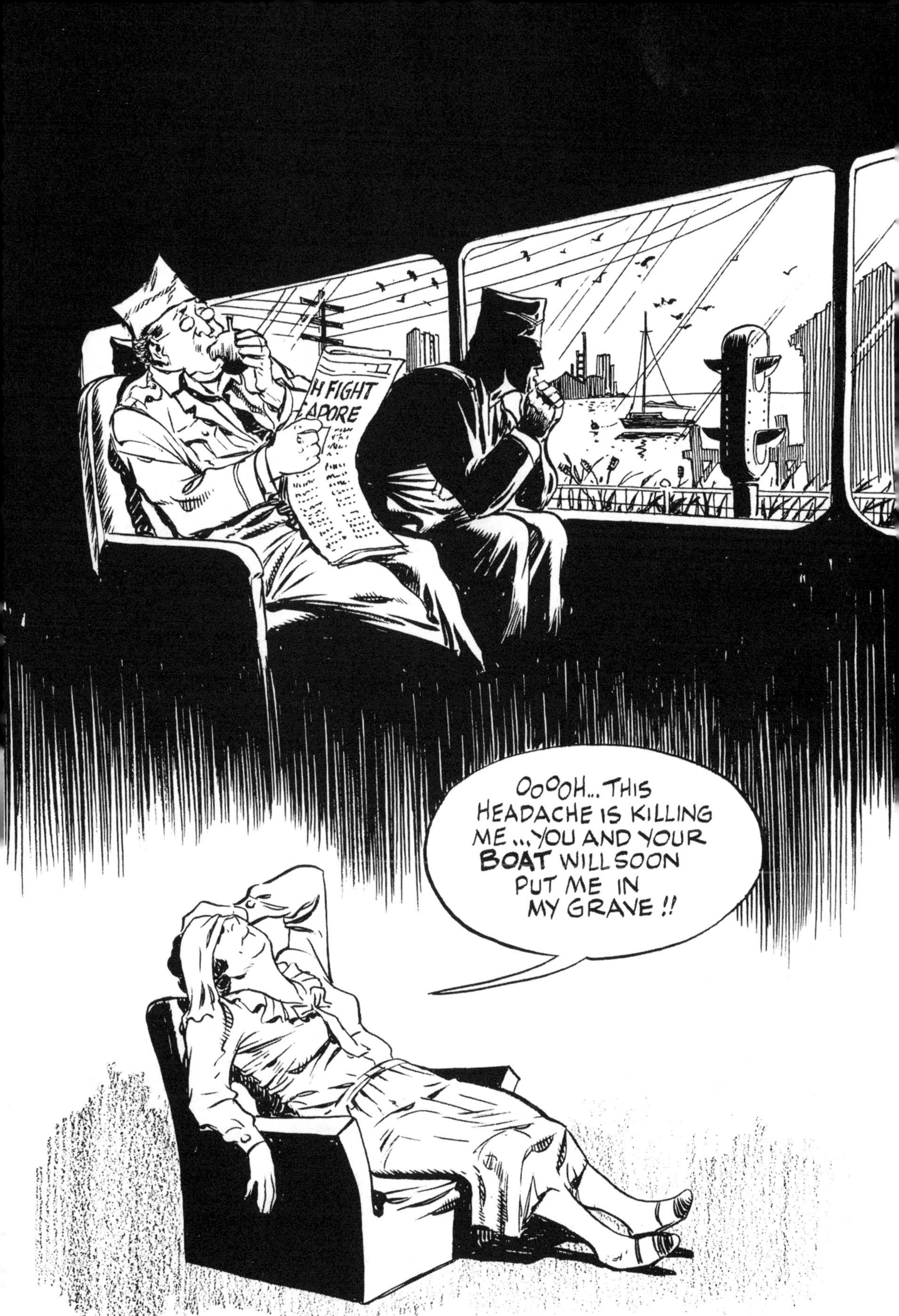
H FIGHT
APORE
OOOOH... THIS HEADACHE IS KILLING ME ... YOU AND YOUR BOAT WILL SOON PUT ME IN MY GRAVE !!

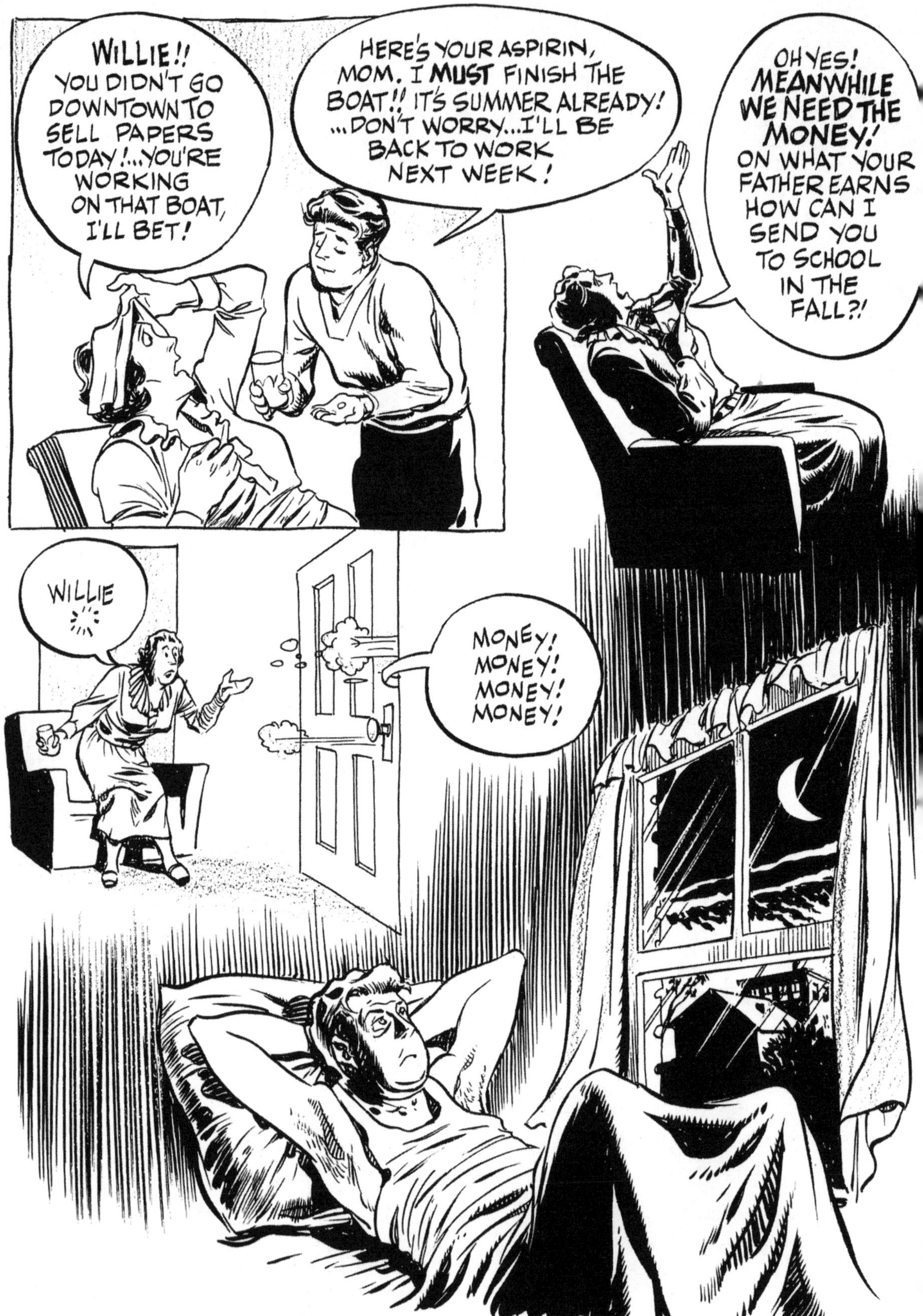
WILLIE!! YOU DIDN'T GO DOWNTOWN TO SELL PAPERS TODAY!...YOU'RE WORKING ON THAT BOAT, I'LL BET!
HERE'S YOUR ASPIRIN, MOM. I MUST FINISH THE BOAT!! IT'S SUMMER ALREADY! ...DON'T WORRY...I'LL BE BACK TO WORK NEXT WEEK!
OH YES! MEANWHILE WE NEED THE MONEY! ON WHAT YOUR FATHER EARNS HOW CAN I SEND YOU TO SCHOOL IN THE FALL?!
WILLIE
MONEY! MONEY! MONEY! MONEY!

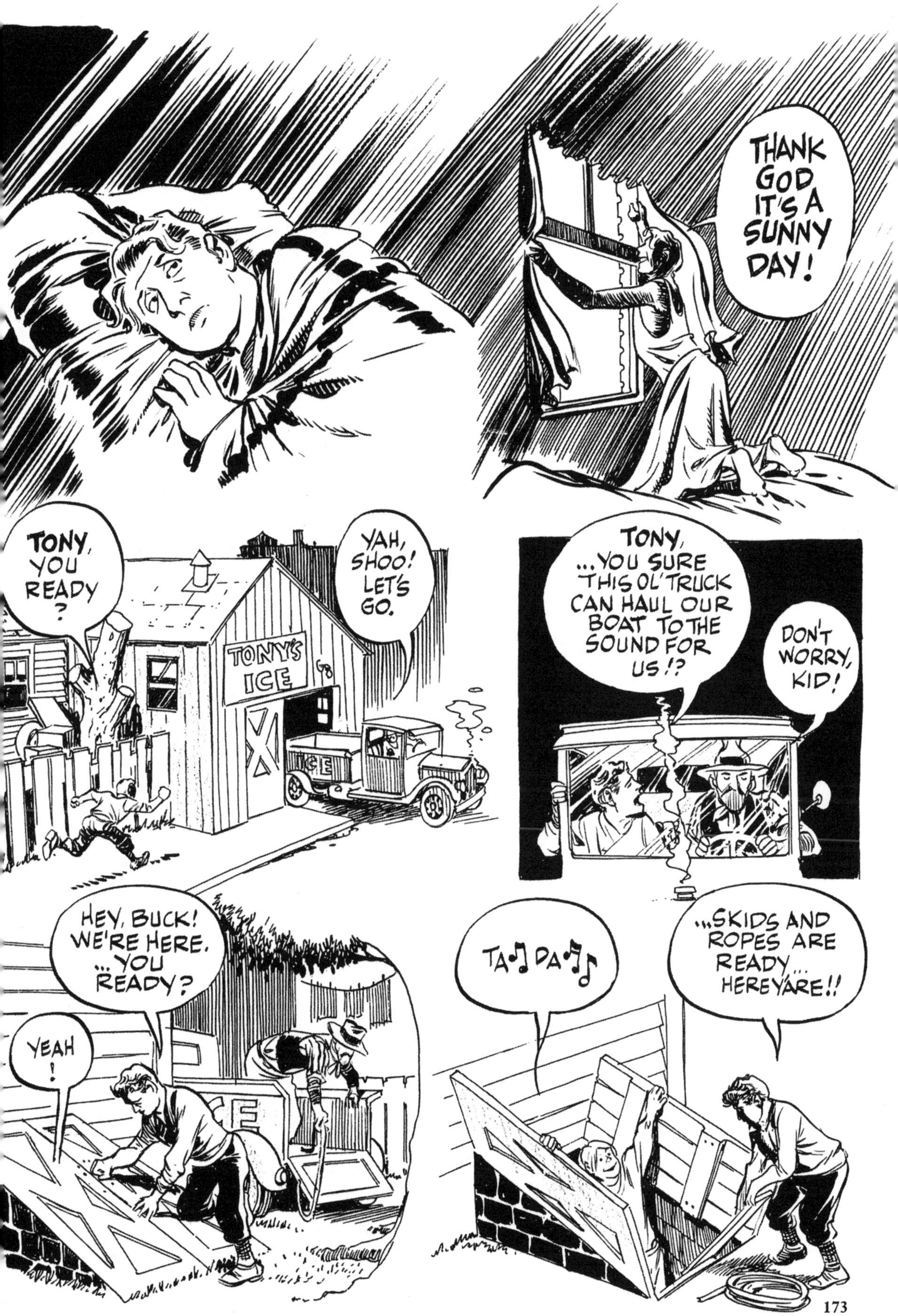
THANK GOD IT'S A SUNNY DAY!
TONY, YOU READY?
YAH, SHOO! LET'S GO.
TONY'S ICE
ICE
TONY, ...YOU SURE THIS OL' TRUCK CAN HAUL OUR BOAT TO THE SOUND FOR US!?
DON'T WORRY, KID!
HEY, BUCK! WE'RE HERE. ...YOU READY?
YEAH!
TA♫ DA♫♪
...SKIDS AND ROPES ARE READY... HEREYARE!!

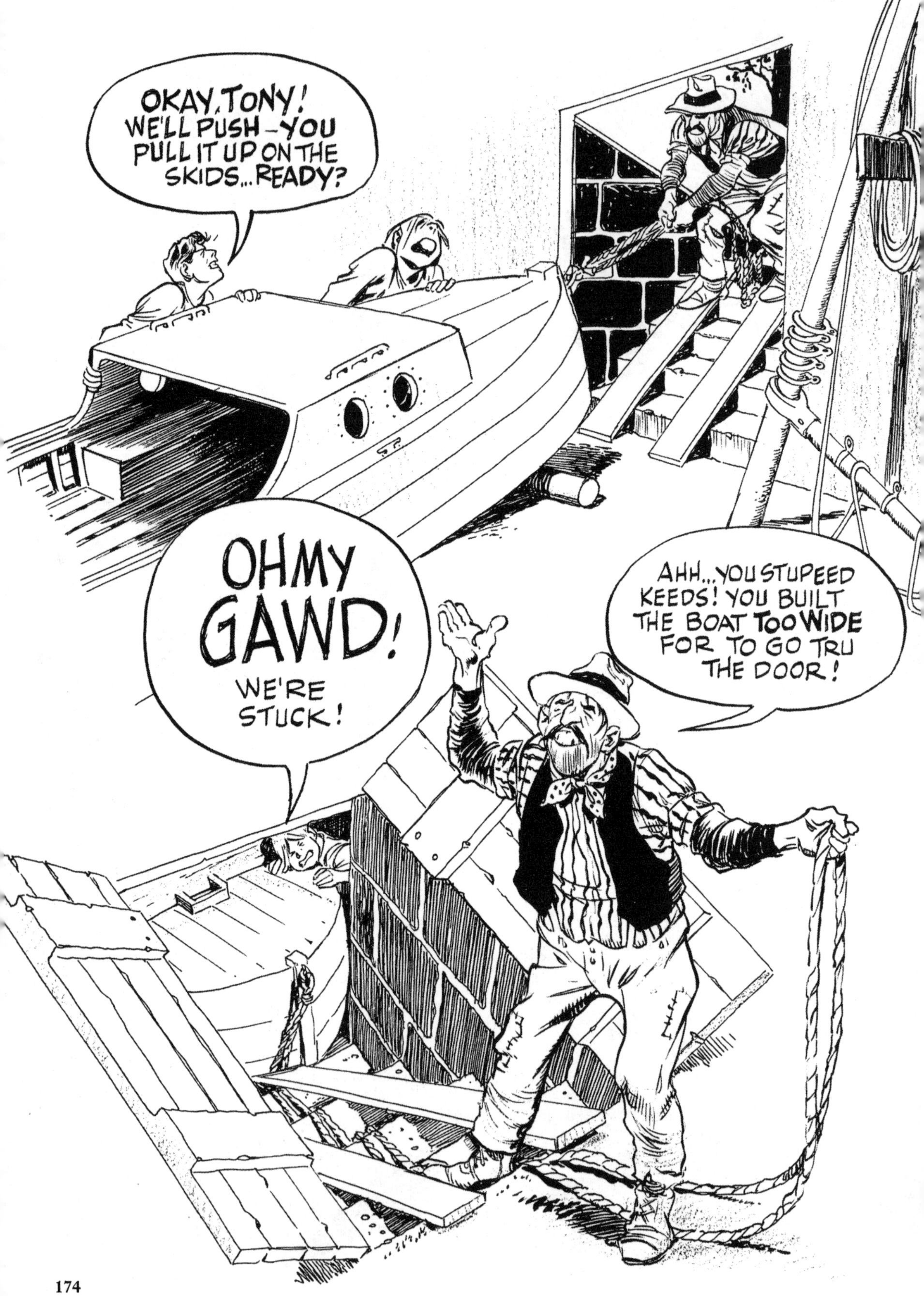
OKAY, TONY! WE'LL PUSH – YOU PULL IT UP ON THE SKIDS... READY?
OHMY GAWD! WE'RE STUCK!
AHH... YOU STUPEED KEEDS! YOU BUILT THE BOAT TOO WIDE FOR TO GO TRU THE DOOR!

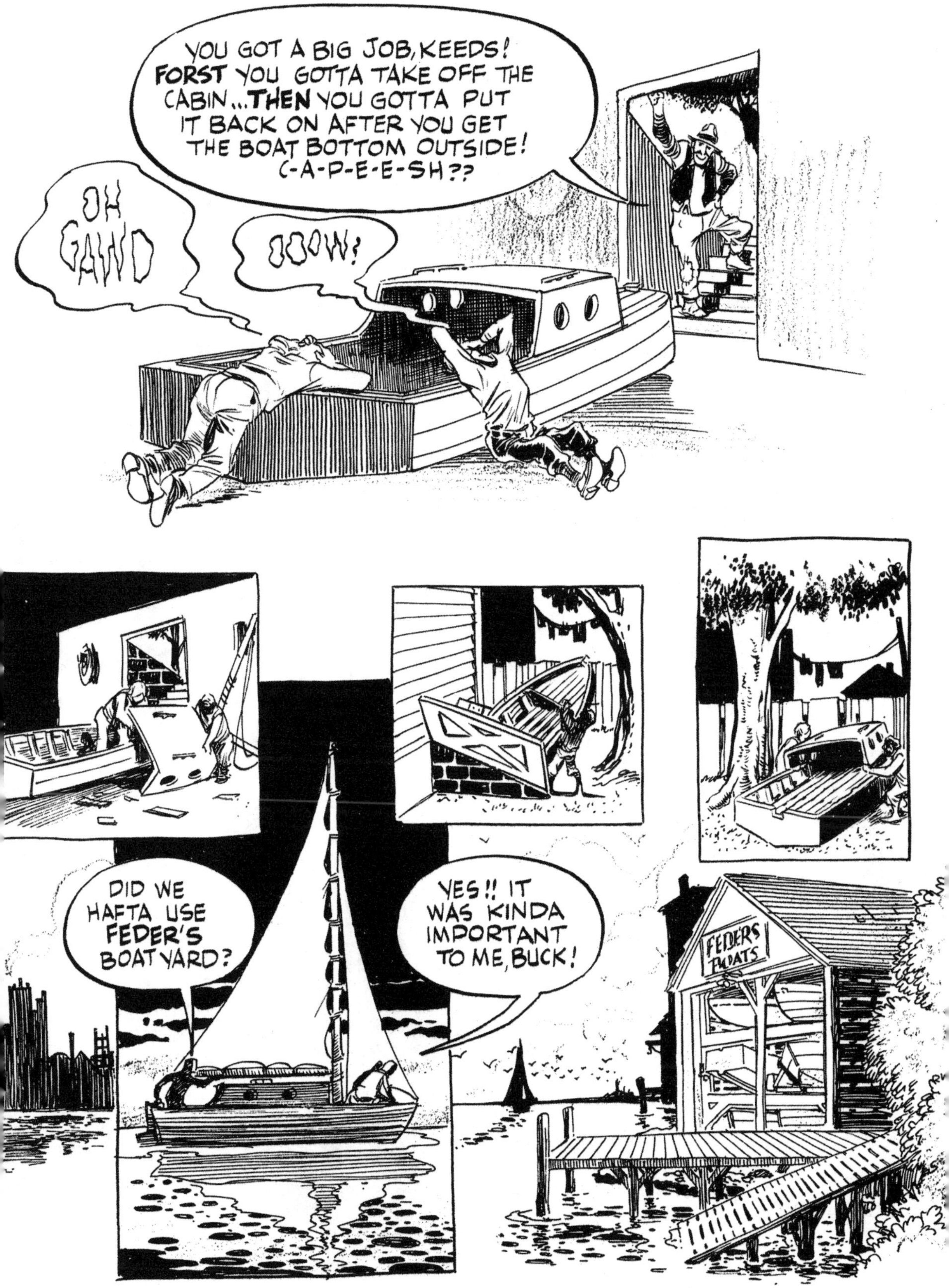
YOU GOT A BIG JOB, KEEDS! FORST YOU GOTTA TAKE OFF THE CABIN...THEN YOU GOTTA PUT IT BACK ON AFTER YOU GET THE BOAT BOTTOM OUTSIDE! C-A-P-E-E-SH??
OH GAWD
OOOW!
DID WE HAFTA USE FEDER'S BOATYARD?
YES!! IT WAS KINDA IMPORTANT TO ME, BUCK!
FEDER'S BOATS

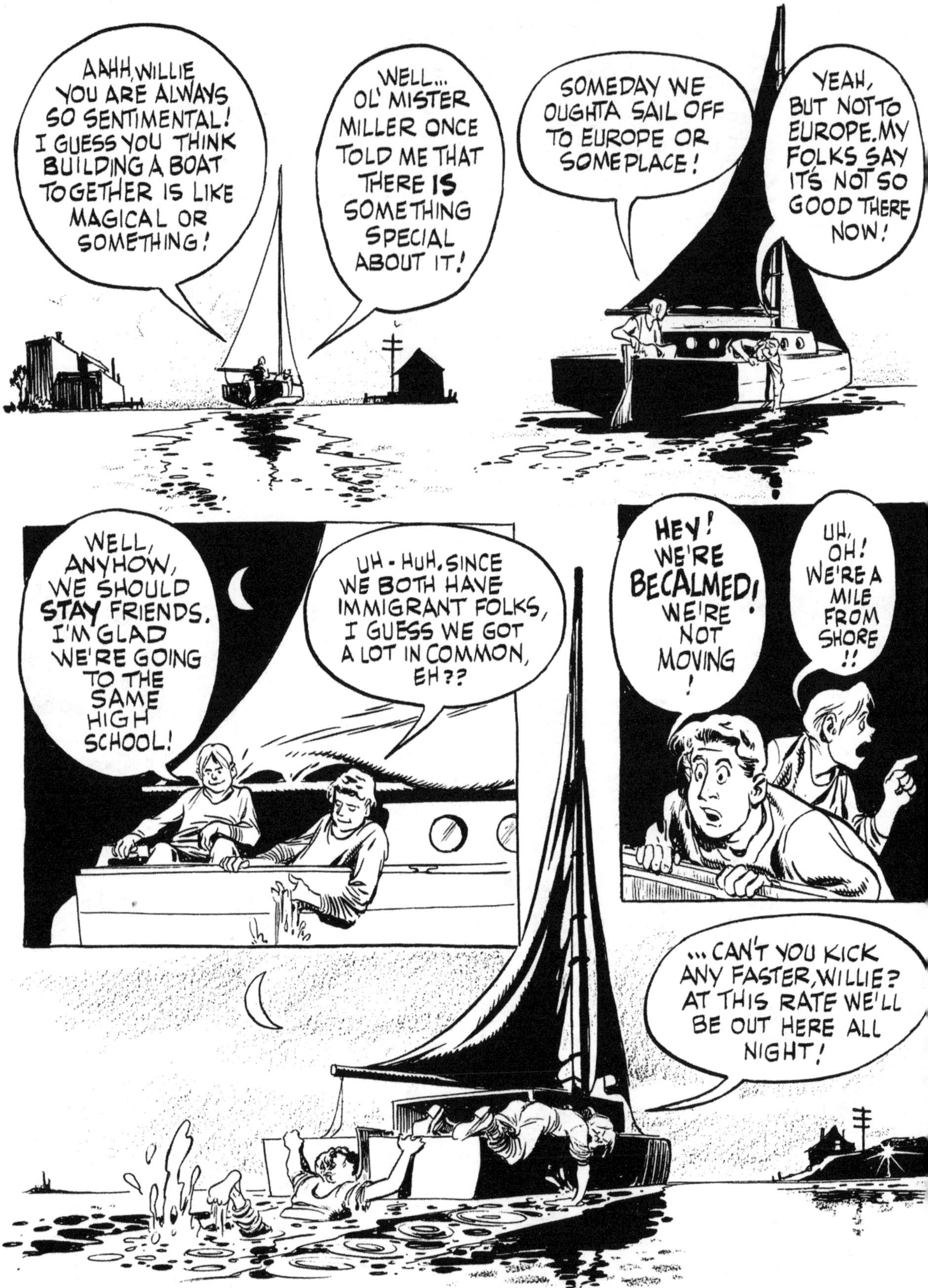
AAHH, WILLIE YOU ARE ALWAYS SO SENTIMENTAL! I GUESS YOU THINK BUILDING A BOAT TOGETHER IS LIKE MAGICAL OR SOMETHING!
WELL... OL' MISTER MILLER ONCE TOLD ME THAT THERE **IS** SOMETHING SPECIAL ABOUT IT!
SOMEDAY WE OUGHTA SAIL OFF TO EUROPE OR SOMEPLACE!
YEAH, BUT NOT TO EUROPE. MY FOLKS SAY IT'S NOT SO GOOD THERE NOW!
WELL, ANYHOW, WE SHOULD **STAY** FRIENDS. I'M GLAD WE'RE GOING TO THE SAME HIGH SCHOOL!
UH-HUH, SINCE WE BOTH HAVE IMMIGRANT FOLKS, I GUESS WE GOT A LOT IN COMMON, EH??
HEY! WE'RE BECALMED! WE'RE NOT MOVING!
UH, OH! WE'RE A MILE FROM SHORE!!
...CAN'T YOU KICK ANY FASTER, WILLIE? AT THIS RATE WE'LL BE OUT HERE ALL NIGHT!

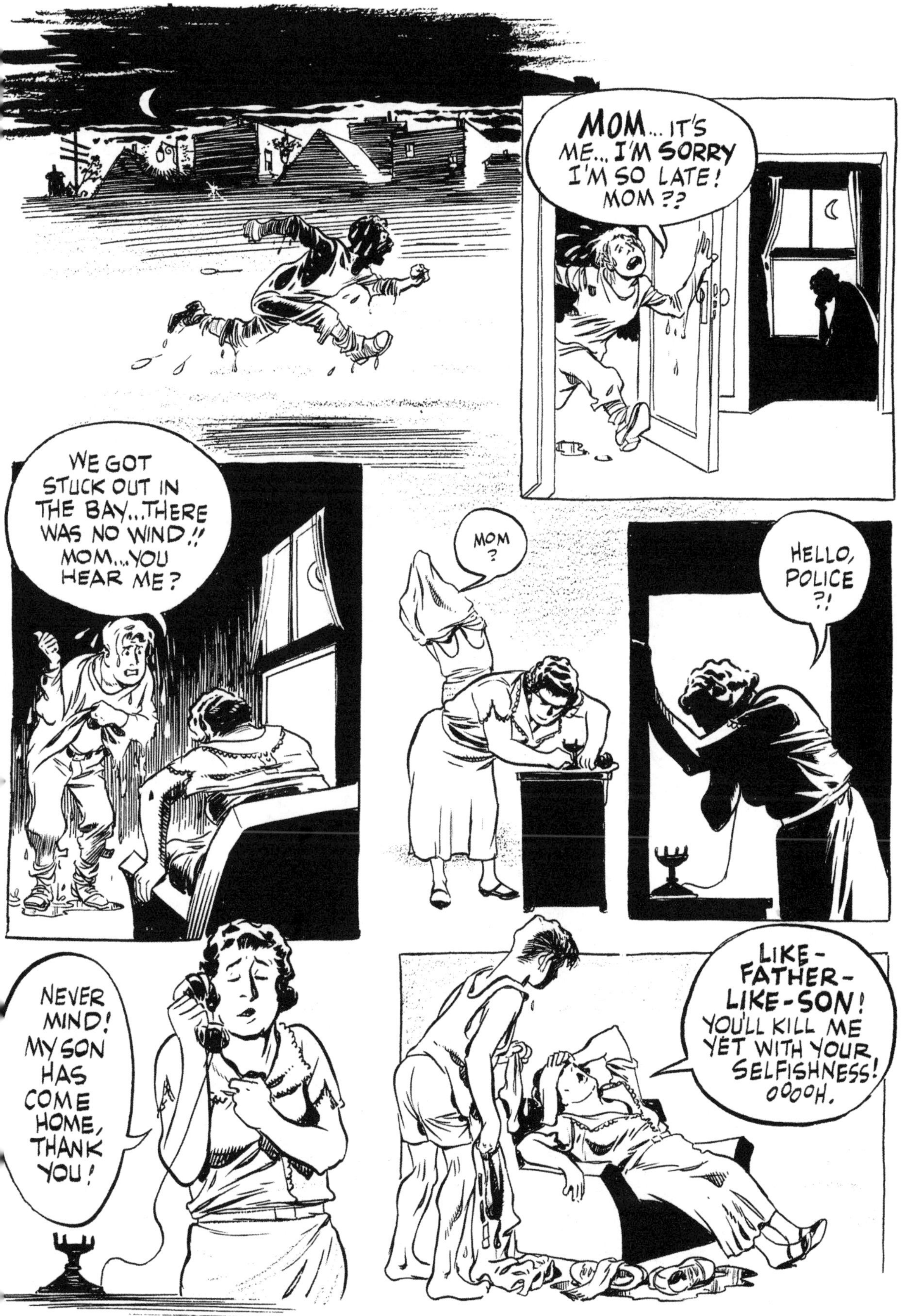
MOM... IT'S ME... I'M SORRY I'M SO LATE! MOM??
WE GOT STUCK OUT IN THE BAY... THERE WAS NO WIND!! MOM... YOU HEAR ME?
MOM ?
HELLO, POLICE ?!
NEVER MIND! MY SON HAS COME HOME, THANK YOU!
LIKE-FATHER-LIKE-SON! YOU'LL KILL ME YET WITH YOUR SELFISHNESS! OOOOH.

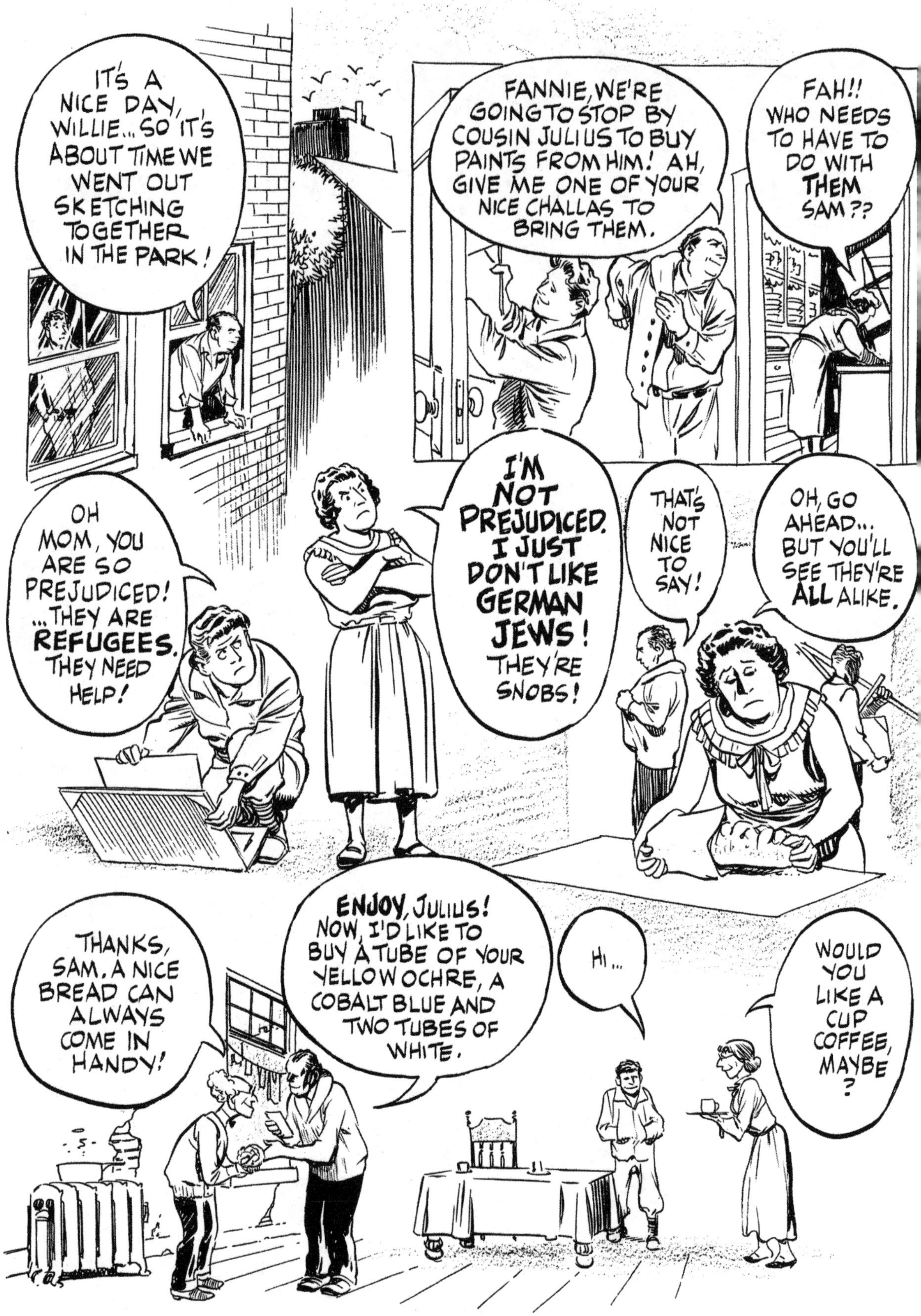
IT'S A NICE DAY, WILLIE... SO IT'S ABOUT TIME WE WENT OUT SKETCHING TOGETHER IN THE PARK!
FANNIE, WE'RE GOING TO STOP BY COUSIN JULIUS TO BUY PAINTS FROM HIM! AH, GIVE ME ONE OF YOUR NICE CHALLAS TO BRING THEM.
FAH!! WHO NEEDS TO HAVE TO DO WITH THEM SAM??
OH MOM, YOU ARE SO PREJUDICED! ...THEY ARE REFUGEES. THEY NEED HELP!
I'M NOT PREJUDICED. I JUST DON'T LIKE GERMAN JEWS! THEY'RE SNOBS!
THAT'S NOT NICE TO SAY!
OH, GO AHEAD... BUT YOU'LL SEE THEY'RE ALL ALIKE.
THANKS, SAM. A NICE BREAD CAN ALWAYS COME IN HANDY!
ENJOY, JULIUS! NOW, I'D LIKE TO BUY A TUBE OF YOUR YELLOW OCHRE, A COBALT BLUE AND TWO TUBES OF WHITE.
HI...
WOULD YOU LIKE A CUP COFFEE, MAYBE?

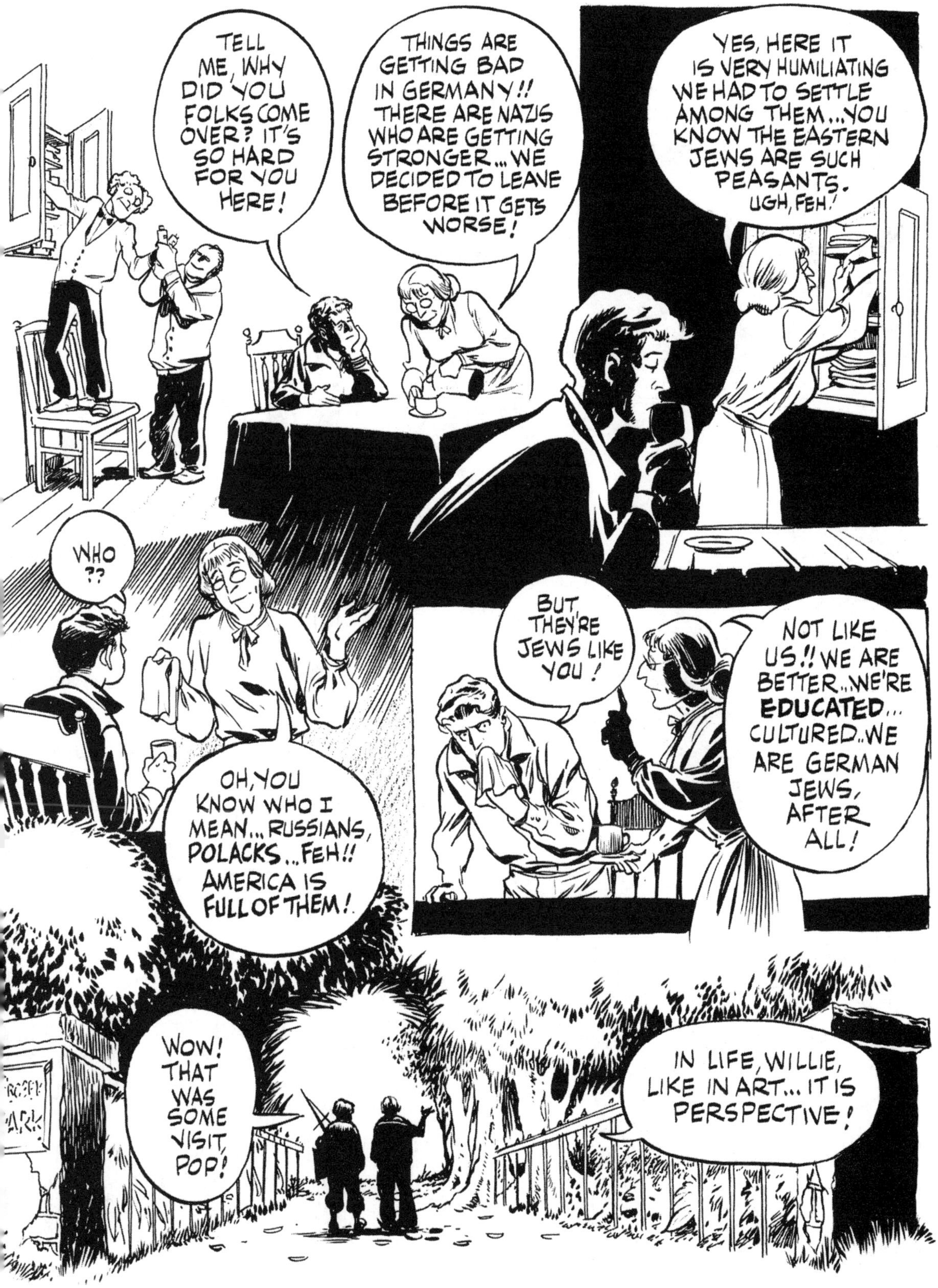
TELL ME, WHY DID YOU FOLKS COME OVER? IT'S SO HARD FOR YOU HERE!
THINGS ARE GETTING BAD IN GERMANY!! THERE ARE NAZIS WHO ARE GETTING STRONGER... WE DECIDED TO LEAVE BEFORE IT GETS WORSE!
YES, HERE IT IS VERY HUMILIATING WE HAD TO SETTLE AMONG THEM... YOU KNOW THE EASTERN JEWS ARE SUCH PEASANTS. UGH, FEH!
WHO ??
OH, YOU KNOW WHO I MEAN... RUSSIANS, POLACKS... FEH!! AMERICA IS FULL OF THEM!
BUT THEY'RE JEWS LIKE YOU!
NOT LIKE US!! WE ARE BETTER.. WE'RE EDUCATED... CULTURED.. WE ARE GERMAN JEWS, AFTER ALL!
WOW! THAT WAS SOME VISIT, POP!
IN LIFE, WILLIE, LIKE IN ART... IT IS PERSPECTIVE!

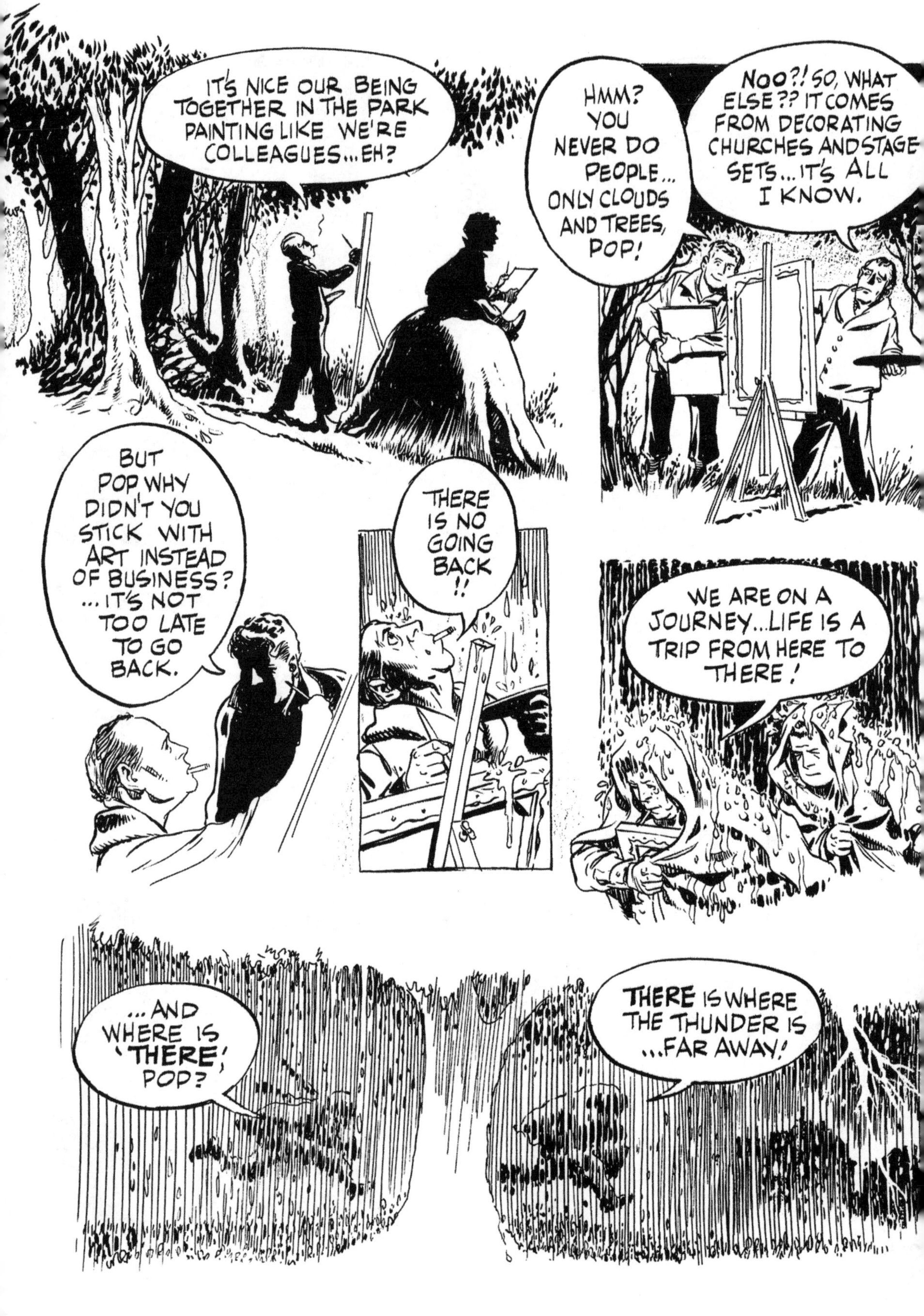
IT'S NICE OUR BEING TOGETHER IN THE PARK PAINTING LIKE WE'RE COLLEAGUES...EH?
HMM? YOU NEVER DO PEOPLE... ONLY CLOUDS AND TREES, POP!
NOO?! SO, WHAT ELSE?? IT COMES FROM DECORATING CHURCHES AND STAGE SETS... IT'S ALL I KNOW.
BUT POP WHY DIDN'T YOU STICK WITH ART INSTEAD OF BUSINESS? ...IT'S NOT TOO LATE TO GO BACK.
THERE IS NO GOING BACK !!
WE ARE ON A JOURNEY...LIFE IS A TRIP FROM HERE TO THERE!
...AND WHERE IS 'THERE,' POP?
THERE IS WHERE THE THUNDER IS ...FAR AWAY!

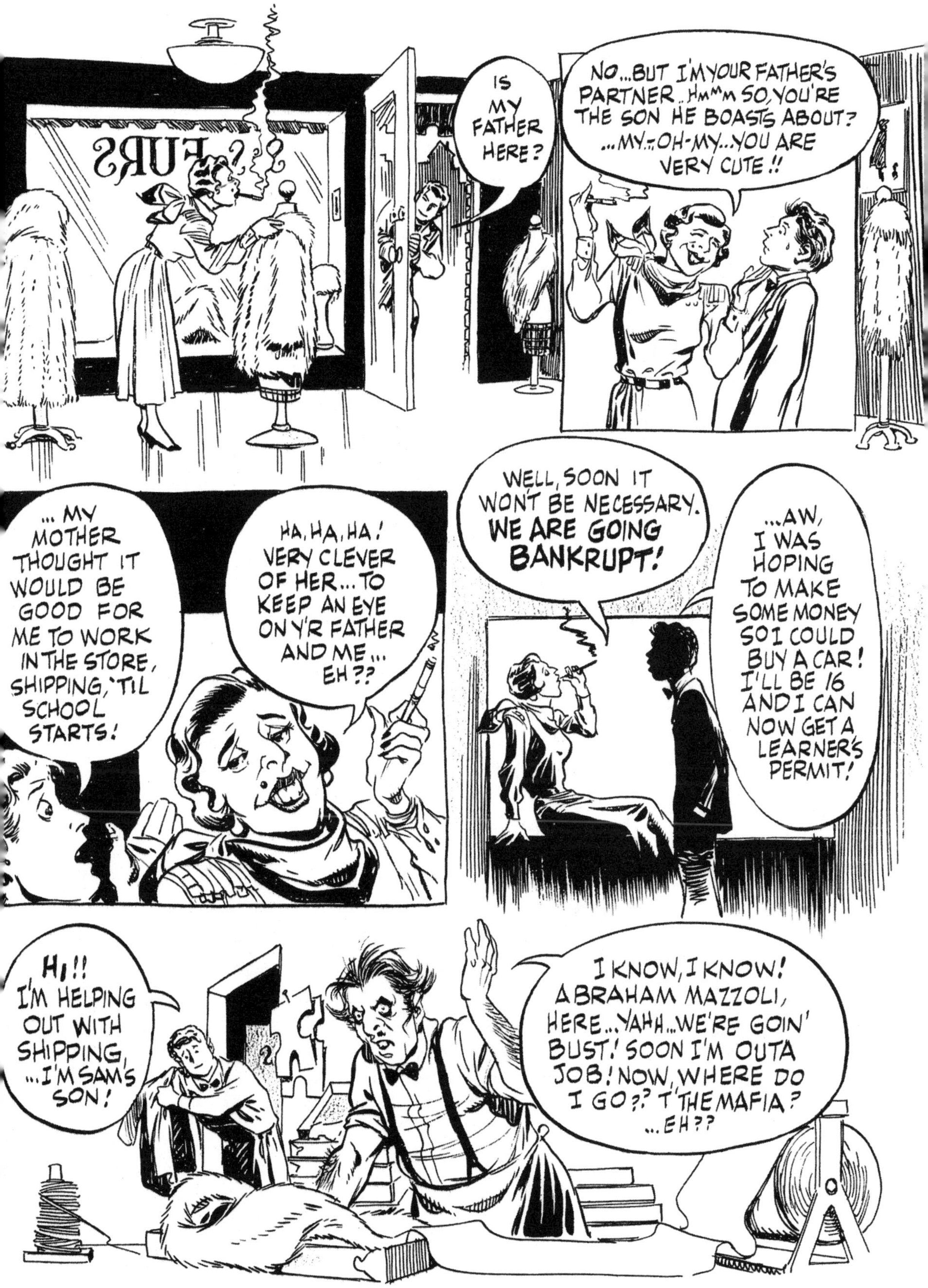
FURS
IS MY FATHER HERE?
NO...BUT I'M YOUR FATHER'S PARTNER..HMMM SO, YOU'RE THE SON HE BOASTS ABOUT? ...MY..OH-MY...YOU ARE VERY CUTE!!
... MY MOTHER THOUGHT IT WOULD BE GOOD FOR ME TO WORK IN THE STORE, SHIPPING, 'TIL SCHOOL STARTS!
HA, HA, HA! VERY CLEVER OF HER... TO KEEP AN EYE ON Y'R FATHER AND ME... EH??
WELL, SOON IT WON'T BE NECESSARY. WE ARE GOING BANKRUPT!
...AW, I WAS HOPING TO MAKE SOME MONEY SO I COULD BUY A CAR! I'LL BE 16 AND I CAN NOW GET A LEARNER'S PERMIT!
HI!! I'M HELPING OUT WITH SHIPPING, ...I'M SAM'S SON!
I KNOW, I KNOW! ABRAHAM MAZZOLI, HERE...YAHH...WE'RE GOIN' BUST! SOON I'M OUTA JOB! NOW, WHERE DO I GO?? T'THE MAFIA? ...EH??

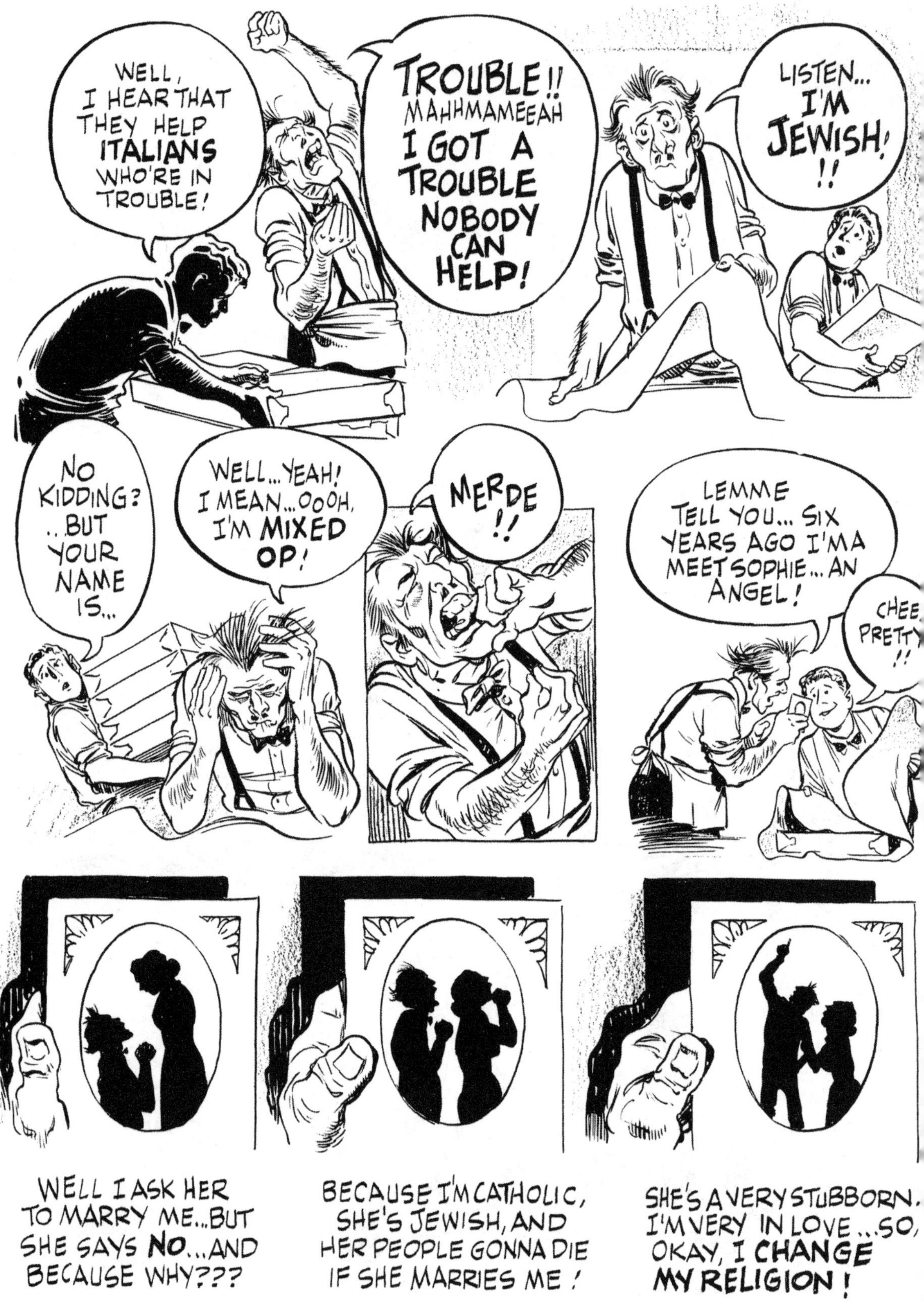
WELL, I HEAR THAT THEY HELP ITALIANS WHO'RE IN TROUBLE!
TROUBLE!! MAHHMAMEEAH I GOT A TROUBLE NOBODY CAN HELP!
LISTEN... I'M JEWISH!!!
NO KIDDING? ..BUT YOUR NAME IS...
WELL...YEAH! I MEAN...OOOH, I'M MIXED OP!
MERDE!!
LEMME TELL YOU... SIX YEARS AGO I'MA MEET SOPHIE... AN ANGEL!
CHEE PRETTY!!
WELL I ASK HER TO MARRY ME...BUT SHE SAYS NO...AND BECAUSE WHY???
BECAUSE I'M CATHOLIC, SHE'S JEWISH, AND HER PEOPLE GONNA DIE IF SHE MARRIES ME!
SHE'S A VERY STUBBORN. I'M VERY IN LOVE...SO, OKAY, I CHANGE MY RELIGION!

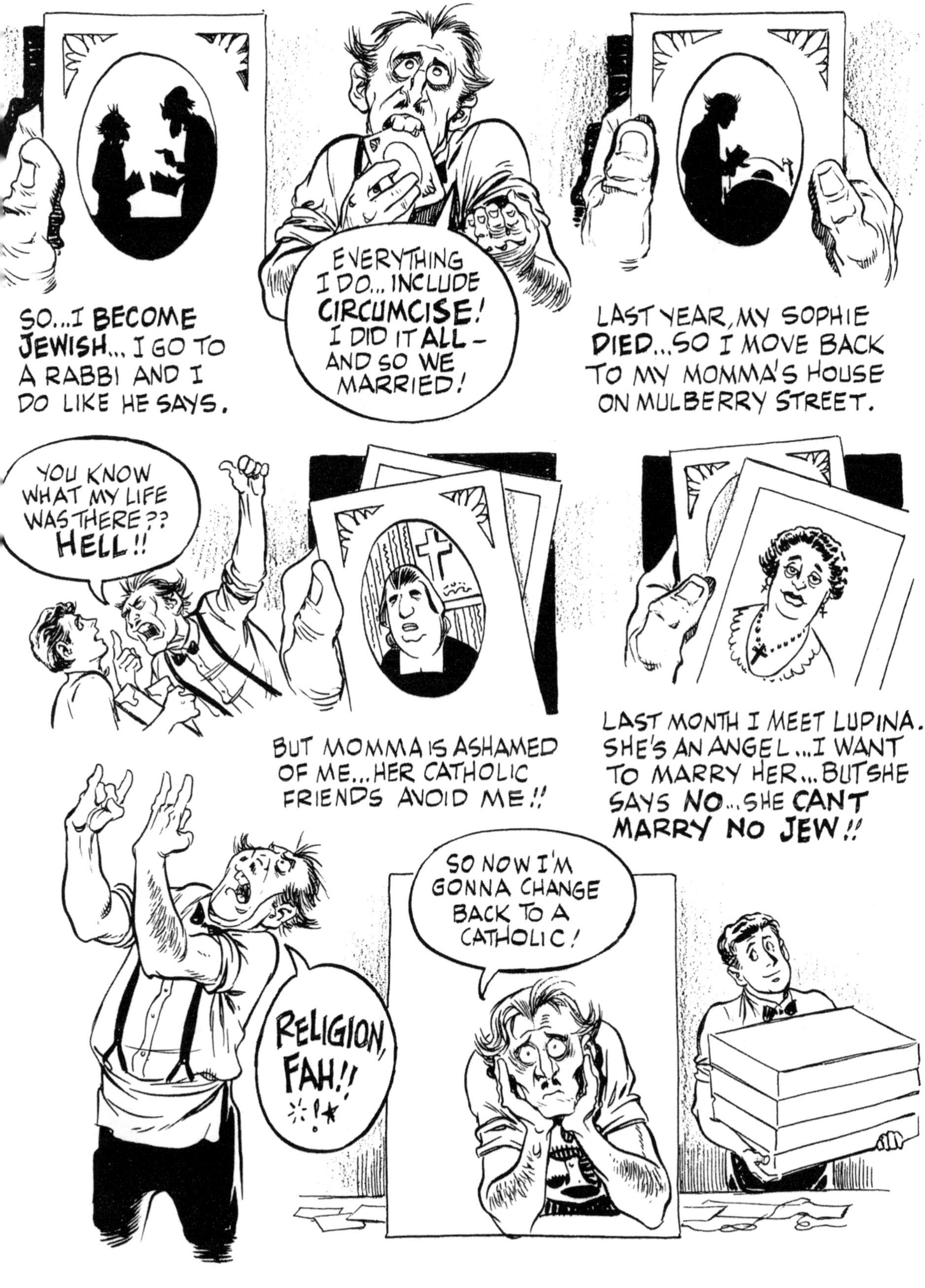
SO...I BECOME JEWISH... I GO TO A RABBI AND I DO LIKE HE SAYS.
EVERYTHING I DO... INCLUDE CIRCUMCISE! I DID IT ALL- AND SO WE MARRIED!
LAST YEAR, MY SOPHIE DIED...SO I MOVE BACK TO MY MOMMA'S HOUSE ON MULBERRY STREET.
YOU KNOW WHAT MY LIFE WAS THERE?? HELL!!
BUT MOMMA IS ASHAMED OF ME...HER CATHOLIC FRIENDS AVOID ME!!
LAST MONTH I MEET LUPINA. SHE'S AN ANGEL...I WANT TO MARRY HER...BUT SHE SAYS NO...SHE CANT MARRY NO JEW!!
RELIGION, FAH!!
SO NOW I'M GONNA CHANGE BACK TO A CATHOLIC!

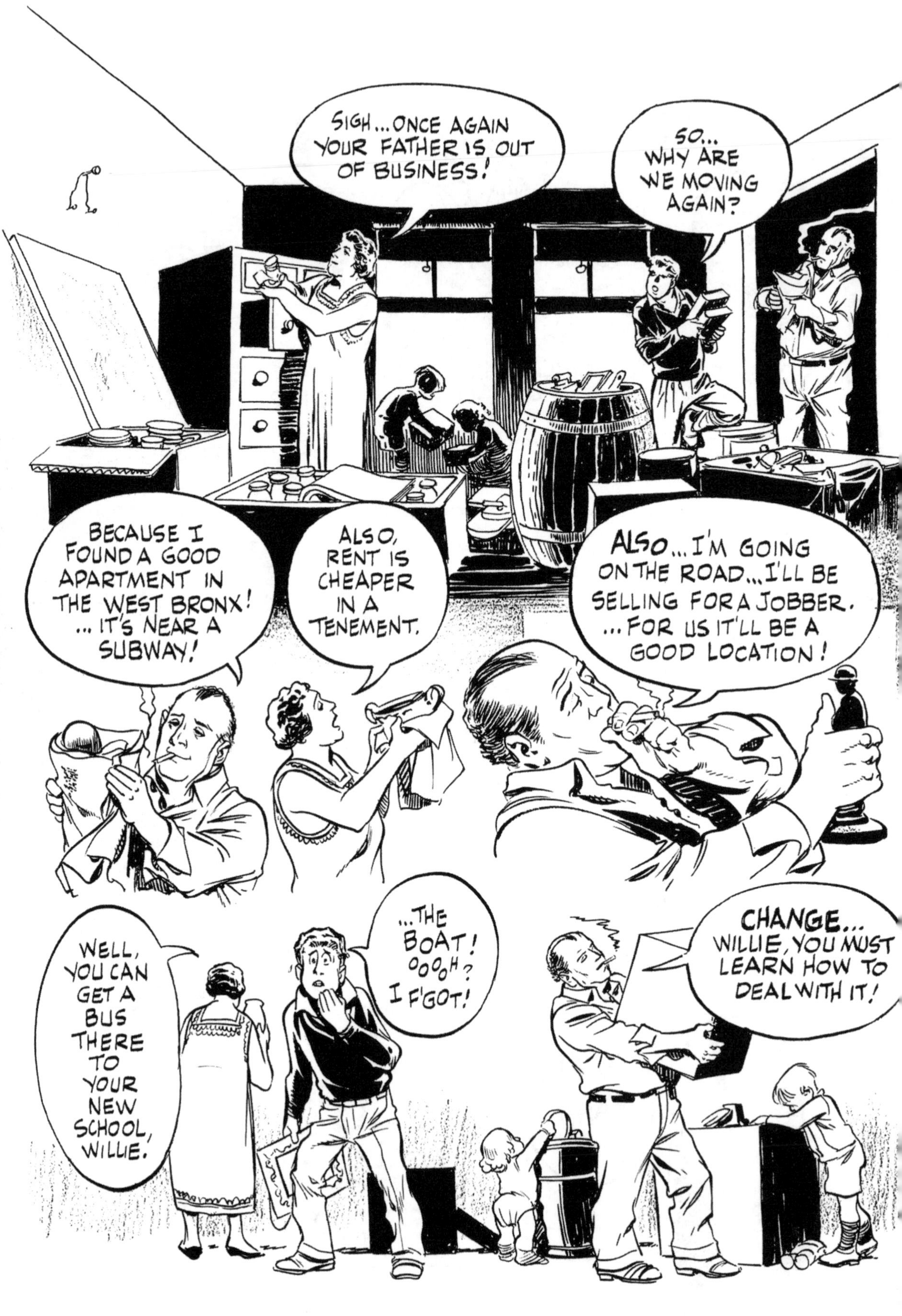
SIGH...ONCE AGAIN YOUR FATHER IS OUT OF BUSINESS!
SO... WHY ARE WE MOVING AGAIN?
BECAUSE I FOUND A GOOD APARTMENT IN THE WEST BRONX! ... IT'S NEAR A SUBWAY!
ALSO, RENT IS CHEAPER IN A TENEMENT.
ALSO... I'M GOING ON THE ROAD... I'LL BE SELLING FOR A JOBBER. ...FOR US IT'LL BE A GOOD LOCATION!
WELL, YOU CAN GET A BUS THERE TO YOUR NEW SCHOOL, WILLIE.
...THE BOAT! OOOOH? I F'GOT!
CHANGE... WILLIE, YOU MUST LEARN HOW TO DEAL WITH IT!

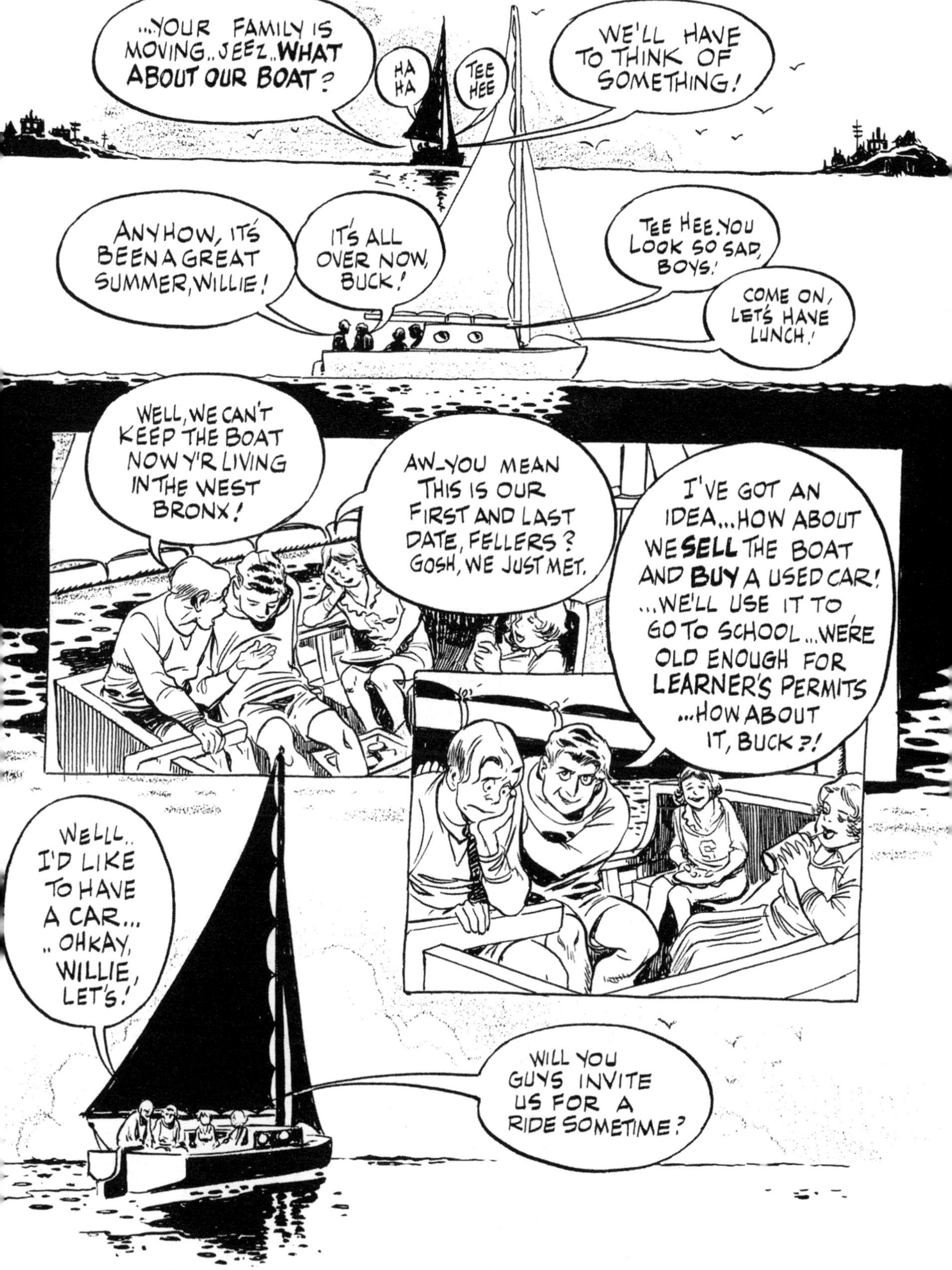
...YOUR FAMILY IS MOVING.. JEEZ.. WHAT ABOUT OUR BOAT?
HA HA
TEE HEE
WE'LL HAVE TO THINK OF SOMETHING!
ANYHOW, IT'S BEEN A GREAT SUMMER, WILLIE!
IT'S ALL OVER NOW, BUCK!
TEE HEE. YOU LOOK SO SAD, BOYS!
COME ON, LET'S HAVE LUNCH!
WELL, WE CAN'T KEEP THE BOAT NOW Y'R LIVING IN THE WEST BRONX!
AW-YOU MEAN THIS IS OUR FIRST AND LAST DATE, FELLERS? GOSH, WE JUST MET.
I'VE GOT AN IDEA...HOW ABOUT WE SELL THE BOAT AND BUY A USED CAR! ...WE'LL USE IT TO GO TO SCHOOL...WE'RE OLD ENOUGH FOR LEARNER'S PERMITS ...HOW ABOUT IT, BUCK?!
WELLL.. I'D LIKE TO HAVE A CAR... ..OHKAY, WILLIE, LET'S!
WILL YOU GUYS INVITE US FOR A RIDE SOMETIME?

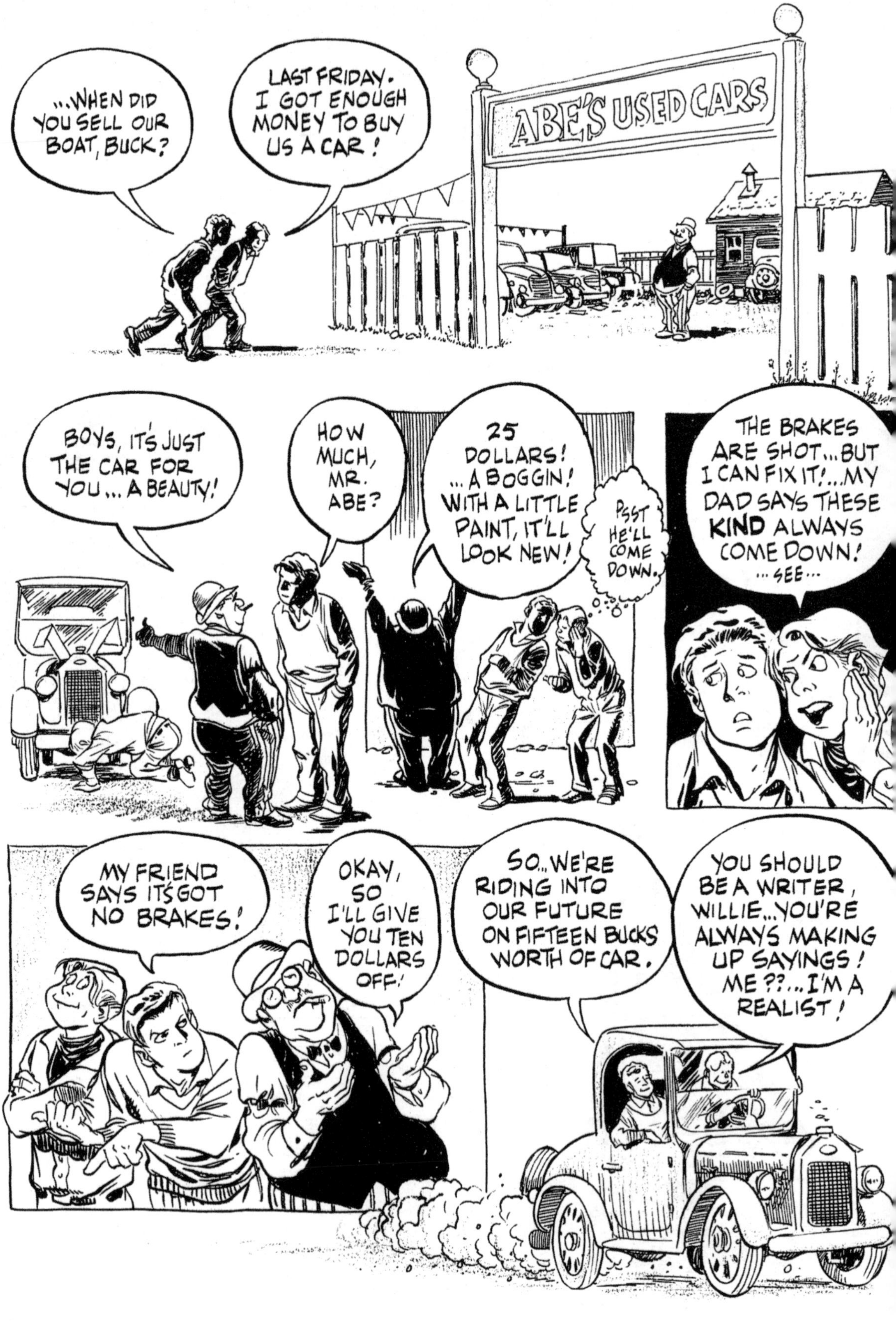
...WHEN DID YOU SELL OUR BOAT, BUCK?
LAST FRIDAY. I GOT ENOUGH MONEY TO BUY US A CAR!
ABE'S USED CARS
BOYS, IT'S JUST THE CAR FOR YOU... A BEAUTY!
HOW MUCH, MR. ABE?
25 DOLLARS! ... A BOGGIN! WITH A LITTLE PAINT, IT'LL LOOK NEW!
PSST HE'LL COME DOWN.
THE BRAKES ARE SHOT... BUT I CAN FIX IT!... MY DAD SAYS THESE KIND ALWAYS COME DOWN! ... SEE...
MY FRIEND SAYS IT'S GOT NO BRAKES!
OKAY, SO I'LL GIVE YOU TEN DOLLARS OFF!
SO... WE'RE RIDING INTO OUR FUTURE ON FIFTEEN BUCKS WORTH OF CAR.
YOU SHOULD BE A WRITER, WILLIE... YOU'RE ALWAYS MAKING UP SAYINGS! ME??... I'M A REALIST!

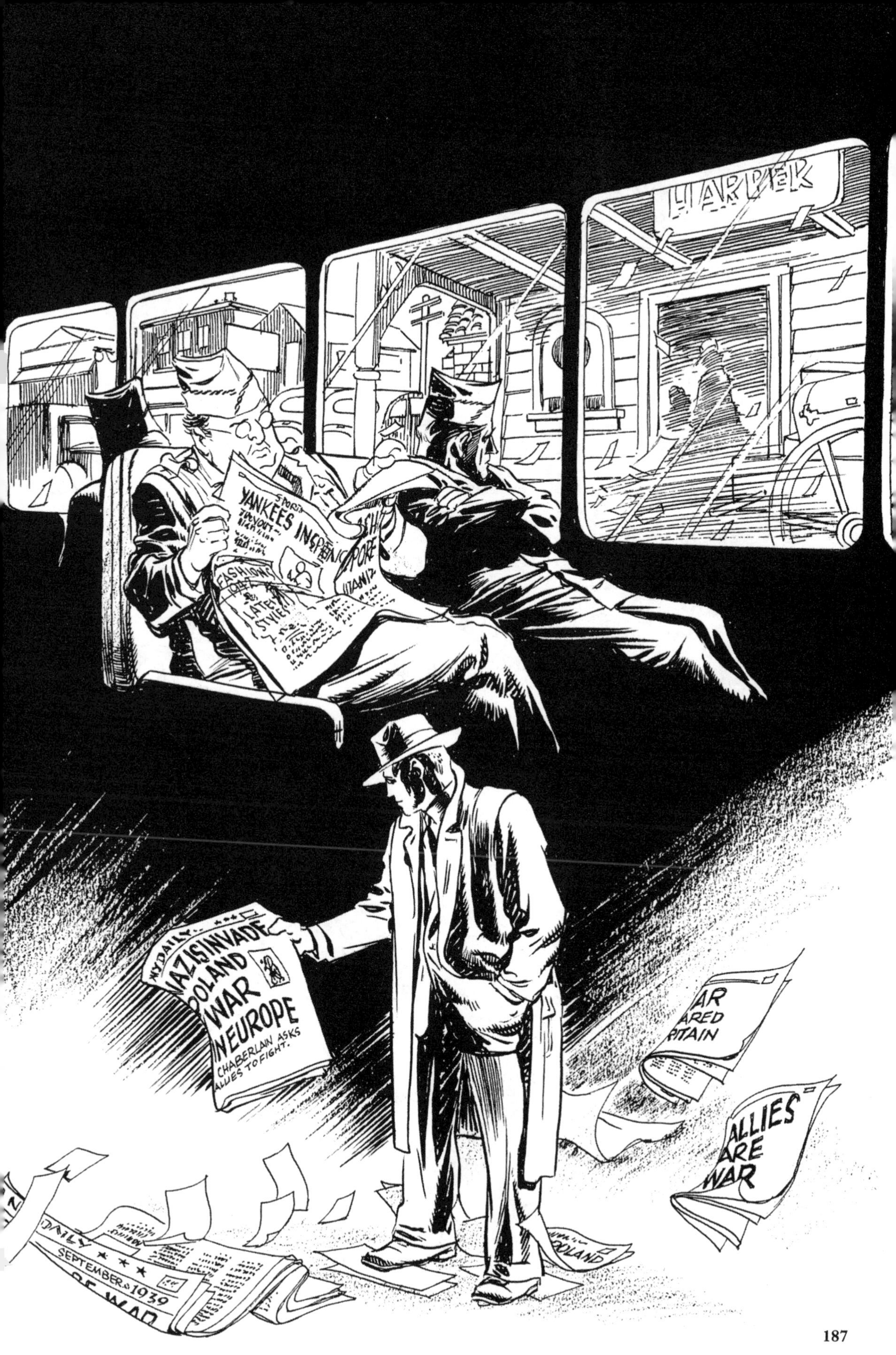
HARPER
YANKEES
NY DAILY
NAZIS INVADE POLAND
WAR IN EUROPE
CHABERLAIN ASKS ALLIES TO FIGHT.
ALLIES ARE WAR
DAILY
SEPTEMBER 1939
POLAND

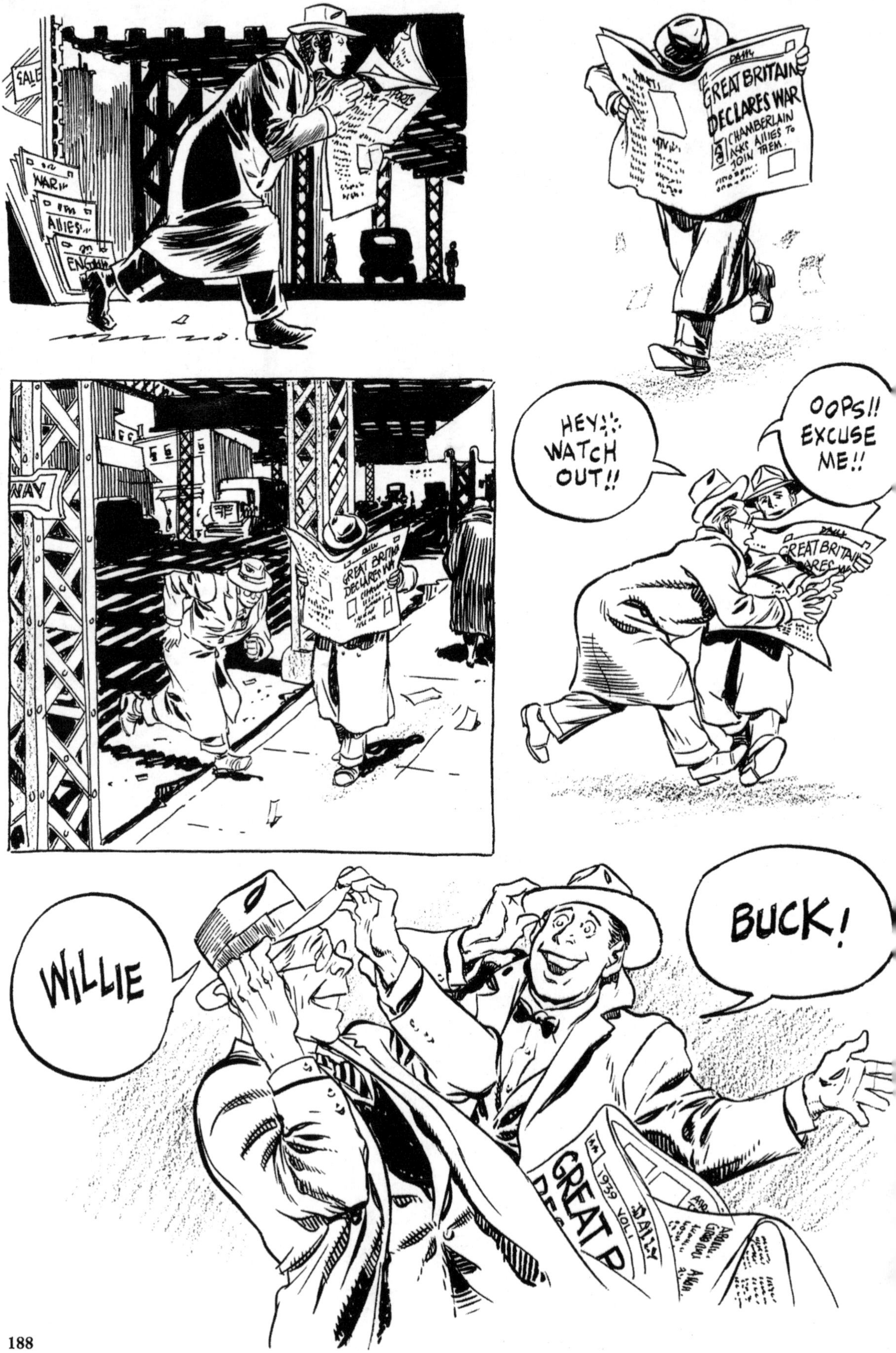
SALE
WAR
ALLIES
GREAT BRITAIN
DECLARES WAR
CHAMBERLAIN ASKS ALLIES TO JOIN THEM.
WAY
HEY!! WATCH OUT!!
OOPS!! EXCUSE ME!!
WILLIE
BUCK!

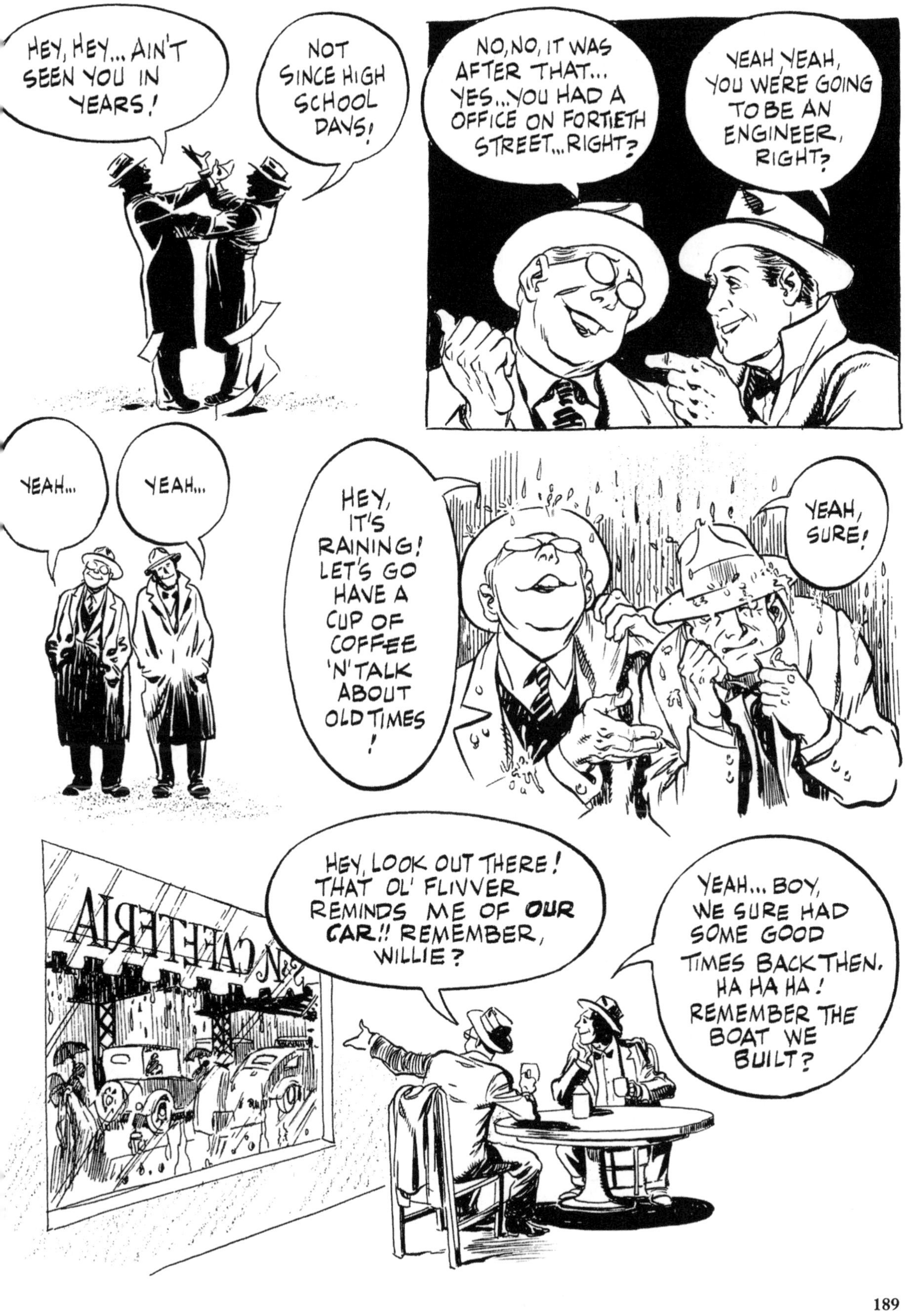
HEY, HEY... AIN'T SEEN YOU IN YEARS!
NOT SINCE HIGH SCHOOL DAYS!
NO, NO, IT WAS AFTER THAT... YES...YOU HAD A OFFICE ON FORTIETH STREET...RIGHT?
YEAH, YEAH, YOU WERE GOING TO BE AN ENGINEER, RIGHT?
YEAH...
YEAH...
HEY, IT'S RAINING! LET'S GO HAVE A CUP OF COFFEE 'N' TALK ABOUT OLD TIMES!
YEAH, SURE!
CAFETERIA
HEY, LOOK OUT THERE! THAT OL' FLIVVER REMINDS ME OF **OUR CAR**!! REMEMBER, WILLIE?
YEAH... BOY, WE SURE HAD SOME GOOD TIMES BACK THEN. HA HA HA! REMEMBER THE BOAT WE BUILT?

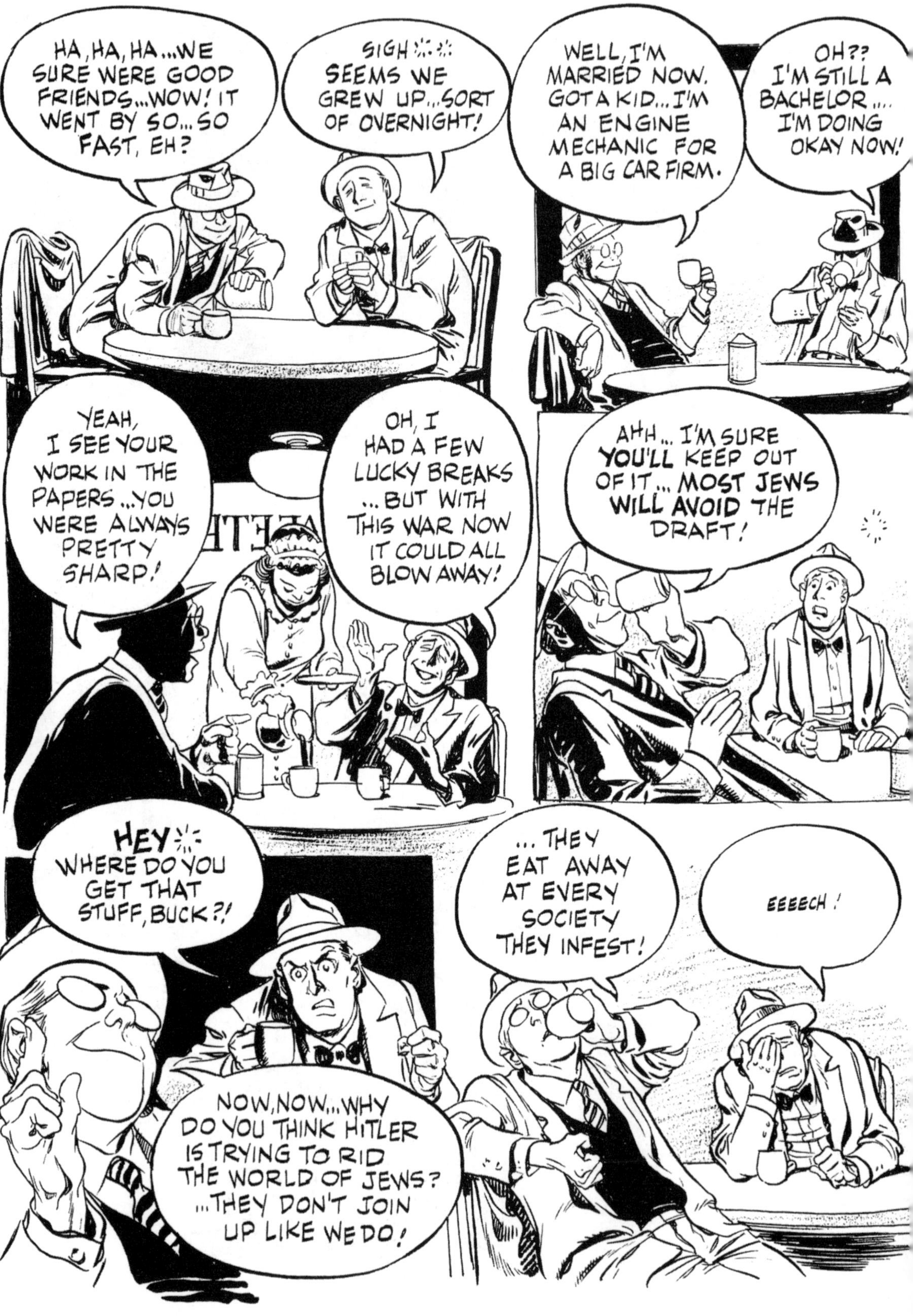
HA, HA, HA...WE SURE WERE GOOD FRIENDS...WOW! IT WENT BY SO...SO FAST, EH?
SIGH
SEEMS WE GREW UP...SORT OF OVERNIGHT!
WELL, I'M MARRIED NOW. GOT A KID...I'M AN ENGINE MECHANIC FOR A BIG CAR FIRM.
OH?? I'M STILL A BACHELOR.... I'M DOING OKAY NOW!
YEAH, I SEE YOUR WORK IN THE PAPERS...YOU WERE ALWAYS PRETTY SHARP!
OH, I HAD A FEW LUCKY BREAKS ...BUT WITH THIS WAR NOW IT COULD ALL BLOW AWAY!
AHH... I'M SURE YOU'LL KEEP OUT OF IT... MOST JEWS WILL AVOID THE DRAFT!
HEY WHERE DO YOU GET THAT STUFF, BUCK?!
NOW, NOW...WHY DO YOU THINK HITLER IS TRYING TO RID THE WORLD OF JEWS? ...THEY DON'T JOIN UP LIKE WE DO!
...THEY EAT AWAY AT EVERY SOCIETY THEY INFEST!
EEEECH!

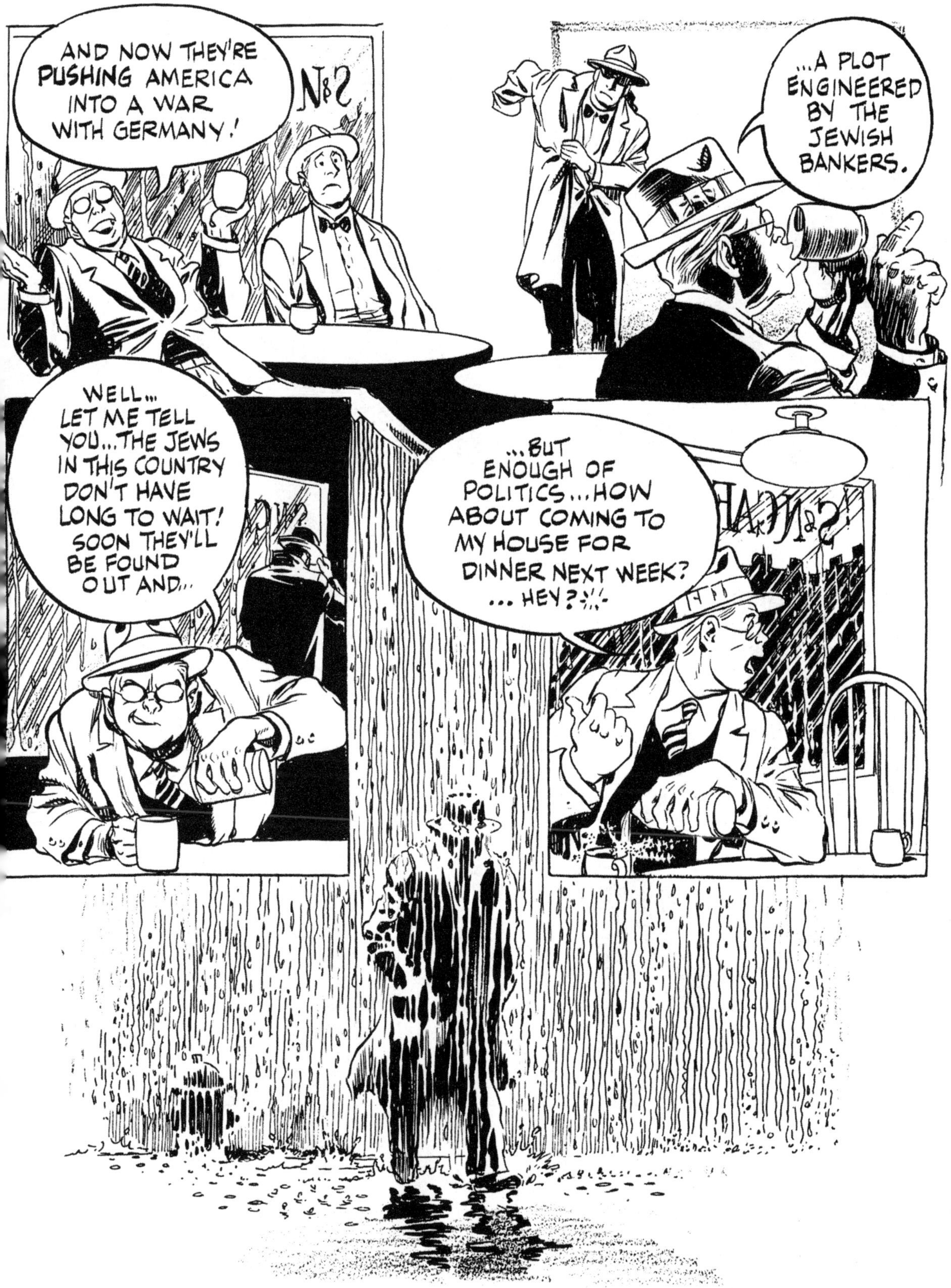
AND NOW THEY'RE PUSHING AMERICA INTO A WAR WITH GERMANY!
...A PLOT ENGINEERED BY THE JEWISH BANKERS.
WELL... LET ME TELL YOU...THE JEWS IN THIS COUNTRY DON'T HAVE LONG TO WAIT! SOON THEY'LL BE FOUND OUT AND...
...BUT ENOUGH OF POLITICS...HOW ABOUT COMING TO MY HOUSE FOR DINNER NEXT WEEK? ...HEY?

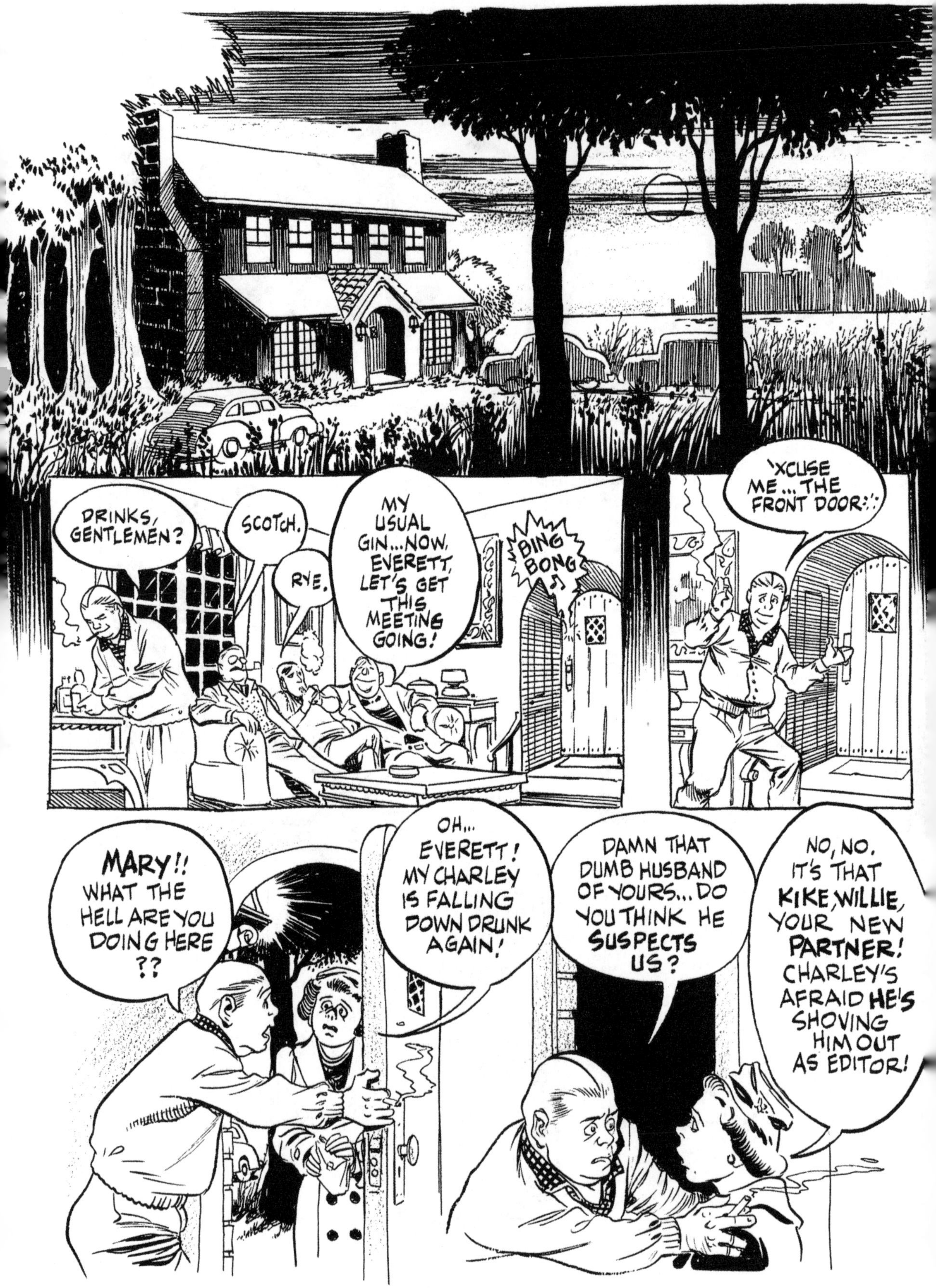
DRINKS, GENTLEMEN?
SCOTCH.
RYE.
MY USUAL GIN...NOW, EVERETT, LET'S GET THIS MEETING GOING!
BING BONG
'XCUSE ME... THE FRONT DOOR.
MARY!! WHAT THE HELL ARE YOU DOING HERE ??
OH... EVERETT! MY CHARLEY IS FALLING DOWN DRUNK AGAIN!
DAMN THAT DUMB HUSBAND OF YOURS... DO YOU THINK HE SUSPECTS US?
NO, NO. IT'S THAT KIKE, WILLIE, YOUR NEW PARTNER! CHARLEY'S AFRAID HE'S SHOVING HIM OUT AS EDITOR!

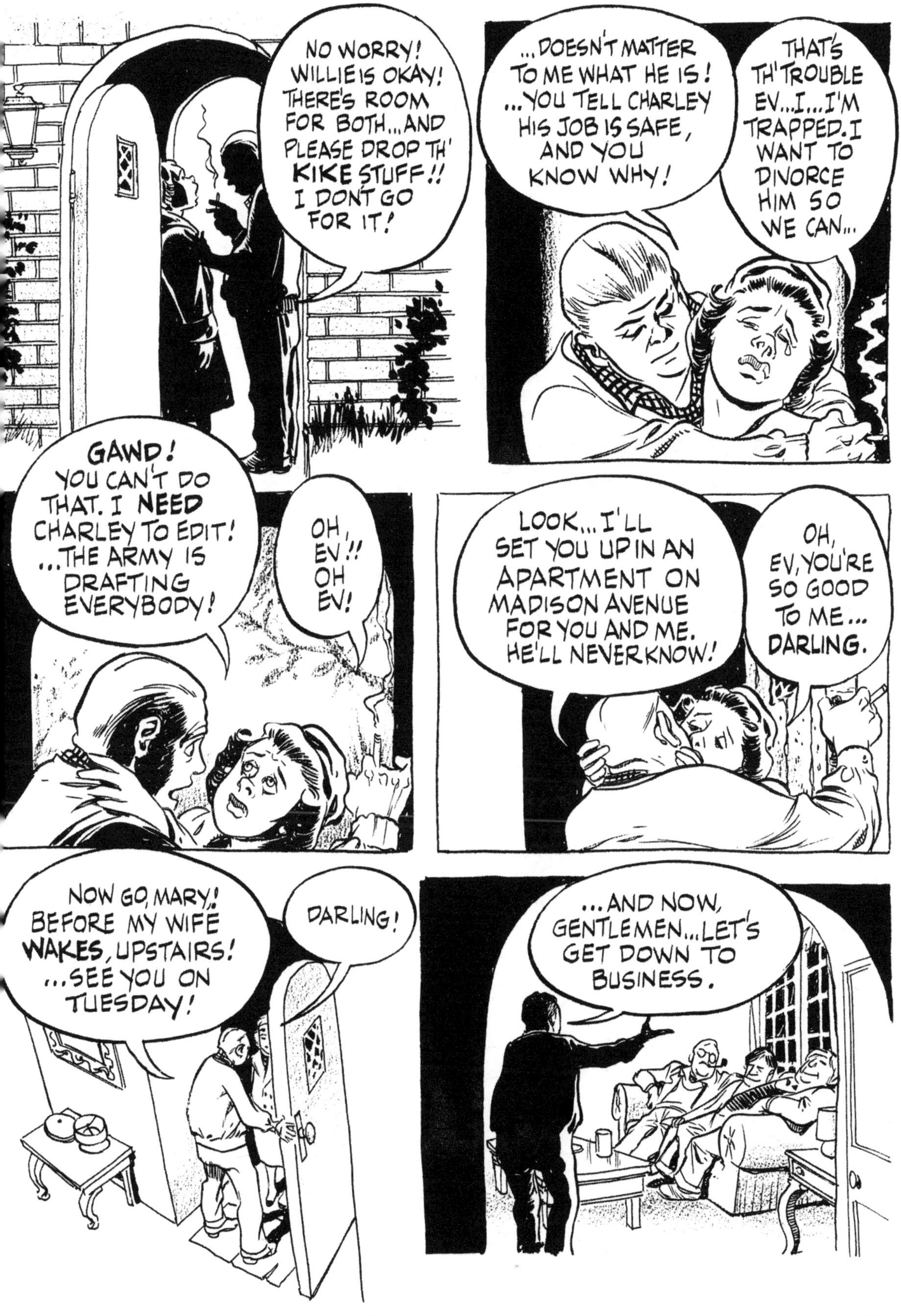
NO WORRY! WILLIE IS OKAY! THERE'S ROOM FOR BOTH... AND PLEASE DROP TH' KIKE STUFF!! I DON'T GO FOR IT!
...DOESN'T MATTER TO ME WHAT HE IS! ...YOU TELL CHARLEY HIS JOB IS SAFE, AND YOU KNOW WHY!
THAT'S TH' TROUBLE EV...I...I'M TRAPPED. I WANT TO DIVORCE HIM SO WE CAN...
GAWD! YOU CAN'T DO THAT. I NEED CHARLEY TO EDIT! ...THE ARMY IS DRAFTING EVERYBODY!
OH, EV!! OH EV!
LOOK... I'LL SET YOU UP IN AN APARTMENT ON MADISON AVENUE FOR YOU AND ME. HE'LL NEVER KNOW!
OH, EV, YOU'RE SO GOOD TO ME... DARLING.
NOW GO, MARY!! BEFORE MY WIFE WAKES, UPSTAIRS! ...SEE YOU ON TUESDAY!
DARLING!
...AND NOW, GENTLEMEN... LET'S GET DOWN TO BUSINESS.

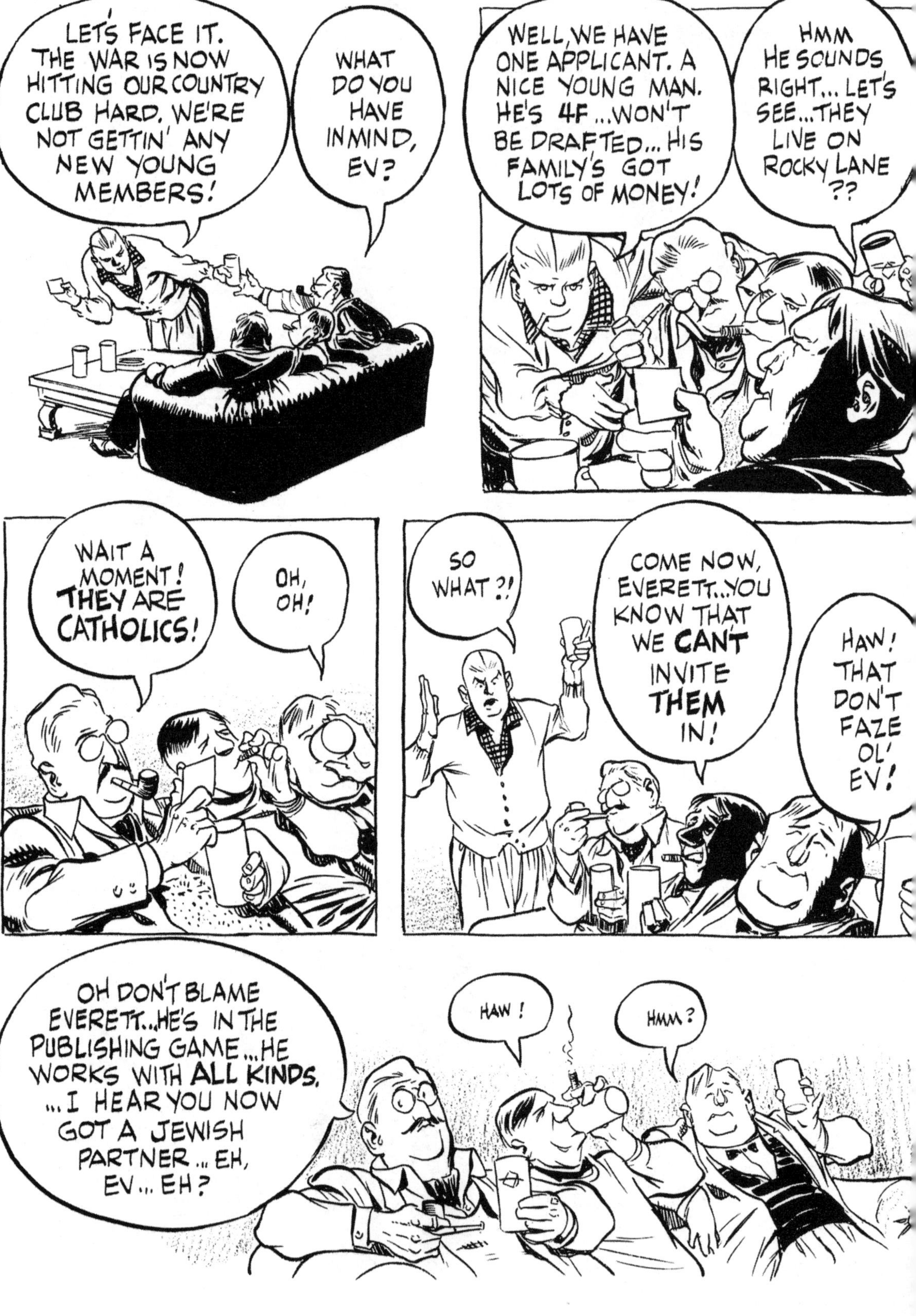
LET'S FACE IT. THE WAR IS NOW HITTING OUR COUNTRY CLUB HARD. WE'RE NOT GETTIN' ANY NEW YOUNG MEMBERS!
WHAT DO YOU HAVE IN MIND, EV?
WELL, WE HAVE ONE APPLICANT. A NICE YOUNG MAN. HE'S **4F** ...WON'T BE DRAFTED... HIS FAMILY'S GOT LOTS OF MONEY!
HMM HE SOUNDS RIGHT... LET'S SEE...THEY LIVE ON ROCKY LANE ??
WAIT A MOMENT! **THEY** ARE **CATHOLICS**!
OH, OH!
SO WHAT ?!
COME NOW, EVERETT...YOU KNOW THAT WE **CAN'T** INVITE **THEM** IN!
HAW! THAT DON'T FAZE OL' EV!
OH DON'T BLAME EVERETT...HE'S IN THE PUBLISHING GAME...HE WORKS WITH **ALL KINDS**. ...I HEAR YOU NOW GOT A JEWISH PARTNER... EH, EV... EH?
HAW!
HMM?

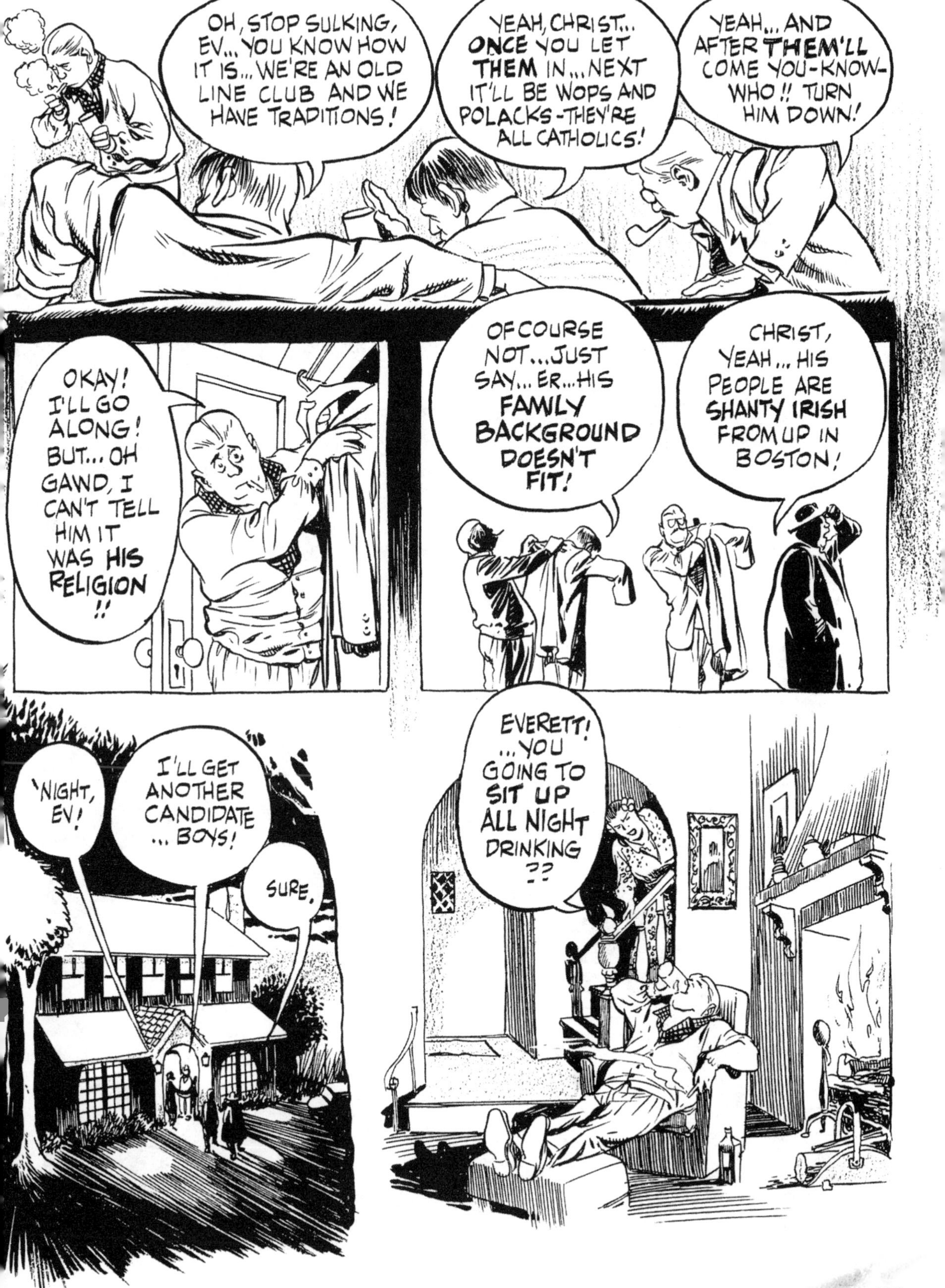

OH, STOP SULKING, EV... YOU KNOW HOW IT IS... WE'RE AN OLD LINE CLUB AND WE HAVE TRADITIONS!
YEAH, CHRIST... ONCE YOU LET THEM IN... NEXT IT'LL BE WOPS AND POLACKS - THEY'RE ALL CATHOLICS!
YEAH... AND AFTER THEM'LL COME YOU-KNOW-WHO!! TURN HIM DOWN!
OKAY! I'LL GO ALONG! BUT... OH GAWD, I CAN'T TELL HIM IT WAS HIS RELIGION!!
OF COURSE NOT... JUST SAY... ER... HIS FAMILY BACKGROUND DOESN'T FIT!
CHRIST, YEAH... HIS PEOPLE ARE SHANTY IRISH FROM UP IN BOSTON!
'NIGHT, EV!
I'LL GET ANOTHER CANDIDATE ... BOYS!
SURE.
EVERETT! ...YOU GOING TO SIT UP ALL NIGHT DRINKING??

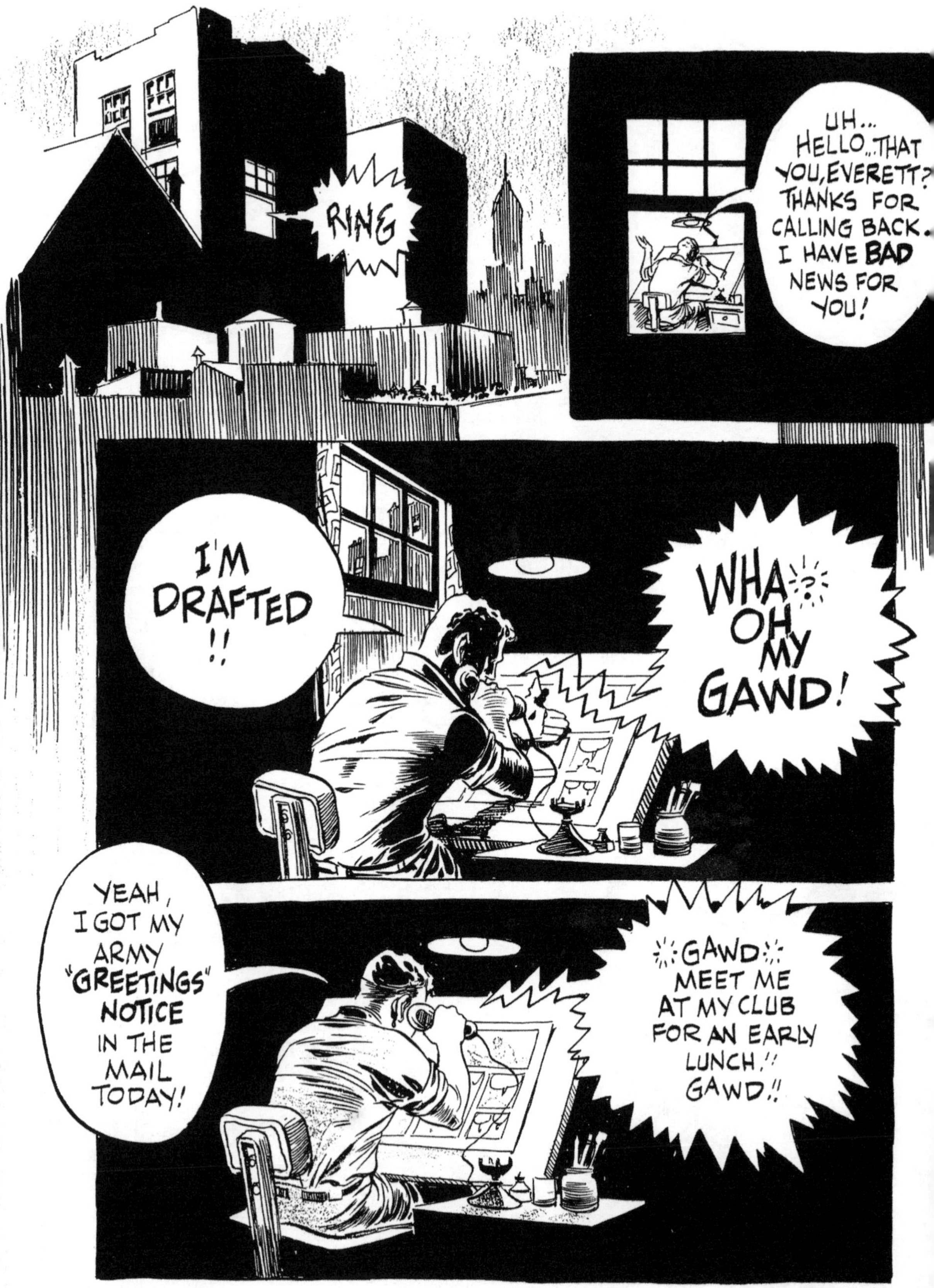
RING
UH... HELLO... THAT YOU, EVERETT? THANKS FOR CALLING BACK. I HAVE BAD NEWS FOR YOU!
I'M DRAFTED !!
WHA?? OH MY GAWD!
YEAH, I GOT MY ARMY "GREETINGS" NOTICE IN THE MAIL TODAY!
GAWD MEET ME AT MY CLUB FOR AN EARLY LUNCH!! GAWD!!

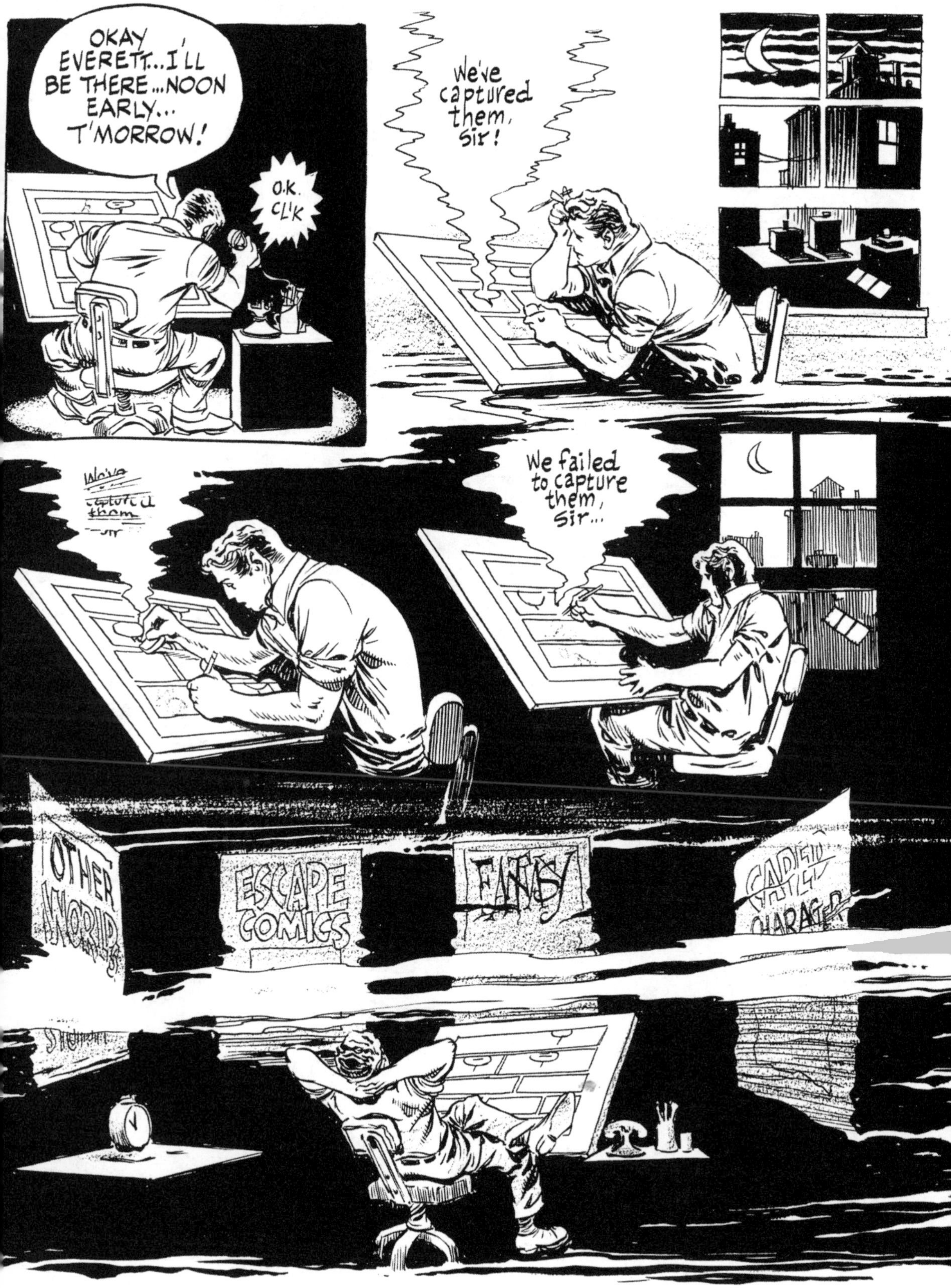
OKAY EVERETT...I'LL BE THERE...NOON EARLY... T'MORROW!
O.K. CL'K
We've captured them, sir!
We failed to capture them, sir...
OTHER
ESCAPE COMICS
FANTASY

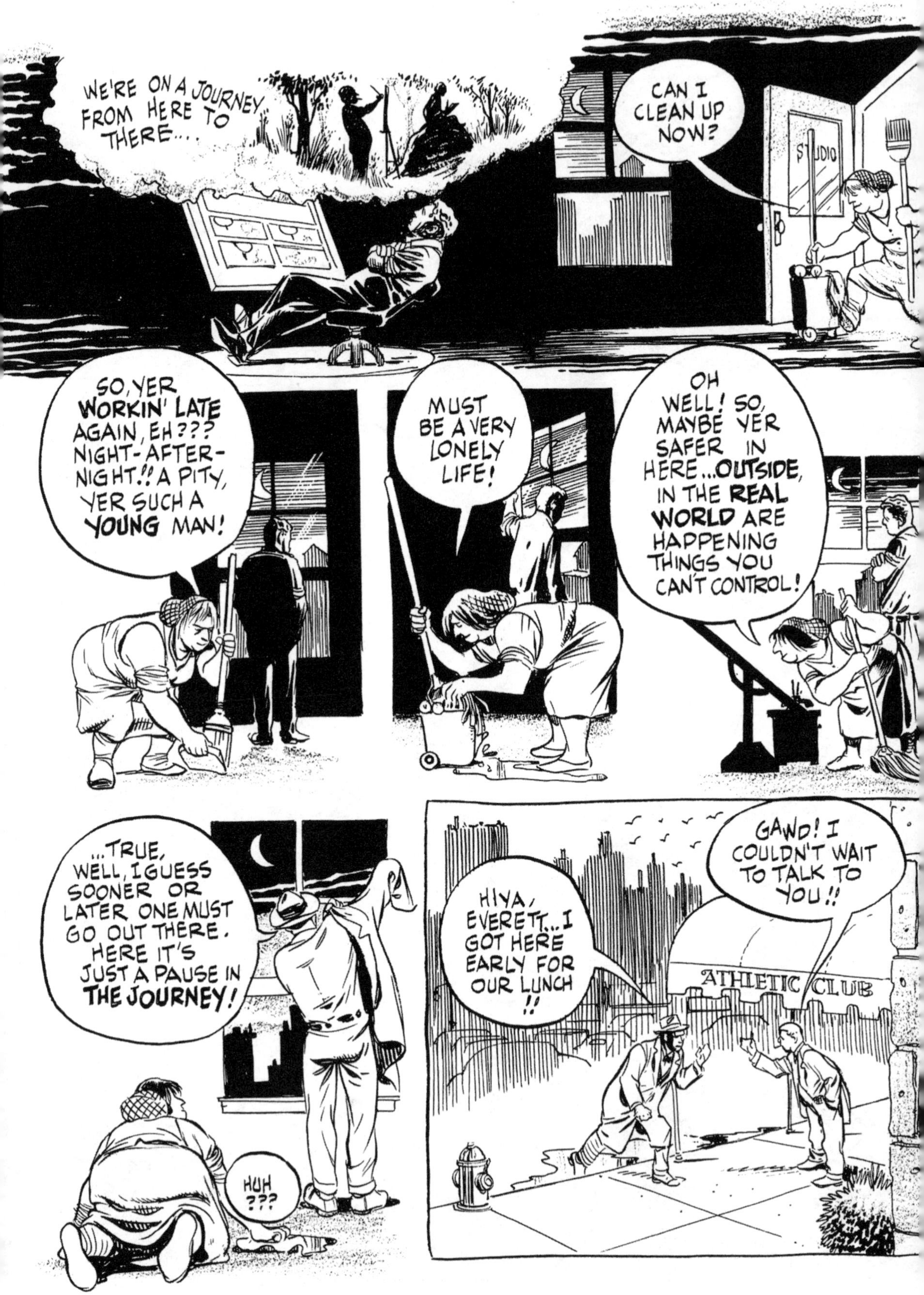

WE'RE ON A JOURNEY FROM HERE TO THERE....
CAN I CLEAN UP NOW?
STUDIO
SO, YER WORKIN' LATE AGAIN, EH??? NIGHT-AFTER-NIGHT!! A PITY, YER SUCH A YOUNG MAN!
MUST BE A VERY LONELY LIFE!
OH WELL! SO, MAYBE YER SAFER IN HERE...OUTSIDE, IN THE REAL WORLD ARE HAPPENING THINGS YOU CAN'T CONTROL!
...TRUE, WELL, I GUESS SOONER OR LATER ONE MUST GO OUT THERE. HERE IT'S JUST A PAUSE IN THE JOURNEY!
HUH ???
HIYA, EVERETT...I GOT HERE EARLY FOR OUR LUNCH !!
GAWD! I COULDN'T WAIT TO TALK TO YOU!!
ATHETIC CLUB

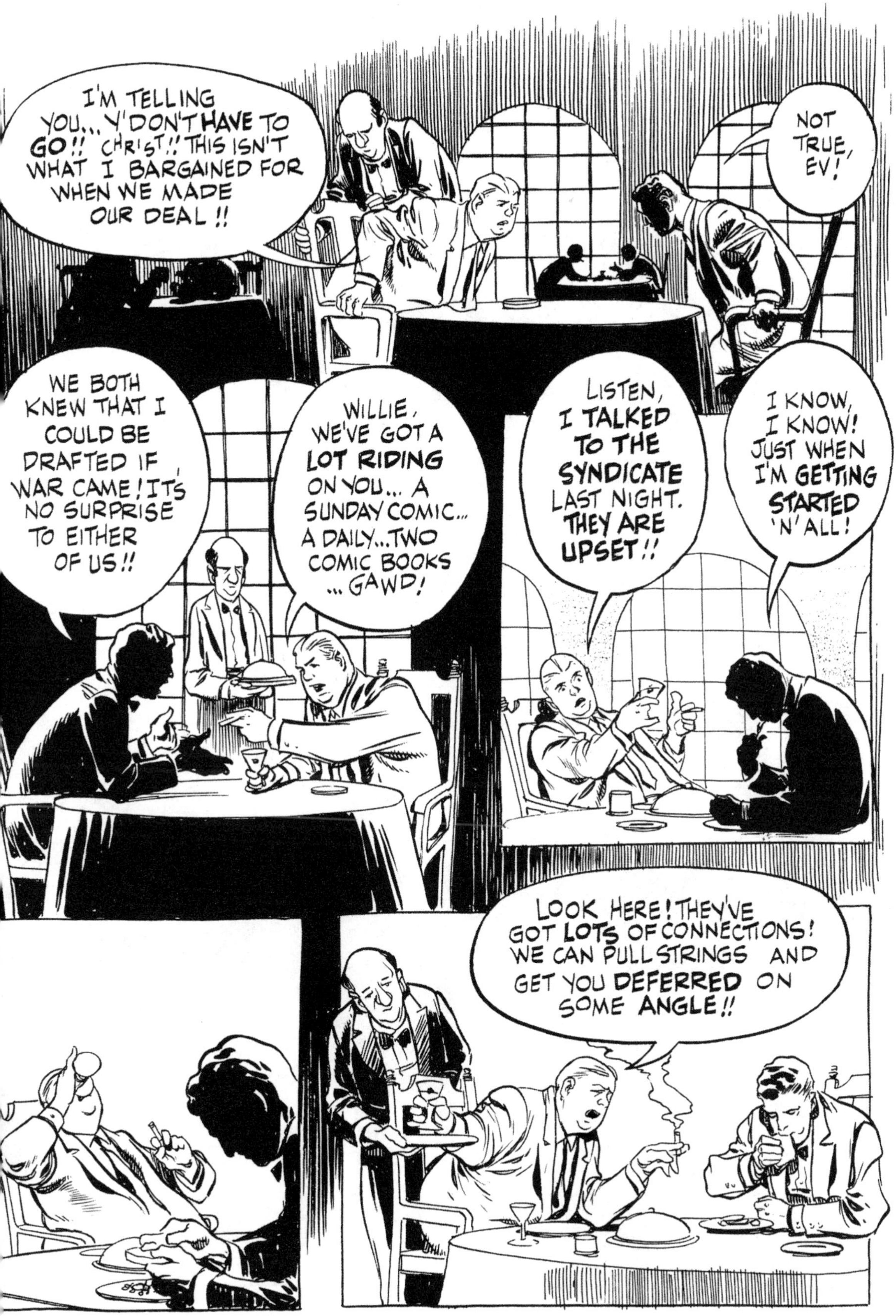

I'M TELLING YOU... Y'DON'T HAVE TO GO!! CHRIST!! THIS ISN'T WHAT I BARGAINED FOR WHEN WE MADE OUR DEAL!!
NOT TRUE, EV!
WE BOTH KNEW THAT I COULD BE DRAFTED IF WAR CAME! IT'S NO SURPRISE TO EITHER OF US!!
WILLIE, WE'VE GOT A LOT RIDING ON YOU... A SUNDAY COMIC... A DAILY...TWO COMIC BOOKS ...GAWD!
LISTEN, I TALKED TO THE SYNDICATE LAST NIGHT. THEY ARE UPSET!!
I KNOW, I KNOW! JUST WHEN I'M GETTING STARTED 'N' ALL!
LOOK HERE! THEY'VE GOT LOTS OF CONNECTIONS! WE CAN PULL STRINGS AND GET YOU DEFERRED ON SOME ANGLE!!

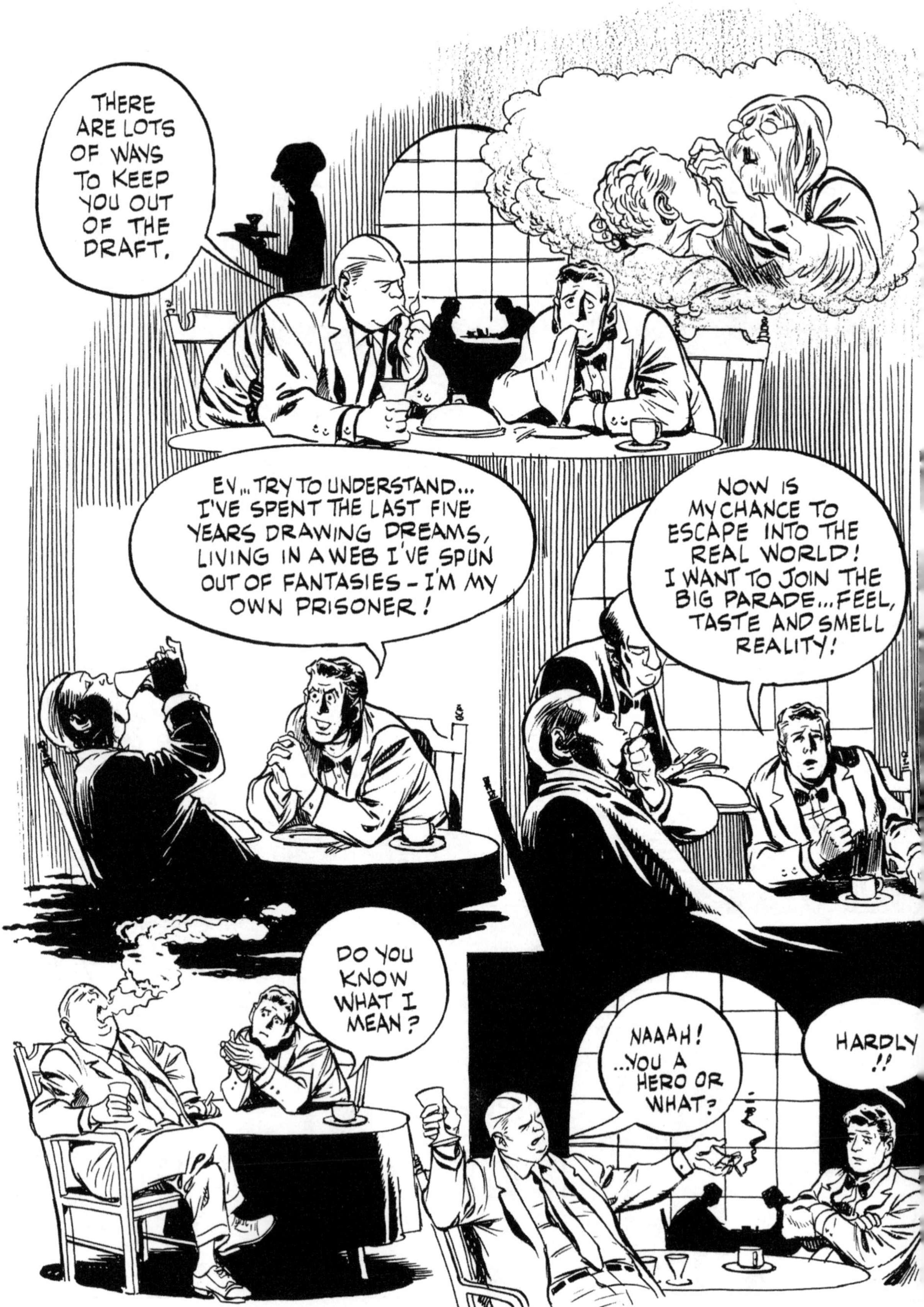
THERE ARE LOTS OF WAYS TO KEEP YOU OUT OF THE DRAFT.
EV... TRY TO UNDERSTAND... I'VE SPENT THE LAST FIVE YEARS DRAWING DREAMS, LIVING IN A WEB I'VE SPUN OUT OF FANTASIES - I'M MY OWN PRISONER!
NOW IS MY CHANCE TO ESCAPE INTO THE REAL WORLD! I WANT TO JOIN THE BIG PARADE... FEEL, TASTE AND SMELL REALITY!
DO YOU KNOW WHAT I MEAN?
NAAAH! ...YOU A HERO OR WHAT?
HARDLY!!

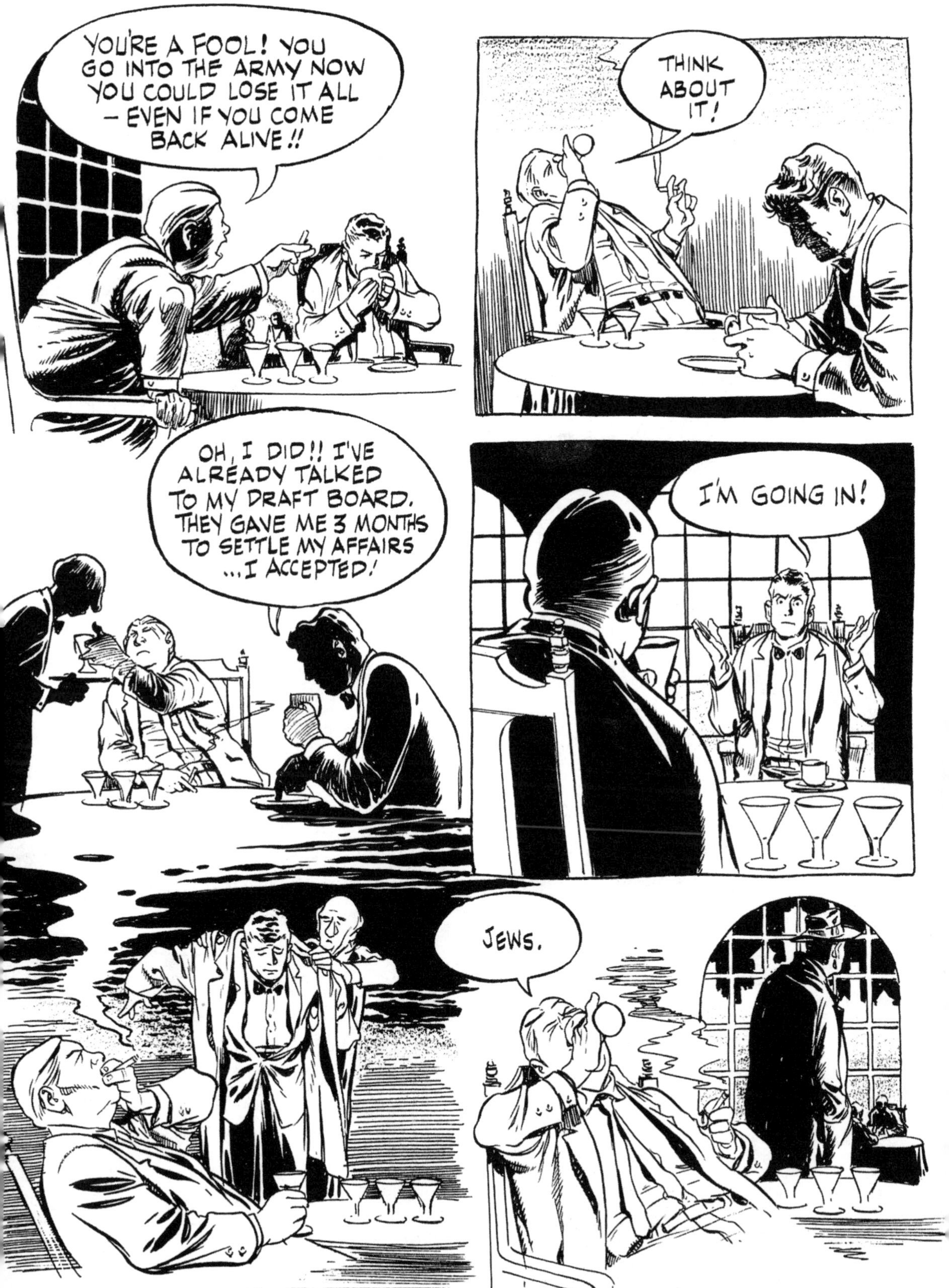
YOU'RE A FOOL! YOU GO INTO THE ARMY NOW YOU COULD LOSE IT ALL – EVEN IF YOU COME BACK ALIVE!!
THINK ABOUT IT!
OH, I DID!! I'VE ALREADY TALKED TO MY DRAFT BOARD. THEY GAVE ME 3 MONTHS TO SETTLE MY AFFAIRS ...I ACCEPTED!
I'M GOING IN!
JEWS.

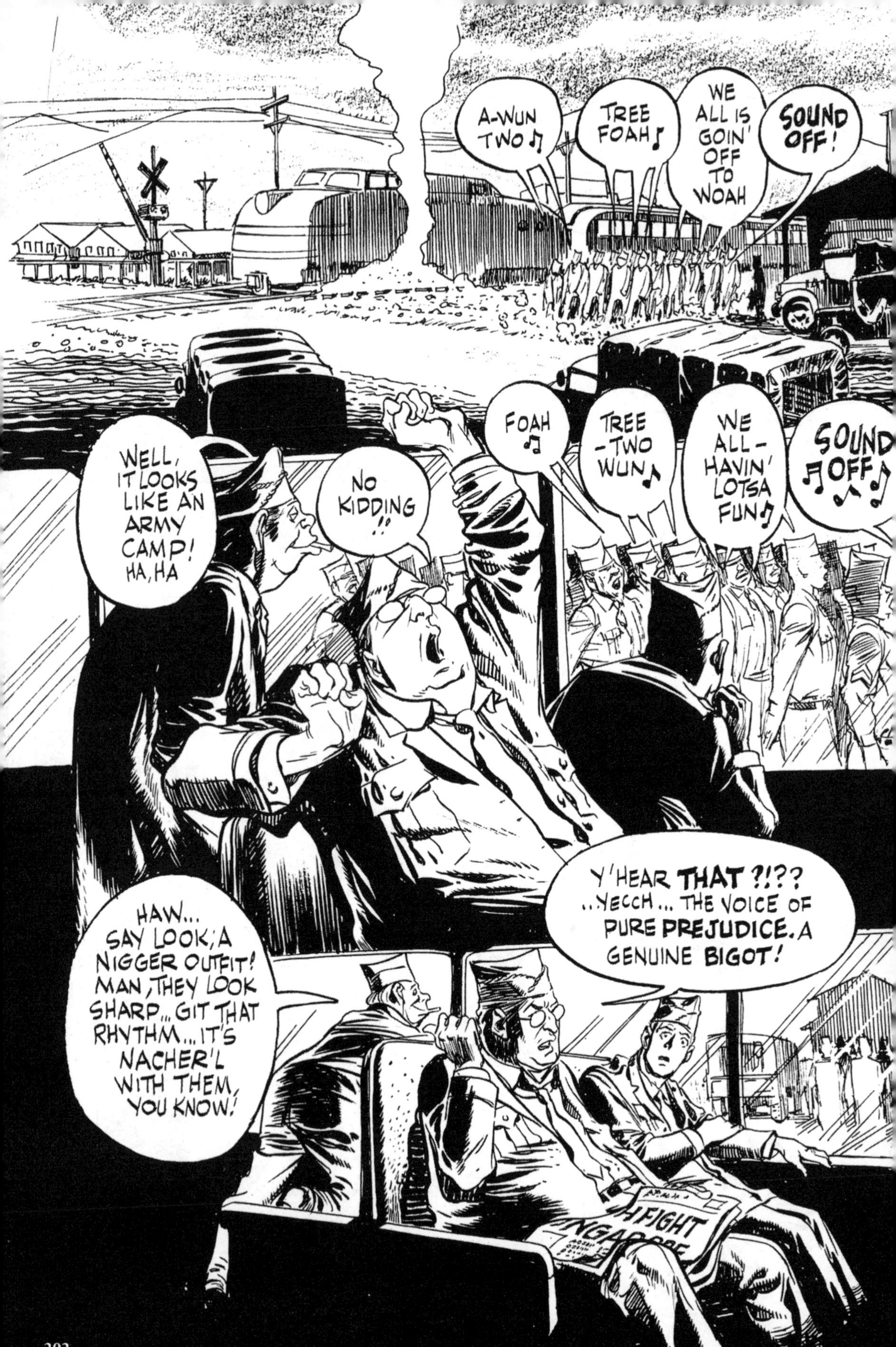
A-WUN TWO ♫
TREE FOAH ♪
WE ALL IS GOIN' OFF TO WOAH
SOUND OFF!
WELL, IT LOOKS LIKE AN ARMY CAMP! HA, HA
NO KIDDING!!
FOAH ♫
TREE-TWO WUN ♪
WE ALL-HAVIN' LOTSA FUN ♪
SOUND ♫ OFF ♪ ♫
HAW... SAY LOOK, A NIGGER OUTFIT! MAN, THEY LOOK SHARP... GIT THAT RHYTHM... IT'S NACHER'L WITH THEM, YOU KNOW!
Y'HEAR THAT ?!?? ..YECCH... THE VOICE OF PURE PREJUDICE. A GENUINE BIGOT!

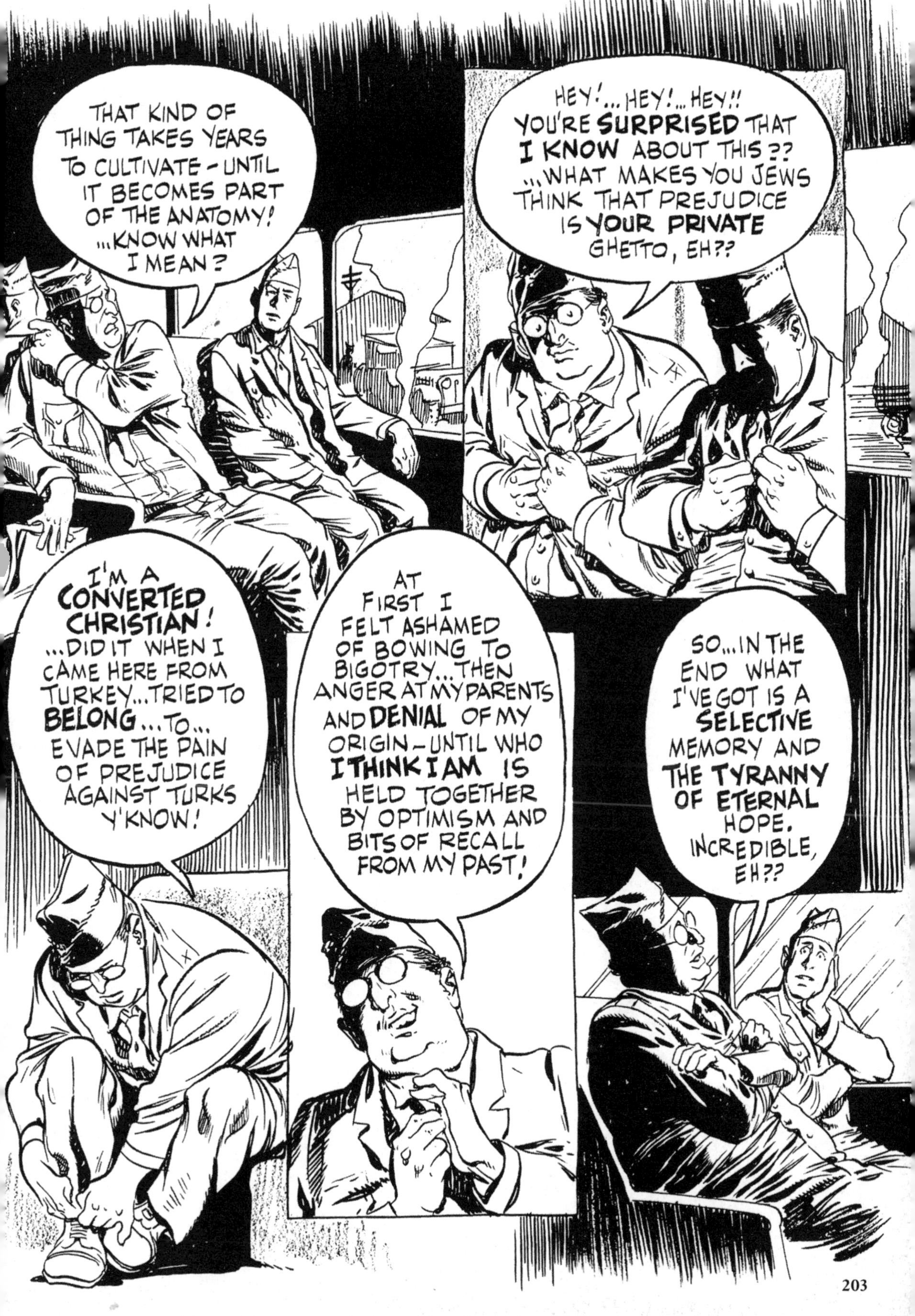
THAT KIND OF THING TAKES YEARS TO CULTIVATE - UNTIL IT BECOMES PART OF THE ANATOMY! ...KNOW WHAT I MEAN?
HEY!... HEY!... HEY!! YOU'RE SURPRISED THAT I KNOW ABOUT THIS?? ...WHAT MAKES YOU JEWS THINK THAT PREJUDICE IS YOUR PRIVATE GHETTO, EH??
I'M A CONVERTED CHRISTIAN! ...DID IT WHEN I CAME HERE FROM TURKEY...TRIED TO BELONG...TO... EVADE THE PAIN OF PREJUDICE AGAINST TURKS Y'KNOW!
AT FIRST I FELT ASHAMED OF BOWING TO BIGOTRY...THEN ANGER AT MY PARENTS AND DENIAL OF MY ORIGIN - UNTIL WHO I THINK I AM IS HELD TOGETHER BY OPTIMISM AND BITS OF RECALL FROM MY PAST!
SO...IN THE END WHAT I'VE GOT IS A SELECTIVE MEMORY AND THE TYRANNY OF ETERNAL HOPE. INCREDIBLE, EH??

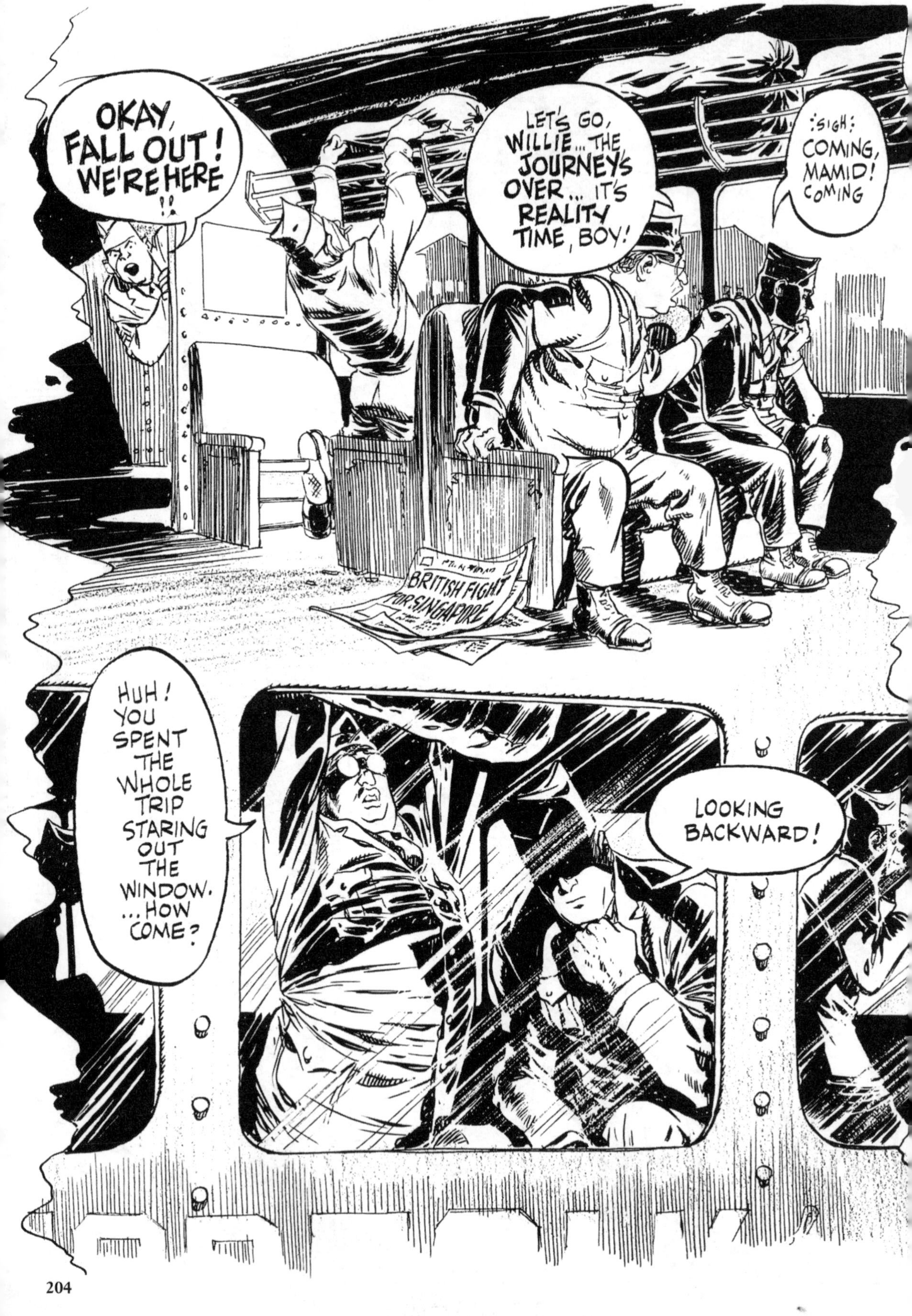
OKAY, FALL OUT! WE'RE HERE
!!
LET'S GO, WILLIE... THE JOURNEY'S OVER... IT'S REALITY TIME, BOY!
:SIGH: COMING, MAMID! COMING
BRITISH FIGHT FOR SINGAPORE
HUH! YOU SPENT THE WHOLE TRIP STARING OUT THE WINDOW. ...HOW COME?
LOOKING BACKWARD!

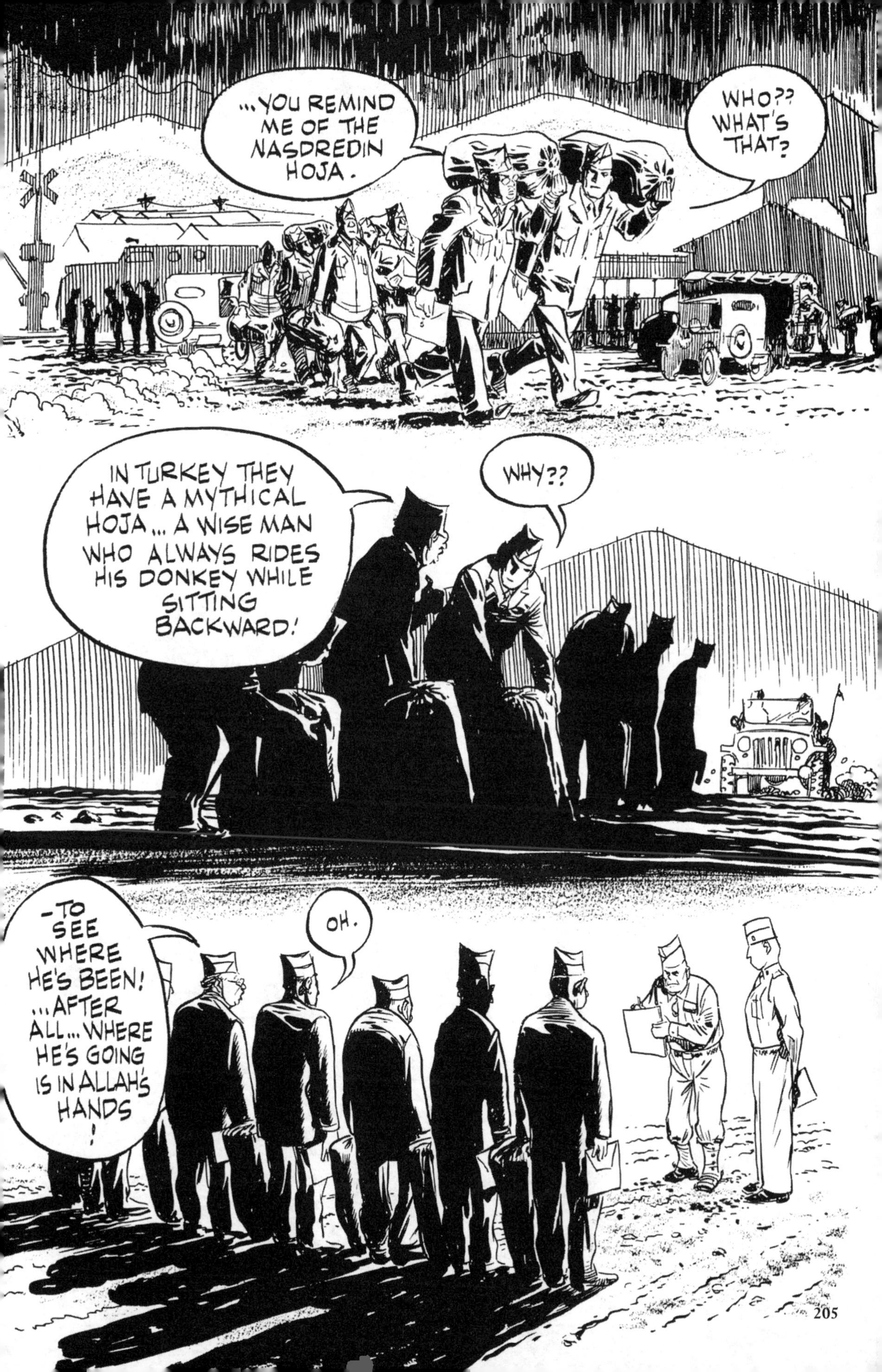
...YOU REMIND ME OF THE NASDREDIN HOJA.
WHO?? WHAT'S THAT?
IN TURKEY THEY HAVE A MYTHICAL HOJA... A WISE MAN WHO ALWAYS RIDES HIS DONKEY WHILE SITTING BACKWARD!
WHY??
-TO SEE WHERE HE'S BEEN! ...AFTER ALL... WHERE HE'S GOING IS IN ALLAH'S HANDS!
OH.

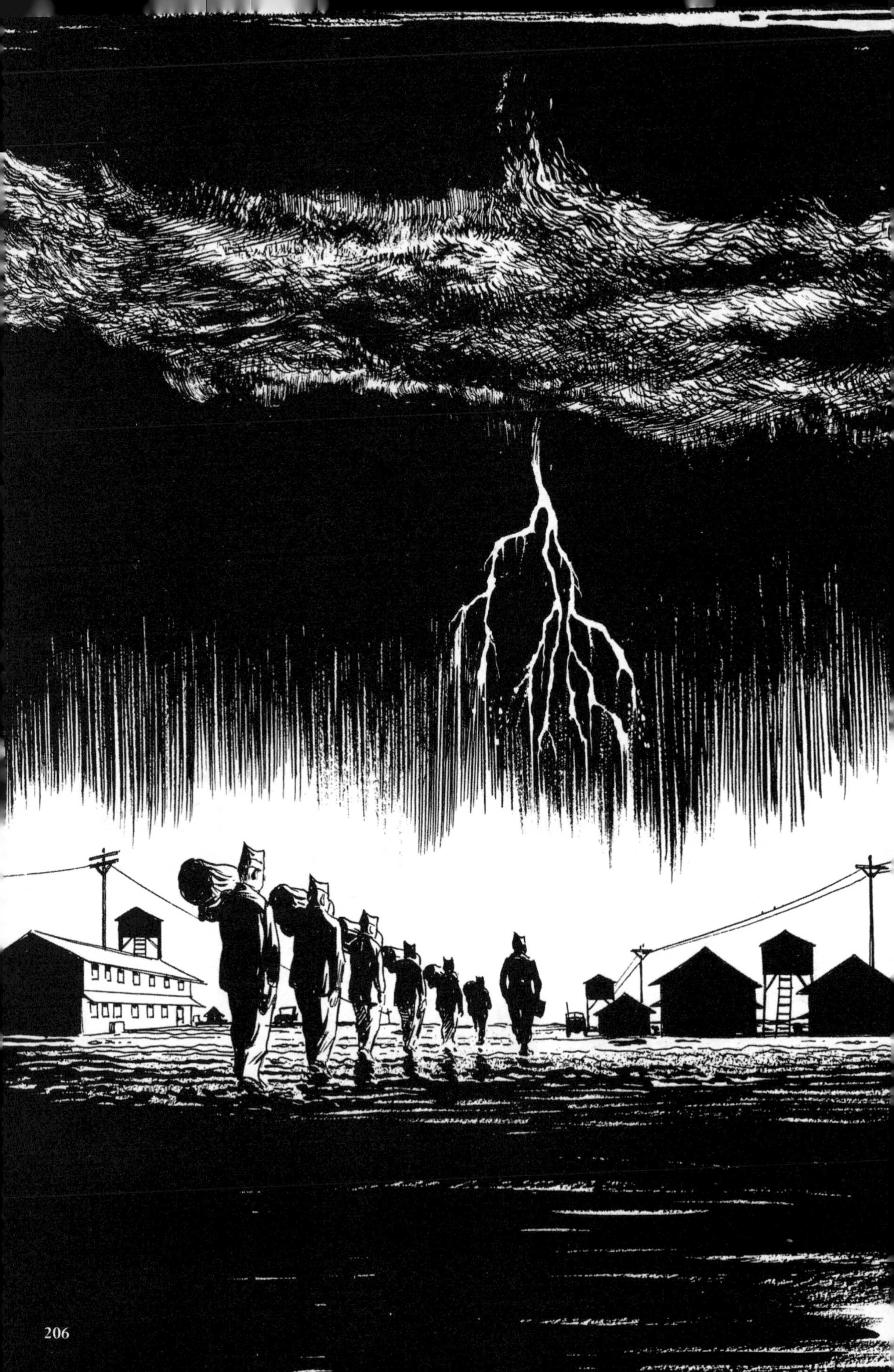

About the Author

Will Eisner (1917–2005) was the grand old man of comics. He was present at the birth of the comic book industry in the 1930s, creating such titles as *Blackhawk* and *Sheena, Queen of the Jungle*. He created *The Spirit* in 1940, syndicating it for twelve years as a unique and innovative sixteen-page Sunday newspaper insert, with a weekly circulation of 5 million copies. In the seven decades since, *The Spirit* has almost never been out of print. As a Pentagon-based warrant officer during World War Two, Eisner pioneered the instructional use of comics, continuing to produce them for the U.S. Army under civilian contract into the 1970s, along with educational comics for readers as diverse as General Motors employees and elementary school children.

In 1978 Eisner created the first successful "graphic novel," *A Contract With God*, launching a bold new literary genre. Nearly twenty celebrated graphic novels by him followed. Since 1988 the comic industry's top award for excellence has been "The Eisner." He has received numerous honors and awards worldwide, including, ironically, several Eisners and only the second Lifetime Achievement Award bestowed by the National Foundation for Jewish Culture (2002).